Politics and Society in Eastern

Politics and Society in Eastern Europe

Joni Lovenduski

Jean Woodall

Indiana University Press
Bloomington and Indianopolis

Manufactured in Hong Kong

Library of Congress catalog card number: LC87–3682

ISBN 0–253–34546–4 (cloth)

ISBN 0–253–28603–4 (paper)

For Ghiţa Ionescu

Contents

List of Tables and Figures

Tables

Figures

Acknowledgements

The authors are grateful to the Nuffield Foundation, which provided financial assistance for the preparation of this book via the Foundation's Small Grant Scheme. In addition, a large number of individuals provided valuable help at various stages of what turned out to be a lengthy process of collecting information, writing and rewriting. We would particularly like to thank Dave Allen, Paul Byrne, Malcolm Hill, George Kolankiewicz, Paul Lewis, Susan Saunders-Vosper, Mary McAuley, Adam Westoby, George Blazyca, Edwina Moreton, Rob Matthews, John Whittaker and Tony Burkett, all of whom read part or all of the manuscript and offered advice and suggestions. Stephen Carter allowed us to see his unpublished work. Mike Hopkins of Loughborough University Library provided considerable assistance in helping us to track down sources, as did the inter-library load staff there. We were particularly fortunate in having access to specialist collections at the British Library of Political and Economic Science at the London School of Economics and the Alexander Baykov Library of the Birmingham University Centre for Russian and East European Studies. Anne Tarver of the Loughborough University Geography Department prepared the map. We are also grateful for the helpful suggestions made by Vincent Wright and for the careful and constructive comments of the publishers' anonymous readers. Steven Kennedy, our sponsoring editor, supported the project from a very early stage. With Keith Povey he patiently and painstakingly saw the manuscript through to publication. Colleagues, friends and family all provided support and reassurance as the work progressed, and special thanks are due to Patricia Swift, who once again proved miraculously patient and cheerful as she typed various drafts of the manuscripts and reorganised its tables. Finally the authors feel obliged to mention that the inspiration for this book came from our experience as the graduate students of Ghiţa Ionescu at Manchester University. He bears at least indirect responsibility for this text. The direct responsibility is ours.

JONI LOVENDUSKI

JEAN WOODALL

The authors and publishers wish to thank the following who have kindly given permission for the use of copyright material:

George Allen & Unwin Ltd for a table from *Blue Collar Workers in Eastern Europe* by Jan F. Triska and Charles Gati (eds), 1981.

Cambridge University Press for material from 'Real GDP Per Capita For More Than One Hundred Countries' by Irving B. Kravis *et al.*, *Economic Journal*, 88, June 1978.

Pergamon Press for figures from *Society, Schools and Progress in Eastern Europe* by Nigel Grant, 1969

United States Information Agency for a table from 'Social Change and Stability in Eastern Europe' by Walter Connor, *Problems of Communism*, Nov–Dec 1977.

The University of Wisconsin Press for figures from *Soviet–East European Relations* by Robert L. Hutchings. Copyright © by The University of Wisconsin Press.

Westview Press for a figure from *Politics and Change in East Germany: An Evaluation of Socialist Democracy* by G. B. Scharf. Copyright © 1984 by Westview Press, Boulder, Colorado.

Every effort has been made to trace all the copyright-holders, but if any have been inadvertently overlooked the publishers will be pleased to make the necessary arrangement at the first opportunity.

1

Introduction: How We Know What We Know about Eastern Europe

Introductory chapters to textbooks are often used to provide background material or to give a foretaste of the book's contents. They are sometimes used to describe the authors' purposes, intentions and motivations in writing the text and occasionally used to discuss the methods employed and the assumptions made in analysing the subject to be studied. In this, very long, book on state socialism in Eastern Europe we are mindful of avoiding repetition, and aim therefore to order material in a way which maximises what may be presented. Thus background material is provided at appropriate points in the text rather than all at once in the beginning. In this chapter we concentrate on a discussion of the methods employed in gathering, analysing and presenting information on the eight state socialist countries of Eastern Europe. We believe it is important that students using a textbook on politics should be aware of both the approaches favoured by and the predispositions of its authors. Such awareness is essential for those who wish to make independent judgements and assessments. Hence we present here in our introduction the main concepts which we use in the text and explain how we define them. We are aware that this somewhat abstract exercise will seem tedious at times, but we hope readers will bear with this brief introductory discussion.

East European politics tends to be seen by scholars and commentators as something exotic, as a world apart. We disagree. Our purpose in writing this book has been to provide

1

students with a systematically comparative study of the politics of the state socialist systems of Eastern Europe which points out not only the differences but also the similarities between these and other European states. Using methods of comparative study, we have tried to show that East European politics may often be understood by reference to the same concepts, models and theories as are utilised in the study of Western liberal democracies.

There are of course differences, and it is to make these clear that we utilise the terms state socialist and liberal democracy. As we use these terms in a very specific way, it is worth defining them carefully here. The structures of state socialism derive from Bolshevik ideology, the experiences of the Russian revolution and the establishment of the Soviet state. In his study of the political system of the USSR David Lane (1985) provides a full definition of state socialism, which he characterises as a hierarchical structure of political incorporation. The hierarchy contains five levels: at the top are the party, state and economic leadership; next are the official economic and professional organisations, followed on the third level by regional and local agencies; the fourth tier consists of various minor associations while at the bottom are social groups and the population at large. Popular participation is widespread but channelled through party-dominated networks and concepts of democracy derive from notions of class power, a revolutionary tradition and communist party leadership. Relations between the tiers are based upon complicated sets of 'exchanges', with power running from the top downwards, as it is the first tier which sets and enforces the major values. Tiers two, three and four exert control on behalf of the leadership, but in exchange for benefits of a moral and material kind. For example, provincial industrial managers accept control by the party in exchange for economic reform and high incomes. Party cadres accept the high levels of commitment required of them and receive both career mobility and greater access to information than is available to the population at large.

In such a configuration elites must fulfil the expectations of the population, an obligation which they undertake within constraints of resources, organisation and ideology. Popular

loyalty and support are conditional upon the effective performance of the system in both ideological and material terms.
As the frequent disturbances in Poland since 1970 show only
too well, elites ignore this at their peril.

Our definition of liberal democracy on the other hand is
supplied by Macpherson (1966), who conceptualises it as
arising from the conjunction of market society and liberalism.
Western liberal democracy was brought into being as a late
product of market society, the first need of which was a liberal
state but not a democratic one. Historical developments in
eighteenth-century England illustrate this point well. The
liberal state was at first designed to operate by competition
between political parties responsible to a narrow and limited,
but economically powerful, electorate constructed on a
property-based franchise. Between 1688 and 1832 the power
of monarchs was limited by the great court parties, the Tories
and the Whigs. Only as industrialism spread and the working
class grew to have numbers, organisation and strength sufficient to achieve entry into the electorate did a popular
democratic franchise become a component of the liberal
British state. Liberal democracy was thus the historical product of a successfully developing capitalist market society.

Liberal democratic states vary in structure, but all contain
representative institutions and are based upon the rule of law,
the formal accountability of leadership and the formal guarantee of basic civil rights. Significantly the laissez-faire market societies which first generated liberal democratic institutions and practices no longer exist – if they ever did. The
original political structures have been modified to accommodate economic concentration and state intervention. The
hallmarks of this accommodation – the welfare state, complex
industrial and regional policies and government macro- economic strategies – exist in almost schizophrenic tension with
the tenets of nineteenth-century capitalism. The example of
British industrialists who at the same time call for deregula-
tion and increased state aid for industry illustrates this point.
So in liberal democracies too the state has increasingly been
held responsible by citizens for economic performance. Here
too political loyalty is contingent upon government output.

Clearly then, state socialism and liberal democracy are not

dichotomous. As types they overlap and intersect at many important points. In affirming this we differ from many analysts of communist politics who implicitly or explicitly regard liberal democratic forms to be part of a world that is both separate and superior. We believe that the considerable common ground between the two types of system may be used not as a basis for making ethical rankings, of identifying and categorising which system is morally better or worse, but as a basis for systematic comparison. Our contribution to such an undertaking is our use of the same methods and concepts which are used in the study of Western systems. Thus we point repeatedly to the different sets of value judgements which inevitably appear in analyses of state socialism. Such value judgements are an occupational hazard for social scientists. They occur not least because the systems in question have the above-mentioned substantial set of common characteristics. Yet value judgements themselves may not be analysed, assumed or denied away, rather they must be acknowledged. Differing values permeate the different theories and models which are used to analyse political systems. Nowhere is this more apparent than in communist studies, where the major theories may be classified according to the values they reflect.

Theories about state socialist society have two main purposes which are sometimes contradictory. On the one hand they have been developed to characterise, to indicate in a few words, the nature of the regimes under scrutiny. On the other hand they are offered as an analytical framework for scholars interested in furthering their knowledge and understanding of the systems. Tension between the two purposes is inevitable and understandable, but it does make for considerable confusion about the theories and concepts which have been employed to analyse state socialist regimes.

Different scholars would classify theories about state socialism in different ways, depending both upon their own areas of interest and the purposes of their enquiry. In preparing this text we have drawn on the three major approaches which have informed the post-war literature on the area. Each of the three approaches may be seen as a set of similar theories: neo-Marxist theories, industrial society theories and regime self-assessments. Each of the three sets of theories makes statements about who controls, how control is maintained and how change occurs. Western neo-Marxist theories tend to be variants of Trotskyism, according to which a privileged stratum of rulers controls the means of production and thereby dominates the working class of the Soviet Union and (by extension) the societies such as those in Eastern Europe which are held to mirror it. Variations turn on the question of whether the ruling stratum is a ruling class in the Marxist sense, that is over whether the bureaucracy in state socialist societies is a ruling class. Such views are held by a range of Western neo-Marxists. (See Bellis, 1979, for a full account.) East European neo-Marxists also draw on Hegelian and Weberian constructs. Writers such as Bahro (1978), Feher, Heller and Markus (1983), Konrad and Szelenyi (1979) disagree with the Trotskyist formulation that contemporary state socialist societies are transitional types. Rather they are unique configurations in which the intelligentsia with its operational core in the bureaucracy is in the dominant ideological and political position. They regard the working class as subordinate and impotent in societies in which an ideology of rational redistribution is contradicted by a reality in which social needs are not met. Control is maintained by modes of ideological dominance underpinned by pervasive bureaucratic structures reinforced by the division of labour. Under such conditions both Western and East European neo-Marxists have difficulty in locating the dynamic of social change. They reject the possibility of reform or of gradual change in state socialist societies and argue that the pathologies which obtain there may be corrected only by political or cultural revolution of some kind.

Industrial society theory has its foundations in the works of early sociologists such as Saint-Simon, Emile Durkheim and Max Weber. Its most important outgrowth is convergence theory, which is related to development theory, with its examination of the transition from traditional to modern industrial society. Convergence theories stress the similarities in the patterns of economic and social control which occur between East and West. For example, bureaucratic forms of authority and similar structures of industrial production may be observed in both systems. In this theory both types of system are regarded as transitional, evolving to a common 'higher' type. Change is seen as being technologically determined, a homogenising process which produces similar post-industrial formations (Woodall, 1982b, p. 6). In consequence social forces such as labour movements are less likely to generate revolutionary change than are the army of applied scientists and the better (higher) educated in general. It will be the computer rather than proletarian revolution which will lead the way to a society of abundance.

Regime self-assessments also postulate a transitional model. While it is widely believed that state socialist Marxist–Leninists view the course of proletarian revolution as passing through the intermediate stage of socialist revolution which precedes the communist millennium, in reality their theorising is more complex. Stalin's 1936 declaration that socialism had been largely achieved was reassessed in the 1960s and 1970s. In conditions of what is officially termed 'developed socialism' political control derives from extensive consultation and participation, enabling the party to act out its leading role. That leading role is predicated upon the party's strategic, theoretical and ideological superiority, as manifested in its management of planned economic and social development. As in convergence theory, technology is acknowledged to be an important facilitator of change. The difference under developed socialism is that here technology goes hand in glove with Marxist–Leninist ideology (Woodall, 1982a, pp. 4–7).

Theories generate models and often the two terms are used interchangeably, the distinctions between them regarded as abstract and rather remote from empirical concerns. For the purposes of this text, if theories enable us to assess political entities, it is models which facilitate their specific analysis. Models may thus be regarded as sets of categories and other concepts according to which we organise our empirical observations. Rather than simply describing a series of individual, idiosyncratic systems, they provide checklists against which structures and processes might be compared. In this text we make use of a number of models of politics, introducing each at the point at which we first apply it. But two examples may usefully be described here: the six-point checklist provided by the totalitarian model and the multiplicity of sources of policy inputs suggested by the interest group model.

Arguably the totalitarian model might now be regarded as a historical artifact. Its use dominated scholarly study of the Soviet Union and its European satellites during the 1950s and 1960s but the model was discarded in favour of more flexible approaches (see Chapter 10), while the term itself continued to have a considerable lay usage. We introduce it here partly because it is a good example of a particular type of model, but more importantly because of its continuing influence upon the literature on state socialist societies. The very fact that the major studies of the first post-war decades were ordered by its premises continues to influence our understanding of the politics of those years. Moreover, much of the methodological innovation which occurred during the 1970s and 1980s was in part a response to the inadequacies of the totalitarian model. There are therefore good reasons why students should be familiar with its contents and application.

Briefly, the totalitarian model sets out to demonstrate how control of the state socialist political system takes place, emphasising the political nature of control and the major role of the state. According to Friedrich and Brzezinski (1956, pp. 9–10), its six features are an official ideology embracing all significant aspects of human existence, a single mass party normally led by one person, a system of terroristic police control, a technologically facilitated state monopoly of the means of mass communications, a state monopoly of the means of effective armed combat and a centrally directed and controlled economy. These six items are meant to be defining features of societies in which the masses play only a subject role. It is possible to assess the presence or absence of each characteristic in a given state and as a result determine whether or not it is analytically useful to characterise that state as totalitarian.

As it happens, the totalitarian checklist suffers from an overstatement of its case, in particular from an inability to reflect change. Its use implies, for example, an equation of the Soviet Union in the 1930s and Yugoslavia and Poland in the 1970s, a characterisation which is patently unhelpful. Essentially the totalitarian model today enables us to determine only that the resemblance of the East European states to the form it outlines is superficial. It permits little in the way of detailed comparison.

The interest group model, which derives from group theories developed for the study of liberal democracies, is more sensitive, providing classification schemes which suggest a focus upon possible sources of group activity in the systems to which it is to be applied. Various schemes have been offered, ranging in their central preoccupations from an emphasis on social groups such as the artistic intelligentsia and/or the peasantry to an apparatus/bureaucracy orientation which concentrates on such groups as the military, the police and the managers. These are described in detail in Chapters 10 and 11. Such schemes have a considerable comparative utility, enabling analysts to make generalisations about such things as sources of demands for reform or of policy innovation of other kinds in the systems to which they are applied. In practice, however, the interest group model also has shortcomings; notably it fails to delimit discrete group structures other than those with an institutional base, so that it assumes rather than demonstrates a direct group influence. Logically it might lead the researcher to infer, for example, that additional financial allocations to the defence budget were the result of military influence, whereas a stronger and more convincing analysis would include a demonstration of the manner and means of the military's influence.

The fact that it is flawed should not lead us to dismiss a model out of hand. Whilst none are entirely perfect, models are, it may be averred, invaluable analytical aids. Any particular model should be adopted, however, only insofar as it enhances rather than obscures our understanding. A model which seems to close rather than open areas of enquiry should be discarded. Accordingly, we might use the interest group model carefully whilst the totalitarian model is probably best avoided.

The usefulness of theories and models is not only internally constrained but affected also by the availability and quality of sources of information. There are two basic problems with the information, especially with the statistical data, available on Eastern Europe: verifiability and coverage. Aggregate statistical data comes to us from both Western and domestic sources. Western sources are, however, only as good as the data supplied by domestic government statistics offices. Often there is no possibility of independent verification. Clearly we need to be circumspect about taking such data at face value, but this is not to say that official statistics should be dismissed out of hand. While economic growth rates are reported differently than they are in the West, they none the less are indicators of change over time (see Chapter 4). Demographic, education and health statistics may be used to construct a set of social indicators which may be used as a basis for systematic comparisons of policy output between state socialist societies and liberal democracies as well as for comparisons of the state socialist systems themselves. Examples here are the number of hospital beds and physicians per thousand of population, mortality rates and age-group participation rates at varying levels of education (see Chapter 12).

The problem with aggregate indicators is that they may conceal important differences between strata, groups and regions. Only by disaggregating the data are we able accurately to identify redistributive effects. Often such disaggregation is impossible, and even where possible it is difficult to interpret without a good knowledge of the relevant political and cultural context. We must not flatter ourselves that statistics in Eastern Europe are collected to meet the requirements of Western social scientists. Rather they are gathered to serve the needs of domestic policy development. Such objectives may well not coincide with the investigative requirements of foreign observers, a deficiency which may be compounded by regime concern to maximise success and minimise failure. Hence we have not a falsification of statistics so much as the maintenance of silence on some matters, a syndrome from which Western governments are not always exempt. Western governments have not been forthcoming on the medical effects of increasing levels of unemployment, and neither sets of governments have been candid about deaths from radiation-induced cancers. And what government chooses to publish its intelligence service or security police recruitment statistics? East European governments have been less than forthcoming on such matters as unemployment, or access to housing by social group, but have been more frank about specifically economic matters. Thus Western observers were well appraised of the problems facing the Polish economy at the end of the 1970s.

Other investigative constraints are also culturally derived. Few analysts have knowledge of the Russian, German, Czech, Serbo-Croat, Hungarian, Polish, Bulgarian, Romanian, Turkish and Albanian languages! In the economic climate of the 1980s research and travel money and time are limited. Such constraints inhibit comparative study. They lead to a tendency to rely heavily upon media sources and the work of individual native speakers, whose research is enhanced by an ostensibly intuitive knowledge of the country concerned. That very intuitive knowledge may be regarded by other scholars as simply a bias, an impediment to systematic generalisation. A further result of such reliance is coverage which is uneven both in terms of country and by topic. Coverage tends to reflect emigré concentrations, Western foreign policy preoccupations and indigenous social science traditions rather than the requirements of comparative research. Thus Poland and the GDR receive the most sustained scholarly investigations. Yugoslavia, as a non-aligned state, also receives considerable attention, as has Romania since its dramatic debut on the international stage in 1965. As Hungary's trade with the West increased during the era of detente, her economy has interested a growing number of scholars. But except during periods of crisis Albania, Bulgaria and Czechoslovakia have attracted less Western interest. Albania's intransigent Stalinism, Bulgaria's unswerving loyalty to the USSR and Czechoslovakia's interrupted de-Stalinisation have made these countries not only less amenable but also apparently less attractive to study.

Disciplinary imperatives may also be constraints. Whilst scholarly monographs on individual countries are invaluable both for their detail and their cultural insights, they often do not cover many topics which are of importance to social scientists but are not so regarded by those whose training is essentially linguistic or historical. Yet it is on these that we rely for much of our knowledge about the individual countries of Eastern Europe. Historians and linguists seldom if ever undertake systematic comparative studies of such phenomena as elite recruitment or working-class composition. A temptation to overdraw on their knowledge of particular systems leads often to unfounded generalisations about others. An overpreoccupation with protest and dissent, evident in even a cursory inspection of the literature, illustrates this tendency. Scholars were quick after the rise of Solidarity in Poland to predict (a) the demise of official unionism elsewhere in the region, (b) imminent USSR invasion, (c) imminent Warsaw Pact invasion, (d) general system collapse. Few considered the option of regime normalisation, something which comparative consideration of antecedent regime crises in the region would have indicated.

A further cultural constraint on systematic study is the considerable variation in the development of particular indigenous East European national social sciences. Relatively well developed interwar social science traditions in the GDR, Hungary and Poland have led to concomitantly richer social science data bases as well as a more broadly conceived scope of enquiry in these three countries than is the case in the other five systems. Social scientists in the three countries, although to some extent constrained by regime priorities, are nevertheless well acquainted with Western social science discourse. Yugoslavia also features a considerable Western social science influence. Such influences are particularly apparent in the areas of social stratification research and of social policy analysis. On these topics our knowledge is therefore greater on the GDR, Hungary, Poland and Yugoslavia than it is on Czechoslovakia, Bulgaria, Romania and Albania.

Taken together such constraints provide a powerful and cautionary explanation of why so few systematically comparative studies of East European politics have appeared since the pioneering works of Giţa Ionescu (1967) and Gordon Skilling (1966). Such texts as have appeared have been restricted to particular topics (for example, local government, legislatures, the working class or the parties) or have extended their brief beyond Eastern Europe (White *et al.*, 1982). Normally these are presented on a country by country basis, often having been prepared for conferences and symposia for which little has been required in the way of a common methodological core. Such works provide possible foundations for more far-reaching comparative analysis but because of their narrow focus lack the necessary scope of an encompassing comparative methodology. There is, however, nothing to prevent their findings from being incorporated into a system level comparative study, a point which might be better understood after a consideration of the nature of comparative inquiry.

The conceptual armoury of comparative political study was, it is true, accumulated mainly for the purpose of analysing liberal democracies. Most of the newly devised comparative concepts were, in the cold war climate of the 1950s, regarded as inapplicable to what were styled undifferentiated totalitarian states. Following the thaw in East–West relations in the early 1960s, scholars by the end of the decade had tentatively adapted concepts and approaches to what was perceived as an increasingly differentiated state socialist bloc. The discarded fashions of Western scholarship became the *dernier cri* of communist studies. Faced with an onslaught at home, pluralism, in its group theory guise, travelled East where, in suitably modest form, it showed signs of replacing a now discredited totalitarian model. By the early 1970s the behavioural approach was making its tardy appearance in the analysis of East European politics. Studies of political culture, political socialisation, mass participation and public opinion were all undertaken. Development studies also enjoyed a passing vogue. A later import was policy analysis, which drew heavily upon the bureaucratic or administrative model of politics. Finally, in the wake of world economic recession, students of both communist and liberal democratic politics met on the common ground of legitimation theory.

Such methodological innovation was often extremely fruitful, yielding many insights into the processes as well as the structures of East European politics. The Lane and Kolankiewicz (1973) study of social groups in Polish society is a case in point here, as is Ludz's (1970) work on East German elite recruitment. But concepts were also often misused, often redefined in order to be applied to Eastern Europe without any account being taken of their applicability in the West.

Political participation is a case in point. Defined in the West as action resulting in control over political leaders by rational informed citizens, it was regarded in communist systems as manipulated or coerced hyperactive support of policies formulated by malevolent leaders unconcerned with public opinion. In short, state socialist participation was not participation at all. As it happens, neither definition adequately describes the phenomenon it seeks to explain. Mindful of this, Little (1976) has pointed out that the concept has comparative utility only when redefined in a more careful and more modest way. Accordingly he limits his attention to mass participation, which he defines as the association of individuals in various types of political activities. This more limited formulation makes a simple comparison of liberal democratic and state socialist citizen participation a relatively straightforward undertaking, as he illustrates in the cases of the USA and the USSR (see below, Chapter 10). Rigorous concept definition is all-important in such cross-system comparisons. A failure at this level is at best unhelpful and at worst may lead to comparing actual state socialist practices with idealised liberal democratic stereotypes.

Attention to rigorous definition may also prevent undue concept-stretching. As we have seen, the early promise of interest group analysis of communist systems was blighted by insufficient attention to the limits of such an approach. Inferences about a groups policy impact tended, as we have indicated above, to be made from mere demonstrations that the group existed. Insufficient attention was paid both to the process of formulating demands and their communication to policy-making elites. Moreover, boundaries between policy-making elites and institutional groups were often ill-defined.

But the effect of conceptual experimentation during the 1960s and 1970s was to enhance and enrich East European studies. More rigorous analysis and more systematic comparison became possible. Today the comparative study of East European polices has at its disposal the resources of official data, the insights of emigrés, linguists and historians, as well as the conceptual apparatus of both indigenous and Western social science. The chapters which follow draw on all of these.

Our approach is unshamedly eclectic and our coverage is

extensive. Apart from our strategy of using the range of social
science concepts designed for the study of liberal democracies,
we do not provide a theoretical case which informs the entire
text. In accordance with the logic of this strategy we have
taken considerable care both over definitions of concepts and
the presentation of material. Where debates over the nature
of the regimes or their policies have taken place, we describe
them, and where we hold opinions, we state them, offering
students a varied menu from which they may select information and make assessments. We begin with chapters on
history and culture and proceed through accounts of the
economy and the social structure. These are followed by
detailed accounts of political institutions and processes. The
ruling parties are described and analysed in Chapters 7 and 8.
Chapter 9 covers state institutions, while Chapters 10 and 11
are devoted to participation, interest articulation and dissent.
Chapters 12 and 13 describe social and foreign policy, and in
Chapter 14 we take up the current debates on the legitimating
strategies of the contemporary East European regimes in an
attempt to assess the political 'success' of state socialism there.

2

Interwar Eastern Europe

State- and nation-building

Albania, Bulgaria, Czechoslovakia, the GDR, Hungary, Poland, Romania and Yugoslavia have followed both common and varying paths of development, sharing traditions with both East and West as well as individually distinctive cultures. Their history is a chronicle of diverse nationalities, religions and cultures set, with few exceptions, in broadly similar economies. Common efforts to establish Communist Party rule in the years after the Second World War were prefigured by similar experiments in establishing liberal democracies in the interwar period. Thus in the diversity of interwar East European history it is possible to identify a number of common themes and similar experiences. In addition to their geographical proximity, the eight countries share an economic history in which industrialisation came late, if at all. Economically they were less developed than most of their West European counterparts. This had important sociological effects, notably the failure of a confident middle class to emerge. Geographical, economic and sociological factors converged in an unfortunate array of political problems. Attempted solutions to long-standing boundary problems generated neither nation states nor genuine multi-national communities, and led to nationality difficulties, local irredentism and great power hostility. New political institutions were ill-suited to the class structures on to which they were

15

imposed, and encouraged unstable multi-party systems often led by individuals uncommitted to liberal democratic norms. As centre and liberal parties lost credibility, and communist and socialist parties were banned, fascist parties rose to present the political alternatives of the extreme right. Matters were eventually 'resolved' by the outbreak of the Second World War, but each development was to have effects which lasted far into the post-war period. In this chapter we attempt to account for those effects by outlining first the geographical context and cultural setting of interwar nation-building. We then discuss the interwar economies and social structure, and finally we trace political developments through to the outbreak of war in 1939.

Nations are forged from diverse traditions, via numerous routes and out of all manner of historical events and processes. Crises such as invasion, war, revolution and civil war often play a major part. No modern state has come into being without experiencing major difficulties. But, either by geographic or historical good fortune some states have had an easier passage than others.

Such good fortune did not attend the emergence of the countries which today comprise the state socialist systems of Eastern Europe. By any standards their establishment as nation states was a difficult process. One state, the German Democratic Republic (GDR) was a post World War Two creation, its history and traditions lodged in the Second Reich, the Weimar Republic and, finally, the Third Reich of a larger German nation. In many respects therefore the GDR was to be an exception in the East European bloc. As a state, it is normally dated either from Yalta or Potsdam (February or August 1945) or from its formal creation in October 1949. Clearly a part of contemporary state socialist Eastern Europe, the origins of the GDR are to be found almost exclusively in the unified German Reich of Bismarck and his successors. Geographically it consists of the German north-eastern territories beyond the Elbe, a substantial part of Berlin and the whole of Saxony and Thuringa, two Laender which had become highly industrialised at the end of the nineteenth century.

Krejci (1976) refers to work by German historians which

suggests that the contemporary division of the German state is a culmination of historic differences. But, he argues, both the Second (Hohenzollern) and the Third (Nazi) Reich and the Weimar period between them, together stretching over 75 years, exerted a strong unifying influence upon what was then Germany. During those years the fruits of the industrial revolution became more evenly spread across the country, a unified educational system was established, and the types of government in the individual Laender became more standardised. Whilst slight differences in the levels of urbanisation, in religious affiliation and in support for the political centre are to be found in the two countries prior to their separation, Krejci concludes, convincingly, that inherited historical differences were small. We may assume therefore that social and economic indicators for interwar Germany as a whole obtained in the East German lands and may be used to describe the developments with which this chapter is concerned. As Scharf (1984, p.2) writes, the sweep of German history had always encompassed the region which is now the GDR.

The geographical and cultural setting

The peoples of the other seven countries have also a history of a continuous presence in the region, but nationality for many found expression in state institutions only after World War One. The areas referred to as Eastern Europe have always been vaguely defined, with shifting historical boundaries and political structures. The nations covered in this study have some territorial contiguity but are not a coherent geographic unit. Since 1914 it has been a zone of small states, but before that it was a region of great empires. From early modern times Eastern Europe had been ruled by four dynastic empires which were hostile to the idea of the nation state: Austria, Russia, Prussia and Turkey. During the eighteenth century Turkey was gradually removed from Europe, a process finally completed in 1912. Throughout the nineteenth century, Austria became gradually weaker and more dependent upon Germany. But Germany and Russia continued to pursue activist policies in the region, which both regarded as vital to their interests. Possibly both saw the First World War as an opportunity to consolidate their East European interests. Certainly the peace settlement of 1919 was predicated on the fact of German and Russian absence from the area.

Geographically Eastern Europe is divided into three identifiable physical regions. Most open is the eastern section of the North European plain. The plain itself extends from the Atlantic to the Urals (in Russia), which are normally considered to be Europe's natural eastern border. It is here that Poland is situated, bounded on the north by the Baltic Sea and the south by the Carpathian and Sudeten mountains, but exposed to the east and west. It is this openness of her eastern and western borders which has made Poland so vulnerable to invasion from either, and sometimes both, directions. Germany and Russia have always been Poland's natural enemies. Today the GDR lies to her west on the north European plain, sandwiched between Poland and the German Federal Republic.

The second region is the plain which surrounds the Danube from south-west Germany to the Black Sea. This plain is ringed by the Alps, the Carpathian, Dinaric and Balkan mountains and the Bohemian forest. It has for centuries been a route for trade, invasion and migration. Czechoslovakia lies in its northern section, Hungary is at the centre and Romania, which incorporates Moldavia and Transylvania, is to the south-east.

The third region is the Balkan peninsula, which extends from south of the Danube and Sava rivers to the Adriatic, Aegean and Black Seas. Here are Yugoslavia, Albania and Bulgaria (as well as Greece and European Turkey). All three countries are highly mountainous: Albania is protected from the interior by the Dinaric mountains, while Bulgaria consists of two fertile plains cut by the parallel ranges of the Balkans and the Rhodopes. Yugoslavia is the most territorially diverse of the three (Skilling, 1966, pp. 11–12; Mellor, 1975).

The eight countries lie to the east of a line running roughly along the river Elbe down to the Mediterranean at Trieste. Historically this line divides those countries in which serfdom disappeared in the wake of economic forces in the fifteenth and sixteenth centuries from those where it survived until the

FIGURE 2.1

Map

nineteenth century. Serfdom was abolished in Austria- Hungary in 1848, in Prussia in the 1850s and in Russia in 1861. In the areas which had experienced Turkish rule, that is the

Balkan countries and Romania, land reform occurred about the same time but with substantive additional disadvantages for the peasantry. Only with the breaking of Moslem rule in the twentieth century did a significant land redistribution take place. In Serbia and Bulgaria this resulted in the lowest proportion of large estates in Eastern Europe. In both areas the vast majority of holdings were below 30 hectares and the rural population consisted almost exclusively of small and middle peasants (Polonsky, 1975, pp. 3–4; Rothschild, 1974, pp. 267–8; 329–30). Elsewhere more substantial inequalities between peasants and landowners were amongst the legacies of serfdom.

Late economic development had a profound effect on the social structures of the region. The logical corollary of the persistence of serfdom is the late emergence of industrialism, both a product and a cause of the phenomena of poorly developed and politically weak middle classes which characterised most of the regions' social hierarchies. Small concentrated working classes, which accompanied such early twentieth century industrial development as there was, were to be found around the Budapest district in Hungary, Silesia and Lodz in Western Poland, and, in coastal Romania, the petroleum industry. Only in the Czech lands of Bohemia and Moravia and in Germany had industrial development produced an urban proletariat of any size. The main lines of class division before World War One were those between lord and peasant.

However, the precise pattern of that division differed considerably by country. Here it is useful to adopt Skilling's (1966) distinction between what are often called the 'Historic' and the 'non-Historic' nations. The two characterisations enable us to distinguish between the ruling and ruled groups of the empire eras, and between those countries in which the native aristocracies survived empire rule and those where it did not (Skilling, 1966).

The 'Historic' ruling groups were mainly, but not exclusively non-native. They monopolised political power, wealth and status. Their class structures were relatively better articulated, containing at least embryonic business classes, developed professions and strata of political, military and administrative personnel. They are therefore distinguishable from groups which were less stratified and featured little in the way of a middle class. Hungary, Poland and Croatia were the countries with native 'historic' groups. There, traditional aristocracies survived loss of independence but with important effects upon the social and cultural framework. There, gentry attitudes included a disdain for trade and industry, and a belief that service to the state and agriculture were the only careers worthy of a gentleman. Such attitudes permeated these societies, where the country squire way of life enjoyed considerable prestige and formed an important image in the nationalist sub-culture. Under such circumstances it is hardly surprising to find that liberal capitalism was to a significant extent introduced by non-native groups, notably Germans and Jews.

In the 'non-Historic' nations (Bohemia, Moravia, Slovakia, the Balkan nations and arguably Romania) the native aristocracies were destroyed in different foreign conquests. There, nationalist revivals were most often inspired and led by sons of peasants who had moved to towns, producing a political culture noticeably different from that which obtained in Poland and Hungary. The struggle against the economically powerful Germans in the Czech lands of Bohemia and Moravia created a resourceful and efficient Czech petit bourgeoisie. In less developed Serbia and Bulgaria, links between native elites (largely of peasant origin) and the masses were closer than elsewhere. In Romania, the Regatine areas (pre World War One territories) exhibited many of the characteristics of the 'Historic' nations, whilst Transylvania had a Hungarian landowning class and a Romanian peasantry (Polonsky, 1975; Skilling, 1966, p. 2).

Important though the class configurations of Eastern Europe were, differences of nationality were politically more salient at the end of World War One. It was nationality rather than class divisions which exercised the treaty-makers. At least a dozen large nationalities (of a million or more persons) resided in the area. The region, as a frontier territory of various contending empires, had a history of prolonged conflict and bloodshed. National identity was a deeply contentious issue amongst native groups who looked forward to independence and sometimes back to great power status (e.g. the Poles).

The natives of Eastern Europe are mainly of Slavic origin, but large groups of non-Slavs have also long resided there. The Slavs themselves have been deeply divided and may be classified as Western, Eastern and Southern Slavs. The Western Slavs are the Poles, Czechs and Slovaks. The Eastern are the Russians, Ukrainians and Byelorussians, now almost exclusively within the territory of the Soviet Union. The Southern Slavs include the Serbs, Croats and Slovenians of Yugoslavia, as well as the Bulgarians and the Macedonians. The latter have traditionally been regarded as Bulgarian by the Bulgarians, but are today treated as a separate nationality within Yugoslavia. The most important non-Slavic groups are the Magyar (native Hungarians), the Romanians, the Albanians and, of course, the Germans.

Cultural differences between the nationalities are often large, and great linguistic differences exist even within the Slavic nations. Serbs and Croats (Yugoslavs), for example, speak the same language but write it with a different alphabet. Magyars speak a language which is outside the main Indo-European group, bearing a resemblance only to Estonian and Finnish. In the German Democratic Republic German is, of course, the first and the official language, Romanian is a Romance language and the Shiptars of Albania speak a distinctive Indo-European tongue (Albanian). Until World War Two, two further groups were important in the area, the Jews and expatriate Germans, the result of migrations dating back to the thirteenth century (Mellor, 1975; Polonsky, 1975; Seton-Watson, 1975; Skilling, 1966).

Religious differences sometimes blurred and sometimes exacerbated national conflict. Eastern Europe is the site of the historic dividing line between Roman Catholicism and Eastern Orthodoxy. Poles, Czechs, Slovaks, Slovenes, Croats and Hungarians were mainly Catholic, whilst Ukrainians, Romanians, Bulgarians, Serbs and Macedonians were mainly orthodox. But both camps were internally divided. A characteristic feature of Orthodox administrative hierarchies has been that they are co-terminous with national boundaries. In the nineteenth century each of the practising nations produced its own autocephalous church, with only loose connections to the titular head at Constantinople. And Catholic East Europe was divided by the rise of Protestantism, notably in Hungary and Germany, but also amongst Poles, Czechs, Slovaks and expatriate Germans. Further complications to religious patterns arose from the presence of Moslem adherents in the Balkans, a residue of the Ottoman Empire. Thus there were Moslem Turkish minorities and Moslem Slavs among the Bosnians, Macedonians and Bulgarians, whilst the Albanians were almost entirely Moslem. To this day strong Turkish and Moslem cultural influences are observable amongst the Albanians, Bulgarians, Romanians and Serbs. Finally, Jews were for centuries an important presence on the religious map of Eastern Europe, where they had migrated to escape persecution in Germany and Spain. Some were assimilated and some concentrated in the ghettos of the major states. Anti-semitism varied considerably in its degree, reaching its height in Hungary, Romania and Poland. The target of Nazi extermination policies, most of those Jews who were not slaughtered in World War Two emigrated in the post-war period (Skilling, 1966, p. 16).

This mosaic of religions, nationalities and cultures was in the years before 1914 divided politically between four great empires. Moslem Turkish, Orthodox Russian, Catholic Austrian and Protestant German Imperialisms have all had their effects. The early separation between Catholic Roman and Orthodox Byzantine traditions produced differing political cultures. From Rome and Byzantium came different conceptions of government and law, of artistic and literary forms and of language. In each of the empires the political experience was an experience of autocracy. But, except under the Ottoman Turks, the degrees of that autocracy were modified considerably over time as limited modes of popular representation were introduced.

A product of Byzantium, the Turks dominated the Balkans for the best part of four centuries – until 1878 for the Serbs, Romanians and Bosnians and until 1912 for Bulgaria, Macedonia and Albania. In cultural terms the Russian empire too was a successor of Byzantium. Poland was heir both to Rome and Byzantium. Divided between the Russian, Prussian and Austrian empires, until the eighteenth century Russian despotism ruled Poland's eastern territories whilst Prussian despotism ruled her western areas. Galician Poles were part of the Hapsburg empire (Austrian) and benefited there from an appreciable local autonomy and opportunity to gain political experience.

The Hapsburg empire might be seen as a long-lasting attempt to organise much of Eastern Europe into a single political entity. A system of dual monarchy shared by Austrian Germans and Hungarian Magyars gave these two peoples dominance, but other nationalities sometimes enjoyed a token autonomy. The exception was Galicia, in which Poles had majority control of their own affairs and were able in characteristic East European fashion thereby to dominate the Ruthenian (Ukrainian) minority. Thus Austrian Poles had a different political tradition to their Russian and Prussian compatriots, as did both of these to the Prussians. In general the nations ruled by the Dual Monarchy featured the greatest range of political experience before World War One. In the Austrian sectors considerable experience of parliamentary processes was obtained. In the Hungarian areas nationality oppression and Magyarisation forged a different set of political cultures. Resistance against the dominant peoples mobilised many of the subject peoples, who were able normally to form their own political parties and to undertake some political activity, although this was limited. For example, the Czechs and the Slovenes under the Austrian Hapsburgs were included in the general manhood suffrage after 1907. Elsewhere the Serbs, Bulgarians and Romanians also had some experience of independent statehood after the Turks were driven out. Whilst such groups did not experience the full variety of political arrangements offered in liberal democratic systems, they did have some time to adjust to the conventions of constitutionalism. Such experiences were undoubtedly valuable.

World War One and its ensuing peace brought the collapse of the great empires. The various peace treaties signed at Versailles in 1919, designed both for punitive purposes and to resolve nationality questions, created as many problems as they solved, for they produced fourteen 'successor' nation states, mainly multi-national entities, in a region in which a century before not a single independent state had existed. The nationalities were not always territorially compact and very often national, class and religious cleavages coincided. In the twelve states which existed between Germany and Russia in 1921, there were at least twenty-five large national groups. The new governments of these states were faced with monumental tasks of harmonising differences and resolving claims, as well as dealing with disgruntled and sometimes warlike neighbouring states that felt they had fared badly in the peace negotiations. Ultimately the treaty-makers dealt with nationality questions by drawing national boundaries in such a way that most of the successor states contained one or more national minority which would rather have been somewhere else.

In the negotiations at Versailles the question of the nature of the East European political systems was at least as important as the issue of nationality. In most cases an effort was made to implant a liberal democratic system, reflecting the ideologies of the treaty-makers but not necessarily the needs or capacities of the countries' concerned. As it happened, most of the new systems came under strain almost immediately. The new governments were faced from the outset with all the difficulties of forging democratic traditions, of founding new political systems, of fusing disparate nationalities, and re-fusing those which had for a time been disunited. In the case of Poland three administrative and political traditions had to be combined. The Czechoslovaks were required to merge Austrian Czechs and Hungarian Slovaks with Hungarian Ruthenian, German Magyar and Polish minorities. Yugoslavia, heir to the dream of the South Slav state, was faced with welding its various ex-empire south Slav nationalities with Serbia, which had been independent since 1878. In addition to its several nationalities, Yugoslavia contained three main religious groups, six customs areas, five currencies, four railway networks, three banking systems, and, at first, two governments. The remnants of four legal systems had to be assimilated into a common code of law. The idea of Yugoslav unity had, as Singleton (1985, p. 131) writes, meaning for only a very small part of the population.

Domestic difficulties were exacerbated by international ones. Up until 1920 to 1921 and possibly until as late as the abortive 1923 uprising in Germany, the Soviet government still had hopes of fomenting revolution abroad. Although resources were limited, a Comintern policy of destabilising central and west European governments undoubtedly contributed to the generally inauspicious environment.

Not surprisingly, some of the new governments faltered. Hungary's was the first to collapse. The failure of the Hungarian government to prevent a loss of territory led in March 1919 to the establishment in Budapest of a soviet government (modelled on the Russian example) under Bela Kun and various other communist and social democratic leaders (including Matyas Rakosi, an important post World War Two leader and Marxist philosopher Georg Lukacs). Although it had some early successes, notably fending off a Romanian invasion, Kun's regime soon failed, giving way to the regency of Admiral Horthy and 20 years of autocratic right-wing government. In 1920 war broke out between Russia and Poland, largely because of Polish aspirations to annex Russian territory. The Red Army eventually prevailed, although Poland successfully gained territory, her Eastern boundaries being virtually redrawn at the Curzon line in the 1921 Treaty of Riga. Elsewhere problems were considerable, although they did not lead to all out war.

What no one knew in 1919 was that the successor states were to have only 20 years before their boundaries were once again redrawn by world war. The states, once founded, were threatened by the tide of civil unrest which followed the Russian revolution and the Versailles Treaty. There followed some years of comparative stability during which revolutions were suppressed and financial and economic life was subjected to reorganisation. But by the end of the 1920s world recession halted recovery and aggravated the conditions which led to the rise of German National Socialism. By the time the East European regimes were recording their first political and administrative successes, Germany's liberal democratic Weimar Republic had collapsed and war was soon to begin.

To summarise, then, before World War One the states with which we are concerned contained a plethora of divergent groups, and most of them exhibited the class structures of systems barely emerged from feudalism. With few exceptions industry was as yet undeveloped and modern political systems were unformed. The peace treaties drew national boundaries and imposed political structures. Newly established and often politically divided and unstable governments set about the tasks of governing themselves, proceeding with strategies of economic and social modernisation. Except in Czechoslovakia, the political systems did not survive.

The interwar years were not entirely a time of failure, however. Despite considerable obstacles and difficulties the two decades between 1919 and 1939 were a time of state and nation building, of political, economic, social and cultural consolidation. In the remainder of this chapter we attempt to outline and assess the most important characteristics, achievements and failures of those years. We shall focus first upon economic and social developments and then turn to a discussion of the political systems.

The interwar economies

In common with the experience of other societies which were late to industrialise, much of interwar East European economic development was foreign- or state-financed. Based upon distorted class structures and imported imperatives, the economies which resulted featured many of the characteristics of late modernisation which had so afflicted late- nineteenth and early twentieth-century Russia. The import of plant and process from more industrialised societies made for a considerable economic unevenness level, which itself contributed to social dissatisfaction and unrest. Absentee capitalists were predictably less concerned over the well-being of native workforces than domestic entrepreneurs might have been. Neither were they particularly motivated to engender well balanced economies. Although some manufacturing industries were foreign-owned (notably textiles), most foreign investment was in the extractive industries.

Except in Czechoslovakia, governments relied disproportionately upon the landowning classes for their support. Although they recognised the necessity to direct a planned industrialisation, and policy-makers were exercised by peasant and working class discontent, political circumstances inhibited the far-reaching changes needed to bring about a widespread economic restructuring. It was not that, except during the depression, economic progress did not take place – considerable progress was made in some areas. Rather the problem was one of distorted development, of failure to produce the kinds of economies which matched the resources of the area and the needs of the population.

Economic development in Eastern Europe was, not surprisingly, interrupted and in most cases set back by the destruction of World War One. In addition, the dismantling of empires and the establishment of new national units disrupted and slowed the modernisation process. The halts in development came at what were, in most cases, very low levels of industrialisation. Neither heavy industry nor machine industry were well advanced. Poorly developed industrial sectors contributed to the problems of agriculture, where despite, or perhaps because of, land reform in many areas, production also lagged. Little headway had been in either the mechanisation or the chemicalisation of East European agriculture.

In 1919 Bulgaria and Yugoslavia were almost entirely without modern industries. Romania, apart from the petroleum complex at Ploesti, had little. In Hungary some heavy industry existed around Budapest. Poland had pockets of industrialism, including textiles at Lodz, coal and steel in the Dabrowa basin and highly developed coal, steel and chemical industries in the Upper Silesian areas assigned to her by the League of Nations in 1921.

Industrial development had been extensively shaped by the economies of Germany and Russia and considerable adaptation was needed to establish a coherent post-independence framework. Only the Czech lands contained a diversified industrial base. Even this was combined with the less developed economies of Slovakia and Ruthenia, both of which had been closely tied to the Magyar plain, from which they were cut off by high tariffs following independence.

Semi-feudal social organisation left many areas without an enterprising middle class of townspeople anxious for economic progress. The peasantry, overwhelmingly the largest class, lacked the skills, capital and legal freedoms to become entrepreneurs, whilst the landowing aristocracy saw no need to augment or risk its wealth. Such native bourgeoisie as there was lacked sufficient capital and initiative to proceed on its own. Hence newly created industries tended either to be foreign-owned or in state hands. War damage, adjustments to independence and new sets of tariff barriers hampered industrial progress. New national boundaries broke up traditional market patterns and transport networks.

Some advances were made, however. Progressively through the 1920s all the countries became more prosperous. However, rates of economic growth were slow. Although political independence provided some stimulus, Eastern Europe was poorly provided with economic resources and lacked the political conditions necessary to secure the benefits of modernisation. Poorly skilled workforces meant that foreign investors tended to be unwilling to establish manufacturing industries, and most countries had little option but to pursue policies of agriculture-led growth.

The Great Depression of the 1930s hit such strategies hard. As all the successor states except Czechoslovakia were exporters of primary goods, the rapid world-wide fall in the prices of agricultural relative to industrial goods was damaging. Industrial strategies based on large-scale foreign investments, backed by international financial systems, had also to be abandoned. Existing debts were serviced by borrowing as international interest rates rose.

Problems were compounded as the depression took hold and its effect on trade balances worsened. Thus Hungary in 1930 required 50 per cent of her imports bill to service foreign debts. Governments were slow to repudiate debts and pursued draconian deflationary policies which ultimately were unsuccessful, prolonged the depression and resulted in a considerable radicalisation of politics. A further effect was a significant German economic penetration of the weakened states (except Poland and Czechoslovakia) when recovery finally did come (Polonsky, 1975, pp. 9–11). Thus France, the political guarantor of much of Eastern Europe, whose citizenry had been considerable private investors in the area, was largely displaced financially by German state investments. The agricultural sector was also generally backward and inefficient. Land reforms had been poorly designed, leaving large estates intact but producing numerous small landholdings incapable of supporting a family. Rural overpopulation was a persistent problem, exacerbated by a lack of capitalisation, technological backwardness and low yields. Except in Serbia and Bulgaria, a substantial amount of large landholding persisted. This was particularly the case in Hungary as late as 1935. In Czechoslovakia 26 per cent of the total land area was in the hands of 1000 families in 1946. Poland and Romania also had imbalances of this kind. But it was probably the large estates which provided such agricultural exports as were produced, tending as such estates did to be efficient and well run by comparison to the smaller agricultural units. They were, however, a source of bitterness, aggravated by the fact that landlords often differed in nationality from their peasants and were in many cases connected to the pre-independence regimes.

The problem of peasant poverty dogged all the states, which were for a variety of reasons politically unable to produce the patterns of land ownership that could give rise to viable medium-sized farms. Interwar land reforms gradually excluded non-native landlords but redistribution policies on the whole protected the holdings of native landlords. Medium sized farms played a limited role. In Poland units of over 100 hectares comprised a negligible proportion of the total number but covered about 43 per cent of the land surface in the late 1930s. There were 100 times more poor peasants than there were rich landowners but the poor peasants possessed only 34 per cent of the land. Calculated in units of surface land, one landowner equalled about 300 peasants (Kagan, 1943).

Disproportionate reliance upon the landowning classes inhibited the role of the state in the agricultural sector of all the economies except Czechoslovakia. Where possible, however, the state did play a leading economic role, establishing credit and finance systems and undertaking the ownership of infrastructure requirements such as transportation networks. In Poland in 1937, although just over 40 per cent of joint-stock companies were foreign-owned, approximately half of all bank credit originated from state banks. The state, as well as owning the railways and airlines and having a monopoly of the production of alcohol, tobacco and armaments, also held large shares in the chemical, coal, iron and steel industries. In 1932–3 Polish state enterprise accounted for about 17 per cent of the general turnover of industry and commerce (Lane, pp. 2–3).

Despite some economic progress, by the outbreak of World War Two most of Eastern Europe was overwhelmingly agrarian and economically undeveloped. Only the Czech lands and the Laender which were to become the German Democratic Republic were fully industrialised. The rest of the area still exhibited the social ills which we normally associate with underdevelopment. High population growth aggravated problems of low income, inadequate food, housing and clothing, high infant mortality, low life expectancy, low literacy rates and generally low levels of education. Patterns were not uniform, however, and considerable differences persisted within the region. According to 1937 National Income statistics, per capita incomes expressed in United States dollars were Czechoslovakia 170, Hungary 120, Poland 100, Romania 81, Yugoslavia 80, and Bulgaria 75. In Britain the same year the figure was 440 dollars, in Sweden it was 400 dollars, in Nazi Germany it was 340 dollars. Average per capita annual income across Europe was 200 dollars in 1937. Whilst improvements were evident on most economic indicators (Moore, 1945, *passim*), the East European states lagged well behind their West European counterparts.

Interwar social patterns

Late dependent development had important social effects, the most significant of which were the persistence of a large peasantry and the absence of a well articulated and confident middle class. The overwhelmingly agrarian and rural nature of interwar Eastern Europe was reflected in a peasant majority in most of the populations. In 1930 Czechoslovakia, with only 33 per cent of her population employed in agriculture, was unique in the region. In the other successor states the peasantry formed a majority of the population. The percentage of the population dependent on agriculture around 1930 was 80 in Albania, 76 in Yugoslavia, 75 in Bulgaria, 72 in Romania, 60 in Poland, and 51 in Hungary (Moore, 1945, p. 26). In Western Europe the equivalent proportions ranged downward from 50 per cent in Spain to 5 per cent in England and Wales, with an average of around 20 per cent or below. In Germany the figure was 20 per cent. Thus the largest social class in interwar Eastern Europe was the peasantry. The persistence of feudalism, with its attendant division of society into landlord and serf, acutely inhibited the development of native intermediate classes before World War One. So great was the size of the gap between landlord and peasant that it effectively precluded mobility between the two classes. Intermediate occupations tended to be performed by groups which differed in language and religion from the majority populations, further inhibiting the emergence of native middle classes. Thus, outside of Czechoslovakia, the native bourgeoisie which eventually developed was small and weak and tended to remain so.

But the class structures were more complex than a three-part scheme consisting of peasants, workers and gentry suggests. Szczepanski (1961), writing about the complex interwar Polish social structure, identifies six distinctive strata, including a landed gentry, an upper middle class, the intelligentsia, the petit-bourgeoisie, the peasantry and the working class. The landed gentry were those aristocrats who retained their lands and enjoyed great traditional prestige. The upper middle classes were the owners of the large and medium sized commercial, financial and industrial enterprises. These two groups formed the ruling class.

The emergent bourgeoisie was the weakest section of the middle class. Its industrialising interests depended for their promotion on the ruling classes and their governments, whose policies favoured the development of a commercial class only insofar as ruling class interests could be protected. Separating the ruling class from the emergent bourgeoisie is analytically difficult in most of the states. Large numbers of the Hungarian landowning aristocracy, for example, sold their land after the nineteenth-century agricultural crises, finding employment in the civil service and liberal professions. A middle class which had the mentality of an aristocracy thus began to form. The Hungarian commercial class was at first mainly Jewish, but after a generation became largely Hungarian. In the interwar period the ruling class was an aristocratic residue of landowners, higher level clergy, military leaders and a few industrialists. Together these were about 6 per cent of the population after 1920. The middle class, about 8 per cent of the total, were bureaucrats, professionals and business people (Toma and Volgyes, 1977).

In Poland circumstances were similar but the process had begun earlier when the 'szlachta' or gentry, became impoverished during the nineteenth century. As in Hungary, a mainly descendant middle class emerged (Seton-Watson, 1945, pp. 123–5). According to Szczepanski, the interwar Polish middle class developed out of the intelligentsia, which he describes as a stratum of non-manual workers earning their living through intellectual, professional and clerical activities. Separated from the classes beneath them by educational achievement, the intelligentsia was linked to the classes above it by shared patterns of social life. In Poland and to some extent in Hungary the intelligentsia was a culturally distinctive group, intertwined both in its own view and in the public imagination with the idea of nation. In the 'Historic' nations the intelligentsia tended to take over the values of the landed aristocracy, with the belief that it embodied the conscience of the nation and had a special responsibility for its survival. Feelings of special mission also pervaded the intelligentsia of the 'non-Historic' nations despite its largely peasant origins.

The original Polish intelligentsia appeared in the nineteenth century and consisted of downwardly mobile gentry who espoused humanist values, aped aristocratic life styles and disdained the activities associated with commerce and trade, which would have diluted their particular character and way of life but given them independent economic strength. Instead, when they had insufficient personal means or could not earn a living from the arts, they preferred to enter white-collar, academic or military employment. The character of the Polish intelligentsia changed considerably during the twentieth century, expanding when the restoration of the state was accompanied by the development of a new salaried class in the 1920s and 1930s (Gella, 1971). The size of the intelligentsia varied as the state developed. In 1931 there were about 665,000 non-manual workers of various types, who comprised about 2.1 per cent of the population and about 25 per cent of those employed by state organisations. Throughout the interwar period this group increased both in number and functions. Hirsowicz (1978) argues that, as it increased in size, the intelligentsia divided into an intelligentsia proper and a white-collar clerical stratum. Moreover, as the Polish educational system developed, the composition of the intelligentsia altered to include large numbers of individuals of peasant and worker origin (Szczepanski, 1961). The intelligentsia supplied the government with functionaries, the political parties with ideologists, journalists and activists and was increasingly productive in scientific and creative fields (Hertz, 1942).

In both Poland and Hungary there is clear evidence that an 'official' class was developing within the state which provided a more substantial base for the middle class than did industry or commerce. State-rooted middle classes are not atypical in countries which are late to industrialise and where economic development is state-led and dependent on foreign finance. Their fundamental characteristic, however, is their dependence, which renders them politically weak, unable independently to press for bourgeois democratic forms. They are forced therefore to rely upon other classes for political muscle and have historically been either pushed aside by the rising working class or held in check by the ruling aristocracy.

The working classes of the region were small and concentrated in 1919, their growth mainly an interwar development. Comparable exact data on the size of the East European urban proletariat are not available, but Moore (1945) supplies figures on the proportions of gainfully occupied males in industrial employment in 1930 which give us a rough indication of its size in the interwar years. In Czechoslovakia the figure was 41 per cent, in Hungary 26 per cent, Poland 22 per cent, in Yugoslavia 14 per cent, in Bulgaria 13 per cent, and in Romania 11 per cent. By contrast, in Britain, Germany and Belgium the comparable figure was 50 per cent (Moore, 1945, p. 125). The working classes did show some signs of a developing class consciousness and amongst skilled workers in the three northernmost countries trade unions prospered as close associates of the social democratic parties, while in Weimar Germany strong christian and communist trade unions also emerged. Elsewhere less powerful unions either had no party connections or were allied with the communist party. In Poland there were also Catholic trade unions, as there were in Czechoslovakia and Slovenia. The fortunes of the unions followed the development of the economies. Their skilled worker base enabled the unions of Poland, Czechoslovakia and Hungary to survive until the outbreak of war, whilst the weaker organisations in Romania and the Balkans were more easily suppressed (Seton-Watson, 1975, p. 188).

The main interwar problem of the peasantry was the pressure of numbers on the land, or rural overpopulation. Ill conceived and poorly executed land reforms left most peasants with holdings barely adequate or inadequate for their subsistence. Their condition was aggravated by rapid population increases and the disappearance of opportunities for emigration. In Yugoslavia, although the proportion of the population employed in agriculture decreased by a few percentage points between 1920 and 1941, its actual numbers increased by 30 per cent (Singleton, 1985, p. 153). The overavailability of rural labour impeded the introduction of agricultural technology, compounding the problem of low international competitiveness in agriculture, hence aggravating the impoverished peasant lot.

The Polish and Hungarian patterns of growing working classes, an over-large and disgruntled peasantry and a weak, dependent middle class were followed by Romania and Croatia, but on a less developed scale. Serbia and Bulgaria were essentially peasant nations which, after independence, developed a middle class of army officers, small town shopkeepers, artisans and rich peasants. Industrialising business classes developed slowly on these bases (Seton-Watson, 1945, pp. 123–5).

Albania had barely changed since the fifteenth century. Important differences between the north and south persisted into the interwar years. Northerners (Ghegs) spoke a somewhat different dialect than the southerners (Tosks). Social differences were more dramatic. The Ghegs formed a tribal society similar to that of the early Scottish clansmen. They were Moslem, with the exception of one important Catholic family. The tribal lands were poor, mountainous and overpopulated. The Tosks were led by large landowners or 'beys'. Their land was more fertile, especially in the coastal plains, and they also had the substantial towns of Tirana, Durazzo and Valona. The land tenure system was of a Moslem feudal type which left the majority with little land. Industry was little in evidence, and such as there was was in the Tosk areas.

In terms of class structure Germany and Czechoslovakia were the exceptions. The ruling class in the Czech lands was a strong commercial bourgeoisie containing a balance of commercial, intellectual and bureaucratic elements which recruited from both the peasantry and the industrial working class during the interwar years. A study of Czechoslovakia's social composition in 1930 (Hajda, 1955, pp. 88–101) divided the total population of 14 million into five classes: an upper class consisting of capitalists, intellectuals and bureaucrats (120,000 or 0.85 per cent); an upper-middle class of the same types as the upper class, but less wealthy and powerful (810,000 or 5.8 per cent); a lower-middle class of merchants, farmers with 2 to 30 hectares of land, small entrepreneurs, and teachers (4,150,000 or 29.6 per cent); an upper-lower class of mainly peasants, small shopkeepers, white-collar workers, and skilled industrial workers (3,490,000 or 24.9 per cent); and a lower-lower class of semi-skilled and unskilled industrial and agricultural workers (5,430,000 or 38.8 per cent). Land reform in Czechoslovakia had been more successful than in other East European countries and, whilst feudal residues were rather more apparent in the Slovak than the Czech lands, the society as a whole was a well articulated and modern one (Ulc, 1974, pp. 45–6). The German class system was also modern. Despite state-led industrialisation under

Bismarck, by the interwar period the German middle classes had considerable independent economic strength. However, their development had perhaps been distorted by early dependence on the state, as they became the most reliable of Hitler's supporters (Lipset, 1960, ch. 5).

East European social structures changed considerably in the decades between the two World Wars. The most important of these changes were those which accompanied industrialisation and national consolidation. A prevailing chauvinist *Zeitgeist* gradually displaced privileged minority groups, a process which was completed in the upheavals of World War Two. The introduction of compulsory education was another source of change. Throughout the period educational provision was increased, illiteracy reduced, and the skills and abilities of the population upgraded. In Poland, by the 1931 census, three-quarters of the population were literate. Such reforms provided a basis for further industrial progress. Yet by 1939 the region was still overwhelmingly agrarian. If the rigid class structures of feudalism had mostly been exorcised, the complex stratification patterns of industrialism were, for the most part, not yet in place.

Interwar politics

The transitional nature of the interwar East European class structures led to poorly articulated social stratification patterns which found reflection in their accompanying political systems. The eventual collapse of the various liberal democracies mainly resulted from the severe class divisions and the lack of sufficient commonality of interests between ruling classes who lived and thought like landowners at the top of the system and the impoverished masses at the bottom. Evidence for this view is to be found in the fact that the only successor state which had a fully articulated class structure was also the only country in which democratic constitutionalism survived. For a variety of reasons class politics were never really played out in Eastern Europe. The middle classes were far too weak in the interwar period to demand and establish liberal democratic forms, which had to be delivered to them by the peace treaties. Imperatives other than class division thus determined initial constitutional arrangements, a circumstance which led to predictably unstable political institutions.

That instability was both reflected and aggravated by the types of parliamentary arrangements which were chosen. In common with the Weimar Republic, the constitutions adopted in Eastern Europe after Versailles were formally extremely democratic ones, characterised in practice by politically weak executives and powerful parliaments. A common problem with such constitutions is that they accommodate numerous parties in legislatures which have the capacity to prevent executives from governing but not to fill the vacuum at leadership level which results.

Arguably strong leadership was called for in the Eastern Europe of 1919. Governments were presented with tasks of unification, harmonisation and the creation of liberal democratic forms in countries in which neither the political traditions nor the supporting socio-economic structures were present. Threats of German, Italian and Soviet expansion also created problems. It is hardly surprising then that, except in Czechoslovakia, one by one, each country adopted a form of absolutism. Hungary after a brief experience of communist rule submitted to the regency of Admiral Horthy in 1920. Albania became subject to the absolute monarchy of King Zog in 1928, Yugoslavia adopted a royal dictatorship in 1929, and Germany accepted Nazi rule in 1933. In Bulgaria, Romania and Poland the constitutional systems lasted rather longer, but experienced both coups and periods of political repression. Bulgaria and Romania became subject to royal dictatorships under Kings Boris and Karol respectively during the 1930s, whilst Poland developed what might be termed a form of incremental presidential autocracy after Pilsudski's coup in 1926. Even the Czechoslovak system experienced difficulties.

There was, however, considerable variation in the degree of autocracy that obtained. Except in Nazi Germany, a variety of political parties and organisations continued to exist. If their role was limited, they nevertheless gained valuable experience of parliamentary politics and political bargaining.

A problem for all the successor states was the establishment of rational administrative systems. Initially these derived from the component empires and states of the pre-war period and their quality and character varied considerably. Predictably problems arose where a nationality with a more primitive structure acquired control over one accustomed to more advanced practices. Seton-Watson (1961, p. 11) writes of a rational and reasonably open 'western' system of administration in the Czech lands and a dictatorial, irrational and corrupt 'eastern' system to be found in the Balkans. These might be regarded as polar types establishing a parameter along which the other administrative structures might be ordered.

It was the party system, however, which most faithfully reflected the political divisions within national cultures. With their parliament-centred constitutions and systems of proportional representation, most of the states experienced an early emergence of multi-partism. Party systems mirrored the class, nationality and religious cleavages to be found in each population. Political parties were built on sectional interests and often institutionalised the most divisive factors in national life. But multi-partism was not in itself an insuperable obstacle to political stability. A multi-party coalition government was the norm in interwar Czechoslovakia. The coalitions successfully dealt with nationality problems aggravated by the economic difficulties of the Great Depression. Other political successes included the submission of the army to political control, the acceptance by the German population (during the 1920s at least) of the legal bounds and framework of the state, the unification of the Slovak and Czech Agrarians into a national party of government. To this might be added the successful pursuit of a wealth-producing strategy of industrial development, the establishment of redistributive welfare policies and the survival of the democratic constitution itself.

Thus the parties were the products of their specific cultures and were often somewhat constrained by their limited roles under autocratic systems. In many cases they played a representative role, providing an outlet for participation but having little influence on policy, Often opposing parties within a particular system had more in common with each other than with the parties which occupied the equivalent part of the political spectrum elsewhere. In addition, patterns were complicated by the presence of a range of national minority parties. But, subject to such provisos, it is possible to detect five main types of political party in the interwar successor states: (1) parties of the conservative right and the bourgeois centre, (2) agrarian or peasant parties, (3) the socialist and social democratic parties, (4) the communist parties and (5) the parties of the radical right, which became especially important in the 1930s.

After the first few years it was normally parties of the conservative right and the bourgeois centre which played the major governing role. The conservatives were supported by the landowning classes and the large and medium sized commercial and financial enterprises. The centre parties tended to be of liberal political persuasion and led by urban middle-class professionals whose policies in the main favoured the business classes. During the 1930s economic problems underlined the differences between these two political groupings and the impoverished mass electorates of most of the states. The conservative and bourgeois parties tended to be nationalistic, which had two important effects. Firstly nationalistic symbols were used to divert attention from domestic problems. The second and more complex effect occurred where, in a multi-national state, one nation obtained control and attempted to impose its symbols and aspirations upon the other nationalities, thereby aggravating and radicalising minorities. Such syndromes may be part of the explanation for communist party support which developed in some agrarian areas during the 1930s.

In Hungary, which boasted no bourgeois democratic parties in the interwar period, the right became ascendant after Miklos Horthy, an admiral of the defunct Austro-Hungarian fleet who organised the armed forces of the countergovernment during the period of Bela Kun's rule, established himself as regent until deposed by the Germans in 1944 (see McCartney, 1957; Rothschild, 1974). Soon after Horthy's rise to power the franchise, which had been introduced under

Entente pressure, was restricted to only 27 per cent of the population. Elections held under this system in 1922 gave an absolute majority to the right-wing government's Party of Unity. Success in this party became the key to a political career. Opposition to it consisted of extreme right wing splinter groups and liberal and social democratic parties. The Communist Party was illegal. Interwar Hungarian governments were interested in the recovery of at least those parts of its pre-war territories in which Magyars resided. Sixty-seven per cent of Hungarian pre-war territory and 58 per cent of its population had been removed by the 1920 Treaty of Trianon. A further government objective was a return to the tightly knit oligarchy which had ruled the country before 1914. Its ruling class was unwilling to share power either with the peasantry or the new urban proletariat. Conservative intransigence, combined with widespread revulsion for communism, socialism and liberal democracy in the political class, was reinforced by the memory of the 133-day Hungarian Soviet Republic in 1919.

Poland's interwar problems were caused mainly by fragmentation. Three different political and administrative traditions, a number of nationalities and a highly individualistic intelligentsia required integration into a coherent political unit. War destruction and military operations against the Soviet Union between 1918 and 1921 placed a severe strain on the economy. Proportional representation institutionalised political fragmentation and by 1925 there existed ninety-two registered political parties, thirty-two of which were represented in the Sejm (parliament), where they were organised into eighteen parliamentary clubs. Stable and lasting governments proved difficult to construct. Fourteen successive governments took office between independence and the Pilsudski coup of May 1926, after which the system gradually became more authoritarian until the general's death in 1935. However, the representative institutions, political parties and interest groups continued to function until the outbreak of World War Two. Before the coup the middle class party was the National Democratic Party, which was closely linked to the Catholic Church and after 1918 was also the strongest party. It went into opposition under Pilsudski and came under the influence of fascism during the 1930s, its anti-Germanism alone preventing it from falling prey to Nazi propaganda.

In Yugoslavia the rising Belgrade capitalist class of the interwar period gave its support to the Serbian Radical Party. The democratic elements of this party proved weak and broke away to become the Democratic Party as the Radicals became the privileged mainstay of King Alexander's dictatorship after 1929. Romania was dominated by the National Liberal Party, which represented big business interests (Seton-Watson, 1961, pp. 25–40).

Czechoslovakia benefited considerably from the political and administrative experience its Czech citizens had been able to gain under the Austrian Hapsburgs and from its more stable social and economic base. Fortunate both in a constitution which provided for a strong executive and in the election of the widely respected Thomas Masaryk as its first president, Czechoslovakia experienced uninterrupted liberal democratic constitutionalism in the interwar decades. After two socialist-dominated cabinets, which lasted from July 1919 to September 1920, power passed to a five-party coalition which dominated the political system until 1939. The pre-eminent party was the Agrarian party, which represented the prosperous and conservative Czech peasantry. The rival focus was the 'castle group', formed from the moderately left-wing National Socialist party of Eduard Benes. Socially radical and strongly nationalistic and anti-clerical, this party attracted the support of the professionals and state officials as well as some from the working class. Strongly liberal democratic in its outlook, Benes' party was a useful political counterbalance to the more interest-orientated Agrarians.

Agrarian or peasant parties were a particularly striking feature of the successor states. At first adherents of peasant radicalism with clear class programmes and organisations, the agrarian parties grew more conservative as they came to be dominated by landholding peasants. Exceptions were found in Bulgaria and Poland. In Bulgaria the peasant leader Stamboliiski took power in 1919 and introduced a radical agrarian regime based upon a land reform which did away with the few remaining large landholdings in the country.

Distrusted by urban politicians and guilty of a certain amount of corruption, Stamboliiski's government was overthrown and he was murdered in a coup in June 1923. However, the Bulgarian Agrarian Union remained committed to radical agricultural reform. The Polish Peasant Party, founded from a number of smaller groups in 1931 resisted the conservatism and 'kulakisation' which befell the peasant parties elsewhere. Efforts by the right-wing Nationalist Party to gain peasant support made little headway. The Polish peasant's political experience was one which produced and encouraged a deep political cynicism, but which also gave to the peasantry a sense of itself as a nation. This feeling survived World War Two, from which the peasantry emerged with its traditions more or less intact (Lewis, 1973, pp. 36–8). Elsewhere, however, peasant organisations became incorporated into the right, leaving the poorer peasantry to seek political redress via the industrially based parties of the left.

Throughout Eastern Europe the Socialist movement after 1919 was divided into Socialist or Social Democratic Parties on the one hand and Communist Parties on the other. The division followed disagreements among socialists over the nature of the Bolshevik revolution, but also reflected deep-rooted differences between reformist and revolutionary conceptions of socialist politics. The movement had been long established in Poland, Hungary and Czechoslovakia, but elsewhere was mainly a post-1918 development.

The Polish Socialist Party (PPS) was founded in Paris in 1892 and operated (mainly illegally) in Russian Poland. In 1900 it split over questions of nationality into Rosa Luxemburg's internationalist Socialist Democracy of the Kingdom of Poland and Lithuania (SDKPL) and the nationalist PPS. In 1918 the PPS left and SDKPL united to form the Polish Communist Party. The remains of the PPS from the three empire territories met at Cracow to found a unified party. While the communists became progressively weaker, the PPS gained the major influence over the trade-union movement and received widespread working class support. It formed strong links with the Polish Peasant Party in conjunction with which it had achieved sufficient popular support by 1939 that historians have since argued that socialism rather than communism is the natural ideology of the Polish left.

The Czechoslovak Social Democratic Party was based historically on the Austrian party founded by Victor Adler in 1889. Although the communists were in the majority after the party split in 1921, by 1930 the two parties were about equally popularly supported. The Hungarian Social Democratic Party ws founded in 1890 and had attracted the support of the Budapest working class by 1914. In the aftermath of war its left formed a communist party which did not recover from the events of 1919. But the Social Democrats themselves were tolerated throughout the interwar period, allowed to operate on the understanding that they did not extend their activities to the peasantry. A cautious, conservative organisation, its major interwar achievement was its survival. The Romanian Socialist Party was also compromised during the interwar period (by its collaboration with the Karol II dictatorship).

In Yugoslavia weak socialist movements in Croatia, Slovenia and Bosnia and a slightly stronger party in Serbia united in 1919 under left-wing leadership to become the Communist Party of Yugoslavia. In Bulgaria, too, the socialists were unable to compete with the communists. Germany boasted the strongest Social Democratic Party (SPD) in Europe. Already internally divided, its left split away to form the Communist Party of Germany after the failed uprising of 1918. Although the SPD experienced periods of government under Weimar, both singly and in coalition, the communists gradually increased their electoral support, mainly at SPD expense, until elections ceased to be held.

Socialist movements throughout Europe thus produced communist parties which emerged after 1918 in all the successor states except Albania. Often at first thriving mass movements, they soon placed themselves under the guidance of the newly formed Communist International, or Comintern, founded in 1920. By 1923 the Comintern was in control of its member parties, which were reorganised along Soviet lines and expected to assume an orientation to Moscow (see Chapter 7). Comintern policy was, for a variety of reasons, notoriously insensitive to national imperatives. The Polish party, for example, was dissolved in 1920 during the Red

Army's advance towards Warsaw, when it became a bureau of the Russian Party. No account was taken of the strong anti-Russian character of Polish nationalism, which was well rooted both in the peasantry and the growing working class. Examples of such insensitivity combined with the fact that most of the parties had been made illegal by 1929 reduced a former mass movement into a set of small, sectarian organisations. Only in Czechoslovakia were the communists able to operate openly. There they obtained about 20 per cent of the popular vote during the 1920s, a proportion which increased over the next decade. The Bulgarian party had achieved about 20 per cent of the vote by the time it was outlawed in 1926 and the Yugoslav party, too, showed some signs of strength in the election it was allowed to contest in 1920, when it turned out to be the third strongest party in terms of popular support. The one election contested by the re-formed Polish party (in 1929) yielded 7.9 per cent of the popular vote.

The fact that most of the communist parties were required to assume a clandestine existence in the interwar period makes membership figures difficult to determine. For Poland, the figure before the party's 1938 dissolution by the Comintern is put at a maximum of 30,000 including its affiliated youth organisation. Other sources estimate membership at between 10,000 and 12,000. These were said to be mainly intellectuals, although about 10 per cent were industrial workers and 31 per cent were peasants (Lane, 1973b, p. 4; Hiscocks, 1963, pp. 72–3). The membership of the Hungarian party never exceeded 1000 in the interwar years. In Hungary only between twelve and fourteen communists were in contact with each other by the end of World War Two, although official sources estimated that there were around 3000 members by the time the Soviet army took Debrecen in 1944.

By 1945 the Czech party had a membership of 80,000, a figure which reflects rapid early post-war recruitment. The Yugoslav party by 1939 had around 20,000 members, after falling to as few as 1000 members in 1932 from a high of 65,000 in 1920. In Albania a few communist groups existed during the 1930s but no organised communist party appeared until 1941, when one was formed with a membership of about 200 under the leadership of a schoolteacher called Enver Hoxha.

Apart from Czechoslovakia and Albania, the parties' fortunes reached a low point in the late 1920s, gradually beginning to recover during the 1930s. Recovery may have in part been due to the adoption by the Comintern of popular-front policies in 1935. But Comintern influence continued to take its toll. Stalinist purges were conducted on the East European parties during the 1930s when many leaders were executed, either in Spain where they were actively engaged in support of the republican side during the civil war or in Moscow where they had been summoned by Stalin. Those party leaders who survived Spain and those who did not opt for Moscow exile in the years of illegality and war gained significant underground experience which placed them well for the organisation of resistance activities. In many cases it was to be their wartime resistance records which finally provided a means for the illegal parties to obtain support.

On the extreme right, fascist mass parties came into being in Poland, Hungary and Romania, the countries with the largest Jewish populations. Elsewhere the pre-existing right-wing regimes simply adapted their structures to suit the Axis powers but never developed indigenous popular movements. In Poland the urban middle class supported the National Radical camp, whilst Hungary and Romania boasted the Arrow Cross and the Iron Guard respectively. Such parties favoured policies of anti-semitism, anti-capitalism and land reform. In Hungary in the 1939 elections the Arrow Cross received 750,000 of 2 million popular votes. The Romanian Iron Guard was also able to achieve a fairly widespread popular support, as did the Croatian movement. But although efforts were made to establish government parties in the states which came under Nazi rule, fascism in the successor states lacked the demonic force which gave German Nazism its dynamism. That this was so may have been due to the presence of what were already fairly conservative regimes, which had the effect of denying the fascists the opportunity to bargain with a politically frustrated right. Or, more simply, it may have been to do with the relative absence of a middle class (see Sugar, 1971; Woolf, 1968).

For a variety of reasons, by the end of the 1930s in Eastern Europe the political right and centre had been discredited and the left had amassed considerable support. The pre-war political indicators were for radical solutions to the region's problems. What was unclear was whether those solutions would come from the radical right or from the revolutionary left. The outcome of a struggle between the two would have been far from a foregone conclusion. As it happened, war was once again decisive in the determination of Eastern Europe's political fortunes. This time, however, it was to be a future to which the different states would be able to bring a historical coherence and recognisable political traditions.

3

War, Communism and Stalinism

Contemporary Eastern Europe comprises a set of state socialist societies which were first established in the years following
World War Two. Their nature and type were a matter for
discussion between the treaty-makers, and in this sense they
may be regarded as products of war. But they are also the
result of events which took place in the years following
liberation as well as of developments in the international
communist movement. In particular, their general political
shape and form owes much to the evolution of the Soviet state
during the 1930s. Stalinism was at its height in the Soviet
Union at the time the East European states were being re-
established. It soon became apparent that it was to be the
dominant political model. But indigenous influences were also
at work, so that each system contained forces which modified
Stalinism in different ways. In an attempt to account for the
establishment of East European state socialism we discuss in
this chapter the impact of war, of liberation and of Stalinism
on the region.

World War Two

World War Two brought profound political, economic and
social change to Eastern Europe. Under German rule the
Jewish population was virtually eliminated and Slavs were
declared *Untermenschen* (sub-human), worthy only of exploitation and dispossession. To varying degrees the educated

classes were decimated by arrests and deportation. Industrial plant which was needed for the war effort was Germanised, the rest left to atrophy.

The war was a watershed for all of Europe, but its political impact varied considerably. The Germans accorded a range of statuses to the East European nations in line with their different forms of government. In many cases the new systems of administration were not exactly co-terminous with inter-war national boundaries. Some states remained self-governing allies of the Third Reich, other states or parts of states were either absorbed directly into the Reich, or experienced direct or mediated German rule. In practice the degree of mediation of German rule corresponded inversely with the degree of brutality of wartime administration.

Bulgaria, Hungary and Romania fought on the German side as allies of the Nazi Reich. Politically they became virtual satellites, but they did escape German occupation. Their economies were integrated into the Reich economy and many died fighting in support of the Nazis. However, except for their Jewish populations, these three countries escaped the brutal subjugation which accompanied occupation. They avoided large-scale destruction until the final stages of the war, when they were caught between the advancing Red Army and the retreating Nazis.

The other countries experienced varying types of German occupation and these fared markedly less well. Czechoslovakia was perhaps the most fortunate in terms of loss of life, but none the less suffered considerably. Some areas were annexed directly by Germany: Slovakia was granted an 'independent' status until 1944 while Bohemia-Moravia became a protectorate administered by the German authorities via corresponding Czech ministries. The army was disbanded, secondary schools were dramatically reduced in number and the intellectual class was targeted for destruction. The German plan was to preserve the Czech peasant and working classes for the duration of the war. Half the Czech nation was to be assimilated, the remainder to be eliminated by various means.

Yugoslavia also experienced mediated Nazi rule, losing 11 per cent (1.75 million) of its total population in the course of the war. Over half of these were slaughtered in the 'independent' State of Croatia established by the Germans. There, Ante Pavelic's 'Ustasa' ran a fascist state. In what remained of Serbia a pattern of occupation was established in which Serb authorities were responsible to occupying Germans. Half of Slovenia was absorbed by Germany and experienced a programme of Germanisation. The remaining lands went to Italy, Italian Albania and Bulgaria.

Elsewhere Nazi rule was direct. Poland, along with the occupied areas of the Soviet Union, was the site of the worst and most sustained German atrocities. Western Poland was incorporated into the Reich. The remainder of the state was treated as a colony, its occupants regarded as slaves. The German Protectorate of Poland did not contain a substratum of Polish authorities through which administration took place. Occupying Nazis administered policies of compulsory labour, large-scale arrests and executions and the banning of the Polish language in schools in the annexed territories. The educated classes were particular targets, approximately 35 per cent losing their lives. In addition, schools were closed, as were universities and other academic institutions. The country was subjected to a systematic slaughter which eventually took 6 million lives, including those of 3 million Polish Jews. The concentration camps with the highest death tolls were all in Poland.

Morris (1984) writes that between 1941 and 1944 two wars were fought in Eastern Europe – one against the Germans and their allies and the other for people's minds. A resistance emerged in all the countries – strongest in Albania and Yugoslavia, where native leaders led movements of significant strength. In Poland, too, the well developed resistance movement comprised a virtual 'secret state', administering the population as well as undertaking military activities. Resistance activities drew support from across the political spectrum, but communists were a force to be reckoned with in each national struggle. After the Nazi invasion of the Soviet Union on 22 June 1941, the Soviet government determined to reorganise the East European communist parties, which, except in Bulgaria, Czechoslovakia and parts of Yugoslavia, where there were traditions of some friendliness toward

Russia, were extremely weak. The communists had both advantages and disadvantages in their bids to increase their support. Stalin's 1941 call for guerrilla warfare behind enemy lines was an about face in Comintern policy, which previously had expected East European communists to offer no resistance to the invading Germans under the terms of the von Ribbentrop agreement (sometimes called the Hitler–Stalin pact), a treaty which caused considerable difficulties for native communists. Another obstacle to recruitment was that Romania, Hungary and Poland were profoundly anti-Soviet and historically anti-Russian. But Stalinism had been built on important qualities of determination and critical organisational skills, which were used to activate communists throughout Europe. By the spring of 1942 a major education and training operation had been launched and communists played an important role in resistance movements. Within the rejuvenated parties differences became apparent between those educated in Comintern schools, who were closely attached to the leadership of the Soviet Union, and the more parochial native-trained underground leaders, who had important resistance responsibilities. During the war years the two groups were able to unite but later their differences were to prove important. The domestic parties worked with socialist and peasant parties in the resistance, a cooperation which became the basis for popular-front governments in the immediate post-war years.

In Yugoslavia the clandestine interwar experience of the Communist Party equipped it well for resistance activities. Tito, a domestic communist leader of considerable ability, responded to Stalin's initiative by calling for a national uprising. Although the partisans were politically divided over many issues, the communists were able to establish their leadership over the resistance, in part because underground status during the 1930s had enabled them to retain a functioning organisational structure. The party politbureau was transformed into a central military staff, and there were local staff headquarters in operation from as early as 1942, by which time Tito had nearly 80,000 soldiers under arms. By 1945 Tito's partisans comprised an army of 300,000 seasoned troops and the national liberation movement numbered

800,000 members. The movement was in effective control of local administration in the liberated areas.

Elsewhere communist leaders were less in evidence but played a significant role, not least because they had advantages in being on the spot whilst other groupings were led by governments in exile. This had profound effects in Poland, where the 1944 Warsaw rising cost the lives of a large proportion of the resistance fighters, who waited in vain for the Red Army to cross the Vistula to assist them. The London-based emigré government was subsequently out-manoueuvred by the Russians, who were able to secure international recognition for the Soviet-backed, Lubin-based Polish Committee of National Liberation. The question of whether the Red Army could have assisted the Warsaw rising has been a subject of dispute ever since. Certainly an outcome in which many able non-communist Polish leaders were killed proved convenient for subsequent Soviet policy. However, the fact that the results were convenient is not, of itself, adequate evidence that the failure of the Red Army to intervene was deliberate. A recent authoritative study indicates that the military situation was much more complex than such arguments allow, and that, in the event, Soviet troops were in no position to assist the resistance fighters (see Erikson, 1983).

The countries which today comprise state socialist Eastern Europe were liberated by the Red Army, a fact which is often regarded as having been decisive in determining their political futures. But war brought other important effects. In Poland, for example, every single village, town and city was affected. Almost three-quarters of its livestock were lost. Total material damage was estimated at 18.2 billion United States dollars and comparable losses accrued elsewhere. The war's end coincided with a severe famine as well as large-scale population migration. Such factors, combined with boundary changes and net population losses amongst some groups, left behind a more coherent East European ethnic map. The successor states were largely returned to their pre-war dimensions, but Estonia, Latvia and Lithuania became part of the Soviet Union, which gained territory from Poland, Czechoslovakia and Romania. Poland, exceptionally, was shifted 125 miles to the west, losing territory to the Soviet Union but gaining highly developed and fertile western territories from Germany. Czechoslovakia ceded Ruthenia to the Soviet Union. Germany was divided, its eastern sector gradually prepared for statehood within what was to become a European bloc of Soviet states.

Liberation and communist ascent

The analysis of what are often termed political 'takeovers' by communist parties has exercised a number of scholars, many of whom have concentrated their attention upon the East European systems (see, for example, Burks, 1964; Hammond, 1975; Seton-Watson, 1961; Tucker, 1968). Various typologies or classification schemes of takeovers have been offered as a result of those analyses. Normally the classification scheme takes into account whether the communists in a particular country came to power mainly as a result of indigenous or external forces. For such purposes Albania and Yugoslavia are usually deemed to have had indigenous revolutions, while the GDR, Poland and Romania are regarded as having had communist regimes imposed upon unwilling populations (Burks, 1964; Hammond, 1975; Tucker, 1968). But Bulgaria, Czechoslovakia and Hungary are sometimes regarded as intermediate types. Thus Burks (1964) sees these three states as examples of parliamentary infiltration by parties with a large popular following. Such strategies were combined with coercion at the point at which progress by parliamentary means faltered. By contrast Hammond (1975) cites Czechoslovakia as the sole example of a semi-legal takeover by a party with considerable popular support. Such disagreements are revealing in that they indicate the variety of ways events in Eastern Europe have been interpreted by Western scholars. But they also point up the difficulties of settling on a single, all-embracing typology of communist party ascent. The great number of disagreements in the literature on this topic are well described by Holmes (1986), who wisely counsels students to concentrate on the factors which contribute to the success of communist bids for power. That is the approach we have chosen here.

The presence or absence of a history of independent statehood, collaboration or non-collaboration with the Axis powers, the survival of non-communist political forces and liberal traditions either at home or in exile and the balance between Soviet, Western and national liberation were all factors which were important in determining post-war political patterns. In Eastern Europe the years between the war and 1948 were characterised by a power struggle in which communists were able by a variety of tactics to take advantage of their control of the media, the army, the police and local government first to undermine and later to destroy their political opponents. These were years of major transformation, involving the restructuring of systems of industrial and agricultural ownership, the movement of national minorities and the overturning of traditional ruling elites. The pace of this change was extremely rapid in Romania, Bulgaria, Yugoslavia and Albania, but slower in Czechoslovakia, Hungary and Poland, reflecting different political circumstances and the need to operate through quasi-democratic forms in those countries in which the Western Allies took a greater interest and where domestic opposition to the communists was stronger and better articulated. In East Germany events proceeded slowly but elsewhere the communists were well established by 1948 – new constitutions were in force, the economies socialised and the collectivisation of agriculture was under way. What has often been referred to as a process of Stalinisation, in which a form of rule devised in the Soviet Union was more and more uniformly applied to the East European states, had begun.

The post-war political map of Europe was drawn in agreements made by the Allies at Yalta and Teheran. The Teheran Conference between 27 November and 3 December 1943 came just before the final Allied attack on Europe. There Churchill, Roosevelt and Stalin agreed to divide the continent into two exclusive zones of influence. The Soviet sphere was to cover Hungary, Romania and Bulgaria. At Yalta (4–11 February 1945) the Western Allies sought to secure agreements about the preservation of the integrity of East European politics. Principles of joint responsibility were proclaimed, but by this stage events had already decreed that the West would have relatively little, if any, influence.

In accounting for the rise of the East European Communist Parties much has been made of the effect of the presence of the Red Army on their success. But Soviet troops played only a small direct role in dealing with opposition. Their presence had an undoubted psychological impact, but the emerging regimes had their own muscle power. In Poland and Czechoslovakia a large contingent of native forces trained in the Soviet Union joined the Red Army in liberating their homelands in much the same manner as De Gaulle's Free French Forces operated with the British and United States' armies. The Polish troops, who were commanded by General Rola-Zymierski, numbered 280,000 soldiers by early 1945. The Czech forces under General Svoboda were a significantly larger number than those who fought with the British. The Romanian Tudor Vladimirescu Division had been recruited by Anna Pauker in the USSR. In Yugoslavia Tito commanded the strongest military force under East European control. In addition, various paramilitary units organised to fight the fascists, such as the Bulgarian partisans and the Romanian 'Apararea', were able to play roles similar to those played by the Russian Red Guard in 1917.

The remnants of Nazi forces surrendered in May 1945 when the Allied armies met in Berlin. Like their counterparts in the West, Red Army commanders in liberated areas needed to secure communications, house and feed troops and administer and keep in order local populations. Everywhere this was dealt with in the same manner. Locals were appointed to oversee the administration of the civilian population. Naturally such individuals were chosen on the basis of their reliability in the eyes of the occupying power in question.

In Eastern Europe former elites were not restored in this process. Within the region a different mode of treatment was accorded those states which had been enemy allies and those which had not. Romania and Hungary, both of which had taken an active part in operations against the USSR, were placed under coalition governments headed by Generals

Santescu and Miklos respectively. These governments contained a modest local Communist Party representation. In both countries a number of fascist activists took the precaution of joining the Communist Party in the confusion of the early post-war years. In Bulgaria, where war against the USSR had literally lasted for only a few hours, power was seized by the Fatherland Front and a government which had considerable Communist Party participation was formed under General Georgiev.

The Bulgarian Fatherland Front was organised by local partisans as an underground resistance movement of agrarians, social democrats, radical independents and communists. They were well placed to seize power by coup in Sofia as Soviet troops entered the country. With its inclusion of noncommunists, the Fatherland Front was a good example of the use of popular-front tactics during this period. Many leading positions were held by political activists who had been opponents of the previous regime. Particular attention was paid to drawing in peasants, but socialists who were direct opponents of the communists for working-class support also participated. Wartime cooperation had erased much of the bitterness between the two parties, so that common stances and commitments to economic and social improvements were emphasised and communists adopted postures which stressed a separateness from the USSR. In September 1946 a plebiscite resulted in the elimination of the monarchy and the establishment of the Bulgarian Republic. In October elections were held for a Grand National Assembly (Sobranje) which was empowered to enact a new constitution, and Georgis Dimitrov, the Communist Party Fatherland Front leader, formed a government. When enacted in 1947, the new constitution became known as the Dimitrov Constitution.

In Romania and Hungary events took a slightly different turn. In Romania the Soviet Union's Deputy Minister of Foreign Affairs, Vyshinsky, established a government under the leadership of Petru Groza, a leader of the radical peasants' Ploughman's Front. This was a nominally coalition government, dominated in fact by the Communist Party. Western pressure at the December 1945 Moscow conference led to the expansion of the coalition to include more non-communists, but later efforts to broaden the basis of Romanian government were unsuccessful.

In Hungary Soviet liberators established a provisional government at Budapest in December 1944 which comprised a temporary legislature based upon five political movements, including a small Communist Party. There were a plurality of communists in the legislature and the party also secured control of the police forces. But at this stage real power lay with the Red Army, and especially with the Allied Control Commission chairman, Kliment Voroshilov. Free elections based on universal suffrage were held in November 1945. The Smallholders Party did best, whilst the Communist Party obtained 17 per cent of the vote. A coalition was formed in which the communists, led by Rakosi, obtained the post of Interior Minister, thus retaining control of the police. In May 1949 elections organised by the Hungarian People's Front for Independence presented voters with a single list of candidates and resulted in full Communist Party control.

In the Soviet-occupied sectors of Germany a rather more protracted course was taken. The Red Army was in complete control of East Germany except for Berlin, which was under joint allied occupation. Initially no government was formed, but local leaders under Ulbricht, who returned with the Red Army, were allowed to re-establish the German Communist Party in May 1945. In June Christian Democrat, Liberal and Social Democratic parties were licensed. In July 1945 all the parties joined the Anti-Fascist Democratic Bloc, which was later renamed the Democratic Bloc of Parties and Mass Organisations and in October 1949 became the National Front. The establishment of a government in East Germany was delayed pending national reunification. A constitution was enacted only in 1949 and formal sovereignty was not conceded until the mid-1950s. Although the Socialist Unity Party (SED), a 'coalition' of communists and social democrats, was in clear control of the system from 1949 onwards, a number of other political parties continued to be represented in the legislature (Volkskammer). Another lasting feature of the East German state dating from this period is the continued presence of approximately twenty Soviet divisions, amounting to 400,000 troops.

Elsewhere Soviet occupation policy took somewhat different forms. Mindful of the interest of Western Allies and to a lesser extent of the prerogatives of exile government, account was taken of local political formations in Yugoslavia and Czechoslovakia, whilst Poland and Albania were each, for different reasons, special cases. There was no Soviet occupation of Yugoslavia, where the Red Army withdrew immediately after taking Serbia and Belgrade. The London-based exile government was a coalition of mainly Serbian pre-war parties under King Peter. This was rivalled at home by Josef Broz Tito's partisans, who were multi-party and multi-national in composition, but unquestionably communist in leadership and programme. A competing resistance movement was led by the exiled government's Minister of War, General Mihailovic, who engaged Tito's partisans in civil war and eventually collaborated with the Nazis in the hopes of ousting the communist-led partisans. But it became increasingly evident that it was the Titoists who commanded local support. Receiving (belated) assistance from the Allies, Tito was able to liberate and therefore administer a considerable part of Yugoslavia. He was well entrenched by the time the Red Army arrived. Thus Tito's assumption of state power was a foregone conclusion, although the Yalta Conference successfully demanded the inclusion of two members of the exiled cabinet in his first government.

In Czechoslovakia the resistance movement was not widespread, although a major revolt of communists and non-communists occurred in Slovakia in 1944. The government in exile under President Benes enjoyed good relations with Moscow after 1941 and was able to conclude a military alliance and agreement over the administration of territories occupied by the Red Army. Agreement was also reached between the Benes government and Czech and Slovak communists in Moscow. Upon liberation a Government of National Unity was formed, with Benes as president, but in which communists had a substantial share.

Relations between the USSR and the Polish government in exile were nowhere near as good. Considerable acrimony was generated by the Soviet acquisition of interwar Poland's eastern territories in 1940, after which relations were strained.

In 1942 Moscow agents founded a new workers party in Poland, headed by native communist Wladislaw Gomulka. Meanwhile German troops announced the discovery of mass graves of Polish officers in the forest at Katyn in eastern Poland. The exiled government in London accused the Soviets of the crime, causing the USSR to break off relations. As Poland was liberated, a series of communist-dominated Committees of National Liberation were formed, with their headquarters at Lublin. The Lublin committee soon proclaimed itself to be Poland's provisional government, alarming the London Poles. The provisional government recognised Soviet sovereignty in eastern Poland, securing in exchange the right to administer the liberated lands. The home army, which was organised by the London Poles, received no Soviet aid when the Warsaw rising took place (see above, p. 00). The rising was crushed by the Germans and numerous leading supporters of the exiled government died. Thus, once the Germans were expelled by the Red Army, the provisional government was in command of the country. But after intervention by the Western Allies at Yalta, the government was reorganised as a coalition of five parties. This time the peasant leader Mikolajczyk was included as a representative of the London Poles. The Yalta conference conceded the Soviet claims to the eastern territories and promised as compensation territorial concessions in the north and west.

The status of the three exiled governments differed considerably, with that of the Czechoslovaks having the most credible claim to legitimacy. The authoritarian interwar sources and almost exclusively Serbian basis of King Peter's cabinet, combined with the widespread support given locally to Tito, helped to destroy its case for governing Yugoslavia. The Polish case, however, was less clear cut. That the exiled government was able to command considerable domestic support was evident from both the activities and size of its 'home army', the mainstay of the Polish resistance movement. But the experience of war, occupation and liberation generated changes in political attitudes which were reflected in a growing popular support for the left. However, that support did not extend to the point of favouring Soviet-style communism in a country in which war-hardened anti-German opinion did not alleviate the strong anti-Russian feelings and deeply felt nationalism which were important elements of the political culture. Awareness of the existence of this particular cocktail of attitudes is crucial to the understanding of postwar Polish politics. Their strength during the period when communist rule was being established partly explains why Poland has presented the greatest obstacles to the legitimation of communist party government of any country in the region.

Albania's wartime and liberation experiences bear a passing resemblance to those of Yugoslavia but were in many respects unique. Occupied first by Italy and later by Germany, Albania was engaged in hostilities against Yugoslavia and Greece. At home a civil war took place between rival partisan forces. The Liberation Front led by communist Enver Hoxha was able to seize power in 1944 without any assistance from the Red Army. No government in exile existed, so that there was no need to make any gestures to the West, and Hoxha was able to set about establishing and maintaining a Stalinist form of rule from the outset, a programme he continued until his death in 1984.

By the end of 1945 communist parties led the governments of seven of the eight states. (East Germany was at this stage still under direct military control.) Under Soviet auspices they were normally the dominant partners in coalitions of anti-fascist parties. Initially communists took care to acquire control of the media and normally either held the post of Interior Minister or made sure this went to a reliable fellow traveller. Police forces were purged, the politically reliable being appointed to key posts and former officers with useful skills and pasts which made them potentially politically reliable recruited for police work.

As well as controlling police forces, ministries of the interior had the responsibility for organising and running elections. Between 1945 and 1947 more or less free elections were contested by those parties which were members of the communist-led popular fronts. The returns showed significant but not decisive levels of popular support for the communist parties. In Czechoslovakia the communists obtained 38 per cent of the vote. In Bulgaria the Fatherland Front stood unopposed, owing to opposition abstention. The front obtained 348 of 414 seats, of which 73 were communist-held. Widespread violence and intimidation characterised the Polish elections of January 1947, where the government bloc obtained 80 per cent of the vote and 392 of 444 seats. The coalition phase was coming to a close.

The next phase was the creation of single united parties by amalgamations between communist and socialist parties. The 1947 United States Marshall Aid programme accelerated this process. Moscow, which could not hope to match the US offer, placed considerable pressure on the East European governments to reject Marshall Aid and to phase out the 'front' governments. Accordingly, socialist and communist parties merged, were declared the effective government and then purged. The new arrangements were given institutional shape by a set of new constitutions proclaiming the establishment of people's democracies. The earliest of these was enacted in Yugoslavia in 1946, the latest in Poland in 1952.

Such events often included coercion and alarmed non-communists. The 1948 political crisis in Czechoslovakia arose from attempts to stop Communist Party appointments in the police. In fact communists were able to make good use of their control of various judicial institutions as they sought to consoldiate their power. 'Plots against the state' were unearthed and the accused were subjected to widely publicised trials, the first of which were held in 1946. Opposition leaders were purged. Thus the trial of Mihailovic in Yugoslavia in 1946 was followed by trials of leaders of 'other' parties in Bulgaria, Romania, Hungary and Czechoslovakia in 1947. Only Poland did not hold such trials.

An objective assessment of the political disposition of Eastern Europe in the late 1940s must include some acknowledgement of a considerable popular support for communist parties in the region. Although post-war communist success involved coercion and violence and drew strength and inspiration from the existence of a powerful model of established socialism in the USSR, these were not its sole basis. As Morris (1984, pp. 25–6) writes, the commitment of communists to change caught something in the prevailing mood, which had been significantly radicalised by war. There was a widespread conviction that the political and economic systems which had led to total war were morally wrong. A swing to the left characterised elections across Europe as communists entered governments in Italy and France and Churchill was seen off by a British Labour Party landslide. The popular-front governments were able to harness similar moods in Eastern Europe. By the end of the war popular sentiment strongly favoured their policies of nationalisation and land reform. It was widely agreed that the return of industry to its pre-war owners would be impracticable. It was further agreed that property owned by the retreating Germans should be redistributed. Moreover, the idea that state control would be needed to oversee the conversion of war economies to peacetime work was also readily accepted. In short, the key elements of the communists' political programme – nationalisation, land reform, the redistribution of confiscated property, the organisation of trade unions, the establishment of welfare systems – were popular.

Stalinism

Stalinism as a system of rule began properly in the Soviet Union in 1934, but it was based on foundations laid before that date. The characteristic features of Stalin's Russia which were transplanted to Eastern Europe were threefold. First were sets of practices associated with the personal dictatorship, including not only the 'cult of personality' but also terror, purges and authoritarian rule. Second were sets of institutions, including hierarchies, councils, assemblies, executives and planning and administrative organs, whose coverage included most areas of political, social and cultural life. The most important institution and the one which dominated all the others was the democratic centralist communist party. But rule over rather than through the party was accomplished by police penetration of the administrative apparatuses of both the party and the state. Finally there existed sets of economic policies centred on the establishment of a planned, command economy. These included an industrialisation drive conducted at the fastest possible pace, the collectivisation of agriculture over a short period of time and strict centralisation of the economy.

The organisational keynote of Stalinism was dual control. Within both the party and the state responsibilities over-lapped and were duplicated. No one network or individual enjoyed a permanent advantage over another. Rivalry, suspicion and insecurity were encouraged in a system in which Stalin's control over personnel gave him the necessary scope for adjusting the balance. The specific characteristics of his rule were relative ones. It was its wide scope, its personal nature and the unpredictable manner in which it was exercised which made Stalinism distinctive. Its effect cannot ultimately be reduced to a mere list of characteristics, which ultimately must fail to convey the general atmosphere of oppression Stalinism generated.

The important preconditions to the establishment of Soviet Stalinism had been fulfilled by the collectivisation and nationalisation programmes implemented between 1928 and 1934. From 1934 onwards Stalin's personal rule over the Soviet Union became increasingly well established. As his dictatorship took hold, the position of individual party members became ever more insecure and the party itself declined in significance. Under Stalin it was the newly established professional bureaucrat rather than the old style revolutionary leader who was influential. Stalin's hegemony extended to the whole of the communist movement and he habitually interfered in the politics of the European Communist Parties, breaking the careers of many Comintern leaders while providing backing, training and sanctuary for others. Within and outside the USSR new leaders owed their careers to Stalin. In the Soviet union domestically minded nationalists became ascendant. Power came more and more to be concentrated in the party politbureau, which evolved into a unique training ground for its members. They gained enormous experience as all types and orders of decision were referred to the top. But the knowledge and experience which survivors gained were countered by the inhibiting baggage of the fear of initiative which the system carried with it.

Like any personal dictatorship, Stalinism took its point of

departure from the system over which it was imposed. In the USSR this was not a well established system, but a society in transition from revolutionary upheaval to a more ordered set of forms. The post-war East European states were also in some disarray and certainly might be regarded as transitional. But they differed significantly from the Soviet Union of the 1930s and were, in varying degrees, rather less receptive to Stalinism. Nevertheless attempts were made to impose the model on the East European states between 1948 and 1953.

The 'Stalinisation' of the East European states was never really completed. It met with two major obstacles. The first was a lack of system receptivity. It arose from the fact that Stalinism in Eastern Europe was applied in a concentrated form, with all of its properties appearing at more or less the same time. What had evolved over two decades in the Soviet Union was intended to be established full blown in Eastern Europe. But the shorter experience of Stalinism there meant that ultimately some of the transplants simply did not take root. Differences between the post-war East European states and Bolshevik Russia are important here. As we have seen, the countries of Eastern Europe harboured important traditional institutions of sufficient strength to require accommodation. Peasant organisations and churches, for example, were often so powerful that it proved easier to retain them than to continue with policies of persecution. Moreover, the higher degree of commitment to democratic institutions in interwar Eastern Europe than in pre-revolutionary Russia made for greater resistance to some of the transplanted institutions. A relatively weaker popular commitment to socialist revolution caused initial diffidence about accepting the new order, a hesitation which was compounded by the brutal manner in which that order was presented. Finally, the domination of the USSR over countries which had long been traditional enemies limited the extent to which nationalism could be harnessed as an instrument of political mobilisation (Brus, 1977).

The other important obstacle to Stalinist legitimation resulted from the fact that isolation from abroad never became so complete in Eastern Europe as it had in the Soviet Union. Regime successes could therefore be (and often were) negated by knowledge of more impressive accomplishments elsewhere. The spectacular achievements of economic growth in the 1930s in the Soviet Union occurred during a catastrophic western depression. The more modest achievements of the early years of state socialism in East Europe were easily overshadowed by the fact that the West was experiencing an unprecedented economic boom.

Stalin's wish to take control of the specific policies of the satellite governments also produced problems, which were manifested most spectacularly in Tito's 1948 break with the USSR and the subsequent expulsion of Yugoslavia from the Cominform. There followed purges of 'Titoists' and other 'Revisionists' throughout the region. Once again Poland was the only country which did not try, purge and execute native communist leaders. During the Stalinist period political trials in 1949 in Albania, Hungary and Bulgaria led to the executions of Koci Xoxe, Laszlo Rajk and Traicho Kostov. In Czechoslovakia Rudolf Slansky was tried and executed in 1952. In Romania the trials of Lucretiu Patrascanu and Vasile Luca were held in April and October 1954. Only many years later was it officially admitted that all been tried, convicted and executed on charges which were false.

Despite its excesses Stalinism was a powerful unifying force for communists. The cult of personality provided an important sense of direction and purpose for party cadres, who found it difficult to adjust first to Stalin's death in 1953 and later to the revelations about the iniquities of his rule made by Khrushchev in his famous 'secret speech' to the twentieth congress of the Communist Party of the Soviet Union (CPSU) in 1956.

Although some changes had already been introduced in the Soviet Union (Malenkov's New Course), Khrushchev's speech marked the beginning of a wide-ranging process of de-Stalinisation. But the new policies were not uniformly welcomed by party leaders attached to Stalinist methods. In a number of cases far-reaching disturbances resulted. Changes in the GDR led almost immediately to revolts by industrial workers in Berlin, while Czech workers revolted in Pilsen. Economic concessions brought the Pilsen workers under control but Soviet troops were used in Berlin. In Poland changes came only after a revolt by workers in Poznan was suppressed. The rehabilitation of native leader Gomulka and his installation as leader of the Polish United Workers Party received grudging Soviet assent. In Hungary what might be regarded as a full-scale revolution reached a climax in 1956, when the Soviet Union used direct military intervention to quell the rebellion.

The five years after 1956 witnessed varying degrees of de-Stalinisation, with the greatest changes occurring in Yugoslavia and the least probably in staunchly Stalinist Albania. In 1961 Khrushchev led a renewed assault on Stalin's political record at the twenty-second congress of the CPSU, bringing new crises in its wake. The years since Stalin's death have been characterised by increasing differentiation between the states. Poland, Yugoslavia and Hungary have tended to be most innovative while Bulgaria, Romania, the GDR and Czechoslovakia more cautious. Indeed Czechoslovak Stalinism lasted until at least 1958 and continued in only a slightly modified form until 1968. Only then did a large scale party-led questioning of the system generate widespread demand for change in what has become known as the Prague Spring, which resulted in the invasion of Czechoslovakia by military forces on behalf of the five Warsaw Pact countries that August.

Apart from Yugoslavia, which early and assertively chose an independent course, Poland was perhaps the country in which Stalinism was least effectively imposed. There the peasantry remained largely uncollectivised, a peasant party was retained and a relatively greater degree of separation between state and society was preserved. The unique factor in the Polish de-Stalinisation process was the availability of Gomulka, disgraced and jailed, but not executed as so many other East European leaders had been. Poland had an alternative. But Gomulka's regime failed to rise to the challenge of establishing its legitimacy. It became progressively more illiberal, finally falling after the massacre of striking shipyard workers in Gdansk in 1970. His successor, Edward Gierek, inherited both a weak party and a stagnant economy. Gierek's failure to deal with either led to further workers' risings and eventually to the rise of Solidarity, an independent trade union. Solidarity's increasing success and radicalism in the face of a disintegrating party provoked the imposition of military rule at the end of 1981.

Elsewhere de-Stalinisation, normalisation and reform left recognisably comparable systems of government in place, in which party rule is exercised through an array of what have become increasingly stable state institutions. These managed and oversaw complex social and economic transformations, adjusting both to national imperatives and varying degrees of Soviet interference. In the next three chapters we shall trace and describe the economic and then the social orders which have resulted from those transformations.

4
The Structure and Development of Centrally Planned Economies in Eastern Europe

A distinctive feature of the state socialist societies of Eastern Europe is that, with the partial exception of Yugoslavia (and to some extent, Hungary since 1968), they are all centrally planned economies. The level of output of manufacturing industry is the most frequently cited yardstick of successful economic performance. This level of performance is, along with the pattern of distribution of national product, an important element of the claim to legitimate rule of the Marxist–Leninist parties. We start this chapter with a brief consideration of the performance of the East European centrally planned economies (CPEs) in comparison with the West. While mindful of the great difficulties they face, we should also not forget that their achievements are impressive. We shall then outline the distinctive features of the communist pattern of industrialisation, which produced the Stalinist model of economic planning and management. A summary of the debates on economic reform of industry along with a more detailed country-by-country description of the experience of implementing reform and current problems of economic policy will be left to Chapter 5. Here we focus particularly on industry, but it is important to remember that, for most of Eastern Europe in 1945, agriculture was the major source of employment for at least one-third of the working population. It is therefore necessary to understand how developments within the agricultural sector determine, and are in turn affected by, what occurs within the industrial sector. Equally the manner in which the interests of managers and workforce are represented will be briefly mentioned (an analysis of their role within the wider political system will be found in Chapters 10 and 11). However, the interrelation between sectors of the domestic economy are not the sole focus of our study, but detailed examination of foreign trading patterns will be left to Chapter 13.

Eastern Europe is different

All too often evaluation of the performance of CPEs is founded upon the assumption that they are inherently inefficient, and achieve a sub-optimal level of output, compared with the Western market economies. As this is a one-sided judgement, we need to give some thought to the way in which the CPEs are analysed and evaluated. A central platform of their claim to legitimacy is that they have broken with capitalism, and are based on a socialist 'mode of production' which itself is undergoing a further transformation towards the attainment of a higher communist stage. Marxism–Leninism emphasises the forms of ownership and control of economic activity, and asserts that the source of all measures of what is valuable (and therefore the prices at which goods exchange) is 'labour power' and not the 'invisible hand of the market'. Social ownership of the means of production (in finance, industry, trade and agriculture), and the direction of economic life in accordance with a centrally formulated plan, are presented as the insurance against the 'anarchy' of the market. In recent years there has been considerable debate within neo-Marxist circles on the exact nature of the 'mode of production' within CPEs (see in particular the work of Tony Cliff, Ernest Mandel, Paul Sweezy, Charles Bettelheim, Hillel Ticktin, and Rudolf Bahro), on whether this public ownership is 'social' or 'statised' (Brus, 1975), and on whether 'rationality' can ever be wholly achieved within the framework of an economic plan without the aid of the market in some form. However, what is obvious from the reading of any East European textbook on economics is that indigenous theory bears little resemblance to the sophistication of classical Marxist political economy. Alex Nove (1983) argues that the architects of the CPEs are unable to provide us with a 'Political Economy of Socialism', and that at the same time Marxist economics is either irrelevant or misleading in respect of the problems that must be faced by any socialist economy (Nove, 1983, pp. 58–9). Certainly a number of problems are left unresolved: the labour theory of value; the consequences of scarcity; the need for a division of labour and bureaucratic organisation in a complex economy; the limitations upon ex-ante planning, the role of material and moral incentives; and, not least, that of human freedom of choice.

But the acceptance that CPEs have inbuilt difficulties should not lead us into an uncritical acceptance of Western neo-classical economics, whose central tenet is that firms are price-takers and can only optimise their 'production function' once they have costed alternatives. In such a theory the absence of a free market to register costs and prices means that by definition a CPE will be inefficient. As Alec Nove (1980, p. 367) reminds us:

> we ought not to compare Soviet economic performance and efficiency with the idealised world of the text book, whether a 'bourgeois' text book or one expressing the Utopian hopes of a neo-Marxist enthusiast. Criteria of judgement applied to the real world, whether in the Soviet Union or anywhere else, should relate to the possible, and the place and time.

Thus it is wrong to compare 'model' with 'muddle' in any system, and his remarks are as pertinent to the East European economies as they are to the USSR. Like Nove, we take the juxtaposition of the polar opposites of 'plan versus market' to be misleading; in any feasible socialist economy (or capitalist economy for that matter) both must co-exist (Nove, 1983). It follows therefore that we need to understand the CPEs on their own terms, as developments from specific historical and institutional circumstances.

Interestingly, examination of the achievements of the CPEs with respect to a number of key macro-economic variables indicates that their differing structures and experiences have produced patterns of economic activity that are not widely different from those to be found in the Western industrialised countries (see Table 4.1). One comparative study of the OECD and East European economies for the period 1950–79 has concluded that there are no significant differences between aggregate growth rates of GDP, that growth is slowing down at similar rates and showing similar fluctuations in sectoral output (with the exception of agriculture), and that in both sets of countries rates of growth of gross fixed capital investment are more or less comparable. Apart from performance in agriculture, the main differences lie in the much higher labour participation rates and associated labour shortage of Eastern Europe, while growing unemployment is the major problem facing the OECD, and the more highly developed service sector in the West (Pryor, 1985, pp. 205, 212, 216–17). It is of course questionable whether macro-economic data can provide a sufficiently accurate picture. It is possible that the main difference lies at the micro-economic level, with sub-optimal performance of firms, farms etc. being more marked in the Eastern bloc. It is also possible that official statistical data for these countries is highly unreliable. Yet it is undeniable that in a period of 40 years the East European countries have built up manufacturing industry and public services such as education, health and housing from a very low level, and avoided the great personal and social privation common during the interwar period. As we have seen, only the GDR and Czechoslovakia were industrialised before 1945. Current economic indicators would suggest that most countries have advanced along the road towards industrialisation since then (see Table 4.2).

It should be noted at the outset that differences exist in the way in which economic performance is evaluated in the two types of system. For a start, East European National Income is calculated in a different way from that usually found in Western economies. In the centrally planned economies it is called Net Material Product (NMP), while in the West it is known as Gross National Product (GNP). Drawing upon the

TABLE 4.1
Average growth rates, 1950–79 (%)

	Relative per capita GDP 1970	GDP per capita	GDP	GDP per economically active	Industrial production	Agricultural production	Gross fixed capital investment
EASTERN EUROPE: OFFICIAL GROWTH DATA							
Bulgaria	37.3	—	—	—	11.44	2.15	10.89
Czechoslovakia	62.0	—	—	—	5.90	0.25	6.11
East Germany	63.9	—	—	—	6.22	1.73	8.52
Hungary	42.7	—	—	—	7.12	0.83	8.85
Poland	35.4	—	—	—	8.46	1.46	9.70
Romania	31.2	—	—	—	12.05	2.86	11.33
USSR	46.9	—	—	—	8.90	2.30	8.02
Unweighted average		—	—	—	8.58	1.66	9.06
EASTERN EUROPE: RECALCULATED DATA							
Bulgaria	37.3	5.43	4.69	4.91	9.48	2.51	—
Czechoslovakia	62.0	3.67	3.02	2.80	4.38	0.62	—
East Germany	63.9	3.77	4.04	3.71	4.68	1.54	—
Hungary	42.7	3.64	3.22	2.96	4.81	1.20	—
Poland	35.4	4.12	2.98	2.61	6.78	1.56	—
Romania	31.2	5.81	4.78	4.71	9.45	2.39	—
USSR	46.9	4.95	3.64	3.62	6.99	3.04	7.03
Unweighted average		4.49	3.77	3.62	6.65	1.84	—

	25.8	5.87	4.84	4.91	8.93	2.66	7.48
Yugoslavia							
OECD							
Australia	69.6	4.54	2.56	2.15	—	1.82	4.43
Austria	63.1	4.74	4.38	4.76	5.35	1.82	5.95
Belgium	72.0	4.00	3.51	3.53	5.11	0.61	4.36
Canada	81.9	4.57	2.69	1.88	5.46	1.49	4.36
Denmark	83.3	3.81	3.15	2.97	4.79	0.87	5.42
Finland	63.1	4.48	3.92	3.95	5.82	1.06	4.54
France	73.2	4.86	3.93	4.24	5.84	1.79	6.41
West Germany	78.2	4.85	3.87	4.31	5.55	1.93	5.69
Greece	38.7	6.20	5.51	6.40	8.74	2.92	7.16
Ireland	40.5	3.45	3.06	3.75	—	—	5.66
Italy	49.2	4.92	4.22	4.62	6.71	1.91	4.79
Japan	59.2	8.35	7.23	7.06	—	—	11.43
Netherlands	68.7	4.58	3.39	3.59	5.92	3.18	5.10
New Zealand	64.6	3.46	1.78	1.38	—	—	—
Norway	68.4	4.15	3.37	3.53	4.88	-0.16	4.95
Portugal	27.1	5.43	5.07	4.72	7.63	0.86	6.49
Spain	48.9	5.53	4.52	4.86	7.81	2.49	7.43
Sweden	86.6	3.69	3.08	2.88	4.60	0.22	4.18
Switzerland	72.4	3.72	2.52	2.33	—	—	4.63
UK	63.5	2.72	2.29	2.39	2.67	2.17	4.29
USA	100.0	3.39	2.05	1.67	3.46	1.18	3.09
Unweighted average		4.54	3.62	3.66	5.65	1.52	3.09

(Yugoslavia row values: 25.8, 5.87, 4.84, 4.91, 8.93, 2.66, 7.48)

Source: Frederic L Pryor (1985) 'Growth and Fluctuations of Production in OECD and East European countries', *World Politics*, Vol. 27, No. 2, January, pp. 209–210.

TABLE 4.2

Main economic indicators

	Albania	Bulgaria	Czecho-slovakia	GDR	Hungary	Poland	Romania	Yugo-slavia	USSR
1 Share of sectors: NMP 1982 (%)									
Agriculture	—	}19	7.4	}8	}14.7	}16.5	}19.7	14.5	}15.3
Forestry	—		1.0					0.8	
Industry	—	54	61.6	70	37.2	48.9	55.7	40.1	51
Construction	—	10	10.1	6	9.9	11.0	7.4	9.6	9.9
Transport of freight	—	8	4.3	4	}38.2	}23.6	}6.4	8.1	6.0
Trade and public catering	—	6	11.9	9			}10.8	19.7	17.0
Other	—	3	3.7	3				7.2	
2 Annual Average % change in NMP by volume									
1979		6.6	3.1	3.8	1.9	−2.3	5.9	7.0	2.2
1980		5.7	2.9	4.4	−0.8	−0.6	2.9	2.2	3.9
1981	6.0–6.4 (planned)	5.0	−0.1	4.8	2.5	−12.0	2.1	1.4	3.2

	1	2	3	4	5	6	7	8
1982	2.9a							
1983	4.2	−0.2	2.6	2.6	−5.5	2.6	0.7	3.5
1984	3.0	2.2–2.7	4.4	−0.5	6.0	3.4	−1.3	3.1
1985	4.6e	3.2e	5.4	2–2.5e	5.0–6.0e		1.5e	3.1e
3 Population								
Total (in millions)	8.9b	15.4a	16.7b	10.7b	36.7b	22.6b	22.6b	275.0a
Working population	4.1c	7.849c	8.368	4.779b*	11.563b	10.428+	10.077	40 (1978)
By sector of employment (%)								
Agriculture	}23.3b	}13.1e	}10.6	}21.8	}8.7	}29.0		
Forestry								
Industry	34.2	39.4	38	31.7	38.4	36.5		
Construction	8.5	9.5	7.0	7.5	9.4	7.7		
Transport of freight/communication	7.3	6.3	7.4	7.9	9.0	7.3		
Trade and public catering	8.6	9.4	10.2	10.0	9.60	5.9		
Others (%)	18	22.3	26.8	21.1	24.9	13.6		
Registered unemployed							9.7	

Key: a = 1984; b = 1983; c = 1982; e = estimate; * = excluding private agriculture, industry and services; + = including private agriculture

Source: The Economist Intelligence Unit (EIU) 'Regional Review: Eastern Europe and the USSR 1985', London: The Economist Publications, 1985.

distinction in Marxist political economy between productive and unproductive labour, NMP measures production (produced tangible goods), including repairs and maintenance, transportation and commerce, and excludes certain services, namely public administration (state and municipal), health and education. Net Material Product (distributed refers to the destination of the national product: either to accumulation (investment) or consumption, taking account of the balance between exports and imports, losses incurred and any statistical discrepancies. Accumulation refers to that portion of national income that is spent internally on additions to fixed assets in both the productive and non-productive sector, and to increases in inventories and circulating funds. Consumption is that portion of national income used for both private and public consumption.

The use of different categories and concepts obviously creates some difficulties in making a comparison with Western countries. These are complicated further in the case of statistics on industrial performance. It is CMEA (the Council of Mutual Economic Assistance, or COMECON) practice to include mining, manufacturing, electricity, gas and water, but not construction. Thus most of the East European aggregate statistical series for the volume of production omit services and focus exclusively upon net or gross material product. The consequent tendency for the service sector to be neglected means that differences in output compared with the West may be exaggerated (Pryor, 1985, p. 206). But, contrary to popular preconceptions, East European statistical sources are sufficiently reliable, with some adjustments, to make comparisons possible. Only when we use fiscal data generated by the official budget in order to infer policy developments do we have to exercise more caution (Bahry, 1980). Thus care to avoid substituting preconceptions for analysis and an informed use of the available data are the key elements of a balanced assessment of the East European economies.

The strategy of industrialisation

The path followed by the East European economies has

largely been conditioned by the experiences of the USSR. But the Stalinist model of planning and management was not the original point of departure and subsequent distinction for their economic development after 1945. Only between 1948 and 1956 did the Stalinist model prevail.

In just the same way as the concept of 'totalitarianism' has acquired several synonyms, so has the Stalinist model of the economy. It has also been referred to as the 'command', 'directive' or 'centralised' model, and has been described by one Polish economist as a 'sui generis war economy' (Lange, 1970). Its features arise largely from the strategy of industrialisation pursued, as follows:

1 Preference for fast economic growth.
2 Preference for import-substitution as a consequence of a closed economy (autarchy) and the need for self-sufficiency.
3 The presumption that the larger the proportion of the social product allocated for accumulation, then the higher will be the rate of growth.
4 The insistence that the production of industrial producer goods – iron, steel, coal and machinery ('Department A') – should exceed that of consumer goods ('Department B').
5 A very high degree of centralisation of economic planning and management in order to mobilise resources and implement the strategy.
6 A reliance upon 'great and sudden spurts' to achieve success and reduce the technological gap with the West (Fallenbuchl, 1970).

The end product of such a strategy is the Stalinist model of the economy which entails:

(a) Domination of economic activity by a legally binding and centrally determined plan.
(b) The establishment of an extensive bureaucratic hierarchy within which communication tends to follow vertical channels and control over production units is assured by the principle of one-man management. At each level of the

hierarchy a single person is accountable for performance to his superiors. Usually this necessitates a three-tier hierarchy: industrial enterprise, central administration and industrial ministry.

(c) Within the bureaucratic framework planning calculations are carried out in physical ('volume') terms, rather than through a measure of value such as prices. The major instrument is the set of 'material balances' (a series of tables linking physical inputs and outputs throughout the production process). Where used in the process of transactions between production units or in relations with administrative bodies (as opposed to consumer sales), prices serve mainly as a unit of account or ex-post evaluation.

(d) It follows from the above points that planning and management are not activities for the workforce. Workers' interests are 'represented' by the trade unions, whose role is mainly to mobilise labour and to attend to social welfare needs rather than to encourage direct autonomous participation in management decision-making.

(e) The counterpart in agriculture is collectivisation for the purpose of transferring resources to industry.

(f) Industrial effort is directed primarily towards military goals.

There has been considerable debate about whether the strategy of industrialisation, the resultant economic model, and the accompanying political controls of a one-party state were inevitable in Soviet and East European conditions. Given the high priority accorded to industry in Marxist–Leninist ideology, the strategy of industrialisation adopted in Eastern Europe was crucial to economic success. Studies of the process of economic development have concluded that there are many patterns of growth. We may not automatically assume that all developing countries catch the train of economic growth at the same 'station' and pass along the same route. The Soviet model of industrialisation is one of many and is distinctive in that the state took a key role. Fallenbuchl argues that the Soviet economic model is based upon the assumption that a high level of growth can be achieved only by industrialisation. In the USSR such a strategy was possible and probably the only one available (because of the low level of demand within the rest of the economy for manufactured goods and a hostile international atmosphere).

But there is little ground for assuming that the same was true of post-war Eastern Europe. Low rates of industrial growth started to appear in the 1954–5 period, and despite renewed attempts to reverse these in 1956–7, further deceleration took place in 1959–60. The result was what has been described as a two-stage process producing an 'extensive' pattern of industrialisation:

> High rates of growth are achieved by large increases first in the quantity of labour, and later in the quantity of capital. During the first stage, the large inflow of untrained labour from agriculture to non-agricultural activities must adversely affect labour productivity and real wages. During the second stage, the large-scale additions to capital stock must reduce its productivity and it becomes necessary to keep consumption and real wages low in order to maintain the high level of accumulation needed to overcome the high capital-output ratios (Fallenbuchl, 1970, p. 478).

East European economists were conscious of the effects of such a strategy of industrialisation. From the early 1960s they followed the lead of the USSR in calling for a shift to a strategy of 'intensive development' which relied upon extracting greater productivity from factors of production and on the selection of particular sectors for high levels of investment. Advantage was also to be taken of the 'scientific and technological revolution'. In this respect the path followed by the East European countries did not deviate greatly from that adopted by the USSR. Emphasis was placed upon priority for the chemical industry (during the Krushchev leadership) and engineering (under Brezhnev), and upon the need to concentrate production and technological research and development into larger and more integrated units. The possibility of a process of industrial development which prioritised small-scale light industry, and products destined for the consumer market, could not be entertained. But for most of the East European countries the pure Stalinist model of industrialisation was relatively short-lived (from the late 1940s to the mid-1950s), and by the early 1960s most governments were aware of the need for a change.

The mechanism of implementing this strategy of industrialisation also came up for discussion. A considerable debate over whether such an approach to running an economy was inevitable in the USSR has its origins in the debates within the Bolshevik party in the 1920s (Ehrlich, 1960), and has been taken up by western scholars of the post-1917 period. Yet the issue of whether it was relevant to the experience of Eastern Europe after 1945 is less frequently raised. Here the Stalinist economic model was not imposed overnight, and as late as 1948 many of the more advanced countries appeared to be following Keynesian economic principles within the framework of a mixed economy (Douglas, 1953; Zauberman, 1964), while the lesser developed economies built upon pre-war traditions of a strong state presence. The nationalisation of manufacturing industry took place in two successive waves. Steel, energy and finance were the first because of the need to assist post-war recovery. Public and private ownership co-existed. Even after 1948, when nationalisation was extended to all other industries, a sizeable private sector continued to exist throughout the Stalinist era (especially in small-scale handicrafts and services).

Similarly in agriculture, the land reforms of 1945-8 only broke up the very large estates and placed a ceiling upon the size of holdings. Land redistribution was significant only where territorial gains meant that landless peasantry were relocated, which occurred on a large scale in Poland. In the face of peasant hostility towards more　dical measures, loose forms of cooperative were set up. Efforts at collectivisation proved on the whole to be disastrous. When Stalin died in 1953, only Bulgaria had over 50 per cent of its land collectivised. A few years later collectivisation was interrupted in other countries (permanently as it turned out in the cases of Yugoslavia and Poland), to be renewed elsewhere in the late 1950s.

The Stalinist model of planning and management was thus not adopted out of preference by the East European countries, as may be illustrated by the debates that arose over the issue of 'national roads to socialism' in 1948. However, by the outbreak of the Korean War little scope remained. In November 1950 Stalin instructed the satellite countries to make upward revisions of their targets for heavy industry, and to break off any trading links with the West, and encouraged autarchy (self-sufficiency) by instructing states to minimise trade with each other. The result was a pattern of trade which created dependency upon the USSR for raw materials and energy in order to raise output levels in engineering, a large proportion of whose products were destined for the Soviet Union (Smith, 1983, pp. 29–30). On the death of Stalin, only the GDR had adopted the Stalinist economic model in its entirety. By that time economists were aware that it encouraged managerial inefficiency in industry, that it depressed living standards, and that in the foreseeable future economic growth rates would start to decline.

What we might term a process of economic Stalinisation was accompanied by political Stalinisation as forms of what were regarded in the west as totalitarian rule emerged throughout the region. But Alec Nove cautions us against assuming an immutable bond between Stalinism, rapid industrialisation and economic planning. While central planning and state ownership of the means of production are necessary conditions for Stalinist rule, the converse is not necessarily the case. To put it another way, it is possible to have state ownership and centralised planning unaccompanied by Stalinist political controls. The one-party state is not necessarily the cause of centralised planning. The experience of the USSR illustrates this point. There the early development of a one-party state was not accompanied by Stalinist economic controls, which came 10 years later.

The Stalinist model may have been 'inefficient' in terms of resource utilisation across a range of industries, but it was 'effective' in terms of meeting 'priorities'. Indeed, the Stalinist economic model was more than inefficient, it had a 'pathology' all of its own. Efforts at tight control induced evasive behaviour patterns and a mode of functioning which had its very own unintended logic. For example, the 'cult of gross output' (Smith, 1983, p. 52) comprised setting plan targets of output in physical/volume terms, and resulted in all sorts of unintended behaviour in the process of plan formulation and implementation. The operation of the 'ratchet effect' meant that industrial enterprise management preferred targets that could be achieved comfortably with the aid of guaranteed supplies, but that central planners preferred an incremental increase over the previous year's output. Thus enterprise managers tended to understate their productive capacity while the central planners endeavoured to raise targets as high as possible. The resulting 'taut planning' made it increasingly difficult for firms to secure scarce supplies for which demand had become overheated. Thus what might seem by Western business standards to be irrational manager- ial behaviour became entirely rational in the context in which it occurred: hoarding of materials and labour, high stock inventories, the acceptance of any inputs offered (no matter how useless) on the grounds that they could be tradeable, 'storming' towards the end of the plan period, vertical integ- ration of the production process within the enterprise (as an insurance against uncertainty by extending control over the manufacture of input needs), and complete disregard for cost-effectiveness so long as target numbers were met. Above all, what has been labelled as 'plan fetishism' prevailed: fulfilment of the plan took precedence over all else. Suppo- sedly a far-sighted activity integrating developments over a 5- year period, planning in practice began to look more like budgeting. The annual plan was far more important than the 5-year plan and sometimes the major concern would be the quarterly or even monthly plans. Even then, planning calcu- lations had a wide margin of error because of the time lag between the information used in the material balance and the years for which the plans applied (Montias, 1979).

Any airing of dissatisfaction and discussion of alternative approaches to planning and management had to wait until after the death of Stalin. In the ensuing 'thaw' in the USSR, the 'New Course' shifted the economic emphasis toward agriculture and light industry. At the same time a more open debate on economic policy became possible in Eastern Europe.

Agriculture

The classic role for agriculture in the Stalinist model is as a source of 'primitive socialist accumulation' of investment resources for industry. It necessitates the forcible expropriation of a private landowning peasantry, their direction into collective farms, and the payment of low prices for agricultural products and low wages to farmers. This was of course the experience of the USSR during the first 5-year plan. However, it must not be forgotten that other policies were under consideration in the USSR in the 1920s. Tolerance of an independent landowning peasantry and the gradual encouragement of cooperation by fiscal measures were the preferred strategy of Bukharin and the Right Opposition. Indeed this practice was largely followed during the NEP period (between 1921 and 1928). Nor is it inevitable that a 'communist pattern' of industrialisation (cf. Fallenbuchl, 1970) will be accompanied by collectivisation. In the USSR forcible collectivisation awaited the end of the first 5-year plan (Smith, 1983). Finally, the pre-1945 pattern of landholding and agricultural production in Eastern Europe was on the whole much more varied than that existing in Tsarist Russia. Private estates and smallholdings were particularly significant in Yugoslavia and Poland and are an important factor in explaining the resistance to collectivisation. The strong parliamentary representation of peasant parties during the interwar period had implications after 1945. These parties re-emerged (except in Czechoslovakia and the GDR) in the post-war anti-fascist front governments and were a further obstacle to immediate collectivisation.

Thus in 1945 all that was initially possible were measures to limit the size of landholdings. It has been estimated that around 20 million hectares (30 million acres) were redistributed to 65 million peasants between 1945 and 1947 (Wädekin, 1982, p. 33). However, land was confiscated only if holdings were above a range of 20–30 hectares (with much higher ceilings of 115 ha in Hungary and 100 in Poland). When collectivisation was fully implemented after 1948, it was not always done by the imposition of an alien Soviet model. For example, a pre-war history of peasant cooperation in Yugoslavia doubtless accounts for the speed of 'collectivisation' there. Similarly, the experience of those lands occupied by the Nazi Reich had already been introduced to compulsory delivery quotas, limits upon private market sales, state monopoly over agricultural supplies and taxation of peasant income.

Thus, the development of East European agriculture has been complex and must be analysed with care. Initially it is best to treat collective and private sectors separately. There is a third category – the state farms – but although larger than some private sectors in some countries, nowhere was it dominant in the early 1980s (Table 4.3).

TABLE 4.3
Landholding by sector of ownership (percentage of both arable and pastoral area), 1983

Country		Collective	State	Private
Bulgaria		87		13
Czechoslovakia		74	21	5
GDR		94	–	5
Hungary		73	15	12
Poland		4	19	77
Yugoslavia	(1968)	1.2	13.7	84.7
Romania		85		15

Source: RFE, Background Report 224, 20 December 1984.

Collective farms

Collective farms are the dominant organisational form for agriculture in all the East European countries except Poland and Yugoslavia. Yet there is little uniformity of structure: they vary from 'lower' types that are little different from producer cooperatives through 'intermediate' types, where equipment is collectively owned, to the 'higher' types, which resemble state farms. The range and type of variation are artefacts of the successive drives towards collectivisation. The first was inaugurated in 1948. Apart from Yugoslavia (for the reasons already mentioned), Bulgaria and Czechoslovakia were the earliest to implement collectivisation. None the less, the process was very slow. By the early 1950s only 5–10 per cent of land was under the control of higher type collectives in Poland, Romania and Albania, while it had reached 20 per cent in Hungary, 25 per cent in Czechoslovakia and 50 per cent in Bulgaria (Wädekin, 1982, pp. 37–9).

The death of Stalin and the inauguration of the New Course in the USSR in 1953–5 illustrate the manner in which successive political events were to have repercussions for agriculture. The political relaxation of these years was reflected in the relaxation of the collectivisation drive in the GDR, Poland and Romania (and to a lesser extent in Hungary and Czechoslovakia). Meanwhile, the rift between Yugoslavia and the USSR was marked by an abandonment of collectivisation and a switch back to private ownership in the former (although collective farms were not completely dismantled until the late 1960s). Similarly, the 1956 events in Poland marked the end of collectivisation, but this was not the case for Hungary. In contrast, complete collectivisation was achieved in Bulgaria by 1958! Pre-war systems of landholding and the model of collectivisation adopted also provide part of the explanation for the differing paces and degrees of success of collectivisation. The final 'drive' began in the late 1950s, and was completed in Czechoslovakia and the GDR by 1960, and Hungary and Romania by 1961 and 1962 respectively (Wädekin, 1982, pp. 63–4). Yet even in staunchly Stalinist Albania there were still tracts of mountainous area untouched by collectivisation before the mid-1960s.

The size and organisation of collective farms ranges from the small and simple in Albania to the very large complex agro-industrial concerns in Bulgaria, where by 1977 most of the former collective and state farms had disappeared. Farms are also large in the GDR and Hungary, but the process of vertical integration with industry has not taken place to the same extent. In Hungary, Czechoslovakia, the GDR, Bulgaria and Romania, the Soviet-inspired Machine Tractor Station was an important nucleus of collective farm organisation, but these were abandoned elsewhere.

The most successful collective farm organisation is found in

Hungary. Central state and party interference is restricted and compulsory delivery quotas are rarely resorted to. Prices tend to be negotiated between farmers and the state and reflect relatively realistic market costs. Farms are free to choose their suppliers. Although outside labour may not be hired for necessary small-scale industrial and craft activities, members can elect to undertake some of these as part of their employment. Reasonably high rates of pay, a comparatively plentiful supply of consumer goods and the existence of private plots all provide incentives for the members. 'Kadarism' seems to have paid off in Hungarian agriculture, and it is claimed that the difference between urban and rural living standards and industrial and agricultural incomes is not as high as in other states. The need to extend the benefits of social citizenship to collective farm workers was generally of greater political urgency in Eastern Europe than the USSR. Social insurance and pension benefits were made available to collective farm members in 1948 and 1959 in the GDR, in 1953 in Czechoslovakia, and in 1957 in Hungary and Bulgaria. Not only has this affected the level of social integration of the peasantry, but it has also determined whether agriculture is a successful contributor to national income – a fact that has become extremely important in the context of foreign trade developments in the 1970s.

The private sector

The private sector in East European agriculture has a distinctive feature. In two countries most of the land is in private ownership. However, the importance of the private plots on the collective farms in their contribution to total agricultural output should not be overlooked. In the Soviet Union these contribute up to 30 per cent of output, a pattern which is repeated in those East European economies whose agriculture is primarily collectivised. Private plots account for around 30 per cent of output in Hungary and Romania, 28 per cent in Czechoslovakia, and 25 per cent in Bulgaria. The percentage is much higher if particular product markets such as market gardening and dairy farming are considered. Given the disproportionately small size of private holdings relative to output in these countries, the private sector appears to have a much higher rate of productivity than the socialised sector. In Hungary in 1974, and in Czechoslovakia in 1979, the governments realised this and stepped up support to smallholders. But how much of this is actually due to the nature of the productive process and how much to the favourable market conditions for specific products? Home-grown tomatoes at Christmas may command an exorbitantly high price on the free market, but wheat and potatoes fetch the same state-fixed price all year long! The issue is further illuminated by an examination of the two countries where the bulk of agriculture is largely in peasant hands.

Poland

The tenacity of peasant resistance to collectivisation is born out of the pre-war system of landholding. Despite the acquisition of large estates in the West in 1945, Poland's peasantry were not employed on large latifundia estates, such as were common in Czechoslovakia, Romania and Yugoslavia. Most of the land was in the form of very tiny holdings run as small family concerns. These have persisted to this day, averaging around 5.4 ha. The characteristic underemployment of an earlier period has declined to the extent that there is now a labour shortage and an ageing and increasingly female agricultural labour force. Industrialisation has also created a hybrid category of workers: peasant–workers and worker–peasants. The former left the land permanently for industrial occupations in the cities, but the latter were forced to leave the land because of poor job opportunities. They return at crucial times during the agricultural year because of labour shortage and the peasants' inability to afford hired labour. Ever since the mid-1950s, when collectivisation was abandoned, state policy has been directed towards ensuring that for the majority of small farmers there were disincentives and costs to persisting with their way of life. Modern agricultural equipment was withheld, and available only at high rent from state centres (such as the Agricultural Circles set up after 1957, and the pesant self-Help agencies, set up in 1972). Compulsory delivery quotas have been abolished, but prices are still fixed by the state. Seventy per cent of public sector purchases are through these agricultural cooperatives. State insurance schemes for sickness and old age were withheld from peasants and their families, and educational opportunities, welfare benefits, and general living standards were inferior by comparison to what was available for those employed in industry or elsewhere in the public sector (see Chapter 12). Inefficiency, a sluggish growth in output, and a long-term agricultural manpower shortage were the consequences. The state passed legislation in 1968, 1973, and 1979 to pay rent and pensions to peasants who handed over their land in exchange. A sickness insurance scheme was made available to the peasantry in 1974, but contribution rates were higher than for public sector employees, and cover was not made mandatory before 1980. Financial incentives to amalgamate holdings led to the disappearance of the very smallest units and a decline from 3.2 to 3.1 million farms during the 1960s. Although there was a marginal increase in the state-owned sector, still 77 per cent of all land and 85 per cent of the total sown area was privately owned by just over 3 million households.

The long-term effects of this on the rest of the Polish economy became apparent in the agricultural problems of the late 1970s. Besides the poor harvests at the end of that decade, animal feed was in short supply and had to be imported. State pricing policies made livestock farming such as pig-breeding more lucrative than arable farming. To check this development the distribution of imported animal feed was rationed or withheld. The result was that animals were fed high quality grain, at high cost, putting further pressure on imports (Wädekin, 1982, pp. 127–9). At a time when Poland had chosen a path of development through import-led growth (see Chapter 5), it was unable to pay off the increasing debt burden in the traditional way, by the export of animal produce. It is true that agricultural exports did increase after the mid-1970s, but at a considerable cost to both the farmer and the consumer. At best, private agriculture in Poland has received a grudging tolerance from the government. There was no attempt to explore ways in which it could be made more profitable and yet still be dependent upon the state until the reform of 1982. Neither the domestic nor the Soviet political leadership are sympathetic to such solutions.

Yugoslavia

Comparison between Poland and Yugoslavia is illuminating, especially as Yugoslavia has always had a higher percentage of the population dependent upon agriculture for its livelihood (it was still around 30 per cent in 1970). Like Poland, the farms are relatively small and under private ownership (2.6 million in 1969), and the number appears to have increased in the 1970s, though with a consequent reduction in size. Yet in contrast to Poland, there is still a sizeable cooperative sector. Many of the collective farms continued as autonomous units after collectivisation was abandoned in 1953, and subsequently operated as cooperatives. These received further financial encouragement in 1965, but with over 85 per cent of the land in private ownership and employing 30 per cent of the active population, 60–80 per cent of agricultural output, and 20 per cent of national income, there is little prospect of further change towards cooperatives. The major difference between Yugoslavia and Poland is that the government of the former is more ready to accept the existence of the private sector and.to plan for its development. A long-term 'green plan' for the years 1973–85 aimed to increase output by means of assistance to private farmers in purchasing output, and by more sympathetic tax exemption and easier financial loans. A major effect of this has been a fall in the number of farmers who are peasant workers, reflecting the greater security of agricultural income relative to Poland.

Agricultural development

If we hope to understand the political significance of agricultural development in Eastern Europe, then it is not enough just to examine the different forms of land ownership. Despite the attention devoted to the way in which this related to different forms of organisation of agricultural output, it is important to note the interdependence between the sectors.

Furthermore, the prospects for agriculture today may depend on decisions that were taken 20 years previously. Again, the Polish case is a good illustration. Census data reveal that by the late 1970s 30 per cent of farms were managed by someone aged over 60, a further third were run by people with no heir, and just under 40 per cent of all farms were managed by women. The ageing and feminisation of the agricultural workforce is widely believed to be a major cause of poor performance. It cannot be speedily remedied, as it is the cumulative effect of past price and investment policies.

However, it is important not to jump to the conclusion that chronic underinvestment in agriculture is common. A tendency to make an analogy with early Soviet development may lead to a mistaken understanding of present trends. Whereas, with the exception of Bulgaria and Czechoslovakia, the effect of policies in the 1950s was to transfer capital out of agriculture, this gradually changed in the 1960s in all countries except Poland. By the end of the 1960s the outward flow of investment resources had been reversed. But increased investment and higher producer prices were not accompanied by increased output or labour productivity after the mid-1970s. By the late 1970s, in all countries except Bulgaria and Romania, the agricultural sector's share of investment resources exceeded the share of its contribution to NMP, and underemployment continued. Again, those who would emphasise that the industrialisation of Eastern Europe was at the expense of employment in agriculture should recognise that only in Bulgaria did the decline of the agricultural workforce exceed that of the West European countries after 1945, and that this rate of decline was slowest in Poland, Yugoslavia, and the USSR (Wädekin, 1982, p. 142). Only in the GDR and Czechoslovakia were those employed in agriculture a minority (although a substantial one) of the working population in 1945.

Thus agriculture is an important element in any East European strategy for economic growth: for most countries it is the biggest employer and yet the least profitable sector of the economy, and persistently unable to meet demand for food (only Hungary is a net exporter of food). Like the USSR, Poland and Yugoslavia are net importers. Elsewhere grain imports are extremely important (amounting up to a quarter of consumption needs in the GDR and Czechoslovakia). The necessity to import animal feed, especially in Poland in the 1970s, places further strain on scarce convertible currency. But Eastern Europe's failure to meet demand is not just a production problem: rising living standards and general demographic developments created a demand for food that state pricing policies were unable to dampen. The strategy of industrialisation and the organisation of the agricultural sector are distinctive features of the East European CPEs. Yet the processes of day-to-day management are equally distinctive.

Industrial management: control over the production process

Centrally planned economies are clearly very different in their operating principles to any of the Western industrialised economies. In both industry and agriculture the way in which production is organised does not have its counterpart outside the 'Soviet bloc'. For a start, the structure is hierarchical, stretching upwards from the individual enterprises (and their constituent plants) through intermediate institutions (referred to as industrial associations, trusts, combines) to a wide range of central national planning and management bodies. The first set consists of a number of committees for planning, material–technical supplies, prices, wages and labour, and science and technology. The second set consists of government ministries for various sectors of industry, and for finance, trade, and foreign economic relations. Finally, there is the state bank and a central statistical office. Where states have a federal political structure, such as Czechoslovakia and Yugoslavia, these structures may be duplicated at subnational levels. However, the government economic 'apparatus' (for a definition of this term see Chapter 7) is paralleled by the Party 'apparatus'. In particular the departments of the Central Committee Secretariat 'shadow' the work of key government ministries, and party officials in large towns, factories and regional party organisations have responsibility for ensuring that the party carries out its leading role in the economy (see Chapter 7). Apart from Yugoslavia (where since the early 1950s the party has taken a relatively less forceful role in economic life), the GDR (where the party's role in industry was strengthened in the 1960s), and Hungary (where between 1968 and 1974 the industrial ministries were abolished in favour of restraining bureaucratic interests), a similar structure has obtained throughout the Eastern Europe economics (see Figure 4.1).

The organisation of the production process is also of great significance as part of the legitimation formulae of state socialist regimes. 'Socialised' ownership of the means of production is held to place control in the hands of the working collective. However, there is a contradiction between the principle of collective control and the goal of economic modernisation by means of industrialisation. As we shall see in Chapter 6, state socialist societies have adopted a division of labour that shows considerable similarity with that of the West. This has implications not only for the social structure and the basis of political power and influence (see Chapters 6, 10, 11) but also for relationships within the basic unit of industrial production: the enterprise. What stands out is the distinction between worker, white-collar employee, and manager. That distinction is underpinned by ideological tradition, by legal sanction, and by the whole system of wages, benefits and status attributes. The predominance of management in decision-making about the production process is universal, but the political leadership, conscious of this flaw in their claim to be workers' and peoples' democracies, have responded in various ways to create the illusion of workforce participation and control of enterprise affairs.

Irrespective of whether we envisage a managerial interest emerging at the central policy-making level, at the level of the firm the enterprise director is firmly in control. With the exception of Yugoslavia since 1953, Czechoslovakia during 1968, and Romania since 1967, each industrial enterprise is run according to the principle of 'one-man-management'. The origins go back to the early post-1917 period in the USSR, when, anxious about threats to their political authority, the Bolshevik leadership crushed a movement for

FIGURE 4.1

The interrelation of government, party and trade-union apparatus in industry

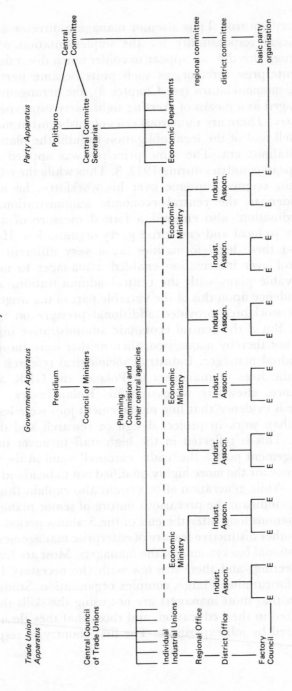

Trade Union Apparatus

Central Council of Trade Unions

Individual Industrial Unions

Regional Office

District Office

Factory Council

Government Apparatus

Presidium

Council of Ministers

Planning Commission and other central agencies

Economic Ministry

Economic Ministry

Economic Ministry

Economic Ministry

Indust. Assocn.

E = Enterprise
Indust. Assocn. = Industrial Association

Party Apparatus

Politburo

Central Committee

Central Committee Secretariat

Economic Departments

regional committee

district committee

basic party organisation

workers' control. Thus a senior managing director acquired sole legal responsibility for the implementation of plans. Although this did not appear to confer much discretion upon the enterprise director, as such posts became part of the CPSU nomenklatura (see Chapter 8), the arrangement was envisaged as a means of exerting tight party supervision over industry. There are numerous tales of misbegotten managers who fell foul of the legal obligation to fulfil the plan during the Stalinist era. The same principle was applied in East European countries during 1947–8. Thus while the enterprise director reigned supreme over his workforce, he was also beholden to the central economic administration. 'Dual subordination' also ensured a formal measure of account-ability to local and enterprise party organisation. However, behind these legal formalities lay a very different reality. Control over information enabled a manager to negotiate achievable plans with the central administration, and the dependence upon this of the variable part of the wages of the entire workforce provided additional pressure on manage-ment. But if the central economic administrative objectives · were not thereby maximised, then neither were those of the individual manager. Industrial sociological research tells us that the lives of managers in Poland, the GDR and, by inference, elsewhere were stressful (Kolankiewicz, 1973b). There is evidence that line management jobs were less desir-able than work in project design or research and develop-ment. This is reflected in the high staff turnover in senior management posts – the 'cadre carousel' – and in the general tendency for the more highly qualified not to be found in such posts. While generation effects could also explain this factor, it does indicate the precarious nature of senior management occupations long after the end of the Stalinist period.

Another distinctive feature of enterprise management is the educational background of the managers. Most are trained in engineering, and there are few with the necessary business skills for running a large, complex organisation. Studies have shown that most managers are not using the skills that they acquired in their education, and those that they do use were acquired by job experience. The first country to respond to the need for more attention to management education was the GDR in 1963 (Granick, 1975). Others followed suit in the 1960s and 1970s, but there is little evidence that senior management in-service training is either of an extensive or intensive nature. The predominance of a background in engineering dates back to the Stalinist period, when all enterprises were legally obliged to have a deputy director with an engineering background. By virtue of the fact that most deputies aspire to higher things, chief enterprise directors were also engineers. Finally, the scope of senior management decision-making is very broad, but too great for one single individual. One-man-management can also mean that other management staff are able to hide their incompetence and remain unaccountable for their actions. Thus there were often attempts to increase managerial powers and tighten up industrial relations law, such as occurred in Poland between 1972 and 1975.

The biggest workforce checks upon management power are the various organs of workforce representation that exist at the enterprise level. Trade unions exist in all the East European countries. They tend to follow the Soviet pattern, in being organised along industrial lines and acting as 'transmission belts' between the workforce and the central administration. As we shall see in Chapters 9 and 10, they operate according to democratic centralism. While not entirely a façade of workplace democracy, on several occasions they have proved deaf to workforce pressures. This gave rise to movements such as Solidarity in Poland.

Whereas the rise of Solidarity was not the first example of troubled industrial relations in Eastern Europe (see Chapter 11), its existence provided the most profound challenge to the legitimacy of the centrally planned economy. As Brus (1975) reminds us, neither ownership, nor control through public ('socialised') ownership, can provide sufficient basis for the appeal to popular legitimacy unless they are matched by high rates of growth of economic output, and a policy of distribution of the product that meets social needs. Declining economic growth, and consequent strain and shortage, have been the cue for Party leaderships to introduce reform. The consequence has been a cycle of acceleration and deceleration of the economy, into which economic reform has been inserted as a political as much as an economic measure (McFarlane, 1984). It is to the general reasons for reform and to a more detailed examination of such measures in individual countries that we now turn.

5

The Implementation of Economic Reform in Eastern Europe

Reforming the Stalinist model of industry: the debates

There is a voluminous literature documenting the successive 'waves' of economic reform in Eastern Europe. The most comprehensive appraisal of developments up until the early 1980s can be found in the two edited collections by Höhmann, Kaser, and Thalheim (1975), and Nove *et al.* (1982). The reforms are generally viewed as falling into two phases: the first during the late 1950s and the second during the 10 years after 1965 (Brus, 1979). The issue of efficiency was a prominent concern in the first 'wave', and that of growth in the second. But before we discuss the reform debates, there are three points which should be understood.

First, when reform debates first began, the Stalinist system had been institutionalised in Eastern Europe for a relatively short period. However, many of the professional economists were people who had trained in the pre-1945 period. They were thus familiar with a wider variety of approaches to economics than those which obtained in Marxist–Leninist political economy. In consequence, the scope of the reform debate was broader in Eastern Europe than in the USSR. Yet the signal that debate and experimentation could be legitimately undertaken could only be provided by the USSR. This did not arrive until 1962 when Evgeni Liberman's article 'The Plan, Profits, and Bonuses' was published in *Pravda*. Not

97

until 1965 did the USSR announce that it too was embarking
on a reform of industrial planning and management. Reform
debate and practical implementation began before 1962 in
Yugoslavia, Poland, and Czechoslovakia, and started in that
year in the GDR. Hungary, Romania, and Bulgaria delayed
the issue until after 1965. In many respects, then, Eastern
Europe was a laboratory for economic reform. In particular
the Polish reform of 1956–8 was the most radical yet unveiled
(Zielinski, 1973). The hallmarks were a greater independence
for industrial enterprises and greater management accountability to the workforce. Yet it would be a mistake to assign all
the substance of the reform debates under the heading of
'market mechanisms'. There was a great variety both in the
perceptions of the problem and in the sort of market elements
envisaged as a solution. At least four main categories of
reform debate may be discerned.

*1 The possibility of making rational calculations under central
planning*

A long-standing debate on the logical and practical possibility
of rational centralised planning focuses on the practical
problem of mathematical calculation: would it be possible to
derive a sufficient number of simultaneous equations to
balance demand and supply of all goods throughout the
entire economy without facing shortages and surpluses? The
now famous reply of the Polish economist, Oscar Lange
(writing originally in the 1930s), was that yes, there was a
solution and that this could apply to conditions where central
planners wished to keep very tight control over investment as
well as for those where they did not (Lange, 1970). His
reasoning was that although the central planning authority
was bound to start off in an arbitrary fashion in fixing prices,
it could then proceed by trial and error to reach market
clearing prices, i.e. to set prices for all goods so that there
would be neither excess demand nor supply. His proposals
were never adopted in full by any of the East European
economies, and Lange modified his views in the 1950s.

2 *Managerial incentives to profitability*

The ability of central planners to simulate the clearing properties of markets was not the central problem for other analysts (or perhaps was so insuperable as to be unworthy of consideration!). Rather, the problem was perceived as one of managerial incentives (overlooked by Lange). Paradoxically, the more that central planners interfered in individual enterprise activity by issuing supplementary binding instructions (directive indices), the greater was the scope for evasive action on the part of enterprise management. Because the target of plan fulfilment was of overriding concern, management would indulge in the 'pathological' behaviour we described above. Any attempt by central planners to restrict these activities resulted only in their displacement in an elaborate ritual of gamesmanship.

How was the centre to induce individual production units to behave in the desired way? The favoured solution was turning such initiative to positive advantage for the economy as a whole, and consequently reducing the number of 'directive indices' (plan targets) that had to be observed. The proposals of Evgeni Liberman suggested that only two basic 'synthetic' (general as opposed to specific) plan indices need now apply: value of total sales and the index of profitability. As the former depended upon the enterprise finding a customer for its goods, and the latter upon keeping the value of fixed assets and running costs low, the interests of the central planners could theoretically be secured, leaving the detailed decisions of day-to-day management where they rightfully belonged. Obviously the successful operation of such a scheme required a carefully monitored reform of prices. It is interesting to observe that Soviet and East European economists were deliberating these issues in the late 1950s, long before they received official endorsement in Liberman's article in *Pravda*. Moreover, it was the GDR that was the first to adopt such proposals fully when it launched its New Economic System in 1963. A partial variation was introduced in Poland in 1964, and in the USSR in 1965.

3   *The compatibility of plan and market*

The issue here was neither one of the state acting to simulate the function of the market, nor of devising the appropriate incentive scheme to modify managerial behaviour. It was a more fundamental argument for a legitimate market role within the framework of a planned economy. Here lay the substance of the debates behind the Czechoslovak Reform of 1965–8 and the New Economic mechanism begun in Hungary after 1968. Planning was to be less pervasive, and to focus mainly on mid-term macro-economic matters, such as growth in national income, technological development, international trade, and investment levels. The annual plan would cease to be operational in terms of setting compulsory targets in relation to output both in aggregate and in terms of specific goods. Furthermore, the centrally administered system of material allocation would be dismantled and replaced by financial 'levers'. These would include prices (many of which would not be decontrolled, especially for retail goods), incomes policy, the financing of investment by means of interest-bearing credits, and the use of penalty rates of taxation upon firms. The main incentive for management and workforce alike would be the profitability of their unit, but they would also be free to determine how this is to be achieved.

In their tolerance of looser controls these proposals verged upon the heretical. While in Hungary reforms were implemented on the assumption that there would be no change in the structure of Communist Party rule, the Czech reformers were arguing that the replacement of a centrally planned economy by a market was a prelude for the introduction of a more pluralist structure of political authority (Selucky, 1972).

A position midway between these two was provided by the former Polish government economist Wlodimierz Brus, in his model of the 'regulated market economy' (Brus, 1972). In common with the Czechoslovak Reform School, he implies that central state and party institutions do not operate in the interests of society as a whole; that the bureaucratic hierarchy of planning and management stifles initiative; and that in the long run reliance upon material incentive to provide criteria of success may be irrational. Thus Brus is arguing for planning to be a more socially open activity. He does not go as far as Ota Sik and the other Czechoslovak reformers in advocating that planning be confined purely to the level of macroeconomic variables – indeed, he acknowledges that many socially desirable goods and practices can only be achieved through central state intervention. However, he rejects specific ad hoc responses in favour of an extensive use of prices where the state and not just the market would undertake the role of adjustment (Smith, 1983, pp. 66–72).

4 Social as opposed to public ownership

In none of the discussions was a departure from public ownership of the means of production envisaged. The economic achievements of Eastern Europe have been made on the basis of a large publicly owned 'socialised' sector of economic activity. Other forms of ownership (cooperative, private) are of marginal importance in manufacturing industry, although in some countries they assume a greater significance in agriculture and services. However, as Brus points out (1975), public ownership has led to 'statisation' reflecting the preferences of the bureaucratic elites, and in no country can it be seen as co-determinous with social ownership. Yet, comparatively early on in Yugoslavia, party theoreticians such as Djilas, Kardelj, and Kidric argued for the introduction of 'free associations of producers', an idea derived from reading Marx. Marx's discussion of the form of a future communist society suggests that the immediate producers would form into associations and thereby make decisions on production and distribution. Legislation in 1950 and 1952 in Yugoslavia inaugurated a series of measures granting greater independence to industrial enterprise management, later accompanied by procedures to introduce 'workers self-management' in enterprises. Its advocates were not content to see it as a method for regulating industrial relations and managing the economy alone. It was ultimately viewed as the basis of a new form of social order and socialist democracy, extending throughout all sectors of public activity and embodying the values of democracy, equality and community (Comisso, 1979).

The theory of workers' self-management entrusts co-ownership to 'Basic Organisations of Associated Labour' (BOAL). However, each production unit is not 'owned' in the normal sense. Rather, its means of production are social property which is 'self-managed' through the BOAL. This means that the state cannot dispose of the means of production, or transfer them to other enterprises, or provide direct grants. On the other hand, the enterprise does not own the means of production, but it is free to determine what it will produce, the combination of inputs necessary to achieve this, and the way in which this will be done. The central principle is that each individual will have a material interest in the prosperity of the whole unit, providing a strong basis for the harmonisation of social interests.

There is in practice a wide gap between the legal entitlement of co-ownership and the disposition of such power. Brus (1975), however, does not consider the Yugoslav type of workers' control to be any better at achieving proper social ownership, as, at best, workers only have control of the firm and have no incentive to take externalities (the unintended consequences of economic activity that incur costs for society that the individual has no incentive to prevent) into account. There is still no mechanism to resolve social problems such as the achievement of full employment, optimal resource allocation and investment.

Thus there is no single agreement on the direction that economic reform should take. The perceived requirements varied according to what was seen as the most pressing requirement facing individual countries at the time. Furthermore, the reform debates were not reflected as a pure unadulterated model when it came to the implementation of reform measures. As we shall see below, in most countries the reform that was implemented was a composite type, was frequently modified in the course of implementation, and was largely shaped by the prevailing constellation of political factors.

From the perspective of the 1980s, a comparative review

(Höhmann, 1982) indicates that the 1960s were the high point of the process of economic reform in Eastern Europe. The reforms were of two basic types: a conservative type involving a 'relaxed, rationalised, administratively planned economy', and a radical type involving the introduction of the 'socialist market economy', which appeared only in Yugoslavia after 1952, Czechoslovakia between 1965 and 1968, and Hungary after 1968. In Yugoslavia and Hungary a greatly modified version persisted into the 1980s. Elsewhere failure to bring immediate improvements in economic growth and productive efficiency led to re-centralisation during the 1970s.

At different times, and with frequent U-turns along the way, scholars of East European economic performance have produced contending typologies emphasising either the degree of 'marketisation' or of reliance upon highly technical calculation (see Smith, 1983, pp. 64–66; and Hare *et al.*, 1981, p. 8). Perhaps the best known such scheme is that of Kaser and Zielinski (1970). Writing in the late 1960s, they observed four different categories of socialist industrialisation between 1950 and 1969 in Eastern Europe:

1 The Soviet system or 'command' economy.
2 The 'reformed directive' or 'state parametric' system.
3 The 'guided market' mechanism.
4 The 'market parametric' system.

While the first closely approximates the Stalinist model, the second and third use prices as parameters (guidelines). But, whereas in the 'command' economy prices are fixed in accordance with the central plan, in 'state parametric' systems they are established by the interplay of government and business. In all three types the organisation of the industrial enterprise is essentially the same, that is it is socially (state) owned, and operates according to the principles of full cost accounting. Only in the case of the fourth model, are assets vested in the worker's collective (Kaser and Zielinski 1970, pp. 12–14).

Except for Hungary and Yugoslavia, therefore, the East European economies are hybrids of the 'command' and 'state parametric' models. In the 15 years after Kaser and Zielinski wrote their text a number of recurrent features brought about some convergence in the models. These included a reduction in the number of plan performance indicators, an increase in plan time spans, and industrial reorganisation favouring larger enterprise groupings and shortened chains of command. Also common were increased incentives to promote worker and management productivity and initiative, an increased orientation of domestic prices to the world level, and measures to boost export competitiveness (NATO, 1980, p. vi).

These points will be considered in more detail below when we discuss the limitations on the prospects for extensive reform. At this stage we should note that the reform processes have suffered reversals but these were partial. The clock has not been put back 30 years. As H. H. Höhmann (1982, p. 8) writes: 'despite all the retardation of the reforms (they) represent a more modern, more relaxed form of planned economy than the initial Stalinist model'. Höhmann's case is best appreciated via an account of the experiences the individual countries had in implementing industrial reforms.

It is impossible in the space available here to do full justice to the experience of implementing reform in all countries, a task best left to the specialist comparative accounts alluded to earlier. Here we shall avoid a chronological account, except insofar as countries are covered according to the order in which they first broached economic reform. As we noted above, Yugoslavia and Hungary apart, it makes little sense to categorise them according to 'models' on the lines suggested by Kaser and Zielinski (1970) because they are now hybrid types. The date of introduction of the first reforms gives no indication of the final outcome, although the absence of change in Albania or the lateness of reform in Romania and Bulgaria do indicate the endurance of traditional anti-reform interests. However, in the case of Romania, the dynastic politics of the Ceausescu family were more the cause of delay than a pro-Soviet stance. Also, the relative lateness of the Czechoslovak and Hungarian reforms is no indicator of the final outcome: in Czechoslovakia market socialism was interrupted in 1969, and there was an almost complete regression to the Stalinist model. In Hungary, on the other hand, market socialism has endured. In all cases subsequent modifications of the original reforms took place on as many as six occasions. Finally, the original causes of reform differ, but we shall leave comment on that to the conclusion of this chapter.

National experience of economic reform

Yugoslavia

Despite Yugoslavia instigating the debate on social as opposed to public ownership, in the late 1940s, this was not fully implemented until the reform of 1965. Although in 1950 a law was passed transferring control of the industrial enterprise from the state bureaucracy to the workforce, the effect was little different from, for example, the operation of a Western nationalised industry such as the National Coal Board in the UK (Singleton and Carter, 1982). Between 1952 and 1964 economic decentralisation took place, but only within the framework of a 'market parametric' model. Full central planning was abandoned after 1953, and what took place was very similar to the 'indicative' planning developed simultaneously in France (Cave and Hare, 1981).

Economic decentralisation was accompanied by considerable political decentralisation, and by the late 1950s pressures were building up from below for more direct participation. The reform of 1965 inaugurated what has been described as a 'polycentric' economic structure (Bicanic, 1973). Central control was so reduced that the centre was split into many decision-making units, and enterprises themselves were further split into self-managing work units, each with its own workers' council. The enterprises also acquired greater autonomy over their own financial affairs. No longer were they dependent upon central and local government, but could now approach Republican Investment Banks. At the same time enterprises acquired the power to conduct mergers and takeovers. However, as we shall see, this generated undesirable side-effects such as illiquidity and general over-heating of the economy. The result was an endeavour towards some recentralisation after 1972 with respect to prices, incomes and foreign trade and to increased local government and Party supervisory powers. Constitutional reform in 1971 and 1974 brought further changes in the system of 'social self-management', whereby Organisations of Associated Labour were in theory free to make self-management agreements on income distribution, product prices, and trading practices, without central interference.

The side-effects of self-management.   The changes in ownership structure and central control brought many side-effects. Overheating of the economy and inflation are common in self-managed systems (Dyker, 1983). Workers are naturally predisposed to consider their own short-term benefits rather than the longer-term profitability of the enterprise. Also, the whole operation of self-management rests heavily upon the banking system. Yugoslavia is unique among East European countries in the autonomy permitted to the financial sector. The Yugoslav banking network has undergone nine major reorganisations since 1950, which have left it largely free of federal and republican government intervention. The easy availability of credit encourages enterprises to take on investment levels far beyond the limits of financial prudence. As a result, many firms teeter on the edge of bankruptcy, while others are drawn into the lucrative lending market. A third factor is the scale of concentration of industrial production. Although this has been a general trend throughout East Europe, by the mid-1970s Yugoslavia had exceeded the level of aggregate concentration characteristic of developed capitalist countries in the mid-1960s (Sacks, 1983, pp. 39–40; Granick, 1975). A fourth side-effect is found in regional policy. The federal government has to keep the 'twelve nations' in harmony, and to balance the interests of the six republics and two regions, all of whom have different levels of development. Regional economic policy has thus received more attention than it has in other East European states (Gregory, 1973) but special regional aid and levy grant systems have provided little evidence that regional inequalities have been levelled and are no longer politically contentious (Comisso, 1979). Economic prosperity and rates of growth are highest in Slovenia and Croatia, and weakest in Kosovo and Macedonia. The effect of all this is highly inflationary.

Measured by the Yugoslav Retail Price Index, inflation was around 3 per cent in the 1950s, but after a rapid leap to 34 per cent in 1965, settled down again to around 11 per cent in 1970. Since the 1970s, however, it has taken off again, and rose to 47 per cent in 1981 (Dyker, 1983; Singleton, 1982, p. 284).

These side-effects of economic reform have been the price of relatively high growth rates in national income (around 7 per cent, 1947 to 1973), but the Yugoslav government is faced with ever less choice. This is largely the result of the international trading position in which Yugoslavia finds itself. Formally outside the main East European trading bloc, the CMEA, Yugoslavia has built upon the pre-war trading patterns developed with Central and Western Europe. Since 1965, industry has displaced agriculture as the main source of export wealth, and the foreign currency remittances of the 1.85 million Yugoslavs who live in Western Europe (many of them as *gasterarbeiter* in West Germany) demonstrate the importance of 'invisibles' to the balance of payments. Yet trading patterns have fluctuated. The growing links with EEC member states since the 1960s have been reversed since 1978. Yugoslavia is now ever more dependent upon invisible receipts from the West, and Western capital has come to have a very important role in the economy. Besides loans from the World Bank governments and other private banking consortia since 1967, inward investment has been possible under partnership agreements permitting foreign firms to own 49 per cent of the equity of Yugoslav concerns. World economic recession, the oil crisis, unemployment among Yugoslavs working abroad, and the decline of the tourist industry have augmented the balance of payments problems with the West. In this context the size of the retention quotas on foreign currency earnings became a highly sensitive issue, especially to the Croat nationalist movement.

In sum, the movement towards a self-managed economy has not succeeded in evading problems associated with the Stalinist model of planning and management, and perhaps has even added a few more. High economic growth rates tailed off in the 1960s, but investment rates grew. Enterprise autonomy has not meant that employees and local and regional authorities alike are willing to accept some of the unpleasant side-effects of the market: closure of firms, demanning and wage controls. Far from attenuating regional inequalities and underdevelopment, decentralisation and self-management seem to have increased them. The gap in terms of the per capita income between the poorest and the richest republics increased from a ratio of 1:4 to 1:6 during the 1970s (Singleton, 1982). Finally, greater openness towards the world economy has brought greater vulnerability to world trends such as rising inflation and deepening world trade recession.

Poland

There have been five attempts at economic reform since 1956 (1956–8, 1964–6, 1968–70, 1972–6 and 1982). With the memory of the debates on national roads to socialism and on the role of central planning and management still fresh in the minds of economists, interest in industrial enterprise autonomy resurfaced in the mid-1950s. A cautious proposal for the decentralisation of decision-making powers to industrial enterprises in 1956 became entangled with the issue of workers' self-management, and the reform of 1956 was accompanied by the emergence of workers' councils. All the reform measures may be described as variations of Kaser and Zielinksi's 'state-parametric' category. The initial concern with workers' self-management was later seen as politically unacceptable and the subsequent reforms shifted to a focus upon 'Libermanism', and concentration of enterprises into larger units. In all cases the central concern was the rate of economic growth and the extent to which domestic or foreign trade policies could contribute to this. This has become ever more prominent since the imposition of martial law. The Polish government has not exhibited a great deal of stamina with respect to economic reform. The general consensus by the 1970s was that it was 'half-hearted, slow, and subject to withdrawal at the first hurdle' (Brus, 1982, p. 94). In the last 10 years governments have been faced with three major problems: industrial concentration, import-led growth and hard currency loans, and consumption and living standards.

Whereas in the 1950s the industrial enterprise autonomy was a central tenet of economic reform, by the mid-1960s improvements in productivity, technological innovation, and foreign trade were held to be best served by concentrating enterprises into large 'commercial concerns such as industrial associations and combines. The launching of 'Large Production Units' in 1972 was a central platform of the reform of that year. Largely designed as a measure to reduce the span of central control, what were previously just sections of the ministerial bureaucracy acquired a quasi-corporate status. By 1976 over 70 per cent of sales in Polish industry were accounted for by such structures. Yet the policy failed. Inertia, central interference and restrictive practices prevented the delivery of more rapid technological innovation and greater labour productivity (Woodall, 1982b; Blazyca, 1980).

Import-led growth was a characteristic of the era of detente in international relations. Opening up trade with the West and permitting enterprises to sign participation agreements with Western firms were not new in Eastern Europe (Yugoslavia and Romania had begun this in the 1960s). However, Edward Gierek's government believed that by purchasing licenses, equipment and know-how from the West on a large scale, Polish industry would be able to apply modern technology and rapidly modernise. The intention of exporting more technologically up-to-date goods to raise the convertible currency to pay off the debts proved sadly misplaced. Imprudent borrowing by the Polish government was tolerated by Western financial institutions – even when the economic recession of the 1970s reduced the demand for exports, pushed up interests rates, and increased debt-servicing charges. Attempts to reschedule debts and cut imports from convertible currency areas in the late 1970s led to a serious reduction in living standards.

The link between economic reform and living standards is close. There is an element of truth in the assertion that Polish economic reforms were partial and half-hearted because they were over-ambitious measures rushed through after successive waves of worker protest. On at least two occasions (1956, 1970) revisions in bonus schemes for industrial workers, and on three occasions price increases of basic necessities (1970, 1976, 1980), have resulted in protest and the promise of further reform. Yet the link does not always hold. For example, there was a marked improvement in living standards between 1971 and 1975 (in both wage rates and the availability of consumer goods). After that date problems in the balance of trade cut the import of consumer durables and increased the export of agricultural produce, thereby accentuating tendencies towards repressed inflation, black markets, and queues. An adjustment to the economic reform after 1977 did not rectify the situation, and the spiral of declining economic growth and living standards was carried over into the period after martial law. The current economic reform is confronted with the same problems of declining output, high foreign currency debts, and low living standards. The modest improvements in agriculture cannot go far to resolve them.

The German Democratic Republic

The New Economic System launched in 1963 was the first comprehensive attempt to implement the Liberman proposals in the Eastern Bloc, but itself marked the relatively late departure of the GDR on the road to economic reform. Largely on account of its geopolitical position (see Chapter 13) Stalinism endured longer here. As one of the most politically loyal and also most economically advanced states, the GDR was the first to receive cautious approval from the USSR for what was an ambitious reform. Yet, at the same time, the GDR was suffering from a crisis of legitimacy in relation to its neighbour in the West: the German Federal Republic. The latter had reached the full flowering of its 'Economic Miracle', and the prospect of life there proved so attractive to East German citizens that as many as 2.7 million refugees had left, mainly by passing through to the Western sector of Berlin, between 1949 and 1961. That such a drastic measure as the construction of a wall across that city was resorted to underlines the desperation of the GDR's quest for legitimacy. The New Economic System was to provide a basis for that legitimacy.

In accordance with the Liberman proposals, industrial enterprises were permitted considerable management autonomy within the framework of a centrally fixed plan and a system of centrally fixed parameters. Indirect regulation of enterprises and the conduct of their business upon a contractual basis were to be facilitated by a reform of the pricing mechanism between 1964 and 1967, and by an administrative reform. The latter comprised extensive industrial concentration of enterprises (VEBs) into industrial associations (VVBs), and later combines (Leptin, 1975).

In practice, indirect regulation failed. The reform of the pricing mechanism was incomplete, enterprise plans were still set by central institutions, and between 1968 and 1971 enterprise autonomy was gradually whittled away as a recentralisation of control took place. Political developments in neighbouring Czechoslovakia and Poland were no doubt responsible in shifting policy towards a more pragmatic orientation, involving raising labour productivity, modernising industrial structure, and improving social-infrastructure investment, as well as continuing the programme of industrial concentration, so that by 1979 all enterprises had been vertically integrated into 129 combines or horizontally integrated into 13 VVBs (Jeffries, 1981; Melzer, 1981).

The modification of reform proposals was no doubt affected by GDR trade policy. By the 1970s a large proportion of exports were destined for the USSR (50 per cent of these were engineering products) but they commanded a lower price than that on the world market. In addition, the USSR negotiated deferred payments. The GDR was also unenthusiastic about the range of goods it was able to import from the USSR, preferring to take advantage of trade with the West, especially with the Federal Republic, from which better quality and technologically more modern goods could be purchased. Such an inflexible trade structure encouraged a balance of trade deficit and surely impeded the effectiveness of the reform.

Despite the original radical intentions in 1963, the GDR should not be viewed as providing evidence of radical achievements. While it has the most consistently high industrial growth rate of all the CMEA economies, and has achieved a higher GNP per capita than Western countries such as the UK, this has not been by means of extensive decentralisation of decision-making or use of market mechanisms. It is still one of the most centralised of the CMEA economies, though there has not been any change away from, or reversion back to, the Stalinist model. What exists is a hybrid form of the command and state parametric models.

Czechoslovakia

The experience of economic reform in Czechoslovakia has been traumatic. Yugoslavia apart, it underwent the most radical shift from the Stalinist model to market socialism in the years 1965–8, and then reverted back to the command model in 1969, from out of which the Czechoslovak economy cautiously emerged in the late 1970s. Yet it is a mistake to over-focus on the reform of 1965–8. A fully fledged command economy was in operation in 1951, but as early as 1958 a limited decentralisation of decision-making to industrial enterprises echoed developments elsewhere in Eastern Europe. By 1963 this initiative had run out of steam and power had been recentralised. At the same time, the Czechoslovak economy experienced a profound shock: national income fell for the first time in post-war Eastern Europe. This provided the cue for debate on the economic model, which was to result in the dramatic changes to the system of planning and management in what became known as the Prague Spring of 1968.

The movement for this comprehensive reform took place in the early 1960s (Kusin, 1973; Skilling, 1976). Between the official endorsement of reform by the Czechoslovak Communist party in 1963 and the year 1965, work took place on devising a blueprint, on the basis of which the reform was gradually implemented in 1966 and 1967 (Kyn, 1975). There was a wide gap between the pro-reform lobby and conservative forces associated with the First Secretary of the KSL, Antonin Novotny. His removal from office in January 1968 opened the way to launch the radical April 1968 Action

Programme. This contained proposals that were not only radical but also heretical, in that they implied the dilution of the political controls necessary for the maintenance of the Stalinist system. The accompanying political changes were short-lived, but the experiment with the guided market mechanism did not come to an end until the summer of 1969, and not until May 1970 were the underlying principles denounced.

There is much debate as to whether it was the wholesale implementation of reform that caused chaos and military intervention. However, it was the political implications of the Czechoslovak reform that were the ultimate source of difficulty. The disappearance of binding obligatory plans, a departure from a material balance of centrally listed commodities, the transition to free market prices – all would have been tolerated had it not been for the proposal to remove economic activity from the control of the Communist Party. The separation of industrial administration from party and state structures, and the weakening of the party 'nomenklatura' (see Chapter 8) by handing over the appointment of enterprise managers to elected workers' councils, were the major causes of alarm among members of the Warsaw Pact. Above all, when the Czechoslovak Communist Party itself showed a disinclination to emphasise its leading role in political life and a willingness to contemplate a more pluralistic political system, the result was the invocation of the 'Brezhnev Doctrine' (see Chapter 13) and invasion.

The political climate after 1968 was certainly not propitious for economic reform. It must then seem surprising that in 1977 and 1978 a new reform project (Kosta, 1982) was developed, with the purpose of moving to a more centralised parametric system of planning, and a management system that relied upon the market. However, this project was experimental, covering only a small section of the economy (150 industrial enterprises, nine others in foreign trade and twenty-one research and development units). The outcome was a decision in 1980 belatedly to follow the trend towards industrial concentration (Jeffries, 1981, p. 21). As elsewhere, the fall in economic growth rates during the 1970s, the decline in labour productivity, and the problem of rising world commodity prices, especially for fuel oil, were an important stimulus. The balance of trade was unhealthy. A high percentage of exports were destined for the CMEA, but the slow increase in exports to the West did not cover the growing import bill from this area. Also industrial production was highly capital-intensive. By the late 1970s nearly three-quarters of investment was destined for the 'productive' sector of the economy – and then mainly for traditional heavy industry (Kosta, 1982, pp. 143–51). An acute labour shortage (by 1970 95 per cent of the male population aged between 15 and 60 were in employment) could not be resolved either by increasing labour participation rates of 'marginal' workers (women and pensioners), or by greater mechanisation of agriculture. Presumably it was anticipated that industrial concentration would bring a rationalisation of production and a subsequent shake-out of labour. On the whole, since 1970, Czechoslovak central economic authorities have exhibited a cautious approach, clinging to the security of a slightly modified command system, and a traditional approach to foreign trading patterns.

Hungary

The short-lived experiment with a market parametric system of planning and management in Czechoslovakia may be contrasted to its institutionalisation in Hungary since 1968 (though subject to substantial changes during the early 1970s). As a small country belonging to the less industrialised group of East European states in 1945, the Hungarian economy depended heavily upon imported raw materials and fuel in order to carry out its industrialisation programme. Today, exports account for around 50 per cent of national product (Hare, 1981). This vulnerability to foreign trade goes a long way towards explaining the endurance of the command model between 1950 and 1968. The post-1956 settlement of 'Kadarism' had traded economic growth and improved living standards for the retention of a highly centralised system of planning and management. But economic reliance upon foreign trade became an important factor in diverting interest towards economic reform. Until the mid-1960s Hungary had been shielded from Western competition, as most of its exports were destined for Eastern Europe. The development of trading relations outside the bloc necessitated the import of Western technology. This in turn meant that convertible currency would have to be earned, and larger quantities of better quality goods exported to pay for it. Economic growth and foreign trade, then, were the principal reasons for interest in reform.

Market-parametric principles.   The preparation of the reform was very detailed. The chief objective was the abolition of the procedures of command planning, and especially the de-emphasis of annual economic plans in favour of manipulation by means of economic parameters. Thus, after 1968, a number of changes took place. First enterprise management decision-making was not controlled by any Directive Indices (commands). Enterprises were free to decide upon the volume and type of goods produced, the numbers of workers employed, wages, raw materials, purchasing and sales. The central state planning authorities regulated enterprise decisions by means of price, taxation and incomes policies. Investment policy left replacement and rationalisation of fixed capital to the enterprise concerned, but infrastructure investment and the total investment budget were still under central control (Vajna, 1982, p. 195) largely through the indirect means of the banking and credit system.

Secondly, in a market-parametric system the pricing mechanism becomes very important as a means of ensuring that enterprises make decisions which are in harmony with the system. In Hungary this necessitated a major recalculation of producer prices to stimulate response to market signals, but only for the most basic materials, and the prices of some semi-fabricates and foodstuffs are centrally fixed by the state (Revesz, 1975; Hare, 1983, pp. 13–14). Freely formed prices operate for about 40 per cent of industrial output and 25 per cent of retail trade. Thirdly, administrative changes took place to guard against the obstacle of bureaucratic interests. Not only were mergers of enterprises encouraged (already a fairly pronounced trend), but there was a reorganisation of central industrial ministries. The replacement of the 'sectoral' ministries for each industry by 'functional' ministries concerned with specific problems, such as finance, employment, and wages, was intended to break up vested interests. Finally, in order to bring enterprises into much closer contact with foreign customers, a number of the larger ones were allowed to export and import directly, and foreign currency exchange rates were adjusted to 'real' values.

Modifications.　A number of problems arose soon after the reform began. Almost immediately, difficulties with the labour supply and wage rates occurred. Disputes over differentials between white- and blue-collar workers affected bonuses, and the offer of higher wage rates elsewhere encouraged labour turnover (Vajna, 1982, pp. 188–90). The central regulation of investment policy was affected by excess demand, underestimation of true costs, and overestimation of potential enterprise rates of return. In foreign trade more central intervention was required to adjust for the variable profitability between branches and enterprises. The declining share of foreign trade with CMEA countries and a growing share of imports from the West meant that in a time of economic recession, and world commodity price increases, problems of a convertible currency trade deficit were not entirely resolved (Hare, 1981). Large firms freely used the possibility to set prices to their own advantage, and restrictive practices ensued. This resulted in fifty of the largest enterprises being brought back under direct state control. Administrative change was also short-lived. During the 1970s the industrial branch ministries reappeared and reasserted their controls over enterprises (Hare, 1981, pp. 15, 31–3) but were merged again in 1981 (Hare, 1983). Certainly average growth rates of net material product improved during the early 1970s, but this disguised the improvised performance in agriculture and a slow-down in industrial output. High rates of investment, wage drift, and low labour productivity persisted. Further reform initiatives in 1977 and 1979 brought little change (Vajna, 1982, pp. 205–7), although after 1980 there were renewed attempts to break up trusts and encourage small enterprises (Hare, 1983).

The second economy. It is impossible to discuss the effects of economic reform on the Hungarian economy without reference to the second economy. It is best described as economic activity that is neither planned nor organised by the state and which takes place outside the publicly owned and managed sector. By definition it is partly visible and not amenable to precise calculation, but it has been estimated that it contributes as much as one-third of Hungarian NMP! Vestiges of such activity are present in all of Eastern Europe but it appears to be most pronounced in Hungary, where its scope has expanded enormously in the last 20 years. Transactions take place in a variety of 'coloured' markets (Katsenelinboigen, 1977), from the 'white' legalised private sector to the highly illegal 'black' markets. It can take place both within and outside the public sector, and affects everyone, workers and consumers alike (Kemeny, 1982). As none of this appears in the level of economic activity officially registered with the Hungarian statistical services, it is possible that the level of real economic activity in Hungary is grossly underestimated. The immediate causes of such coloured markets are not clear. Incomes policy and restrictions upon taxation of the self-employed have been cited. More generally, state industry cannot respond to all profitable opportunities, and private individual initiative is severely curtailed. It is unlikely that coloured markets will disappear, and they may be a permanent feature of any market-parametric mechanism – even one which has undergone the degree of recentralisation experienced by the New Economic Mechanism since the early 1970s. Ultimately it is debatable whether the second economy impedes or assists the implementation of economic reform.

Bulgaria
Yugoslavia apart, the Balkan economies attracted little scholarly attention before the 1970s. Since they belong to the least industrialised of the CMEA states, only their methods of

organising agriculture have been systematically studied by Western scholars. Investigation of their industrial perform- ance has suffered relative neglect. Yet Bulgaria and Romania are the two countries whose rate of growth of industrial output has been consistently above the CMEA average.

Although similar to those taking place in Czechoslovakia, Hungary and Yugoslavia, the reform debates in Bulgaria between 1963 and 1966 went unnoticed, perhaps because the blueprint for reform revealed in 1965 proved to be largely rhetorical. It proposed that industrial decision-making should be decentralised to the enterprise, whose only constraint would be four binding Directives Indices. There was also much talk of using parametric instruments such as prices, taxes and penalty rates of interest. However, rhetoric it did remain, as in the wake of events in Czechoslovakia in 1968 it was decided to halt implementation.

Of all the CMEA economies, Bulgaria is perhaps the most integrated with the USSR, with which three-quarters of its trade is conducted. During the 1970s it was faced with two problems: the need to raise labour productivity in what is primarily an agricultural economy and the need to be more competitive in trading patterns to counter the CMEA trend towards closer trading relations with the West. Between 1948 and 1964 the number of farmworkers had fallen by half, and industry needed to be technologically modernised in order to raise productivity. But what took place was administrative reform rather than economic change. This took the familiar form of integrating enterprises, but even from its early beginnings in 1963 the creation of these State Economic Organisations brought together both agriculture and industry (Jeffries, 1981, p. 18). Concentration into bigger units took place after 1976 (especially in the chemical industry) and the relatively novel development of agro-industrial complexes (after 1979) brought a high degree of monopolisation to the Bulgarian economy. All this appears to have been ac- companied by frequent reshuffles of top administrators, including ministers and party secretaries (Feiwel, 1982, pp. 237–40). Since the early 1980s Bulgaria has made a determined (although belated compared with the rest of

Eastern Europe) effort to open up trading relations with the West, not just in terms of imports and exports but also by permitting Western firms to own up to 49 per cent of 'share' capital in Bulgarian firms. Its motives were similar to those of the Gierek government 10 years previously. However, the method used is different and the Bulgarians have been more careful to avoid financial indebtedness to the West (Wiedemann, 1980, p. 31).

Romania

Along with Albania, Romania was the last of the East European economies to debate and introduce reform, perhaps because of the idiosyncracies of politics under the personalised rule of the Ceausescu family. However, sensitivity to the West was not precluded by nepotism. Romania was one of the first East European countries to open up diplomatic and trading relations with the West (it was the first formally to join the International Monetary Fund). Yet until 1967 it kept its foreign economic relations within a highly centralised framework. In 1967 reform proposals were announced, and implemented in the years 1969–72. Further administrative changes took place between 1973 and 1978. In the latter year a dramatic, but deceptive, move towards market socialism and collective management was proposed.

In 1967 the aim was to decentralise decision-making to the industrial enterprise but there was no acknowledgement of the need to relax the high degree of 'planner-tension' (Kaser and Spigler, 1982, p. 254; Smith, 1980, pp. 38–9). Indeed, the economic aspects of the reform are less important than its political and administrative implications. The 1967 reform was part of the process of reshaping the whole constitutional and administrative structure for the purpose of enhancing party control. In consequence, the reform may be seen as a compromise struck between party and state interests over the amount of state control needed in plan formulation and implementation. Although decentralisation to the enterprise was announced, enterprises were reshuffled into more tightly integrated units (*centrala*) in order to reduce the amount of government ministry interference. Also, one-man management may have been replaced by collective management boards and workplace consultative councils (worker's committees after 1971), but in practice there was a highly formal interlocking of the party and government bureaucracy under a unified political command (Smith, 1980, p. 40; Kaser and Spigler, 1982, p. 255; Jeffries, 1981). At the same time, wider constitutional reform was being used by the Ceausescu faction to secure its political pre-eminence. The bewildering appearance and disappearance of new central government planning and management institutions, and the apparent move to collective decision-making and greater employee participation, should really be seen from this perspective. Between 1969 and 1972 the central control over enterprises actually increased, so that they were even more tightly controlled than in the USSR (Granick, 1975) and this continued in the 1980s.

In 1978 new proposals to develop a market socialist system by means of greater reliance upon monetary and fiscal parameters, workers' control and profit-sharing are misleading in terms of what actually happened. It is really safest to assume that Romania remained one of the most centralised economies of Eastern Europe. The political climate continued to be its major determinant. While bureaucratic politics were the motive for the first reforms in the late 1960s, by the late 1970s world trade and concern at the political consequences of declining living standards were the major stimuli.

Albania
More than any other East European economy, Albania defies reliable analysis. With a social structure that had not yet emerged from feudalism in 1945, with its peculiar diplomatic relations with the rest of the world, and with its unerring faithfulness to Stalinism, Albania is an anachronism. Its economy continues to be based significantly on agriculture (in 1970 this still contributed one-third of NMP). The development of any industry took place exclusively during the post-1945 period. The consequences of this arrested development were a number of anomalies. Contrary to the rest of Eastern Europe, which was toying with the

notion of markets, in 1966 the Albanian party affirmed its commitment to the 'pure' command model of planning and management, with continued commitment to the political and mobilising roles of the party and trade unions (Kaser and Schnytzer, 1982, pp. 314–20). The complete rejection of a parametric approach can be seen in the ruthless pruning of the government statistical service in 1967. Yet policy change is difficult to divine. Changes of leadership in the ministries of industry, education and agriculture in 1975 are seen as a symptom of internal party dispute over economic growth strategy at a time when the production of consumer goods exceeded that of industry (Artisien, 1985). There were hints at some relaxation of central control over industry after 1970, but recentralisation occurred after 1977, largely following the end of economic aid from China and the ensuing diplomatic break, over which no conciliation took place until 1983.

Summary

The gap between the principles enunciated in the various reform debates and their practical implementation even 20 years later is wide. Successful reform presumes a stable domestic and international environment. However, in most East European countries, declining rates of economic growth, high rates of capital investment, and by the late 1960s falling labour productivity were the crucial factors that swayed political leaderships to accept reform. As Zielinski remarked, most reforms were introduced when economies were under strain – conditions which make success even more elusive (Zielinski, 1973). Although the successive waves of reform in the 1970s added no new economic mechanism, they did bring changes in the organisational structure of economic management and in foreign trade. Industrial concentration into 'socialist corporations' changed the context of the discussion of decentralisation: the autonomy of the individual industrial enterprise was sacrificed for the promise of rationalisation, economies of scale, and innovation. Some countries took advantage of the period of detente in the early 1970s to redirect their foreign trade to Western Europe and the US (Poland, Romania, the GDR, and Hungary). Others were more restrained (Czechoslovakia and Bulgaria). They all suffered in one way or another as a result of the recession of 1973–4. The need to earn more convertible currency imposed an additional strain. Those economies for whom trade with the West was particularly important to their national development (Romania, Yugoslavia, Hungary and Bulgaria) resorted to inward investment and joint ownership with Western firms. This was seen as less risky than import-led growth on the scale adopted in Poland. Yet the logic of Western business interests has been to pursue their own advantage rather than that of the host country, even when it entails insuperable debt for the latter.

Finally, with the exception of Hungary and Bulgaria, economic reforms were concerned with industry, which (for reasons we alluded to earlier) is seen as the only legitimate source of long-term prosperity for state socialist societies. A capital intensive, high productivity, agricultural sector was not envisaged, and so the level of agricultural investment remained relatively low until the 1970s. However, the failure to integrate agriculture into the plans for economic reform had a dampening effect upon the prospects for economic growth, living standards, and trading relations with the West. Agriculture, distribution, and the service sector remain relatively underdeveloped throughout Eastern Europe, in comparison with the West.

Conclusion: the politics of economic reform – who benefits?

The bulk of this and the preceding chapters have been devoted to explaining why the economies of Eastern Europe are different from those of the West, the USSR, and from each other. The emphasis has been upon economic models of planning and management, economic reform debates, and economic performance. Ultimately, the touchstone of regime legitimacy is what happens in the economy. Accordingly, the political dimension of economic policy-making and reform needs also to be explored. This area usually receives little attention from economists, who tend to assume that the political oppressiveness associated with the command model is sufficient to spur a pro-reform lobby into action, or that the imperatives of mobilisation and advanced industrialism will stimulate both professional economists and the managers of industry to clamour for reform. Other academics would argue that the economic reform movement can then spill over into a broader movement for political reform.

To take the last point first, it may seem superficially tempting, but it is also contentious. Brus (1979) is emphatic in his assertion that economic reforms can never be a decisive factor in political change. Although he concedes that the history of the second wave of reforms (1966–75) shows evidence of a direct connection between the political attitude of the dominant power and the ultimate fate of the reform (Brus 1979, p. 263), this observation must be qualified by the following point: that the decision to reform is taken under the impact of adversity and attendant political pressure. However, successful reform requires a favourable environment, and so plan tautness must be relaxed, and greater scope for manoeuvre permitted. His conclusion is that far from economic reform leading to political reform, in most East European countries it has not even been given a chance to prove itself. Zielinski (1973) expressed very similar sentiments in his explanation of the failure of Polish economic reforms after 1964. Contradictory objectives were the problem; and Zielinski (pp. 310–16) cites the following illustrations of this:

1 The simulataneous use of administrative orders and economic parameters.
2 The preservation of the basic features of the traditional economic system with changes in enterprise behaviour.
3 The simultaneous use of annual plan targets and long-term financial norms.
4 Simultaneous decentralisation of decisions to enterprise and industrial association.
5 The simultaneous preservation of 'taut' planning alongside changes in the management mechanism.
6 A 'false policy of transition'. This can include over-

cautiousness, inadequate preparation of the introductory
stage of the reform and of vital factors such as pricing
policies, and an overall lack of consistency in what was
frequently a piece-meal approach.

We may conclude that economic reforms are impeded by
political barriers from achieving full implementation, but
political crises provide the impetus for economic reform in that
political elites try to counteract the undesirable effects of
investment cycles with reform (McFarlane, 1984).

There is a further dimension of the politics of economic
reforms. It turns on the question of who supports and who
opposes them. The line-up is not always immediately obvious,
and the study of some reform experiences can throw up some
surprises. For example, Nove cautions us not to see the economic managers as a pro-reform lobby. Rather, as we have
seen, they operate in a world of such uncertainty that they may
prefer to minimise the disruption associated with reform rather
than risk all for the gain of greater autonomy of decision-
making. Studies of managerial careers and interest politics
show that in all countries managers have a varied career.
Nobody is an 'organisation man' employed in the same enterprise for life. As a general rule, managers seek to advance their
careers from smaller to larger enterprises situated in priority
sectors of industry. At the same time they will tend to favour
measures that enlarge their sphere of autonomy. This can
produce contradictory positions. For example, Hungarian
enterprise managers were reported as basically in favour of the
1968 reforms but association management was hostile to what
they perceived as an erosion of their powers. In Poland
(Woodall, 1982b) and the GDR (Melzer, 1981) both ministerial officials and enterprise managers acted to obstruct the
merger of enterprises in WOGs and combines, and Romanian
enterprise directors objected to reform proposals to dispense
with one-man-management during 1967–71 (Kaser and
Spigler, 1982, pp. 258–9).

It is not obvious either that the industrial workforce should
be in favour of economic reform. Bureaucratic as much as class
politics may determine their response. In a situation of structural shortage of capital and labour, the shopfloor power of

various work groups may be considerable. This can be used to exploit factional disputes over economic strategy among the elite (Sabel and Stark, 1982, pp. 439–75). Thus workers are not powerless in a centrally planned economy, as shortage and planner's tension enable small groups to engage in a form of disguised collective bargaining. So the advocates of economic reform must offer them tangible benefits if they are to enlist their support for economic reform. In any case automatic support for reform is unlikely on the part of the working class. Thus one study has argued that in 1982 the Hungarian trade-union bureaucracy sided with the political elite against work-force pressure. While in Czechoslovakia the workers allied belatedly with the reformers in 1968, in Poland in the 1970s they differed in their support of reform according to sector of industry and size of firm (Sabel and Stark, 1982). Greater managerial autonomy might mean less accountability, and although more efficient production processes benefit all customers, changing criteria for efficiency might lead to a reduction in bonuses and wages. With market-parametric or market-socialist models of reform, a greater mobility of resources consequent upon the relaxation of controls over supply allocation, labour recruitment and wages can imply less job security, a greater risk of being forced to move job, unemployment and no automatic bonus. Concern about such consequences was expressed by Hungarian trade unions after 1968 and Polish union activists in 1970. The move to a new method for calculating bonus payments caused workers' discontent long before the price rises and riots of December 1970. In a system whose logic is to sustain overmanning, labour shortage and high rates of turnover in employment are common. While this is a perennial problem for management, it is a source of bargaining power for the worker, who can apply the threat of leaving for another post when faced with attempts to change work practices or to raise labour productivity. Should the incentive for managers to hoard surplus labour disappear, this power is withdrawn. Indeed there are strong grounds for arguing that the industrial manual working class has little predisposition to favour economic reform.

There are always conservative interests who are against reform at any price. Often referred to casually as the 'bureaucracy' or 'apparatus', such people need to be identified more closely with sectional interests and circumstances. Notably the Communist Party apparatus is in an ambiguous position. Reform could be the ideological boost required to salvage a sagging popular image. Yet if reform causes an organisational change that affects the manner in which the party exerts its 'leading role' (see, for example, the change from the 'territorial' to the 'production' principle in the GDR in 1965), lower level party apparatchiki and activists may not be especially sanguine. Within the central economic administration itself, a variety of positions are indicated. The planning offices and other academic institutes tend to be the originators and foremost supporters of reform (although of course there can be profound divisions, as in Romania in the 1960s or Czechoslovakia before 1967). However, this is not the case with agencies responsible for allocating supplies or fixing wages and prices. The strongest hostility of all tends to be encountered among the officials of the industrial branch ministries. As there is yet to be a reform proposing an actual increase in their powers of control over industrial associations and enterprises, the ministries appear to be the certain administrative losers in any economic reform. So strong is the lobby in defence of their interests, that efforts to dismantle their power have been effectively resisted in Romania (1967–72) and Hungary (1968–71) (Smith, 1983, p. 40; Hare, 1981, p. 40). Elsewhere, in Poland for example, the industrial branch ministries were successful in limiting the devolution of power to the Large Production Units, and after the Economic Manoeuvre of 1976–7 they actually succeeded in increasing their control and influence (Brus, 1982, pp. 121–2). Thus the bureaucracy or apparat is unlikely to take a uniform stance on economic reform: its position is more likely to reflect a conglomeration of differing, shifting interests whose position is contingent upon events.

The type of economic reform adopted may have wider implications for political leaderships. A 'computopian' solution along the lines of the state parametric model is inherently centralist. It is a way of remedying the flaws in the command model, without having to abandon it entirely, and thereby enabling the regime to retain its grip on the economy. On the other hand, a market-socialist solution may weaken party supervision of compliance with central plan instructions and may cause considerable institutional change, such as occurred in Yugoslavia in the post-1953 period and in Czechoslovakia in 1968. Political unacceptability as much as the wider economic climate explains why most reform proposals have not been fully implemented (Martin, 1977).

Even if we take account of the different levels of institutionalisation of the communist parties, and the recruitment and turnover of their elites as a barometer of the scope of political support for economic reform (see Chapter 8), we would still do well not to forget the international context in which these parties operate: namely the relationship with the USSR. The views of the Soviet leadership are an important constraint. Official approval and endorsement have been necessary for all but Yugoslavia after 1948 and Albania after 1961. This is not to imply that these countries always have to copy Soviet experience. Obviously the New Course of 1953–5 and the Twentieth Party Congress of the CPSU in 1956 provided the climate in which economic reform could be broached and collectivisation of agriculture be relaxed. Less obviously, policy initiatives of specific CPSU leaders such as Khrushchev's interest in the chemical industry or Brezhnev's support of engineering were echoed in several East European countries. However, the diffusion and emulation of ideas and practices has not all been in one direction. It should not be forgotten that the USSR did not embark upon its own economic reform until 1965, and that this has turned out to be cumbersome and slow. Reform was contemplated and tried out in several East European countries long before this date (Poland, Czechoslovakia and the GDR) but Soviet sanction and blessing were necessary. The signal to launch the 1963 reform in the GDR came from the USSR, but strong party control over the economy and society permitted an ambitious experiment. The opposite conditions applied in the later stages of implementation of the Czechoslovak reform of 1965–9. In Hungary, the market-parametric model was traded in exchange for an unquestioning loyalty to the USSR. Perhaps the relative absence of loyalty on the part of Romania delayed the appearance of reform. On the other hand a high degree of dependence upon the USSR could have the same effect, as illustrated by the Bulgarian case. The international political dimension is thus an equally important constraint upon the diffusion of reform throughout Eastern Europe. Along with contradictory objectives and the various interests of managers, the apparat, and the workforce, this factor shows just how politically and historically contingent economic reform really is.

6
Equality and the Social Order

As we have seen, one of the predominant goals of the post-war East European regimes was the production of an industrial economy. Elites aimed to harness the wherewithal of industrialisation to the creation of a new socialist individual who was tolerant, conscious of obligations to others and collectivist in outlook. The required changes were large, but of a once-for-all nature; they aimed at the alteration of the perspectives and outlooks of one generation. Once change was accomplished, the newly mature industrialism would require rather less in the way of government as the social order became self-regenerating. The use of coercion for the purposes of initiating a new social order was regarded as justified by elites.

The foundation of that order was to be the industrial working class. However, at the beginning of the 1950s the majority of those at work in Eastern Europe were peasants. Even in the more advanced states of Czechoslovakia and the GDR, 38 per cent and 25 per cent respectively of the working population were employed in agriculture. Industrialisation policies had a dramatic effect on these figures and between 1960 and 1980 movement from agricultural to industrial work took place on a massive scale in Eastern Europe (Table 6.1).

By the criteria of the percentage of the workforce employed in industry Eastern Europe was by 1980 industrialised. It was also urbanised, although, capitals apart, there was a striking lack of large cities, with the typical urban centre at that time about the size of a Western market town, attractive perhaps to a rural dweller but too small to provide the full range of

TABLE 6.1
**Percentage of the workforce employed in agriculture in 1960 and 1980 in
Eastern Europe**

	1960	1980
Albania	71	62
Bulgaria	73	24
Czechoslovakia	38	13
GDR	24	10
Hungary	49	24
Poland	56	26
Romania	74	30
Yugoslavia	70	33

Note: The way in which these data are collected suggests that the shift from
agriculture is slightly underestimated by these statistics.

services and facilities which might be found in a city (Morris,
1984, pp. 117–19). Populations had grown everywhere except
in the GDR, where low birth rates and a massive exodus to the
West before 1961 resulted in a 1984 population over 2 million
below the 1948 figure of 19 million. In the mid-1980s the
largest country was Poland, with a population of nearly 37
million, and the smallest was Albania, with just under 3
million (Table 6.2).

Eastern Europe did not avoid the social disruption which
has everywhere accompanied industrialisation; indeed it is
arguable that the forced nature of industrialisation there
intensified such effects. Labour mobility, which was most
dramatically expressed in the movement off the land, was

TABLE 6.2
East European populations in 1984

Albania	2,906,000
Bulgaria	8,969,000
Czechoslovakia	15,420,000
GDR	16,717,000
Hungary	10,681,000
Poland	36,887,000
Romania	22,683,000
USSR	274,860,000
Yugoslavia	22,997,000

Source: Staar (1985).

perhaps no more disruptive of traditional patterns of life than the changes in family structure which occurred as increasing numbers of women were encouraged (or obliged) to take paid employment outside the home. But a population recently emerged from the destruction of world war proved surprisingly amenable to such changes, not least because a widespread rejection of the inequalities of the old order meant that the communist promise of social equality struck an important responsive chord.

State socialist systems are unique neither in their rhetorical commitment to combating inequality nor in their imperfect egalitarianism. But they are distinct in that from the beginning their legitimacy has been firmly linked to egalitarian values if not always to practices. A core debate in both Western and East European sociology turns on the question of whether communist party rule has made significant progress in combating social inequality by comparison both to national pasts and to other types of industrial system. This chapter focuses on the evidence which informs and the arguments which structure that debate. After an initial discussion of key theories of social inequality and political domination, we turn to an account of the relations between social stratification and social mobility, followed by a description of the status and conditions of key social groups. We discuss in turn the peasantry, the manual working class, the intelligentsia, women and the national and ethnic minorities. Finally we consider the political implications of social stratification in an assessment of the significance of social inequality.

Social inequality and political domination

The study of social stratification and its attendant inequalities requires the delineation of the social groups which are to be regarded as important. Normally such delineation is undertaken to determine the relation between political privilege, economic inequality and social rank. Lately such phenomena as managerial subordination and work autonomy have also been regarded as important. The perspectives of Marxist and non-Marxist sociologists diverge over such issues. Marxists have tended to concentrate on socio-economic class divisions, which they have defined in terms of ownership inequalities. Non-Marxists and some neo-Marxists have defined inequality more widely, regarding income, power, wealth, property, prestige, life style and honour distributions as also having significance. Further differences obtain between those who regard equality of opportunity as the desired goal (meritocrats) and those who would concentrate on equality of reward or condition (egalitarians). Such divisions result in a wide and confusing variety of theories which are often not directly comparable and which comprise one of the most difficult areas of the social sciences. Of the major types which have been offered, the most important for this text are regime self-assessments, the various neo-Marxist critiques, the neo-Weberian theories and the totalitarian models mentioned in our introduction.

A useful way to select from the array of contending explanations and contradictory evidence is to consider carefully our reasons for undertaking an analysis. As we have argued above (see Chapter 1), theorising about class (or any other social group) demands identification, classification and characterisation normally in order to make statements about who controls, how they control and how change occurs. Different approaches reflect different perspectives. State socialist sociologists consider social stratification from the viewpoints of harmony, consensus and hierarchy rather than conflict and dichotomy. Differences in income, power and prestige are regarded as justifiable and inevitable, a part of the efficient and effective operation of socialist society in which some legitimate inequalities exist. Inevitably other theories are more critical than such regime self-assessments. As we have seen, western neo-Marxists have since the 1940s pointed to what they regard as a privileged stratum of rulers of state socialist societies who dominate the working class through their political control of the means of production. In Eastern Europe this view was put as early as 1966 by Yugoslav dissident Milovan Djilas, whose critique conceptualised the party as a ruling political class.

Neo-Weberians have also sought to identify a new class in attempts to determine whether the state confers important rights and privileges upon a limited circle of individuals located in the party and state bureaucracies (see Lane, 1982, pp. 141–3). They advance what are essentially convergence theories in which managers become capital personified under both monopoly capitalism and state socialism. In the most sophisticated of such theories large groups of educated professional and technical white-collar workers bound together by the ethics of professionalism are given cohesion by a distinctive language, and a politically united vanguard, expressing the elite ambitions of the new class, which is distinguishable by its possession of cultural capital. Weberian categories have been adapted by avowedly Marxist native critics such as Konrad and Szelenyi (1979) and Bahro (1977, 1978), who apply variants of the new class thesis, focusing upon patterns of control over distribution and its base in the party, the bureaucracy and the police. In such conceptualisations social exploitation under state socialism has not diminished so much as altered in nature, and the prospects for political change derive from the dynamics of the division of labour. Possibly the most sophisticated of the neo-Weberians are the Hungarian dissident intellectuals Feher, Heller and Markus, who regard the bureaucratic apparatus as the determining social institution, seeing its incumbents as a corporate ruling group who are the trustees of productive property. This stratum exercises what is typed as 'dictatorship over the needs' of the mass of the population through the command economy, which underpins the privileged bureaucratic elite at the same time as it imposes its own definition of the economic, social and cultural needs of individuals.

The Feher, Heller and Markus (1983) model bridges critical Weberian and totalitarian characteristics of state socialist systems. The totalitarian model postulates an exploitative and coherent ruling elite which dominates an amorphous, socially ineffective mass. Its two salient characteristics are the absolutist nature of rule and the deliberately promoted lack of structure in society. Totalitarian theorists do not concern themselves with the detail of social stratification, but concentrate on the outputs of the ruling elite. Analogous to the totalitarian conception of the role of the masses, Markus in the first section of *Dictatorship over Needs* describes the working class as subordinate and impotent. In the second section of the same volume Heller makes this explicit when she characterises all East European societies as totalitarian.

Whether the bifurcated elite-mass model offered by totalitarian characterisations of Eastern Europe may or may not aid an analysis of the implications of social stratification is a question we pursue in the final section of this chapter. What is clear at this stage is that it has little to offer a discussion of the detail of social structure, for which either one or both of neo-Marxist or neo-Weberian models are more appropriate. Both have their advantages and limitations. Marxism, as Hirszowicz (1980) reminds us, describes class structure by relating class divisions to property relations. Two main non-antagonistic classes are officially distinguishable: workers, who are linked to the state-owned means of production and a class of peasants linked either to collective or private forms of land ownership. White-collar employees (the working intelligentsia) are regarded as a stratum rather than a separate class. They share with workers the status of state employee but are a separate category within the division of labour because they perform non-manual work. Class conflict is regarded as having disappeared, although various differences are acknowledged to exist.

A class theory based upon property relations has analytical utility in the assessment of the differences between private and collective farmers. It enables the determination of the extent of differential living standards between workers and private and collective farmers and encourages assessments of the nature of the pressures and constraints to which the different groups are subject. However, sensitive to aggregate economic inequalities though they are, such schemes throw little light on important gradients of power and privilege. They have little utility, for example, for answering such questions as have arisen about the class nature of the bureaucracy or the greater access to power of the intelligentsia. Indeed theories based on property and market relationships have explanatory power in state socialist systems only insofar as differential property relationships and markets persist. More sensitive to the distribution of power and privilege are the neo-Weberian schemes, which take a hierarchical model of the division of labour as their point of departure as well as taking into account sources of inequality other than the economic order. Thus such social factors as family background, style of life, cultural access, urban or rural locality, region of residence, ethnicity and gender may be considered. Generally both Western and official state socialist writers use elements of both schemes. Official Soviet sociology, for example, acknowledges and assesses four main areas of social inequality. These arise from (1) class distinctions such as that between collective peasant and worker, (2) distinctions between rural and urban populations, (3) distinctions between manual and non-manual labour and (4) distinctions associated with various skills, trades and incomes. The four areas provide the basis for most Soviet sociologists' descriptions of social stratification in the modern USSR. Some work has also been carried out on gender and regional differences, but ethnicity tends not to be seen as the stratifying variable that it is.

In Eastern Europe, especially in Poland and Hungary, sociological work on inequality has been more sophisticated, but is hampered by the centrality of the issue to regime legitimacy. The political sensitivity of inequality studies inhibits not only the eventual publication of research results but also the kind of enquiry which is undertaken. Nevertheless a number of domestic studies have been carried out and their results are of considerable value in the assessment of the success of East European state socialism in combating various kinds of social inequality. Such assessments may be of two types: those which compare past and present social structures and those which compare state socialist with the stratification patterns found in other industrial societies. Both kinds of assessment should be sensitive to regime aims. State socialist equality does not necessarily suggest a unitary goal. Under developed socialism meritocratic views of equality prevail over egalitarian ones, but both are present. The provision of equality of reward is a long-term (communist) objective which no regime claims to have met. But the promise of equality in the occupational order is an important precondition for working-class support for the regime. Thus state socialist society may be judged on the basis of the extent to which it provides equality of opportunity whilst at the same time promoting the social, political and material ascendency of the manual working class. Equality goals are thus complex, and may be mutually contradictory, compatible only when there is rapid and extensive social mobility or when differences in reward between strata are so small as to be insignificant. In practice the East European regimes have relied upon combining the social mobility which accompanies industrialisation with a package of social welfare policies in their efforts to juggle both objectives. The welfare policies are analysed in Chapter 12. Here we consider the phenomenon of social mobility.

Social stratification and social mobility

Two kinds of social mobility have interested political sociologists: structural mobility and exchange mobility. Structural mobility arises from an increase in the number of positions available in some statuses, or the creation of new statuses, allowing for an inflow from other statuses, and normally features a decline in the numbers of lower status positions, forcing an outflow to other statuses. Exchange mobility leaves the number of positions constant while the social orgins of new occupants of those positions change. In a fully established meritocratic society the critical performance test will be a comparison of the social backgrounds and current occupational positions held by individuals. Ideally, those who are in the favoured occupations (normally the professions) will have a similar background profile to those in other occupations, and their children will be dispersed across occupational groups in a distribution which is similar to that for the children of other strata. Status differences between the sexes, ethnic groups and nationalities will not be present. In a meritocratic society which is pursuing long-term egalitarian goals, stratification itself, or at least its attendant hierarchies of privilege and reward, will also be disappearing.

How do the East European societies perform on such indicators? The evidence suggests that performance has varied considerably both over time and between states. The

different countries started in different positions, and industrialisation programmes had to accommodate this, providing
differing opportunities. Over time similarities did emerge.
The political revolutions in which the communist parties took
power created a form of exchange mobility as vacancies were
created by the displacement of former elites. Only with the
implementation of the industrialisation policies formulated in
the first few post-war years did a widespread and lengthy
period of structural mobility begin. New social groups formed
and new statuses emerged, the most significant and numerous
of which were the managers, the clerical workers and the
skilled industrial workers themselves. These were new groups,
the majority of whose members had moved upward socially.
Only the peasantry did not experience inflow, continuing to
be recruited from amongst peasants. Outflow from the
peasantry led to a profile change whereby the rural workforce
declined in numbers and strength, coming over time to consist
disproportionately of women, the elderly and the very young.
In both industry and administration inflow was experienced
as the number and size of statuses and positions increased.
Everywhere a process of social mobility from agricultural to
industrial occupations and from manual to non-manual work
took place. Detailed statistical analyses indicate a considerable upward mobility in the early years of industrialisation, a
pattern which had also been evident in the industrialising
USSR.

But at the top of the systems the evidence indicates that
those with the highest qualifications and achievements were
the children of non-manual parents. In other words, new
patterns of social mobility did not break down traditional
patterns of internal recruitment to privileged positions.
Rather they created additional room at the top. As industrialism advanced, the tendency to internal recruitment apparently slowed and some children of non-manual parents
entered manual occupations. After consideration of a number
of East European and USSR mobility studies, David Lane
suggested that state socialist mobility patterns are characterised by three main trends as industrialism progresses. Firstly,
there is a characteristic replenishment of occupational strata
from within. Secondly, upward mobility continues, but at a

declining rate. Finally, an increase in downward mobility, that is from non-manual to manual strata, occurs (Lane, 1982, pp. 115–16). But other writers point to evidence that ideological efforts have succeeded in elevating the status of skilled work and that routine white-collar work has ceased to be thought of as requiring the well educated or the highly skilled (Bryant, 1980). Thus what Lane regards as downward mobility may simply be evidence of a change in the ordering of the occupational hierarchy itself (see Parkin, 1971).

Most writers stress the importance of continued provision for upward social mobility to the maintenance of political stability in Eastern Europe. Indeed Connor argues that exchange mobility is actually lower in state socialist than in other types of industrial society (Connor, 1979). Certainly as mobility has slowed, the importance of provision for worker advancement in education, housing, consumption and control of life and work has become increasingly apparent (Bryant, 1980). Elites have been assiduous in attempting to encourage and to favour the access of manual workers and peasants to higher educational institutions, and the educational systems have been major channels of social mobility. But inequalities persist not least because the cultural resources of families continue to be unequally distributed, to the advantage of the non-manual strata. As in the West, intellectual skills such as language facility have their origins in the home. In Eastern Europe, as elsewhere, the differential ambitions of families for their children tend to be stratified along traditional lines, having tangible effects over such matters as whether families will arrange private tuition for their children. Thus the educational system, although an avenue of upward mobility, has not prevented some crystallisation of East European social structures. If long-term egalitarian goals are ever to be realised, social policy goals should, in response to the onset of such crystallisation, increasingly be directed at the equalisation of reward. Accordingly future assessment of state socialist social change would necessarily turn increasingly on the results of strategies to equalise consumption. Before such assessments are possible, however, the order and scale of stratification changes to date need to be detailed.

The new social structure

Soviet Marxist–Leninists acknowledge that classes will persist until communist society is achieved. Contradictions remain under socialism, but these are regarded as non-antagonistic. A non-antagonistic contradiction is one which is not systemic: it may be resolved by quantitative change, whereas qualitative change is required to resolve antagonistic contradictions. Put another way, antagonistic contradictions between classes may be resolved only by changes in the nature of the system, whereas non-antagonistic contradictions may be resolved within the existing system. This theory has important ramifications for the way in which data on social groups are collected, recorded and aggregated. As we have seen, official domestic interest in state socialist stratification tends to concentrate on differences between very broad occupational groupings. The four main divisions acknowledged by Soviet sociology (see above, p. 135) form an effective data collection grid. In the USSR and much of Eastern Europe status or power rankings are not part of the official discourse and are not reflected in official statistics (Poland and Hungary are exceptions in this respect). Such theoretical constraints limit our knowledge of state socialist society, making it difficult to obtain reliable information on matters which do not, officially, interest the regimes. Moreover, the various statistical offices do not classify their subjects according to the same criteria, leading to considerable problems of intra-region comparability. This is complicated by occasional changes in official practice. Poland, for example, abolished the manual/non-manual dichotomy from official statistics in 1974. Nevertheless, some generalisations may be made on the basis of official figures.

Soviet experience is instructive here not only because of the USSR's leading status in the state socialist camp but also because the initial East European transformations were, except in Yugoslavia, carried out under fairly close USSR supervision. The effect of the Russian October 1917 revolution was to destroy some social groups, to strengthen the working class, and to secure the formation of new groups such as the collective farmers, the commissars and the apparat-based and managerial intelligentsia. Political decisions were constrained by the norms and values of the different social groups. From a very early stage, for example, the desires of skilled workers for higher remuneration were recognised. Moreover, during the industrialisation process, the need for incentives to encourage workers into skilled and responsible jobs and to maintain a stable workforce resulted in even steeper wage differentials. It was only after the death of Stalin that wages began to level (upwards) amongst workers of varying degrees of skill (Lane, 1982, ch. 1).

While industrialisation did not lead to wage equality, it did produce a dramatic change in the occupational structure. The transformation between 1913 and 1939 is shown in Table 6.3. Inequality of reward persisted after the achievement of socialism was announced in the 1936 constitution. Wages had increased in essential industries during the industrialisation process, with the highest paid in engineering, followed by the power industry, ferrous metalurgy, oil, coking, iron ore and coal production. Coercion had also been employed, with some 5 million people in labour camps, working mainly on construction projects (Lane, 1985). After Stalin's death wage equality was more assiduously pursued, but in a context of continuing upward social mobility (Table 6.4).

In contrast to its Soviet counterpart, East European sociology acknowledges the existence of at least some interest differentiation and contradiction in socialist society. Wesolowski (1979) distinguishes between interests derived from class position in a Marxist sense and those which derive from one's place in the social division of labour. Although the abolition of private property abolishes class relationships, the

TABLE 6.3
Occupational patterns in Russia, 1913, and the Soviet Union, 1939 (per cent)

	1913	1939
Workers	17	50
Collective peasantry and craftsmen	0	47
Independent peasants/craftsmen	67	3
Kulaks, bourgeoisie, landowners, merchants	16	0

Source: Lane (1982, pp. 13–15).

TABLE 6.4
Social structure in the Soviet Union (official figures), 1959 and 1979
(per cent)

	1959	1979
Manual + non-manual workers	68.3	85.1
of which: manual	49.5	60.0
non-manual	18.8	25.1
Collective farm peasants	31.4	14.9

Source: Lane (1982, p. 117).

nature of work, of income, of education and prestige continue to produce social differentiation. Under socialism, income and prestige rankings are not so congruent as they have been found to be under industrial capitalism. However, differentiation is sufficient to produce differences of interest and identity and is likely to continue to do so until greater material wealth gradually increases freedom of choice and equality. In short, Wesolowski regards stratification differences as evident but transitory.

Certainly change has been the keynote of the post-war social structures in the region. From 1945 until the mid-to-late 1960s the characteristic social phenomenon was social mobility, both an intra- and inter-generational kind. It is generally agreed that widespread opportunities to improve one's status and to enhance one's material position compensated for the hardships which were experienced, particularly in the early years. At the beginning of the 1950s almost everyone experienced low living standards by comparison to individuals of equivalent status elsewhere and by comparison to persons of equivalent status in the interwar years. Members of the inteligentsia and the manual working class had less purchasing power than they had enjoyed in 1938. Only amongst some of the peasantry was there any evident improvement. But on an individual level most people perceived themselves as better off because they had experienced collective mobility. Dramatic increases in rates of social mobility were apparent in all the states for which data are available. As industrialisation programmes began to take hold, labour demand drew the peasantry into the industrial workforce,

TABLE 6.5

Inter-generational social mobility: percentages born into a particular stratum who have moved to a different stratum

	Manual to non-manual	Worker to non-manual	Peasant to non-manual	Peasant to worker
Bulgaria, 1967	13.5	22.6	10.1	49.5
Czechoslovakia, 1967	29.0	35.9	20.6	50.3
Hungary, 1973	17.2	27.5	10.7	48.8
Poland, 1972	16.9	27.6	10.3	33.7
Romania, 1970	20.0	37.4	14.3	41.1
Yugoslavia, 1960	14.5	27.9	10.7	25.5

Source: Connor (1977, table 1).

while the numbers of posts for the working intelligentsia expanded. Managerial posts proliferated as the working class grew. In Poland, Hungary, Czechoslovakia, Romania and Bulgaria the peasantry yielded up to half its offspring to form the new working class (Table 6.5), and the decline of the peasantry continues into the 1980s (Table 6.6). At the same time manual to non-manual mobility was high (Table 6.7), although, interestingly, not as high as for industrialised liberal democratic countries during the 1950s. Here the significant point is that, although the East European worker in the mid-1950s was disadvantaged compared to 1938 he or she was not actually the same person. Arguably therefore the impact of the sacrifices necessary to establish socialist indus-trialism was on the whole absorbed by advantages accruing to individuals experiencing social mobility. Connor (1979) argues that such success has now produced unavoidable costs because the early pace of social change cannot be duplicated. The transition to slower growth and a stable social structure implies that after a time only exchange mobility is possible, and that social closure frustrates the rising expectations of an increasingly educated population, leading inevitably to politi-cal instability.

Such arguments have found considerable support amongst analysts of the 1980 events in Poland, but have been difficult to transpose to the rest of Eastern Europe. Indeed close analysis of the role of the Polish working class during the

TABLE 6.6

Social stratification in Eastern Europe: proportion of population by occupational group of main source of family income (*) or by occupation of individual – economically active population only (†) (per cent)

Country	Manual worker	Non-manual employee	Peasants	Other
GDR*				
1939	56	18	26	
1970	45	39	13	3
Czechoslovakia*				
1930	57	7	22	14
1950	56	16	20	8
1961	56	28	14	2
1970	60	27	11	2
1975	61	28	9	2
Hungary*				
1949	39	11	39	11
1960	55	16	26	3
1970	55	22	21	2
1973	56	23	19	2
1983	56	26	14	–
Poland†				
1931	26	4	61	9
1950	45		53	2
1960	34	18	44	4
1970	41	23	34	2
1983	37.4	32	26.7	3.5
Bulgaria†				
1956	16		64	
1965	27		41	
1975	42			
1982	42	38	20	–
Yugoslavia†				
1961	22	19	57	23
1971	30	24	43	
1983	33.6	33.9	28.6	3.9
Romania				
1956*	20	9	68	3
1964*	33	10	55	2
1966*	26	19	55	–
Albania*				
1950	11	10	74	5
1960	29	11	59	1
1971	34	13	53	–
1975	36	14	50	–

Sources: Johnson (1981, table 2.1); *Hungarian Digest of Statistics*, 1983; *ILO Yearbook of Labour Statistics*, 1983, 1984.

TABLE 6.7
Male blue-collar workers by father's occupation (per cent)

Country	Father's occupation		
	Peasant	Worker	Non-manual
Czechoslovakia, 1967	37.5	53.6	8.9
Poland, 1972	43.6	50.4	6.0
Hungary, 1973	54.0	42.8	3.2
Yugoslavia, 1962	55.8	34.8	9.4
Bulgaria, 1967	61.5	33.3	6.2
Romania, 1970	65.4	30.5	4.1

Source: Johnson in Triska and Gati (eds) (1981, p. 33). Calculated from Connor (1979).

1970s and 1980s indicates that increasing social inequality may have been more of a provocation to the skilled working class than frustrated material expectations (see Chapters 5 and 11). Thus generalisations about the politics of social equality in Eastern Europe are difficult to make with any confidence. They must inevitably be predicated upon an appreciation of the increasing complexity of class structures as industrialism develops. Moreover, cultural patterns unique to each of the individual states have an important bearing, not only on rates of development and population expectations but also on perceptions of status and life style. The official categorisations of individuals into a two class (workers and peasants) and one strata (intelligentsia) model are not particularly amenable to analyses which are sensitive either to cultural or to temporal differentiations, a problem made worse by the fact that even these aggregate data are not always regularly published (Table 6.6). In short, it is difficult to use the available data for the purposes of systematic comparisons. Official evidence does, however, allow for some generalisations about the three main socio-economic groups. Material which enables us to make assessments of the effects of gender and ethnicity in many of the states also exists. Each of these categories is worthy of separate examination.

The peasantry

It was the peasantry, the largest social group in Eastern

Europe in the interwar period, which experienced the most acute decline in the post-war years (Table 6.6). Of the main social groups, the peasantry was the only one whose membership was not new to it. The traditional peasant has been defined as a country dweller of low status, who is self-supported primarily from small-scale agriculture conducted more as a way of life than a commercial enterprise. The basic unit of production and consumption was the family, which was also the fundamental social institution of the typical small peasant community. Historically the peasant remained outside the urban culture of literacy, social hetereogeneity and rapid social and technical change. Narrowness and parochialism were distinguishing characteristics of peasant life, as was a relative absence of political purchasing power (Lewis, 1973).

Throughout the 1950s and 1960s the East European peasant was very much a second-class citizen. At the bottom of the social hierarchy, the post-war peasantry experienced a large net outflow of population, which left behind a rural workforce increasingly composed of the old, of women and of adolescents. But other changes were also in evidence. First collectivisation and later the combination and upgrading of collective into state farms altered the rural social structure as formerly independent peasants became engaged in state-managed agriculture (see Chapter 5). Under communist party rule and the impact of industrialisation the character of the peasantry has changed considerably from the traditional European peasant type.

The private peasantry was dissolved in two phases of collectivisation, ending in 1962, and covering all the states except Poland and Yugoslavia, where large private sectors were retained (see Chapter 4). Collectivisation had been extremely unpopular, reversing the agricultural recovery of the immediate post-war years and leading to falls both in output and in living standards in the countryside. In Poland, Hungary and Bulgaria the peasantry had been the basis for political opposition to the communists, appearing (somewhat out of historical character) as the group most attached not only to the churches but also to parliamentary democracy. But by the late 1960s attitudes had clearly changed. There was, for example, no move to decollectivise during the 1968 Prague Spring.

As we have seen in Chapter 4, a variety of forms of ownership now exists in the countryside, and the proportion of land which is privately farmed ranges from 9 per cent in Czechoslovakia to 85 per cent in Yugoslavia. Patterns of regime responsiveness to peasant enterprise also vary, with collective farms coming under greater or lesser degrees of central control. During the 1960s the regimes began to introduce policies designed to close some of the more obvious gaps between the industrial and agricultural workforces. Strategies included attempts to equalise consumption both by raising rural incomes and undertaking a range of transfer payments (see Chapter 12). These drives continued through the 1970s, when considerable progress was made in the equalisation of rural and urban areas in Bulgaria, Hungary, Czechoslovakia and the GDR. But great inequalities persisted in Poland, Yugoslavia and Romania, although Polish agricultural incomes did rise considerably in the late 1970s (Morris, 1984, ch. 5; Cieplak, 1979). The problem for policy-makers has been that, even where they were willing to, it is relatively expensive to provide amenities for rural populations, making it difficult to equalise living standards. In Hungary the resultant lack of incentives in the agricultural sector led to the disappearance of the peasantry at a greater rate than was regarded as desirable. There the peasantry declined rapidly as a result of labour mobility, rising technological levels in agriculture and educational opportunities. Seventy-two per cent of farm land is located within commuting distance of industrial centres. Thirty-four per cent of workers on collective farms were over retirement age by the late 1970s and only 25 per cent received credit for more than 200 working days per year. Cooperative farm members tended to perform the minimum work required to be eligible for housing, services and household plots.

Like Poland and Hungary, Romania has also experienced a damaging ageing and feminisation of its rural workforce. There a physical shrinkage of rural areas, as cities and new towns spread, raised problems of land use and management which led to restrictions on urbanisation in the 1980s. Rising demand for agricultural production led to policies designed to keep workers on the land. But such policies bring their own problems. The physical placement of industrial plant in the countryside sets the stage for the later development of towns and cities. Socially it promotes the development of the peasant worker, whose perceptions of relative deprivation may be aggravated by contact with better-off, skilled blue-collar workers. The Romanian peasant is, uniquely in Eastern Europe, the subject of a regime nationalism which relies heavily upon a glorification of peasant folklore, and is a beneficiary of Ceausescu's concern to present himself as one who is deeply concerned with peasant problems. The result has been an increased party penetration of rural areas and a decreasing peasant autonomy (Gilberg, 1979) in the country with the highest urban/rural worker income disparities in the region.

An important development has been the increasing incidence of worker–peasant families, which by the end of the 1970s were a phenomenon throughout Eastern Europe. These are families which are peasant-based but which contain at least one industrially (that is non-agriculturally) employed member. Such arrangements enable the family to benefit from the private plot, secure the family dwelling, and at the same time accrue some of the benefits of access to an industrial income. Regime responses to worker–peasants have varied. While the Polish government taxed them heavily, other regimes, perhaps mindful of urban housing shortages, regarded such individuals as less of a problem in many respects than they otherwise might have been. Romania, for example, has encouraged the worker–peasant phenomenon by the establishment of industrial plant in rural areas.

It is difficult to determine whether worker–peasants are a transitional social type, a manifestation of a temporary phase in industrial development, a new category of agricultural worker or a factor peculiar to the East European industrial *cursus*. In Hungary, Poland and Yugoslavia about 50 per cent of agricultural families derive some of their income from non-agricultural employment. Lewis (1979) feels that they should be regarded as a long-term phenomenon, pointing out that worker–peasants are extremely large proportions of their industrial workforces. Worker–peasant industrial employment has tended to be concentrated in the least skilled sections of industry, but this may be changing as a second generation emerges. While the host sections of industry have a limited capacity for the absorption of additional labour, there is no real evidence of pullback demand from agriculture, which has a labour surplus, although this is sometimes concealed by its distribution. On balance it is likely that a stratum of worker–peasants will persist for some considerable time.

Evidence on the status of the worker–peasants is far from clear. Cross-pressured by family, party and economy, they face a major acculturation process. Some Polish statistics suggest that they are better off than other peasants, but not so well off as urban industrial workers, resulting in a high peasant valuation of industrial employment. Other data indicate that the Polish worker–peasant is worse off than all other employment categories, but these may simply reflect the fact that it tends to be the poorest of peasants who opt to take on industrial employment. Hungarian evidence indicates that the worker–peasant in 1973 was better off than those in blue-collar employment and those in the cooperative peasantry proper. In Yugoslavia, however, a fall in the proportion of worker–peasants accompanied a policy of increased state support for private farmers and reflected a greater security of agricultural income there. Generally it appears that industrial employment provides essential supplementary income to families whose landholdings are insufficient but who are either reluctant to leave the countryside and its more traditional way of life and secure family housing (see Chapter 12).

In political terms the incorporation of the East European peasantry may be regarded as having been successfully achieved. There is some evidence, for example, that peasants on Czechoslovak collective farms have come to identify with these institutions, demonstrating high levels of productivity and participation in management. Such attachments, which are also evident on some Hungarian cooperatives, may fall foul of longer-term state farm aspirations of the regimes. Low-level experiments with collectivisation are also to be found in Poland in the form of agricultural circles. Little evidence of rising peasant discontent exists, and there are numerous examples of their cooperation. However, industrial progress is inevitably accompanied by a continuing decline in the agricultural workforce as well as an alteration in its character. As Connor (1979, pp. 183–5) writes, the contemporary East European village is mobility-orientated. Adult farmers see their status as low and do not seek to prevent their children from leaving the land in search of greater opportunities. The young themselves are inclined to leave. In the long term the disappearance of the traditional East European peasantry is inevitable.

The manual working class

The literature on the manual working class of state socialist Eastern Europe contains three contending models of its general role and position. We may term these the ascendant worker, the adaptive worker and the dominated worker models. The concept of the ascendant worker refers to the official party claim that the workers constitute the leading political class. The second model has been termed the adaptive (*Pravda* 1981, p. 49) or incorporated (Lane and O'Dell, 1979, pp. 41–5) worker. The adaptive worker is a well socialised individual whose attachment to socialism centres on security, stability and relative equality, enhanced in a parochial outlook by feelings of national identity. The adaptive worker is an ideal type, capturing the essence of skilled groups. The acceptance of a strong state is conditioned by welfare provision, but qualified by a penchant to bend the rules in search of some personal liberty and the maximisation of material benefits. Such an individual has only a secondary interest in national politics, but quite a concern about enterprise affairs and local conditions. The adaptive worker falls somewhat short of the socialist ideal, both in the retention of individualism and the lack of social motivation, but is regarded as more than amenable to the hypothetical favoured East European social compact, which exchanges relative material well-being and low productivity for political quiescence. The third model, that of the dominated worker, is put forward by a number of writers, including Konrad and Szelenyi (1979), Bahro (1978) and Feher, Heller and Markus (1983), who are concerned to identify the nature of contemporary class power in Eastern Europe. Konrad and Szelenyi and Bahro regard the workers as a class exploited by the intelligentisa through mechanisms of rational redistribution, which are controlled by the intelligentsia, who occupy the positions of redistributive power. Feher *et al.* see the working class as subordinate and impotent, with even such gains as its freedom from unemployment a negative aspect of paternalistic state control. Although none of the three models adequately describe the increasingly complex status, role and position of the manual worker, there is an element of truth in each of them.

Possibly the most important characteristic of the industrial working class has been its explosive post-war growth, a phenomenon as evident in the developed states of the GDR and Czechoslovakia as it has been in the more backward Balkan states. In the GDR and Czechoslovakia second and third generation workers outnumbered the influx from the countryside, enabling long established working-class communities to enculturate newcomers. Elsewhere the old urban proletariat 'dissolved in a vast mass of peasant migrants' (Bauman, 1971). (See Table 6.7.) The most extreme case was that of Albania, where the number of non-agricultural manual workers rose from an estimated 55,000 in 1950 to 154,000 in 1960, and to 307,000 in 1970, a sixfold increase in only 20 years, i.e. in less than a generation. Poland's pattern of occupational mobility was the median case for the eight countries. The number of non-agricultural manual workers grew from about 2.7 million in 1950 to 4.2 million in 1960, and to 6.3 million in 1970, an average annual rate of increase of about 4.3 per cent. A 1963 survey cited by Johnson (1981, p. 33) indicated that at that time about 50 per cent of factory workers and 60 per cent of construction workers were people who had lived in rural areas until the age of 14. Surveys in the late 1960s and early 1970s showed that an absolute majority of industrial workers in Hungary, Yugoslavia, Romania and Bulgaria were people who had grown up in peasant families. Only in Poland, Czechoslovakia and the GDR did the hereditary proletariat constitute a majority of the workforce, and in Poland that majority was slight.

The contemporary East European workforce is, as Connor (1979, pp. 186–7) has written, close both in chronological and psychological terms to the peasantry, which it uses as a sort of reference point, to which it compares rather well in material and prestige terms. Generally more satisfied with its position, the occupational working class is less mobility-oriented than the peasantry, in the sense of being less likely to aspire to higher status for its children. Whilst in other industrialising economies patterns of oppositionism, and alienated and anomic behaviour, typified new working classes, this was avoided in most of Eastern Europe. Except in Poland the state socialist regimes have had a high degree of success in maintaining integration and have experienced high levels of working-class conformism (Johnson, 1981, pp. 33–4).

Thus the East European working classes are largely new classes shaped to a great extent by the policies of the ruling communist parties. The class as a whole has not been a significant source of political leadership (see Chapter 8). It has, however, been a beneficiary of policies of full employment and increasing welfare provision, although not perhaps to the same extent as the non-manual strata. But the working class is not an undifferentiated social group, and this is especially so in the countries in which class traditions became well developed in the interwar years. Summarising research by Polish academics, Woodall draws our attention to the fact that the Polish manual working class is differentiated by age group, by type of industry and by work process as well as by social origin. It has experienced considerable variation in the transmission of family labour traditions across generations. Traditions are apparently strong in the chemical, engineering and mining industries, and weaker in construction, transport and communications. Differences in wages and skills between branches of industry tend to reflect social origins and educational attainment, with standards apparently lower in the shipbuilding, construction and textile industries than in mining, chemicals and engineering. Moreover, as we have seen above, many workers are not just workers but also peasants. Worker–peasants commuting from farm to workplace may require long periods of absence to attend to farm responsibilities. At first they experienced repeated difficulties of adapting to the discipline of the industrial process and had problems of role contradiction which became sources of tension between them and skilled workers (Woodall, 1981, p. 41). Second generation worker–peasants are less likely to conform to such stereotypes, however (Kolankiewicz, 1980), hence tensions will wane over time.

Although central to state socialist legitimation strategies, the manual working class has been politically passive and has rarely behaved in a manner which confirms its theoretical position as the leading political class. Such reticence is hardly surprising in a social group whose political experience as a large coherent and stable group has lasted less than a generation. The problem is that a reticence based on inexperience and lack of confidence cannot be guaranteed to continue.

The Polish case may be instructive here. In 1980 only 10 per cent of the Polish working class had a pre-war industrial work experience. Fifty per cent had spent their youth in the countryside. A core class numbering 3.5 million was subsumed in a group of manual workers numbering 8 million. Of these, 25 per cent had secondary or post-secondary education, 7 per cent had higher education and 20 per cent had completed only elementary education. Sixty per cent had working-class parents and an increasing number each year were recruited from the routine white-collar stratum. The slow-down in inter-generational mobility began to harden class boundaries, while new patterns of exchange mobility placed articulate and educated individuals in working-class ranks (Kolankiewicz, 1981, p. 148). Events after 1980 indicate that as the class began to stabilise, it also came to acquire an active sense of political identity. An important part of that identity was a willingness to organise when it class status was threatened.

While many of the elements of the circumstances which led to the rise of an independent trade-union movement in Poland were unique to that country, the preconditions for class consciousness of a politically significant kind exist throughout Eastern Europe and are evident at the workplace level in many of the countries (see below, Chapter 11). In each country there is a potential dissonance between an official and actual leading role for the class. In each country (with the possible exception of Albania) there has developed a stable working class which has a skilled and educated core and is able to make its presence felt.

The intelligentsia

Perhaps even more than the industrial working class the contemporary East European intelligentsia is the creation of the post-war regimes whose major clients and supporters its members are. The new white-collar professionals and semi-professionals play a critical role in industrial society, and as a group they have increased vastly in numbers as industrialism and socialism have progressed, reaching the highest proportions in the most developed states of the GDR and Czechoslovakia (Table 6.6).

The critical theories which regard the working class as the party's puppets, see the intelligentsia as its puppeteer. Officially, however, the role of the intelligentsia is more limited. In communist party canon the intelligentsia is a separate stratum of socialist society which performs the leading creative, executive and administrative roles, working in full harmony with the manual working class. In practice it is not a unitary social group, but consists of those engaged in creative, scholarly or artistic work; those in more technical activities, such as executives and organisers of production; and those with some sort of theoretical training, such as factory managers, economists etc. Also included are political officials, whose control over ideology gives them intelligentsia status (Gomori, 1973, p. 152).

Historically the term applied to a social group which arose in nineteenth-century Russia and Poland. Its members were recruited from the children of the gentry and upwardly mobile elements in the military who adopted an urban life style and generally entered the professions of creative writer, poet and social critic. Their development was made possible by the failure of a bourgeoisie proper to emerge. They fell outside the major Marxist worker/capitalist dichotomy in that their capital was primarily of a cultural kind and they were not employed so were not workers. In modern parlance there is some ambiguity in the Soviet use of the term. In the widest sense it is used to refer to all non-manual workers, but it is more properly and commonly understood as a term reserved for the highly qualified executive and technical stratum. In Poland the idea of an intelligentsia has always had a heavy social and political value loading (see Hirsowicz, 1978; Gella, 1971). In the interwar period the intellectual core of the intelligentsia supplied humanistic orientations, while the group as a whole reproduced, as far as possible, an aristocratic life style. In the post-war years the word became more neutral and came to be used to refer to those employed in 'mental work.' Throughout Eastern Europe a nineteenth-century oppositional tradition was harnessed by the radical strategies of the communist regimes.

The diversity of the contemporary East European intelligentsia has been detailed by Polish sociologists Slomczynski and Wesolowski, who detail six major sub-divisions of the stratum. These are (1) the technical intelligentsia, (2) managers and directors of enterprises, (3) the legal and economic experts, (4) teachers and school inspectors, (5) the humanistic professionals and (6) others with higher education. In short, the critical criteria would appear to be receipt of higher education, although Kolankiewicz (1973b, p. 181) reminds us that many had not received such education before achieving senior positions, legitimating their status by the later acquisition of the relevant credentials.

The political position of the intelligentsia has received considerable attention from critics of state socialist society, who draw atention to its cultural capital, suggesting that this enables the stratum, which is sometimes seen as a ruling class, to dominate and control. Konrad and Szelenyi (1979) see the East European ruling elite as only temporarily in power. In the long run the intelligentsia as a whole will gain class power. Although the intelligentsia are fragmented, distributed across several different bureaucracies, the party provides an organisation able to unite them all. In their view the party is a mass party of the intelligentsia, and a cadre party of the working class.

However the diversity of the intelligentsia makes it extremely difficult to characterise it as a cultural bourgeoisie, or indeed, any other kind of a ruling class. Nevertheless a considerable literature exists which indicates that the intelligentsia have been successfully coopted, rewarded with access to power and privilege and far removed from their oppositional roles of the nineteenth century. Whilst there is little doubt that as a group they are well rewarded, it is not apparent that it has the same role as the capitalist bourgeoisie in the sense of being a historical force. It is a very wide stratum whose differentiation creates a range of conflicting interests. Lane (1982, p. 143) cites a wealth of evidence of disagreements over important policy matters. Konrad and Szelenyi (1979) themselves repeatedly refer to the different segments of the intelligentsia. Both Staniszkis (1979) and Hirsowicz (1978) draw attention to the dysfunctional nature of conflicts between political and other officials. But Woodall (1981) cautions against an overestimation of its revolutionary potential, reminding us that even in dissident Poland intellectuals who oppose the regime are a small group. The element of truth in critical theories which place the intelligentsia at the centre of state socialist systems of rule is found in its position of strategic importance to industrial progress, reinforced by its apparently privileged access to goods and services, including in particular housing, health care and education. Members of the intelligentsia have been well able to secure positions of privilege in whatever hierarchies of reward obtain in Eastern Europe.

The social significance of gender

Occupational stratification is not the only significant social division in industrial society. Class cleavages are cross-cut by other social divisions. Both gender and ethnicity are known to have a determining effect on one's place in the social structure, a syndrome from which the state socialist societies have not escaped. These warrant consideration before we may extend our review of East European social stratification to a discussion of its effect on access to economic and political resources.

Regarded in official Marxist theory as artifacts of capitalist culture, inequalities determined by the sexual division of labour continue to accrue in state socialist society. The importance of sexual domination in pre-communist human society is recognised, but class stratification is held as the key to its effects. Hence the abolition of private property was expected by Marxists to transform family structures in such a way that women would no longer be exploited. Feminists, on the other hand, regard the exploitation of women as being grounded in the family itself rather than in the capitalist family *per se*, and argue therefore that special efforts over and above those which are aimed at ending the exploitation of one class by another are necessary to end the dominance of one sex by another. Although that theoretical debate continues outside the state socialist systems, little in the way of a feminist voice is heard in Eastern Europe.

Regime efforts to construct sex equality policies have been directed at the labour force, where considerable efforts have been made to ensure the greater entry of women into a labour market desperately in need of their work. Spinoffs from such policies have included greater freedom within the activities of child-rearing, the provision of a considerable amount of childcare facilities and what are often generous provisions for maternity leave. But sex roles continue to have important sociological, economic and political consequences and women are nowhere equal to men in Eastern Europe when it comes to access to privileged or powerful positions. Perhaps change may only have come as a result of labour shortages and, whatever its motivation, policy has fumbled at the point of attitude change.

Gender inequalities are often obscured in official statistics and sociological studies because of tendencies to consider families rather than individuals as the basic unit of society. State socialist women are more nearly equal to men than their liberal democratic counterparts in terms of levels of paid employment and access to education (Wolchik, 1981). But these basic indicators conceal a number of areas of persisting inequality. Men continue to have the initiative in instituting relationships. In the USSR and to a certain extent elsewhere there exists neither public discussion nor endorsement of individual sexuality and liberation. Modern methods of contraception are at best unreliably available and often of poor quality. Family break-up as measured by divorce (initiated largely by women) is high (see Chapter 12). Studies of time budgets indicate that the amount of free time available to women is about half that for men. Other studies show clearly that the arrival of children has negative effects on a woman's career advancement. Discrimination is particularly in evidence where authority roles are concerned and women's under-representation in political elites has been well documented (Lane, 1982; Lovenduski, 1986).

Traditions in the treatment of women vary greatly in the eight East European countries. Suffrage for most arrived immediately after World War One, but actual opportunities to take part in public life varied with social and cultural norms. Czechoslovak and German women (before the rise of Nazism) had access to education and employment and were active in the cultural and political life of their countries, although rarely as elected officials. In the Balkans, however, women were far less integrated and were particularly restricted in the countries that had been dominated by Islam. Immediately after World War Two women were in the majority in Eastern Europe. Demographic imbalances resulting from wartime losses of men are slowly diminishing as the relevant generation ages. Women were rapidly recruited into the industrial workforce and soon became strikingly high proportions of those employed in traditionally male industries. By 1954 women were one-third of the workforce in mining and manufacturing in Czechoslovakia, Poland and Hungary. By the mid-1970s they comprised over half the workforce in Czechoslovakia and the GDR. But, as in the West, occupational sectorialisation persisted, with some industries almost entirely reliant upon women, e.g. the animal husbandry side of agriculture, food processing, education, the health service, social work, and tourism. Similarly to the West, women were in the overwhelming majority amongst employees in the textile, leather and shoe industries. Further similarities are a general pattern of women taking employment for which they are overqualified and that the industries in which women predominate are the worst paid. Wage planning in Eastern Europe assumes that women earn two-thirds of the male wage.

Sensitivity to persisting inequalities between men and women under state socialism should not obscure the fact that the position of women has altered greatly since the late 1940s. Access to education, for example, has increased dramatically, and by the middle of the 1970s women numbered half of all secondary students and ranged from 40 to 60 per cent of those in higher education. The proportions of employed women in the normally defined as available for work ages of between 15 and 54 ranged from 47 per cent in Yugoslavia to 75 per cent in the GDR and Czechoslovakia to 80 per cent in Poland by 1970. But differences between the sexes continue to affect life chances, and the educational pipeline indicates that differences will persist for some time to come. Girls are still more likely than boys to follow general rather than vocational educational programmes, tending to specialise in the humanities rather than in the more valued science and engineering programmes. Some variations do exist, however. The GDR in particular has, as the country with the most acute labour shortage, made considerable efforts to upgrade the skills of its women workers (see Edwards, 1985).

In Yugoslavia the small two-generation urban household has become the preferred familial mode, and a relative democratisation of households has taken place, a phenomenon which is partly attributable to the intermingling of the sexes in the workplace. The average Yugoslav woman is exposed to two conflicting cultures: the modern public culture and a residual private amalgam of folk values and more ambivalent revolutionary norms. There is a Balkan variant of the feminine mystique which encourages a socialist version of the superwoman syndrome, whereby women become dually burdened with household and employment responsibilities and are exhorted to take on a political role for which they have neither the time nor the inclination. Overburdened, they are unable to pursue the activities which might lead to social ascent (Rosenblum-Cale, 1979).

At the heart of the failure of state socialist societies (relatively) to liberate their women are sexist values supported and encouraged by the persistence of the gendered division of labour in the home. Family sociology has made little effort to investigate and perhaps thereby to undermine the pattern of male dominance in the family, with its attendant distortion of women's social roles. The nuclear family is assumed to be a given in both policy and ideological statements as well as in academic investigations (Jancar, 1978). Efforts to reduce burdens on women are efforts to transfer her responsibilities to the public sphere rather than to promote the sharing of traditional domestic responsibilities with men. As a result, the patterns which constrain women persist and women continue to be less likely than men to hold leading economic, social and political positions.

Ethnicity, nationality and inequality

Both general commitments to equality and legitimation strategies have led to ruling communist party efforts to reducing differences in standards of living between the various national and ethnic groups that are present in many of the states. Some of the ethnic diversity which characterised the interwar period had, one way and another, been eliminated by the end of World War Two, but Yugoslavia and Czechoslovakia continued to be multi-national states, while Bulgaria and Romania contained significant national minorities. In Yugoslavia national differences are intensely felt, particularly those between the Serbs and the Croats and Albanians. Religious, cultural and linguistic divisions parallel Yugoslav national differences, which are largely, but not completely territorially based in the context of a federal system. In Czechoslovakia there are both cultural and linguistic differences between the Czechs and the Slovaks, each of whom is territorially concentrated. Bulgaria contains a substantial but dispersed Turkish minority; and Romania has inherited a culturally and linguistically distinct, and to some extent territorially concentrated, Hungarian minority, which has resisted integration into the less prosperous Romanian community.

Problems of national integration have been closely intertwined with economic issues. In Yugoslavia national economic rivalries are expressed in debates on economic reform and the allocation of funds for economic development in the different states. Yugoslav rivalries may have been encouraged by the decentralisation of political controls over planning and investment during the 1960s, when vested interests among local elites emerged. Economic and administrative matters quicky turned into matters of national honour and equality as leaders confronted each other and attempted to mobilise their constituencies. According to Shoup (1968, pp. 242–8), economic issues supplied a quantitative measure for national grievance, which was given a moral component by ethnicity. The resulting complex configuration severely inhibited pragmatic bargaining between regions. Things came to a head in Croatia in 1971, leading to political recentralisation during the 1970s. Ten years later riots amongst the Albanian minority in Kosovo were clear evidence that the Yugoslav nationalities issue was far from resolved.

In general the idea that the national question is in substance a peasant question has prevailed; hence it has been expected to disappear as industrialism progressed and the size of the peasantry declined. Federalism has been a post-war concession to the nationally segmented character of the Yugoslav population, to whom it provides a parallel structure of relatively independent Republican party apparatuses. But republics are not co-terminous with nations. Only Slovenia is ethnically homogeneous. Occasionally therefore ethnic animosities have found outlets within the boundaries of a specific republic. A continuing tension has been present between the better-off Slovenians and Croatians and the other national groups, especially the Serbs. Slovenians in particular felt threatened by stagnation as large amounts of Slovenian-produced funds were channelled into less developed parts of Yugoslavia. In Croatia resentments became so great that in 1971 Croatian nationalists pushed their cause to the point of declaring the right to secede. The crackdown this inspired became a turning point, producing constitutional changes in 1974. The situation has not been improved by an apparent over-representation of Serbs in the Croatian party, and a disproportionate Serbian presence is apparent throughout the Yugoslav political hierachy. Although party policy has been relatively pluralistic with regard to national groups, and the

Serb position has weakened since the fall of Rankovic in 1966, the balance between Serbs and Croats remains a delicate one. Other groups are less polarised, the exception being the Albanians of Kosovo. Conflict tends to be over distribution, with the weaker and poorer members of the federation prone to demand a more equitable distribution of wealth and the wealthier nations unwilling to contribute what is necessary. Economic differentiation has tended to increase over time, mainly because of a considerably higher birthrate among the poorer ethnic groups than among the richer ones. New jobs have not become available to meet increased supplies of labour because new investment has tended to increase the productivity of those already employed. Thus Slovenia, the richest republic, with one of the lowest birthrates has tended in increase its advantage, while Kosovo, the poorest region, with one of the highest birthrates, has experienced an income decline relative to the national average.

In Czechoslovakia it has been the Czechs who are economically advantaged. Although Slovaks had hoped for equality in the new order, the centralist strategies of the ruling party soon disappointed such aspirations. But Slovak leaders did not press their demands until the late 1960s, becoming especially persistent during the Prague Spring of 1968. Then ethnic relations and the relative statuses of Czechs and Slovaks again became topics for general discussion. Leadership failures to eradicate inequalities were criticised as attention was given to the fact that Slovaks usually had lower wages than Czechs, who were also in receipt of better health care and education facilities (see Chapter 12). An effective federalisation of the state was implemented in 1968 as the administrative manifestation of an equalisation strategy. Since then rulers have sought to bring about a reduction in the differences, not least because the post-invasion party has had better hopes of achieving popular support in Slovakia than in the Czech lands of Bohemia and Moravia.

A study undertaken by Sharon Wolchik in 1983 suggests that Slovakia has made considerable progress since 1969, both in absolute terms and relative to the Czech lands. She examined such indicators as infant mortality rates, numbers in higher education, average wages in the socialised sector of the national economy (excluding agriculture) and patterns of ownership of consumer durables. Although Slovakia still ranks lower on most indicators, policies of sustained investment have resulted in a considerable catching up between the two nationalities (Wolchik, 1983, tables 10.1–10.8).

The Romanian nationalities problem is of a rather different kind than those we have so far described. While perceptions of inequality are at its root, the perspective of the Hungarian minority is one which has developed from a history of relative advantage. The Transylvanian Hungarians have a pre-regime history of privilege compared to other groups. A largely regionally concentrated group, Hungarians regard policies aimed at reducing regional inequalities as persecution. The smaller ethnic groups in Romania, such as the Yugoslavs, Ukrainians and Gypsies, who have not historically been privileged, find it easier to accept egalitarian goals and perceive their limited desires for upward mobility as being met by the regime. But the historically powerful Hungarians deeply resent political domination from Bucharest. Ceausescu's nationalities policy has been one of assimilation, with a public commitment to equality and tolerance combined with economic strategies which reduce ethnic exclusivity. His speeches invariably refer to the country's cohabiting nationalities. Disputes occur regularly, and invoke claims over minority language teaching in schools, reductions in the number of Hungarian publications and suchlike.

Although no information on income by nationality is available, regional statistics show that the minorities are concentrated in the economically more prosperous areas. Hence the aim of equalising territorial production throughout the country does threaten what is an advantageous position for the Hungarians. Evidence of a decline in the size of the Hungarian communities exists, suggesting, in the absence of other information, that the 'missing' individuals are being assimilated (Fischer, 1983a, p. 213). In short, the Hungarian minority problem in Romania is, on currently available evidence, the result of Hungarian perceptions of superiority, an attitude which is at odds with the strong Romanian nationalism of the Ceausescu regime.

In most of the states regional inequalities intertwine with

the national rivalries which had weakened previous regimes. First in the USSR and later in Eastern Europe, new communist party rulers appealed to previously alienated national minorities, basing some of their efforts to achieve legitimacy upon promises to reverse the effects of past discrimination. The parties came to power committed to reducing what in practice were disparities in regional living standards and conditions. Their monopolies over economic investment, wage fixing and welfare transfers gave them a unique opportunity to follow such promises through. But regional equality was only one of many economic goals. Moreover, it was one which conflicted with the overriding commitment to growth. The best growth rates tend to be achieved by concentrating investment in the most advanced sectors of the country. Only after substantial development are sufficient resources created to enable concentration on the poorer regions.

In general, inequalities between regions are often at their greatest at the medium levels of development. Hence Clark in a comparative study of regional policies in industrialising societies hypothesised that under state socialism industrialisation programmes would lead initially to greater inequality, but that, later, attention would be given to the reduction of such disparities. He found that, except in the USSR, no differences were apparent between the levels of success in reducing regional inequalities of state socialist and other types of system. In other words, no apparent advantage accrued to systems of central planning in this regard. The general pattern was one in which attempts were made to produce comparable living standards by pouring in government services, a process which tended not to produce the desired results. On the basis of his investigations Clark argued that regimes sought to reduce regional inequalities earlier in their development than purely economic considerations would have warranted, a view that underlines regime commitment to regional equalisation policies but also points to the elusive nature of goals which remain central to legitimation strategies (Clark, 1983).

The political significance of social inequality

Politically, social inequality is significant in Eastern Europe for two reasons. In the first place, equality in the social order forms part of the implicit ideological contract between leaders and led. Citizens in general, and the industrial working class in particular, have been promised progress toward an egalitarian order, and they may well assess regime performance on the basis of whether and to what extent that promise is being kept. Secondly, the distribution of political power in a society is closely related to its pattern of social stratification. As we shall show in Chapter 8, East European political elites are disproportionately drawn from a particular social stratum. This has led to charges by a variety of critical social theorists that far from abolishing systems of class rule, communist parties have merely exchanged one ruling class for another. Let us consider both of these points.

Having outlined the general shape of East European patterns of social stratification, we turn now to a more general consideration of the associations between stratification and inequality. Bunce (1983, p. 54) has shown that income inequalities continue in Eastern Europe. However, income differentials are not the whole story. Although individual wages may be unequal, it would be misleading to imply that, because of this, skilled workers have a higher standard of living than unskilled workers. Family circumstances such as the number of dependents and the earnings of the spouse must also be taken into account. When such factors are measured in the USSR it is found that it is the non-manual groups whose earnings are the highest. To family incomes must be added consideration of the transfers involved in social security and other government provision such as housing subsidies. Incomes or earnings are best seen as a combination of wages and benefits of various kinds (see Chapter 12), a pattern which will be further complicated by the effects of work in the second economy and differential consumption habits.

State socialist income inequality is of a narrower span that in capitalist countries and is set in a context of rather different distribution and pricing policies. Living standards are a compound of social and private expenditures. The resultant consumption patterns have varied in line with occupational stratification hierarchies which themselves reflect gender and nationality stratification. But regimes have encouraged popular expectations that inequalities will erode and studies of social attitudes have shown that their amelioration has come to be regarded as important in some states. Koralewicz-Zebik's analysis of empirical studies of Polish public opinion between 1956 and 1980 indicates that a growth in inequality will be accompanied by a growth in the popular perception that it should be abolished (1984). But that perception itself is likely to be stratified. Lane (1982, pp. 101–2) cites a number of Polish investigations which show that the majority of manual workers believe that the government should set limits on wage differentials. However, the majority of technical and administrative personnel favoured much greater wage differentials than those regarded as tolerable by workers. Other studies have revealed similar patterns, with, in general, those with the lowest level of education and income the most likely to favour egalitarianism.

The information reported in this chapter and in Chapter 12 supports a conclusion that inequalities of consumption in Eastern Europe follow the occupational hierarchy to a very large extent. The evidence itself is patchy, however, and does not allow us to make systematic comparisons between or within states. It is likely that attitudes play a considerable part, with cultural norms having an important effect on how individuals perceive their position. Thus the relatively prosperous GDR contains a society which compares its living standards to those which are to be found in the German Federal Republic, standards which may be readily identified from television broadcasts receivable in the homes of most East Germans. In Romania, on the other hand, lower standards of living on most measures than are to be found in the GDR or, say, Hungary, are absorbed by a population which still largely has a village frame of reference (Shafir, 1985). By comparison to Western Europe, East European living standards are lower if these are defined by such indicators as the availability of consumer durables or access to housing, but, given their different cultural settings, it is extremely difficult to make sensible use of such data. To what extent does the near guarantee of employment compensate for the lack of a refrigerator? The whole question of how to measure and interpret living standard differences is a research area in itself and its detail is far beyond the scope of a text such as this. We may do little more here than report similarities and differences, cautioning readers about the dangers of making direct comparisons.

An interesting dimension of occupational stratification by income is the extent to which it corresponds to hierarchies of occupational prestige. The socialist value system holds that particular occupations or levels of income should not elevate some individuals above others; that while individuals may differ from each other in various ways they are not stratified in terms of social worth. Consciousness of membership of a social stratum should not occur, and there is therefore no investigative sociology of different perceptions of the social structure qua social structure. But Lane (1982, pp. 99–100) argues that inferences may be made about social relations and rankings from studies of patterns of friendship and marriages. These, if socialist egalitarianism holds, should be formed independently of educational background or level of income, he contends. Where friendship networks and marriages occur predominantly between individuals of similar social background, it may be inferred that social barriers and distance exists between strata. He cites evidence presented by Connor (1979, pp. 270–3) on intermarriage in Czechoslovakia, Hungary, Poland and the USSR. Connor grouped husbands and wives on the basis of their present occupations into elite, routine non-manual, worker and peasant categories. His data revealed a high proportion of homogamous unions amongst married couples in the 1960s. Other studies show that friendships tend to be sought amongst persons of similar background. From these Lane infers that there is a significant differentiation of interest and outlook between people from different occupational groups and that these strongly influence choices of friends and spouses. It is likely, he concludes, that the offspring of different strata are socialised into different sub-cultures. Further support for this contention comes from Hungarian research which shows that not only is wage income differentiated but it is spent on different things, giving rise to different styles of living. The top group spent three and a half times the average on newspapers, thirty-three times the average on books and eight times the average on the theatre. The better educated strata apparently treat themselves to a 'more cultural manner of life' and also eat better kinds of food, utilise more household appliances and are more skilled at making the most of provisions for social consumption (Szelenyi, 1979, p. 282; Feher, Heller and Markus, 1983, p. 47). Such patterns have also been found in Poland and Czechoslovakia (Lane, 1982, pp. 62–3).

Industrial society theorists believe that there is a relatively invariable hierarchy of prestige associated with the industrial system even when placed in significantly different political contexts. East European research tends to confirm this. What are known in the West as the upper-professional occupations are also held in high regard in Eastern Europe. At the other end of the scale come unskilled jobs. Regardless of income rewards, occupations such as physicians, engineers and scientists everywhere are awarded high prestige. Distinctions between manual and non-manual work also continue to be made despite relative wage equalisation. Respondents to a Polish study of children's career aspirations in 1967, in which 3000 respondents were asked to place forty occupations in rank order, nearly all gave the highest rankings to professional and technical employment, while the lowest were awarded to semi-skilled and unskilled work of various kinds as well as shopkeeping. Interestingly, skilled work was given ninth place, indicating that it may be more prestigious in state socialist than in capitalist societies, a finding which has been replicated in a similar Soviet study (Lane, 1976, p. 182).

Whether seen in terms of prestige, income or consumption, there can be little doubt that inequalities continue to exist in East European society. They are, believes David Lane, rooted in four distinct sources. Firstly, there are inequalities which are perpetuated by property relationships. Although large-scale private property has been abolished, private ownership persists in agriculture, and institutional control of wealth not only continues but secures privileges for those who get control. Elites responsible for accumulation have arisen in each system. Secondly, the system of political power perpetuates inequalities via the industrialising process and its accompanying distribution of relative power between groups. Thirdly, the division of labour, highly developed as it is in industrial society, divides individuals between those who do creative work, those who plan and order the work of others and the majority who perform the less exacting and interesting routine jobs. At the very least the rewards of satisfaction from work are not evenly distributed. Finally, the family as an institution (especially the nuclear family) is a source of inequality. Parents may transmit cultural advantages or disadvantages to their children, the family reinforces an oppressed role for women and it transmits values which may or may not be egalitarian (Lane, 1982, pp. 154–6). To Lane's list may be added a fifth source of inequality, that of a history of regional or ethnic disadvantage, the effects of which, as we have seen, prove remarkably difficult to ameliorate.

Taking a completely different approach, Valerie Bunce (1983, pp. 7–8, 19–21) writes that the East European regimes have failed to achieve equality because of their status as Soviet satellites. In her view there is a contradiction between the goal of empire for the Soviet union and goals of satellite domestic growth. In such a view the main question about East European inequality is not why some have more than others, but why different periods have featured different income distributions. She sees East European progress as passing through three distinct phases, closely paralleling Soviet experiences. In the first phase the East European economies featured all the trade-offs of Soviet industrialisation. Stalinisation led to rapid growth and caused large economic inequalities by class and production sector. During the Stalinist period the policy agenda was constrained and kept simple. Growth was to come from ploughing back money, saved by holding down consumption and agricultural costs through a combination of fiat and repression. The result was a widening of income and power differentials between rural and urban areas, between white- and blue-collar workers and between party members and others. De-Stalinisation proved especially traumatic in Eastern Europe. The need for economic reform was first recognised and signalled by the

Soviets. The problem was that its requirements were not necessarily popular and came just as the compensating increase of social mobility was slowing. Domestic elites with a largely external power base sought to enhance their position by the only means possible, the achievement of greater equality between classes. The late 1950s were a time of huge budgetary outlays for social consumption, of significant rises in actual minimum wages and rising costs of government subsidies on basic essential items. Especially in the northern tier of the region, a trend toward income equalisation was clearly apparent.

Bunce perceives such moves as part of a legitimating strategy in which the most constrained reform efforts accompanied the greatest equalisation accomplishments. In her view equality was traded for efficiency during the second period. In the third phase, which began in the mid-1960s and continues to the present, neither equality nor efficiency are achievable. Slowed growth rates mean that redistribution rather than distribution is necessary to achieve equality. This brings numerous conflicts, as a public proves unwilling to reduce consumption and to accept price rises, thereby further squeezing sums available for investment. As the need for reform becomes ever more apparent, the decentralisation which is necessary for its implementation runs against opposition from the centralised planning apparatus, which is unwilling to decentralise itself. Over-institutionalised elites protect their advantaged positions and fail to initiate reforms (see also Martin, 1977).

Bunce's arguments oversimplify what are in fact very complex trends. She does not explain why some countries have succeeded in implementing wide-ranging economic reforms, which have entailed considerable inequality (Hungary and the GDR), and why others have failed. Too little account of decisions made by domestic elites is taken and the role of the Soviet Union in domestic decision-making is overstated. It is also far from evident that the East European domestic elites are as uniformly insecure and poorly supported as she suggests.

The notion that a ruling class has emerged in state socialist society arises from the observation that party, state and economic bureaucrats there are well positioned to enjoy political and material advantages. As we have seen above, such theories encompass that of Yugoslav philosopher and dissident critic Milovan Djilas, who regards party function-aries as a political bureaucracy. The political bureaucracy has a monopoly over property, ideology and government which gives it the essential characteristics of a ruling class, whose dominant position is shored by a monopoly of the ideological apparatus. Its control over the means of production via the state bureaucracy is nothing less than a new form of owner-ship, thus the 'new class' is a ruling class in the classical Marxist sense (Djilas, 1966). At the other end of the range of theories is the view that the intelligentsia as a whole has achieved a class domination over the workers. Konrad and Szelenyi (1979) declare that the intelligentsia controls the bureaucacy and possesses the monopoly of skills and knowl-edge necessary to control redistribution. Markus defines the bureaucratic apparatus as a corporate ruling group with members acting as trustees of productive property (in Feher, Heller and Markus, 1983). Their point is that particular privileged strata in state socialist society run the economy in such a way as to keep the power structure intact, even where this runs contrary to the policy which would produce the maximum surplus or the greatest redistributive capability. In short, elites exist and rule to protect elite rule.

The problem with such theories (and justice has not been done to their subtleties here) is not that they do not contain important elements of truth, but that their proponents tend to overstate their case. In many of the full-blown ruling-class theories, e.g. those of Tony Cliff or Milovan Djilas, many of the critical elements of class dominance, notably the right to transfer property from one generation to another, are miss-ing. Those more subtle characterisations which stop short of proclaiming the existence of a new class nevertheless fail to demonstrate that their corporate group or strata rule in their own, self-defined interests. Nor do they show why party activists often seek to articulate policies which redress imbal-ances.

What all the theories seek to explain is changes in the social structure in maturing economies whereby benefits tend to accrue to technical, executive and professional groups. These groups are not necessarily united, and important differences exist between those who derive authority from the party and those whose position is technocratic and professional. As will be shown in Chapter 8, political strategies are, as far as we can judge, determined by those whose rise has been on the basis of political criteria. Programmes of education and training have been sufficiently successful now that a substantial pool of politically qualified experts exist from which leaderships may be recruited on grounds of political and ideological merit. On the other hand, there is little doubt that the composition and position of the political leadership suggests at least ambiguities in the claim that state socialist elites act solely on behalf of their working classes. Thus theories pointing to the dominance of the intelligentsia, the power of the bureaucracy or the appearance of a new political class are valuable because they raise important questions about the relationships between the intelligentsia and the manual working class.

An alternative explanation of state socialist stratification patterns is to be found in arguments by technological functionalists, who hold that modern technology in an advanced economy has a standardising effect on social structures. This makes for uniformities in industrial societies which are so strong as to override factors which might lead to possible diversity (for example, a political commitment to social equality). Such theories stress increasing similarities in institutional arrangements and social systems as industrialism proceeds. All social structures will experience an expansion of managerial and white-collar work, creating a surge of upward mobility which will produce an elite based mainly on technological skills. But detailed comparisons of mobility patterns in a number of state socialist and advanced capitalist societies show that cultural and political variations make for considerable diversity in elite composition (Heath, 1981). While at an abstract level we may argue that hierarchical stratification patterns and the clear presence of a small political elite indicate that all industrial societies are necessarily not only unequal, but also elitist and technocratic, in practical terms important differences obtain which may only be explained by resort to the different political objectives of liberal democratic and state socialist elites. As a result various studies have shown that class inequalities have been significantly reduced in state socialist societies, although other kinds of inequality persist (Echols, 1981a). If the social transformation in Eastern Europe has been economically determined, it has also been socialist-inspired, raising possibilities at least of the utilisation of political and economic resources to achieve equality.

7

The Logic of Party Rule (I): History, Ideology and Structure

Like their counterpart in the USSR, the communist parties of
Eastern Europe are the main source of authoritative political
decision-making; they are the sole arbiter of legitimate social
values, and draw upon the same fundamental set of political
principles: Marxism–Leninism. However, it would be doing
these organisations a great disservice merely to ascribe to
them identical structures, patterns of membership, functions
and relations with the state. In this chapter we shall see that
there is considerable variation, and that while the experience
of the USSR has had a profound impact upon party programmes and historical development since the founding of
the parties, this has not ensured uniformity. Furthermore, the
issue of a distinct national political identity has been a
continuous problem lurking beneath the surface of the common ideological façade and which from time to time breaks
through to remind the political elites that 'national roads to
socialism' are a *sine qua non* if the Marxist–Leninist regimes are
to build and retain popular and international legitimacy. As a
result, the East European communist parties have encountered more frequent crises of legitimacy than has the CPSU,
and they have had to resort increasingly to more ingenious
methods of crisis management. These have ranged from
periodic recruitment drives among certain social groups to
variations in party structures and their relation to state
institutions. While ideology and structures will be explored in
the course of this chapter, it is necessary to start by giving

173

some thought to what constitutes a Marxist–Leninist party in the East European context.

The Marxist–Leninist heritage and the origins of the communist parties of Eastern Europe

With the exception of Bulgaria, whose communist party history has been very closely tied to that of the Russian movement since the 1890s, and the Albanian Party of Labour, which did not come into existence until 1941 (and continued under Yugoslav patronage until 1948), most of the East European communist parties have their origin in the years 1918–23: the Hungarian Communist Party (HCP) was formed in 1918; the Bulgarian (BCP), German (KPD) and Yugoslav (YCP) Communist Parties in 1919; and the Czechoslovak (KSC), Romanian (RCP) and Polish (CPP) Communist Parties in 1921, largely as a result of political developments in Russia. On the grounds that nothing succeeds like success, the victory of the Bolshevik party in 1917, and the founding of the Third International in 1919, brought greater orthodoxy to the international communist movement. Parties that wished to affiliate to the Comintern had to subscribe to the Twenty-one conditions of membership approved at the Second Comintern Congress in 1920. These endorsed the model of party organisation and activity developed by the Bolshevik Party since its own founding at the Stockholm Conference in 1903. They drew principally upon Lenin's *What is to be done?*, which advocated the 'vanguard' party consisting of highly committed and trained members working in an organisation that aimed to combine the maximum amount of democratic involvement with the strictest centralism of decision-making and action. The Comintern conditions were basically 'exported' to the communist parties working in the very different conditions of the rest of Europe. The example of the Soviet success, plus financial and organisational aid from the USSR, encouraged compliance on the part of the parties who affiliated. As they were often very small groupings of intellectuals competing with a number of rival groupings for popular support, acceptance by the Comintern accorded them greater legitimacy and higher status over their rivals.

At the same time, most of the parties founded in the early 1920s were subject to the tension between 'Russian' and 'Austro-German' Marxism. The foundation of the Comintern was as much an attempt to exclude the latter influence as it was an endorsement of Soviet success. The varying emphases of the 'Austro-German' tendencies, upon a parliamentary road to socialism, upon a strong organisational base in the trade-union movement, and the adoption of a looser mass party structure, were rejected by the Third International. These aspects were the basis of the difference between this organisation and the Second International of Social Democratic parties. While the label 'Social Democratic' has very different connotations today from about 70 years ago, its traditions continued to haunt the communist parties emerging from wartime exile and underground in the post-1945 period. Most parties formed in the 1918–23 period had strong social-democratic tendencies (especially in the HCP, BCP and the KSC). For many the experience was traumatic, as in the case of the German KPD, which broke away in 1919 from what was still the largest mass workers' party in Europe, the SPD. Accusing the latter of treachery because of the brutal repression of the Spartakist uprising in Berlin, when Karl Liebknecht and Rosa Luxemburg were killed, the KPD itself turned to support Hitler in the late 1920s – a move which was disastrous for its popular support.

Indeed, the interwar years produced a curiously changing choreography of positions adopted by the communist parties and principally directed by the Comintern. By the time of the Fifth Comintern Congress in 1924, doctrinal changes constrained their action considerably (Carr, 1964). The condemnation of Trotsky's theory of 'permanent revolution' and the call for 'Bolshevisation' of the member parties placed them under ever closer Soviet tutelage, and subjected them to membership purges of first the 'rightists' and then the 'left', in a manner analogous to the experience of the USSR during the period of the debate between the Left and Right Oppositions between 1923 and 1928. At the same congress social-democratic parties were condemned as 'social fascist', thus precluding a broader alliance (although later in the 1920s the failure of the shift leftwards produced yet another change in direction in the call for the communist parties to form popular fronts with various bourgeois parties). Obviously the implications of this were disastrous for the German KPD, and were none too satisfactory for the parties in Czechoslovakia and Poland. The Czechoslovak party, the KSC, was a very broad coalition that still included many former left Social Democrats and the instruction to expel these 'rightist' elements proved extremely painful to implement. However, perhaps the most painful experience of all in the interwar period was that of the Communist Party of Poland following the Great Purge of 1936–8 in the USSR. First, in the early thirties the suspected Polish Trotskyites were purged, followed by a similar attack upon those suspected of 'nationalistic deviations'. In 1938 several hundred Polish communists who were on Soviet territory 'disappeared' and by May of that year the CPP had been dissolved. So, the effect of membership of the Comintern was generally harmful to the East European communist parties, particularly for the Polish party and for those parties which had been set up in the more advanced industrialised countries such as Germany and Czechoslovakia.

Another factor important to communist-party development was the general level of tolerance of their activity by the interwar governments. Some parties were proscribed soon after their appearance (in Hungary in 1919, in Yugoslavia in 1921, in Bulgaria in 1923 and in Romania in 1924), while others ploughed on with ever-dwindling support to be banned later (the German KPD in 1933) or to face liquidation (the CPP in 1938). Some parties, such as those in Hungary and Bulgaria, changed their names after the ban, or operated under the cover of other parties and front organisations, until they were finally outlawed following military coups. Only in Czechoslovakia did the KSC flourish and openly contest elections as a mass party of a non-Bolshevik nature, and despite 'Bolshevisation' it received a revived support following Hitler's *anschluss* of the country and appeasement by the Western Allies. However, like the other parties, the KSC was dismembered in 1939 and went underground.

The support given to the parties varied, with those in the

more industrialised states faring better than those in the predominantly agrarian states such as Yugoslavia and Romania. The Bulgarian Communist Party was, however, anomalous, as it built up and sustained a large following during the 1940s in what was still a largely agricultural economy. There was also the additional problem of nationalism, both right-wing and liberation-oriented. Thus, for example, the perception of the Romanian Party (RCP) as anti-nationalist (because of its international connections with other communist parties) lost it much potential support. Whereas the appeal of nationalism had been stronger than internationalism in the interwar period, the experience of the war years themselves created further tensions, which were to reappear during the post-1945 decade. Tensions largely arose from events after the dissolution of the parties upon the outbreak of war. Except for Yugoslavia, where the revival of the party was assured by the part it played in the partisan struggle against the Axis powers, and of course disregarding Albania, where the party was itself born of the wartime struggle, there was a fundamental tension.

It arose between the 'nativists' who had remained (either underground or in jail) and the 'Muscovites' who lived out the course of the war in the USSR. Nativist factions who had on the whole learnt to work with other left of centre interests in the resistance movement were uneasy about accommodating the demands of the Soviet-backed Muscovites, especially when they had been so reliant on the Red Army to get into power. This was the case with the Hungarian Party (HCP) in 1944, and again the case of Czechoslovakia is noteworthy: there was a lack of leadership from Moscow, and although the KSC did not win a majority in the 1946 elections (it only acquired 31 per cent of the votes as against 61 per cent for the Democratic Party), it profited from the Kosice programme negotiated with other democratic parties in order to set up a government of national unity. The Czechoslovak Communist Party (KSC) held the key government posts, and emphasised the nationalisation of properties owned by the Nazis and their collaborators. This provided the base for the KSC to build up its electoral support so that by February 1948 it was in a majority at all levels of government. However, by that time the onset of the Cold War, and pressures from the USSR to prevent autonomous 'national roads to socialism', provided the occasion for a coup and a purge. Consequently, since 1948 (with the exception of 1968–9), the KSC has been 'Totalitarian, authoritarian, and semi-elitist in function and character' (Toma, 1979).

Following the Comintern line, other parties pursued a 'popular-front' strategy during the years 1945–8. However, this created two types of problem: firstly, another international body came into existence in 1947 – the Cominform – whose primary objective was to tighten Soviet control over the emerging People's Democracies, including both domestic and foreign policies. The denunciation and later expulsion of Tito in June 1948 marked the break between Yugoslavia and the USSR, and the expression of sympathy from the 'nativist' Secretary General of the Polish Workers Party (PWP), Gomulka, cost him his position in office. Thus sympathisers of a 'national road to socialism' were weeded out of the newly emerging, post-war communist parties after 1948. Secondly, the already low legitimacy of these parties, which resulted from interwar experiences culminating in their dissolution, was aggravated. The parties that emerged in 1945 were in many cases completely new structures, e.g. the Polish Workers Party, founded in 1942. Furthermore, not all were as successful at the ballot box as the Czechoslovak party. In Poland the Polish Socialist Party and other leftist groups commanded greater support. So in contrast to the early years of the Comintern, Moscow instructed the socialist and communist parties to merge. Despite some attempts at compromise, the result was a forcible merger in 1948. Similar mergers took place in Romania as the Social Democrats were absorbed into the RCP (renamed the Romanian Workers Party (RWP) after 1945); in Hungary to form the Hungarian Workers Party in 1948; and in the GDR to form the Socialist Unity Party (SED) in 1946. The Bulgarian Communist Party (BCP) was atypical: Bulgaria had been an axis satellite during the war, and so there was no government in exile planning to take over after the liberation of the country. Furthermore, Bulgaria had not declared war on the USSR, which proved an obstacle to Soviet military intervention and political influence. The result was that the BCP was left outside the post-war coalition government. Only after the USSR declared war on Bulgaria did it have the pretext to intervene and install the BCP in power. Thus except for a brief period after 1945, the communist parties of Eastern Europe (with the exception of Yugoslavia) became subject to Soviet direction.

Marxist–Leninist principles and party life: the role of ideology

Having shown how since their early development the Marxist–Leninist parties of Eastern Europe were influenced by the USSR, it is necessary to give some attention to the principles according to which they operate, and their self-image, before going on to examine their structure, membership and relations with the state. Generally speaking, these parties are held to conform to the model of the 'cadre' party as distinct from the 'mass' parties or electoral 'caucus' organisations of liberal democracy (Duverger, 1962). Unlike the other two, the cadre party places great emphasis upon the role of the individual member:

> A cadre party is small, and derives its power from the quality of members, bringing influence to bear on the basis of individual knowledge, prestige, riches or skill. A mass party has a large membership: its tactics are to make its influence felt by the strength of numbers of members (Duverger, quoted in Lane, 1985, p. 151).

In practice, the parties' memberships vary. While the CPSU has changed since 1917 from being a 'cadre' party of a small committed group to more of a 'mass' party in the post-Stalinist period, the SED started life in 1948 as a leftist mass party with about 1.3 million members which soon increased to 2 million (Grote, 1979). It was during the ensuing Stalinist era that it reverted to being a cadre party. Similarly the Hungarian Workers Party and the Yugoslav Communist Party (League of Communists of Yugoslavia after 1952) claimed membership of around half a million. The member-

ship is organised in cells (later Basic Party Organisations –
BPOs) according to the territorial–production principle. This
means that the individual member has a primary commitment to conduct party tasks in the place of work or residence,
and thus will be brought into maximum contact with the
general population. Because Marxism–Leninism places so
much emphasis upon control over the means of production as
the basis of political power, be it in capitalist or socialist
societies, the party organisation at the place of work has a
higher status than at the place of residence, at least below the
local district level. But the principle of committed membership remains distinctive.

A second principle follows on from the parties' monopoly
of political power, and that is their leading role in society. Its
leading role does not mean that the party makes decisions on
every single issue, which would be impracticable, as we shall
see when we examine some of the weaknesses of party
organisation in certain central state institutions and in the
agricultural sector of the economy in particular. Rather what
it means is that the party's views are dominant and solely
legitimate, implying that there are controls over both state
institutions and personnel. In the first case this means the
monitoring and supervision of non-party institutions such as
central government ministries, factories, schools etc. Such
kontrol cannot extend as far as the actual enforcement of party
preferences. Hence party cadre policy and the device of the
nomenklatura exist to ensure that the recruitment and placement of personnel in senior positions of authority is such that
the party will not experience any difficulty in getting its
policies observed. The *nomenklatura* lists of key posts and
reliable candidates for them are drawn up and held by the
party apparatus at various levels. As we shall see in the
following chapter, the *nomenklatura* system does not always
mean that only party members can hold positions of responsibility. Those who show a strong sympathy and reliability
will also be included.

Obviously besides these mechanisms of control, parties also
want to ensure that arrangements imply more than enforcing
compliance of membership to centrally made decisions. These
parties see themselves as having an equally important ideolo-

gical role. It was Lenin who saw the desirability of combining the need for firm leadership with democratic participation. Hence he synthesised this in the concept of 'democratic centralism', vaguely formulated in 1905–6 and later elaborated in the 1920s and 1930s. While in a revolutionary situation decisive political leadership required the discipline of a unified and centralised organisation, in order to claim to be legitimately representing the people a communist organisation would have to be democratic. Thus democratic centralism as it was produced in the 1930s demanded:

1 The election of all leading party bodies, from the lowest to the highest.
2 Periodical reports of party bodies to their party organisations and to higher bodies.
3 Strict party discipline and subordination of the minority to the majority.
4 The decisions of higher bodies to be binding on lower bodies (CPSU, 1977, quoted in Lane, 1985).

It is the combination of the principles of membership commitment, the leading role of the party, democratic centralism and proletarian internationalism, which comprises the distinctive characteristics of Marxist–Leninist parties. It would be a mistake, however, to assume that such parties espouse a rigid ideological world view.

There is considerable controversy about the status of ideology in state socialist societies. Meyer (1966) sees ideology as having six components, contained in different sets of documents and public statements. While Marxist–Leninist parties are unusual in possessing a body of doctrines that are clearly identifiable in everyday political discourse, the role of this as an instrument of the regime to ensure compliance has been overstressed. In as much as Marxist–Leninist ideology is a pattern of beliefs which justifies the social order, it is also something which explains to the ordinary citizen their historical and social setting. It thus also acts as a constraint upon the activities of the rulers, and gives rise to expectations on the part of the governed which the rulers must fulfil (Lane, 1985, p. 216). ideology thus contains as many clues as to the hopes and fears of Marxist–Leninist party leaderships, as it does to confidence in regime performance. Ideological formulations also change: some concepts are dropped; new ones enter the political vocabulary; and old ones take on a completely new meaning (Taras, 1984). It is difficult to illustrate this without reference to the history of ideological debate, both within and between parties, since 1945.

We will begin with a brief reference to the orthodox ideological basis for assuming power in order to establish a 'dictatorship of the proletariat'. Although the latter term was used by Marx to describe the form of rule needed during the transitional period after the working class seized power, it was given a more precise formulation by Lenin in the context of the Bolshevik revolution in 1917. Lenin made three major contributions to Marxist theory and revolutionary tactics: his theory of imperialism, his theory of the revolutionary party, and the theory of the dictatorship of the proletariat. More of a political strategist and tactician than Marx, Lenin was able to perceive the revolutionary possibilities in such an economically backward country as Russia. The three aforesaid concepts aided him in this. Paradoxically, the dictatorship of the proletariat (i.e. the state embodying through its coercive and ideological apparatuses the interests of the working class) took place in a country where the working class was in a minority. However, for some of the East European countries, this was not the case (Czechoslovakia, the GDR, and, more marginally, Poland), and for many of the others there was a more extensive experience of associational life during the interwar period (despite the emergence of authoritarian regimes, and the suspension of representative democracy in many states). Thus from the start there was some concern that a system of rule that equated state and party would not be appropriate for East European conditions. This concern is reflected in ideological developments. Conditioned by their own past as well as by international pressures from the USSR, these Marxist–Leninist parties each put their own gloss on the ideological orthodoxy. According to the social situation, rank and file party discipline, and geopolitical and military considerations, such aberrations have aroused a mixed response from the USSR. The resulting pattern of similarities and differences may best be understood via a brief examination of the 'operative' ideology (defined as explanations and justifications of policy formulations, Taras, 1984, p. 235) of each party.

We start with the party that was the first to make an open break with the USSR: the Yugoslav Communist Party. From being one of the closest supporters of Soviet policy, in 1947 Tito became one of the most outspoken critics. The result was expulsion from the Cominform, and radical policy changes during the later 1940s and early 1950s. Between 1950 and 1952 there were major efforts at separating party and state, which culminated in a call by the Sixth Congress for the 'Withering away of the party'. This fitted in with the concept of a 'self-managing society', following such policies as the introduction of workers' councils in industry and a general decentralisation of state activities (see below). Finally the development of a foreign policy that espoused non-alignment (see Chapter 13) marked the third major difference from orthodox 'proletarian internationalism'. Yet, as we shall see when we examine the principles of operation of the League of Communists of Yugoslavia (LCY), as the party became known after 1952, it is not very different from its fellow parties – despite the fact that in 1952 it dropped the requirement of candidate membership, and by 1966 had become more of a mass party (Carter, 1982). However, not all ideological disputes have focused on the USSR. The issues of regional autonomy and party reform have been cloaked in a mantle of ideological debate between conservative and liberal factions. The former, led after 1962 by the anti-federalist head of the security police, Rankovic, was supported by Serbian, Montenegrin and Bosnian party members. 'Liberal' pro-federalist interests made a comeback at the Seventh LCY congress in 1966. However, Slovenia and Croatia continued to oppose the policies of the federal government, on national rights, regional development policy and devolution, issues which became embroiled with the call for party reform. A general upsurge of nationalism in Croatia, Kosovo, and Macedonia was dealt with fairly severely. Tito instigated a purge of the 'liberal' elements in the LCY in 1971, and introduced constitutional change in 1974 (see Chapter 9) to keep such tendencies in check, and to prepare a smooth transition in the leadership after his death.

The expulsion of Yugoslavia from the Cominform aroused the strongest feeling in Poland, where the 'nativist' Gomulka defended the right of individual parties to search for 'national roads to socialism'. Unfortunately this only brought about his dismissal as First Secretary of the Polish United Workers' Party (PUWP), and inaugurated a period of Stalinist rule, presided over by the 'Muscovite' Bierut. However, the issue of a 'national road to socialism' has resurfaced several times in ideological debate, and was fuelled by extensive popular support for the Roman Catholic church. In 1956 nationalism was associated with a call for workers' self-management, and in 1968 with pressure for cultural freedoms, anti-semitism and anti-Soviet sentiment. However, the nationalist wing of the PUWP was relatively weak in the 1970s, when, after the events of 1970-1, the ideological focus shifted to the ability of the party to represent working-class and peasant interests. Discussion of the entry into an era of 'Developed Socialism' was legitimised by the Twenty-fourth Congress of the CPSU in 1971 and in the constitutional reform of 1976. The aim of this discussion was to rebuild the legitimacy of Marxist–Leninist parties at a time when the material achievements of socialism appeared less substantial than those of the capitalist West. In Poland this caused little ideological debate, but much of what later became known as a 'propaganda of success', as rhetoric fell increasingly out of step with reality. The trade benefits of the era of 'detente' proved elusive, and popular living standards suffered. The legitimacy problem of the PUWP became more acute, and worker protest erupted in 1976, and was never far below the surface before it broke out on an unprecedented scale in 1980. The face-saving pledge of the PUWP to undergo a process of 'socialist renewal' was inadequate to rebuild its legitimacy. As many as a third of its membership joined Solidarity, and by 1981 a situation of 'dual power' existed in Poland. After the declaration of martial law in December 1981 General Jaruzelski proclaimed a situation of 'class struggle and class alliance'. An ensuing stage of 'normalisation', after the declaration of the 'amnesty' in favour of those interned, was an endeavour to achieve a rapprochement with society.

If the direction of ideological change in the PUWP had been toward bankruptcy during the 1970s, the opposite is true of the East German SED. Following the enforced merger in 1946, and the proclamation of statehood in 1949 by the Federal Republic, the legitimacy of the SED was from the start very low. The unpopularity of its Stalinist policies in the 1950s, and the growing emigration to the West, necessitated a change in style if it was to rebuild and sustain its legitimacy. Although the SED was aided by an unprecedented increase in economic growth in the 1960s, this was achieved within a change in political style and an assertive ideological stance. The introduction of the New Economic System in 1963 was accompanied by a very extensive discussion of the benefits of the Scientific and Technological Revolution. At the Seventh Congress in 1966 it was announced that the GDR was on the threshold of being a 'Developed Social System of Socialism'. This has been interpreted as a de-emphasis of classical Marxism–Leninism; it implies a shift from the 'class vanguard' role of the SED, and from the assertion of the transitional nature of socialism, to a role for the party as the auxiliary of the state, and an acceptance that the socialist stage of development is itself permanent (Holmes, 1981). The suggestion is that applied science and not Marxist theory will be the power-house of further development. Although they are capable of being interpreted in many ways such ideological nuances are pretty heretical. The brazen claims of the SED were checked, when it became apparent that the implementation of the New Economic System was facing difficulties. Moreover the Ulbricht regime was providing an obstacle to the Soviet aim of 'detente', and the normalisation of relations between the two Germanies in particular. Accordingly, the self-image of the task of the SED was reformulated as being the formation of a 'Developed Socialist Society', at the Eighth SED Congress in 1971 (McCauley, 1986). In line with the Soviet developments, the 'dictatorship of the proletariat' was re-emphasised. A further restatement came in 1976, when Ulbricht's successor, Honecker, announced at the Ninth SED Congress that political, economic and social development must proceed along the lines of realistic probabilities. Hence 'Actually-Existing' or 'real Socialism' (a term that crept into political discourse after 1973) was extremely pragmatic, and became the object of criticism by party intellectuals such as Bahro.

Such an ideological minuet is surprising in a party that is otherwise one of the most loyal to the Soviet Union and a key member of the Warsaw Pact. It contrasts strongly with another of the currently most pro-Soviet states, Czechoslovakia. Originally one of the largest and most ideologically diverse mass parties in 1945, the Czechoslovak Communist Party (KSC) changed rapidly to become one of the most Stalinist after 1948. Bitter memories of the purges of the years 1948–52 persisted until the 1960s (especially of the execution in 1952 of KSC officials, including the former general secretary, and Slovak, Rudolf Slansky). While most of the other Soviet bloc parties responded gradually (though with some adjustment to their leadership) to supporting Khrushchev's condemnation of Stalinist crimes, this was not the case for Czechoslovakia and Albania. Between Stalin's death in 1953 and Khrushchev's speech, the general Secretary, Novotny, did not even embark upon a 'new course' of less stringent economic policies. Thus de-Stalinisation was late in arriving in Czechoslovakia. Only in the mid-1960s did a reformulation of policy take place among certain sections of the KSC, and particularly among the leadership of the Soviet KSS. Reformulation of objectives and demands from other social organisations, including economists, writers, journalists, students, and academics, led to the growth of intellectual ferment both within and outside the KSC (Kusin, 1973; Skilling, 1976; Golan, 1971). One interesting ideological development took place outside the KSC and later had an impact upon party ideology. A symposium held by the Czech Academy of Sciences provided a theoretical framework and an empirical survey of the implications of the 'Scientific and Technological Revolution' for Czechoslovak society. It hinted at a changing role for the party in the light of a changing class structure, and the possibility of political as well as social pluralism (Richta, 1969). However, these ideas did not receive official endorsement until the publication of the April 1968 Action Programme of the KSC. The main aims of this proposal were to modify the undue concentration of power in the party–state apparatus, to abolish the *nomenklatura* (see Chapter 8), and to de-emphasise generally both the leading role of the party and the use of democratic centralism as a basis of decision-making in non-party organisations. It was this ideological heresy – 'socialism with a human face' – rather than the issue of market socialism, or the proposal to introduce a form of workers' control in industry, which caused anxiety among the other socialist states, especially the USSR. In this context a series of meetings of the Warsaw Pact took place over the summer of 1968, ending in the invasion of Czechoslovakia and the ensuing proclamation of the so-called Brezhnev Doctrine (see Chapter 13). Agreement to the Action Programme was reversed at the Central Committee meeting in December 1970, when there was a return to ideological monolithism (Rupnik, 1981). Since then there has been little deviation or innovation.

If ideological development went overboard and precipitated military intervention from a 'friendly' power, then the ensuing Czechoslovak experience has been very different from that of Hungary. After the turbulence of 1956, ideological orthodoxy has provided the framework within which considerable policy innovation has taken place. Here the rapid de-Stalinisation in 1956 caused widespread support for doctrinal heresy within the Hungarian Communist Party (HCP), and Soviet military intervention. But the effects upon the HCP were more dramatic, as the HCP was dissolved and replaced by a new party, the Hungarian Socialist Workers' party (HSWP), which faced considerable difficulty in rebuilding its membership and popular legitimacy. Hungary's problems may have well been partly due to the legacy of the immediate post-war period. A lack of electoral success during the interwar period, a heavy reliance upon the USSR and the Red Army in the assumption of power, the instigation of a reign of terror and the banning of all opposition parties in 1947, had produced intense popular dissatisfaction. Historically the Hungarian Party is one of the least stable, having been dissolved/disbanded in 1919, 1936, 1943 and 1956 (Schöpflin, 1985). It is all the more interesting, then, that Hungary has introduced the most radical form of market mechanism, and has one of the most consumer-oriented economies of Eastern Europe (see Chapter 5). This is the hallmark of Kadarism, or, as some East European wit has put it, 'Goulasch Communism'. Kadar, the first secretary of the HSWP since 1956, has operated an 'alliance policy', trading popular support from individual social interests for material well-being. In 1983 he announced that Hungary was 'constructing socialism in a national context'. At the same time ideological digression is not tolerated, and the HSWP has been most outspoken in condemning the toleration of dissent.

Finally we come to the other Balkan countries. Bulgaria has followed Soviet ideological leadership very closely, so that ideological developments are practically indistinguishable. Albania, however, has adopted contradictory stances, owing to its relationship both with the USSR and Yugoslavia. Like the LCY, the Albanian Party of Labour (APL) took part in a common partisan struggle and achieved victory without the need for Soviet assistance and the violet suppression of the population, but unresolved population and border problems have placed the APL frequently in ideological opposition to its neighbour. At the same time, the APL refused to repudiate Stalinism after the Twentieth Congress of the CPSU. It finally broke with the USSR in 1961, when aid was withdrawn, and turned towards China at the time the Sino-Soviet dispute emerged. Criticism of the 'revisionism' of the USSR was couched in a very esoteric and vitriolic rhetoric. An analogy was drawn between the USSR and Yugoslavia, and thereby the former could be indirectly criticised through the latter. In its communications with the outside world strong ideological statements have been prominent, featuring a heavy emphasis upon national self-reliance and revolutionary proletarian internationalism. To justify its position, the APL is scathing in its criticism of 'social imperialism', 'peaceful coexistence' and 'detente'. However, the adherence to the Maoist ideological line in the 1960s (including the instigation of a cultural revolution between 1966 and 1969) started to falter after US President Nixon made his visit to the People's Republic of China in 1972. The withdrawal of aid by China in 1975, and the changes in Chinese domestic policy after 1978, brought the Sino-Albanian alignment to an end until 1984, and was marked by a slight improvement in relations with the USSR and the rest of Eastern Europe.

The remaining Balkan state, Romania, is renowned more for its independent foreign policy stance than for ideological innovation. Nationalism has played an important part in the establishment of the legitimacy of the Romanian Communist Party (RCP), and affected Romania's international position. It surfaced in party debates after 1958, and in 1964 when Romania asserted her right to her 'own road to socialism'. This inaugurated a phase of 'de-Sovietisation' in foreign policy and economic and military relations. The assumption of power by Ceausescu was accompanied by a strongly populist appeal on the part of the RCP, which was expressed in the ideological concept of the 'multi-laterally developed society', denoting an expansion of the RCP's position in society through extending its organisational framework and contacts with the population. This was contrary to the general tendency elsewhere, where parties took on a lower profile and tolerated the emergence of pluralist tendencies (Gilberg, 1979a). A continuous reorganisation of the political machinery of the party and state (see Chapter 8) was instigated, and a personality cult and dynastic power structure surrounding the Ceausescu family developed. Like Yugoslavia, Romania has been very wary of Soviet initiatives in the direction of closer 'cooperation' between Marxist–Leninist parties on a European level. It reflects a fear of Soviet attempts to impose sanctions.

Our brief overview of 'operative' ideological developments might be concluded with the observation that although East European Marxist–Leninist parties have been primarily influenced by the ideological pronouncements of the USSR, this very often provoked an independence of ideological line. Soviet decisions of 1947–8 to bring to an end the 'popular-front' phase of rule in Eastern Europe, and to impose an orthodox model of the 'dictatorship of the proletariat', the 'leading role of the party' and 'proletarian internationalism', were not easily accepted. Opposition was strongest among the Yugoslav and the Polish parties, although factional opposition within the Hungarian and Czech parties caused very drastic purges. The next major Soviet initiative was the 'new course' and Khrushchev's secret speech to the Twentieth Congress of the CPSU in 1956. Intended to signal the appropriateness of de-Stalinisation, it did not engender a uniform East European response. The most radical interpretations of de-Stalinisation came from the Hungarian and Polish parties, but were resisted by Albania, Czechoslovakia and the GDR. Khrushchev instigated further ideological manoeuvrings in 1961, when he declared that the USSR was shifting from a workers' state to a 'state of the whole working people'; that with the aid of the 'scientific and technological revolution' (STR) the USSR would surpass the USA in economic and technological matters by 1970, and be on the threshold of communism by 1980; and that a phase of peaceful coexistence between East and West marked a softening of inter-bloc relations. This caused a considerable furore. Albania found this unacceptable, Romania used it as a means of developing a more independent foreign policy line and of reconsidering the role of the party. Other parties saw this as betokening a lower profile for the party in society, especially the SED, which inaugurated a debate on the STR and 'developed socialism' to legitimise this. In a completely different way, so did the Czechoslovak Communist Party.

Finally the opening of the era of 'detente', was the excuse for the Soviet Union to reassert its ideological superiority, with Brezhnev's Report to the Twenty-fourth Congress of the CPSU that the USSR had arrived at a stage of 'developed socialism'. This assertion of social and economic maturity was expressed in constitutional revision, whose effect was to strengthen party control over state apparatuses and social organisations. This was the context in which constitutional revisions took place throughout Eastern Europe (see Chapter 9). The hollowness of the claims made and the transparency of the rights guaranteed (especially after the signature of the Helsinki accords on international cooperation and security in Europe) in 1975, were the bases upon which the dissident movements in Czechoslovakia, the GDR and above all Poland developed after the mid-1970s. The falseness of 'developed socialism' as a description of the declining living standards in Poland not only meant that the Polish regime was faced with an unprecedented legitimacy crisis. The current position on this has reverted to the more modest claim that it is still 'constructing socialism'. In conclusion, we may state with some certainty, that the ideological developments of East European communist parties are as much shaped by the force of nationalism and circumstance as by proletarian internationalism.

Party structures

One outstanding difference between the USSR and the state socialist countries of Eastern Europe is that the latter are not mono-party systems. This is emphasised in their claim to be People's Democracies. Other parties exist but with restrictions placed upon their autonomy. Within the framework of an election campaign organisation known usually as the National Front (see Chapter 10), but whose role in the allocation of parliamentary seats is wholly under communist party control, varying numbers of parties 'contest' elections and have their 'representatives' in parliament. Thus besides the SED in the GDR there are four others (the Christian Democrats, Liberal Democrats, National Democrats, and the Peasant Party). In Poland two other parties exist: the United Peasant Party and the Democratic Party; in Yugoslavia a separate Peasant Party is tolerated; and in Bulgaria the Bulgarian Agrarian People's Union retains a formal structure, participates in various governing bodies, and claims a membership of 120,000. In Czechoslovakia there are four other parties besides the KSC (which itself is divided along federal lines, as there is formally, if not in practice, a separate organisation for Slovakia, the KSS). Only in Hungary and Romania do such parties not exist.

The role of the 'other parties' has been interpreted in different ways, varying from the charitable justification that they exert 'control without opposition' (Wiatr and Przeworski, 1966), to the more dismissive view that they are a façade devised to boost regime legitimacy. Yet when reviewing the party systems of Eastern Europe, the typical mistake is to draw too stark a contrast between them and the arrangements within liberal democratic systems. In many of the latter party competition is imperfect, or there are electoral barriers against the entry of new parties. The mass of party membership may have difficulty in influencing policies, and, above all, membership numbers are well below those of the East European communist parties, a factor which obviously has a bearing upon assumptions about political participation (see Chapter 10). Whatever opinion is adopted, it is obvious that the role of the minor parties is not identical to that of competing, non-governing parties in Western liberal democratic systems, as the former are imperfect articulators and aggregators of interests, and cannot challenge the basis of communist party rule. Such functions are more often performed by the discussion clubs and groups that have sprung up periodically in times of crisis, such as in Hungary in 1956, in Poland in 1956, 1968, 1976, and 1980–1, and in Czechoslovakia during 1966–8. In these cases the boundary between such organisations and the underground opposition is finely drawn.

Neither can the ruling communist parties of Eastern Europe themselves be presented as identical to the orthodox Soviet model. Since the early 1960s, there has been considerable diversification. However, it would not do to exaggerate this too much: no party (not even the League of Communists of Yugoslavia) has yet abandoned the Leninist formulations of the 'leading role of the party' or 'democratic centralism' in the conduct of its own affairs. An examination of ruling party statutes (Simons and White, 1984) has shown that despite a number of small variations between parties (and over time), specifying criteria for membership recruitment, and the status of the party 'apparatus', it may be concluded that common features are more apparent than differences.

The party statutes all tend to be set out in a similar way. They start with a general introduction, setting out the party's version of its own history and future goals, and the basic principles of Marxism–Leninism. A section on procedure for admissions, and the rights and obligations of membership, is followed by a fairly lengthy outline of the organisational principles of democratic centralism and the leading role of the party. The organisational structures are remarkably similar, although after 1969 in Romania, and even earlier in Yugoslavia, there were some variations (see Chapter 8). In all cases the congress is (nominally) the supreme decision-making body, given ultimate authority to amend rules, elect a central committee and to authorise major decisions. Congresses meet every 4 to 5 years, although in some party statutes there is provision for party conferences to be held to discuss important issues in the interim (these seldom take place). The long period between congresses ensures that substantive power falls upon the 'Politbureau' (consisting of anything from nine full members, as in Albania in 1985, to twenty-two, as in Romania), Secretariat and full-time party apparatus. The former two are elected by the Central Committee (normally consisting of 150–200 members) at congress. Although the Politbureau is the more visible of institutions, it is usually the Secretariat that is the 'power house' of party policy formulation. Headed by the General or First Secretary, it is in a strong position through its departments to monitor the major areas of government activity such as industry, education, agriculture foreign policy etc., as well as the important party-specific activity of the selection of cadres and the 'verification' of fulfilment of party tasks. With the exception of the HSWP and the SED, no party statute deals in great detail with the structure and functions of the central party apparatus. None the less, the Secretariat is in a strategic position within the party, both to provide information and policy recommendations to the Politbureau and Central Committee, and through the device of the *nomenklatura* to control cadres (party membership and recruitment to non-party posts – see Chapter 8), propaganda and campaigns, and the work of the lower regional and local levels of the apparatus.

The Politbureau, Secretariat, and central apparatus are assisted in their work by a Party Control Commission, which supervises membership discipline within the party, and a Central Auditing Commission, which supervises the party's finances and expenditure on resources. Finally, at the sub-central level, there are at least three basic tiers of party organisation stretching downwards usually from a regional (republican in the case of Yugoslavia and Czechoslovakia), district (both urban and rural) to a Basic Party Organisation in the place of work or residence. There are statutory provisions for all of these to hold (from the bottom upwards) a succession of conferences to elect their executive bodies and delegates to the next highest level before the meeting of the party congress. Following this, similar meetings should be held to report back. Ideally, the whole mechanism is designed so that from the bottom to the top the principles of democratic centralism can operate. It is, however, the Basic Party Organisation which communicates directly with the rank and file membership, and which carries out the functions of admission, and ideological and organisational work at the local level. Some statutes mention the existence and tasks of auxiliary and 'feeder' organisations such as those for youth, women, etc. All the parties differ in terms of the number of Politbureau, Central Committee and Secretariat members, congress delegates, the number of Basic Organisations etc. These numbers fluctuate over time, and may be found in the various national party histories for any given year.

Of course it is questionable whether the statutes, used as a 'map' of party organisation, may tell us anything meaningful about the actual functioning of the political process. The general opinion is that just as the constitutions of the communist world fail to provide an accurate picture of political realities, the same applies to the party statutes, and the formal provisions of party rules seem to have been more honoured in the breach than in the observance (Simons and White, 1984, p. 538). However to dismiss any further study of them is overhasty, as the party statutes have frequently been modified to reflect changes in the role and function of the party to which they apply. A change in party statute is often a means of institutionalising desired political change. This can occur because of an internal party crisis, such as in Hungary in 1956, Czechoslovakia in 1968 and 1971, or Poland in 1981. In Hungary the collapse of support for the HWP in 1956, following the Soviet invasion, a change of name to the HSWP, and a new statute in 1957 were designed to mark the return to normalisation. However, persistent problems in recruitment, especially among the younger generation, resulted in the abolition of candidate membership status in the 1966 statutes. A further revision in 1975 was largely occasioned by the difficulties for the operation of the party organisations in industry following the introduction of the New Economic Mechanism in 1968.

In the Czechoslovak case the 1968 draft statute reflected the pressures upon the post-Novotny leadership to transform the KSC from a unitary into a federal-branches organisation, to accept the possibility for party branches to engage in 'horizontal' as well as vertical communication within the party hierarchy, and to agree on the rights of minorities to dissent from majority decisions while still proscribing factionalism. The 1968 statute was never implemented, as the Warsaw Pact invasion took place before the 'secret' Vysocany Fourteenth Congress could endorse it, and in 1971 the statute reverted to the previous model drawn up in 1966, but with stricter provisions to exclude 'opposition elements' from membership. Candidate membership status (abolished in 1966) was reintroduced as a means of screening out people during a probationary period.

Similarly in Poland the revisions to the PUWP statute at the Ninth Extraordinary Congress held in June 1981 included proposals designed to open up party procedures and make them more accountable to the rank and file member: secret ballots and rotation of apparatus officials, more direct and regular supervision of central executive bodies such as the Politbureau and the Secretariat by the Central Committee, and separation of dual state and party office-holding. Greater responsibility for Basic Party Organisations and the possibility for them to engage in 'horizontal' discussions with one another were proposed as amendments to the 1975 statute, largely as the result of pressure from a rank and file horizontalist movement that began in Torun in 1980. All these matters reflected issues that had been hotly debated in the post-August 1980 period. The main issue over which the party leadership refused to give way was the relaxation of the *nomenklatura* and a tolerance of ideological pluralism. As it was, the changes were sufficient to provoke military intervention on the grounds that the future of Polish socialism was endangered.

Other parties have changed their statutes to mark changes in their foreign policy, either *vis-à-vis* the USSR or the West. So the founding Statute of the Albanian Party of Labour in 1941 was amended in 1948 to bring it into line with Stalinist developments, but was reaffirmed in 1956 in the face of totally contradictory movements elsewhere to decentralise and liberalise. In Yugoslavia the statute adopted in 1946 adhered closely to the Soviet model, but was drastically revised after the Sixth Congress in 1952, when the party changed its name to the League of Communists of Yugoslavia. From that date on, with the exception of statute revision in 1974 and 1982, there were changes at almost every congress, marking the shift to an ever more decentralised and self-managed society. This meant allowing greater autonomy to the constituent republic party organisations, and changing the nature of the LCY role in supervising the administration. The changes at the Eleventh Congress in 1978 represented Tito's efforts to prepare for the succession after his death, and to prevent centrifugal tendencies among the republics from leading to a constitutional crisis. Already the statutory changes of 1969 had been devised with this in mind. Tito himself had ensured that there should be a rotation of senior cadres and fixed periods of office, and that he would remain at the head of the party and the state for life. However, on his death such life posts were to be abolished. Indeed, the 1982 changes adhered to these principles. The only significant changes were the provision for a secret ballot and competitive elections for the next republican congresses and for the Thirteenth LCY Congress. Although the validity of the 'dictatorship of the proletariat' and the relevance of democratic centralism for Yugoslavia were questioned by some delegates in 1982, this challenge to Leninism was not upheld.

Another example of changes in party statute being occasioned by an ideological break with the USSR is the case of Romania. Although ideological and foreign policy differences can be traced back to 1958, the arrival of Ceausescu as First Secretary of the Romanian Workers' Party in 1965 not only brought about a change of name to the hitherto Romanian Communist Party but a new party statute which was notable mainly for de-Sovietisation and for relaxing the period of candidacy and requirements for membership. Further amendments came in 1974, but the Romanian party statutes are the most extreme example of how at variance with reality such documents can be. Despite ever-increasing talk of maximising accountability and participation, the actual practice of the RCP has tended towards an increasing rigidity. Efforts to mobilise the population, the ideological control of cadres, the conditions for holding office as a Central Committee member, and above all the entrenchment of the personalised rule of the Ceausescu dynasty are all illustrative of this. In the opposite direction, in line with its constitutional development, the statute of the East German SED, has been coloured with references to the precarious national status of the GDR. Following the signature of the Basic Treaty between the two German states in 1972, the statute introduced in 1976, the fifth in all, made fewer references to the common heritage with the FRG than the previous document of 1963, reflecting this disappearance of anxiety about GDR statehood.

Party–state relations

The very nature of Marxist–Leninist parties means that their structures are entwined with those of the state (see, for example the GDR case as illustrated in Figure 7.1). However, the relative balance between party and state has many dimensions, and has varied over time. The complexities of this duality are best revealed via first an evaluation of the general relation between state and party bureaucracies, and then a consideration of some of the very different interrelations of these structures in individual East European countries.

The party–state system which has evolved in state socialist societies stems, ideologically, from the vanguard role ascribed to the party by Marxism–Leninism and affirmed in each of the state constitutions. It is a political system in which the party oversees authority relations, institutional arrangements, political practices and policy. The party plays a supervisory, coordinating and directing role. Its success in this role depends on the party's control over non-party institutions. The principal mechanism of that control is a form of elite dualism whereby virtually every office of importance in the state and other significant institutions is held by a party member, an overlap particularly apparent at the apex of the various hierarchies. Individuals are obliged to give their first

FIGURE 7.1

Principal party/state, and social organisations in the German Democratic Republic

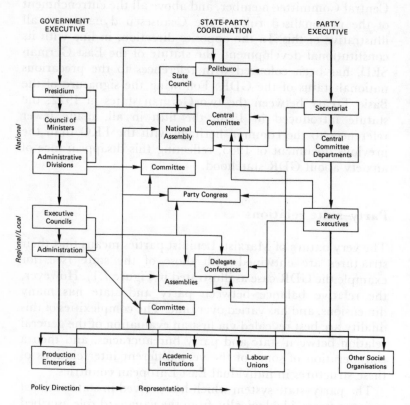

loyalty to the party, and the absence of such loyalty is severely penalised. A consequence of the mechanisms of the party-state system is that, by and large, where conflict arises, it is imported from other institutions to be resolved within the party. Nevertheless party control cannot be complete as the very complexity of government requires a division of labour among various institutions. Of necessity this leads to some political autonomy especially in policy implementation. Hence the status of state and other non-party institutions

might best be described as one of 'limited institutional autonomy within the context of overall political subordination to
the party' (Perlmutter and LeoGrande, 1982, p. 779).

The main trend of party–state relations, then, is for a
formal separation between the two with personnel overlap.
An abundance of empirical evidence shows that in all the
states under discussion here senior party personnel occupy
most if not all the key state offices. Such overlap falls off at
lower levels of the systems, but is none the less present, and
systems of *nomenklatura* ensure that state positions are filled by
personnel who are acceptable to the party. The system is not
without its problems, however. On the one hand, it cannot be
assumed that the interests of party and state officials will be
identical, however carefully state officials are chosen. On the
other, where personnel fusion is high, there is no built-in
mechanism for resolving differences. If in theory the party
controls the state, in reality things are much more interdepen-
dent than that. Although examples of state officials being
sacked when the party requires a scapegoat may be cited
(most notoriously Soviet Ministers of Agriculture), there is
otherwise little evidence of clearly drawn party–state separ-
ations. Leslie Holmes (1981) argues that the party–state
arrangement persists not because of its proven efficiency in
political management but because of its origin in the mobilisation phases of regime establishment, which led invariably to
the production of strong sets of institutions, with a considerable capacity to survive.

The significance of the party–state concept for the purposes
of this text lies not so much in its ability to distinguish
between party and non-party mechanisms as in its assumption
that party rule is not direct. The concept asserts that party
rule is mediated, that it takes place through a greater or
smaller number of non-party institutions, the most important
of which are state institutions. It implies therefore that those
institutions are themselves worthy objects of study for students of state socialist politics, that approaches focusing solely
on party mechanisms will lead necessarily to partial and
distorted analysis of the political systems in which we are
interested. This was recognised by Ionescu (1967) in his
concept of the apparat–state, which extends beyond the party

apparatus. He sees the concept of an apparat as a feature common to many non-opposition states:

> defined as any centralistic organisation, which . . . holds, in proportion to its share of responsibility in the running of the state, a smaller or a larger part of the coercive power of the state; and which together with other secondary apparats, and under the aegis of the main apparat, forms together the all-embracing state–apparat (Ionescu, 1967, p. 16).

He observed eight apparats in all (party, army, state admini-stration, political police, the bureaucracy, the youth organisa-tion, the planning commission and the trade unions). While one may want to amend this list slightly in the light of developments in the last 20 years, the central point is still valid: the structure and organisation of all these apparats is the same, all the secondary apparats are united under the command of one main apparat, and the identity of this one apparat can vary over time. This is a particularly helpful concept for exploring the East European states, and accord-ingly it is used throughout the text. The internal structure of each of the relevant apparats is explored in Chapter 9; here we discuss the relative balance between the party and the rest.

To summarise the current situation, we could say that the separation of party and state has been rejected outright in Albania, subject to increasing merger in Romania, accen-tuated and expanded in Czechoslovakia in order to promote the maximum popular participation in its institutions, and shifted in the direction of over-institutionalisation by new party–state or non-party agencies in Poland after 1971 and 1981 (Sandford, 1983). The balance between the different structures is subject to a variety of political forces. In Yugos-lavia we may see a separation of state and party that does not always denote the preponderance of the League of Com-munists of Yugoslavia. Elsewhere different apparats are pre-eminent at different times. For example, the emphasis upon the production principle in the organisation of the SED after 1958 acted to strengthen the industrial administration in its dealings with the rest of the party, which has organised on a territorial basis from the district level upwards. On the other hand, in Poland the emergence of a country-wide trade-union structure (Solidarity), outside the traditional trade union apparat, constituted the establishment of a situation of 'dual power' in Poland which threatened the supremacy of the party in such a way that the loyalty of its membership was seriously disturbed. In this situation another apparat, the military, was forced to assert itself in order to try to normalise the situation. In Yugoslavia in the early 1960s the security police headed by Rankovic provided another example of apparat challenge to the LCY.

Czechoslovakia and the GDR both experienced an increased centralisation of party control over the state administration in the mid-1970s. Indeed in the GDR, Poland, and Hungary, economic reform in industry caused problems for party control at several levels. In particular, the concentration of industrial production within larger 'corporate' structures or combines disturbed communication between higher and lower party organisations, as the influence of the party declined in the enterprise, as the normal practices of dual-subordination were by-passed, and district party organisations with large combines located on their territory were not consulted. The result in all three cases was to strengthen the organisation and provide extra resources for party branches in combines and industrial ministries after 1976–7. However, on the whole, party structures have lagged behind social and economic change in Eastern Europe.

Despite its obvious utility, caution should inform our use of the apparat–state concept. Although each apparat will be headed by individuals whose primary loyalty may well be to that organisation, we must remember that the device of the *nomenklatura* exists to ensure an overlap of key personnel with what is the major apparat. Secondly, the device of dual-subordination ensures that each level in the state bureaucracy is accountable both to the administration and the party. Furthermore, study of the Soviet Union shows that we should be wary of making too much of the formal distinction between the party apparat and state bureaucrats, i.e. between the political professional and the representatives of particular policy interests (Hough, 1977, pp. 52–3). This is not only because they have all proceeded through orderly bureaucratic career paths, but also because it is unlikely that a successful career will be confined just to one apparat. Indeed, to reach the influential position of a regional first party secretary, it is often necessary to have had experience first in running some large economic undertaking in that or in another region. The *nomenklatura* ensures that there is a 'cadre merry-go-round' switching personnel in and out of party and state apparats. This has implications for the way in which we view the intermediation of interests, and also means that in the every-day policy process it is highly unlikely that regional party officials will be in conflict with regional state interests. Con-versely, it is highly likely that central party apparat officials will be more united in conflict with another part of the apparat itself (such as the regional and district level) than when dealing with their counterparts in the ministries.

To return to Ionescu, he argued that the 'apparat–state must be dictatorial, centralistic and monopolistic', but it also becomes vulnerable to forms of pluralism 'precisely because it attempts to conduct, control and co-ordinate all the activities of the society' on whom it depends for the goods and services necessary to its functioning (Ionescu, 1967, p. 17). It was to his credit that he was the first to reject the argument that the apparat was in full control of society, and that it imposes on society its unchanged plans and aims. Since that time there has been an attempt to integrate an analysis of the policy-making role of ruling Marxist–Leninist parties in state social-ist societies with the models of Western science. Obviously interest-group theory is the most oft-cited example, but other theories of 'brokerage' and 'patron–client relations' have also proved illuminating. Hough's pioneering study of the broker-age role of regional and local party secretaries in the USSR (Hough, 1969) showed how in policy decision-making after 1965, 'leadership assumes the role not of the major policy initiator, but of a broker mediating competing claims of powerful interests' (Hough, 1977, p. 29). A similar pattern has been observed in Poland. Rigby and Harasymiw (1983) have used the concept of 'patron–client relations' to show how senior party officials are courted as 'patrons' and are in a position to exact loyal service and reciprocal favours from their 'clients'. They make the important point that political clientelism should not be viewed as a manifestation of the malfunction of Marxist–Leninist regimes, but point out that just as the second economy is a functional complement to the official 'first' economy, so inter-personal networks and patronage 'cliques' are functional to the politico-administrative system, in the sense that the latter would not only operate less efficiently but would arguably not operate at all without this. Although this tends to overstate the case for most of Eastern Europe, it is useful in helping us understand party–state relations in Yugoslavia and Romania.

In Romania party–state relations have been grounded less in statutory authority than in whatever connections, pull or 'bakshish' can be applied. Although this has usually been associated with the arrival of the 'Ceausescu dynasty' in power, it is probably part of the traditional make-up of Romanian society. The complex relabelling of the Politbureau, Central Committee, and the insertion of intermediary bodies between party and state (Shafir, 1985) represent this. Mechanisms of 'cadre rotation' introduced in 1971, and of self-management are more illustrative of the concern of Ceausescu to consolidate his personal power than increasing accountability. Even in Yugoslavia, despite a decentralisation of political control, ascendancy of the security police ensured that centralised control over top personnel remained when the dominance of the security apparat was terminated with the demotion of its head, Rankovic, in 1966. Liberal political forces were reasserted, accompanied by changes in cadre policy such that de-professionalisation of careers in the party and mass organisations took place. Cohen argues that with the abolition of the personnel department of the LCY central committee in Belgrade in 1966, and the decentralisation of cadre control to the republics and other state apparatuses, a less arbitrary, centralised and personalised form of cadre selection emerges (Cohen, 1983, p. 106). But others argue the excessively small LCY apparat is an indication that political clientelism based on national and local connections, continued to be very important to the policy process (Shoup, 1976).

Conclusion

From this study of party ideology, organisation and relations with the state, we can trace common patterns, if not complete uniformity. A common espousal of Marxism–Leninism has not made the East European communist parties completely acquiescent to the USSR. Relations with the USSR have not always been 'comradely', and the memories of Soviet interference are particularly bitter in Poland, Hungary, and Czechoslovakia. Despite the hegemony of the CPSU over doctrinal and organisational developments, innovations that clearly would not be tolerated within the Communist Party of the Soviet Union have not been precluded in Eastern Europe. Parties have shown ideological flexibility rather than rigidity, and their policy is less constrained by a clear-cut but undebatable ideology (Hough, 1977). But party organisational structures have lagged behind social and economic changes. As a result, they have been dogged by a series of 'legitimation crises' (Lewis, 1984c) not only in terms of the ideological 'package' presented to the mass of the population but also with respect to the effectiveness of internal party channels of communication. This has created problems for local activists and middle system management capabilities. Legitimacy crises may ultimately lead to the collapse of party authority. Such was the case in Hungary in 1956, Czechoslovakia in 1968, and (the most extreme example) in Poland in 1980–1. Whatever the formal basis of party–state relations, it is apparent that informal interactions are extremely important. Inter-personal networks and patronage cliques are often the mainstay of the relation between the party and the other apparats. To understand how this shapes the parties' role in policy-making, we need to look at party membership recruitment, processes, the recruitment and operation of party officials ('cadres'), and leadership recruitment and structures. This will be the subject of Chapter 8.

8

The Logic of Party Rule (II): Power and Representation

Having outlined the historical origins and ideological heritage of the Marxist–Leninist parties of Eastern Europe, we may now examine them as real organisations. Marxist–Leninist principles of party life, and the structure of the party–state, are essential starting points for an understanding of the role undertaken by these parties in national political life, but they provide only the bare bones to which the flesh of the party organism – its membership – adheres. Further examination is needed of why people want to join these organisations, especially when competitive political mechanisms associated with Western Liberal Democratic politics are absent. For people do join, and in numbers which would be the envy of any Western political party leadership. We need to determine whether particular types of people are more susceptible to the invitation to join than others, the social characteristics of membership, and finally what sort of people 'get on' and how the party elite is recruited. Changes over time will also be examined. As David Lane (1976) has pointed out, communist revolutions and takeovers of power are usually led by intellectuals, but during the industrialisation process a change takes place and different types of individual assume leadership positions. This raises the questions of whether the older revolutionaries are displaced by a managerial intelligentsia, whether it is accompanied by a decline in revolutionary ideals, and whether the attitudes and orientations of these people are affected by their social origins and career background. All these questions are addressed in this chapter, which is primarily concerned with the political recruitment of party members and of political elites.

We are also interested in the related issue of the manner in which the parties represent both their members' and the wider social interest. The accusation is often made that either the parties have lost contact with the manual working class or that they never succeeded in establishing such a base in the first place. In consequence the basis of communist parties' claims to legitimacy – that they represent the interests of working peoples – is seen to be fictitious. They are thus at best representatives of the white-collar intelligentsia and at worst a quasi-autonomous self-perpetuating oligarchy. In order to settle this matter we could do well to bear in mind the various interpretations of the concept of representation in usage in the West. Birch (1972, pp. 15–18) has outlined three possible usages. Representation may be viewed in terms of a statistical or physical resemblance to the wider population. Thus a party is representative if it is the 'mirror image' of society in terms of electoral support and membership. Secondly, the notion of representation may be used in the sense of an 'accountable mandate', i.e. an individual is representative because he or she is elected to power on the basis of adherence to a particular programme committing him or her to specific policies. A failure to implement these policies thus renders them unrepresentative. Finally, as long ago as Edmund Burke's letter to the electors of Bristol in the late eighteenth century, the case for representation by an enlightened personage from another social group acting on the behalf, and in the best interests of, the populace has been perceived as legitimate within liberal democratic theory. Here representation is 'symbolic'. We should be mindful of such different usages of the concept of representation not only in the context of liberal democratic politics but also in the context of state socialist societies. The Marxist–Leninist parties base their claim to representativeness on all three grounds. Before we are tempted to dismiss such a claim as being without foundation, we might consider whether any failure of representation is substantially different from similar shortcomings in Western liberal democratic political systems.

Party membership

All parties have three gradations of members after they have served their period of candidacy: the rank and file; the *aktiv*, or as they have been typed in the GDR, the 'propagandists' (Starrels and Mallinckrodt, 1975); and 'cadres'. The term *aktiv* and its equivalents denote an informal organisation in the workplace of people in 'leading positions' which may not necessarily arise from the *nomenklatura* of the party but whose collaboration is vital to the smooth running of the workplace. More important still are the 'cadres', i.e. those who hold positions of responsibility in state organisations and who have been placed in them, via the *nomenklatura*, because of their reliability.

Before looking more closely at recruitment patterns, it is necessary to consider the significance of membership for both the individual and the party organisation. Membership now necessitates an individual giving up some of his private life to be a dedicated 'organisation person' if no longer a committed revolutionary. Usually the prospective member is invited to join, and, depending on social origin or country or point in time, he or she may have to undergo a period of candidacy of up to 3 years. A period of candidate membership has always been the practice in Albania, Poland and the GDR, but was relaxed in a number of states in the 1960s, such as Romania (1965), Hungary and Czechoslovakia (1966). In Czechoslovakia direct recruitment was blamed for indiscriminate incorporation of opposition elements into the party, and was reversed in 1971. However, the earlier relaxation of candidate membership in Yugoslavia was not associated with a threat to party unity, mainly because the self-image of the party is much more relaxed. The other two parties that do not have a requirement for candidate membership, Bulgaria and Hungary, are, surprisingly, very orthodox in other respects. The Hungarian Socialist Workers' Party (HSWP) has faced considerable difficulties in membership recruitment, which may explain the relaxation there.

Any analysis of trends in party membership must be both cautious and careful. Because the Marxist–Leninist parties are the sole legitimate policy-making authorities in the state

TABLE 8.1

Communist party memberships: total and as percentage of population

	1962	1966	1971	1976	1978	1982	1984
Bulgaria	528,674	611,179	699,476	788,211	821,179	821,600	825,876
	6.6%	7.4%	8.1%	9.0%	9.2%	9.0%	9.2%
Czechoslovakia	1,680,819	1,698,000	1,173,183[c]	1,382,860	1,473,000	1,538,179[f]	1,623,000
	12.1%	11.9%	8.2%	9.3%	9.7%	10.0%	10.5%
GDR	1,610,679	1,750,000[b]	1,909,859	2,043,697	2,077,262	2,172,110	2,202,277
	9.4%	10.3%	11.2%	12.0%	12.4%	12.0%	13.2%
Hungary	498,644	584,849	662,397[c]	754,353[d]	770,000	852,000[i]	871,000[g]
	5.0%	5.7%	6.4%	7.2%	7.2%	7.6%	8.0%
Poland	1,270,000[a]	1,848,000	2,270,000	2,500,000	3,037,000[h]	2,870,000[f]	2,327,349
	4.2%	5.8%	6.9%	7.3%	8.5%	7.6%	6.3%
Romania	900,00	1,518,000[b]	1,999,720	2,655,000	2,747,000	3,300,000	3,440,000
	4.8%	7.8%	9.9%	12.5%	12.6%	14.5%	15.2%
USSR	9,981,068	12,357,308	14,455,321	15,694,187	16,300,000	18,717,000[i]	18,500,000
	4.6%	5.3%	5.9%	6.2%	6.2%	6.8%	6.7%
Yugoslavia	1,035,003	1,119,307[c]	1,025,476			2,200,000	2,500,000
						9.7%	10.9%
Albania	53,659	66,327	86,985	101,500		122,000	
						4.1%	

[a] 1961; [b] 1965; [c] 1970; [d] 1975; [e] 1968; [f] 1981; [g] 1985; [h] 1979; [i] 1983

Sources: J. Bielasiak (1981); D. Lane (1985); S. Stankovic, RAD/RFE Background Report/44 – 1982; G. Kolankiewicz (1982); R. F. Staar (1985).

socialist societies of Eastern Europe, it is easy to assume that membership affords entry into a political elite. This is of course partly true, as the party is the main arena of debate and decision-making. However, the total rank and file membership is, in absolute and relative terms, greater than the totals achieved by parties in liberal democratic systems. Party membership statistics also show a great variation in size relative to the total population of state socialist societies (see Table 8.1), ranging from 3 per cent in Albania (1977) to 14.5 per cent in Romania (1982). In between come the parties in Hungary (7.6 per cent in 1982), Poland (8.5 per cent in 1979, but 7.0 per cent by 1981), Czechoslovakia (9.14 per cent in 1979), Yugoslavia (9.7 per cent in 1982), Bulgaria (9 per cent in 1981), and the GDR (12 per cent in 1981). But such figures do not take into account the different demographic structures of the individual countries. A better measure is the proportion of the population over the age of 18, although parties do not regularly publish the statistics on this. This measure has the effect, of course, of increasing the ratios, so that even for the HSWP, membership is over 10 per cent of those aged over 18; in Poland it was 14 per cent, in the GDR it was 21 per cent and for the Romanian Communist Party (RCP) it was a staggering 31 per cent!

The pitfalls of measuring 'party saturation' have been discussed in detail by Hough (1977), who regards virtually all aggregate indicators as misleading. In the case of the CPSU, for example, very few members join before their mid-twenties, men are about three times as likely as women to join, and membership 'densities' increase with levels of education. Thus when we talk about party membership among men, we are speaking of an activity that is extremely widespread compared with typical levels of political activity in the West: as many as a quarter of all male manual workers, and about one-third of all those aged over 30 with higher education are likely to be party members. 'To think of such a Communist Party as a "priesthood" makes no sense at all, and even to call it an "elite", requires us to recognise that it is, indeed, "an elite of a rather peculiar kind"' (Hough, 1977, p. 133). We can draw the same inference from party membership statistics for Eastern Europe, with the proviso that in some cases membership rates are much higher among the younger age cohorts than is the case for the CPSU. In the SED one-third are under 27 and 42.5 per cent under 40; and in the League of Communists of Yugoslavia (LCY) 58 per cent are under 35. However, in the latter case this is the result of a conscious recruitment policy since 1968 (Carter, 1982). As we shall see below, there are also considerable variations in the 'densities' of membership among particular social groups, especially among manual workers, who were the target of 'positive action' recruitment campaigns during the 1960s and 1970s in a number of parties. These met with varying levels of success.

Ensuring a balanced 'density' of membership among particular social groups, especially according to age, gender, class, education, and nationality, has been perceived as a problem by party elites. Obviously all the Marxist–Leninist parties started out as class parties whose prime purpose was to further the cause of proletarian revolution, even though (the Czechoslovak and German parties apart) they drew their membership mainly from intellectuals and white-collar workers outside the working class. The assumption of political power changed parties of revolutionary conspiracy into parties of mobilisation. A high membership drawn from the working class became an important part of the legitimacy of their rule. The membership purges of the late 1940s were partly designed to achieve the desired stratification of composition, but after 1956 the process of de-Stalinisation encouraged a more open and broader appeal to other social groups. The ideological changes at this time, especially the commencement of debate about the benefits of the 'Scientific and Technological Revolution', were part of a wider search for a new formula of legitimacy. The official acknowledgement of change came with Khrushchev's announcement in 1961 that the USSR was no longer a state of the working class but of the whole working people. However, the opening up of membership (especially to members of the intelligentsia) was not without consequences, and inaugurated a secular decline in manual working-class party membership during the 1960s (see Table 8.2). In Hungary, Czechoslovakia, and to a lesser extent Poland, this was a source of great anxiety to the ruling party elites, who sought to reverse this trend in the 1970s.

Despite those endeavours, by the end of the 1970s only in the GDR and Romania were manual workers in the majority. The share of manual workers in the SED had risen in the 1960s, but during the 1970s intelligentsia members increased from 17 to 22 per cent. In the case of Romania this was largely because of a consciously planned long-term strategy.

In Yugoslavia the relative decline in working-class membership was least dramatic of all. It hovered around 30 per cent, increasing to 36 per cent in 1960, with a slow decline thereafter (Shoup, 1976). Rather, the proportion of peasant members fell drastically and this was attributed to the entry of ambitious young career-oriented professionals into the LCY. None the less, manual working-class membership was the lowest in all of Eastern Europe by the mid-1960s. Thus attempts to 'deprofessionalise' and 'reproletarianise' the LCY took place in 1962–4 and again in 1971. Despite this, there was an abolute increase in the number of professionals between 1972 and 1980, although the peasantry was the most under-represented of all groups, constituting less than 5 per cent of members. Throughout the 1960s the manual-worker membership of the Czechoslovak and the Hungarian parties declined, but after 1971 this trend was reversed, with a particularly dramatic increase in the numbers of manual workers in the KSC. The KSC had lost a lot of support among blue-collar workers at the time of the economic reforms in the mid-1960s, and the Soviet invasion in 1968 accentuated the dissaffection with the Czechoslovak Party (KSC). The remarkable increase in the total proportion of manual workers among party members from 25 per cent in 1971 to 45 per cent in 1978 was achieved by ensuring that at least two-thirds of new recruits consistently came from this group.

Attempts to increase party 'saturation' of a particular social category can misfire, as was shown in the Polish United Workers' Party (PUWP) after 1971. The social background of new recruits suddenly changed after that date. Manual-worker recruitment rose sharply from 50 to 67 per cent, levelling out to around 60 per cent after 1975, and by 1980 had raised their proportion among PUWP members from 40 to 46 per cent, with a proportionate decrease in white-collar and intelligentsia membership. What is particularly interest-

TABLE 8.2

Social composition of the communist parties (per cent)

	Bulgaria	Czecho-slovakia	GDR	Hungary	Poland	Romania	USSR	Yugoslavia	Albania
	1962		1962		1964	1960	1961	1961	1971
Workers	37.2		33.8		40.2	51.0	34.5	37.0	35.2
Farmers	32.1		6.2		11.4	22.0	17.5	10.0	20
White-collar	30.7		41.3		43.0	11.0	48.0	36.0	35.8
Others	—		18.7		5.4	16.0	—	17.0	—
	1966	1966		1966	1968	1965	1966	1966	
Workers	38.4	30.2		42.5	40.2	40.0	37.8	33.9	
Farmers	29.2	8.1		6.0	11.4	32.0	16.2	7.0	
White-collar	32.4	30.5			43.0	22.0	46.0	39.0	
Others	—	31.2		51.5	5.4	6.0	—	—	
	1971	1973	1970	1970	1971	1971	1971	1971	
Workers	40.1	44.1	47.1	42.7	39.7	43.4	40.1	28.8	
Farmers	26.1	4.7	5.8		10.6	26.6	15.1	7.0	
White-collar	33.8	31.6	28.1	38.1	43.6	24.0	44.8	45.0	
Others	—	19.6	19.0	19.2	6.1	6.0	—	19.0	

	1976	1976	1978	1982
Workers	37.5	29.0	29.4	29.0
Farmers		5.0	5.0	4.0
White-collar	29.0	41.0	41.0	41.0
Others	33.5	25.0	24.0	26.0

	1976	1979	1983
Workers	41.6	41.6	44.1
Farmers	13.9	13.9	12.4
White-collar	44.5	ca. 44.0	43.5
Others	—		

	1976	1978	1983
Workers	50.0	51.0	56.0
Farmers	20.0	19.0	16.0
White-collar	22.0	22.0	20.0
Others	8.0	8.0	8.0

	1975	1979	1982
Workers	40.9	46.2	42.7
Farmers	9.5	9.4	
White-collar	43.2	33.0	
Others	6.4	11.4	

	1975	1979	1982
Workers	45.5	62.4[a]	42.9
Farmers		10.8	
White-collar	46.1	25.3	
Others	8.4	1.5	

	1976	1979	1981
Workers	56.1	56.1	57.6
Farmers	5.2	5.2	4.7
White-collar	20.0	31.5	31.2
Others	18.7	7.2	6.5

	1976	1977	1978	1981
Workers	41.4	42.0	41.8	42.7
Farmers	23.0	5.3	22.4	N/A
White-collar	35.6	35.2	30.2	N/A
Others	—	17.5	—	

[a] Proportion of membership by social origin.
N/A = Not available.

Sources: J. Bielasiak (1981); G. Shabad (1980); D. Lane (1985); RFE/RAD Background Reports; RFE Situation Report; B. Szajkowski (1981).

ing is the way in which such recruitment was 'targeted' at the more highly trained and educated manual workers. 'Party saturation' was particularly strong among the highly skilled and younger members of the working class. The PUWP may well have sought to be more or less equitably represented amongst all categories of workers, but during the 1970s it aimed to establish a greater presence among such groups as the foremen and brigade leaders in industry, peasant workers, women, youth and students, and in the most rapidly industrialising areas (Woodall, 1982b). This recruitment drive, especially among young people with only a few years' work experience, was also accompanied by a high rate of resignation: of those who were dismissed or who voluntarily left between 1976 and 1978, almost two-thirds were manual workers. Younger, more educated people were being lured into the PUWP in ever greater numbers, but they showed little inclination either to stay the course, or to have passed through an 'apprenticeship' in one of the feeder' organisations such as the Socialist Youth Movement. Given that in the second half of the 1970s the PUWP was attempting to cut the cost of living, to reduce the import of consumer durables, and generally to raise labour productivity, one can only surmise that many working people who joined rapidly became disillusioned with the gap between rhetoric and reality, and left. The PUWP had succeeded in incorporating potentially discontented people into its ranks, up to one-third of whom were later to join Solidarity (Kolankiewicz, 1981, 1982b). The degree to which the PUWP rank and file was 'infected' by such anti-establishment forces goes a long way towards explaining why a military solution was adopted in December 1981, and illustrates how recruitment strategy can misfire.

Obviously the fluctuations in working-class membership have had an effect on the relative balance with the other two major social class categories within the parties: the intelligentsia/white-collar group and the peasantry (see Table 8.2). The non-manual group is difficult to compare cross-nationally, as it is not always clear what the basis of distinction is between the two sub-categories. In Poland this group grew rapidly from 17 per cent in 1949 to 36 per cent in 1954, and 43 per cent at the end of the 1960s (Woodall, 1982, p. 128). Thereafter it remained fairly constant until the mid-1970s, when it took a nose-dive to 33 per cent (reflecting the increase among manual workers and 'others'). The proportion of non-manuals in the Yugoslav League of Communists increased rapidly from 13.6 per cent in 1949 to 32.6 per cent in 1956, and thereafter steadily to 32 per cent in 1960, 39 per cent in 1966, and 45 per cent in 1970. Throughout the 1970s the trend has been reversed slightly to stay at just over 41 per cent in 1976 and 1982. In contrast to Poland this increase has been almost entirely at the expense of the peasantry, whose share of membership fell from 47.8 per cent in 1948 to 17 per cent in 1956, and more slowly thereafter to reach 5 per cent in the mid-1970s.

In Romania the massive increase in manual-worker members from just under 40 per cent in 1965 to 56 per cent in 1983 (RFE SR 10, vol. 9, no. 30, 1984) was almost totally at the expense of the peasantry, whose proportion of membership sank from 32 per cent to 16 per cent over the same period, with only a 2 per cent fall in the proportion consisting of intellectuals, white-collar workers and students. However, in absolute terms, recruitment increased in all categories. Despite the increase in manual-worker members in the Hungarian Party (HSWP), the share of the intelligentsia and the white-collar group remained high at around 40 per cent. Finally, although we do not have a systematic up-to-date series of data on party membership for either the Bulgarian or the Albanian parties, we know that by the middle of the 1970s the Bulgarian party was composed of about 41 per cent of workers, 30 per cent intelligentsia and white-collar, and 23 per cent peasantry. In Albania the comparable respective shares were 37 per cent, 33.5 per cent, and 29 per cent.

Czechoslovakia provides an interesting case of changing patterns of membership composition. Starting in the mid-1940s, the KSC was one of the few genuinely mass Marxist–Leninist parties. However, Stalinisation had the paradoxical effect of reducing the working-class membership from 58 per cent in 1946 to 38 per cent in 1950, and the peasantry from 13 to 10 per cent. The gap was filled by immediate recruitment from among the white-collar groups. A slight fall to 36 per cent from the working class by the mid-1950s levelled off until the mid-1960s, when it fell to desperately low levels. Allowing for the fact that the membership statistics sometimes concealed such trends by lumping together the number of active and retired workers (the latter formed a particularly high proportion of the membership in the late 1960s), it would appear that the proportion of workers rose from 43 to 45 per cent, although the share of active workers in the total membership fell rather sharply between 1966 and 1971 from 30 to 26 per cent. Thereafter it crept up very slowly to regain 30 per cent by 1980 (Wightman, 1983). The Czechoslovaks classify social groups by current occupation, rather than the Soviet practice of 'social position', or classification in accordance with members' occupations at the time of joining the party. This Czech practice will tend to understate the proportions of workers relative to other parties. Such variances in statistical practice generally add to the difficulties of meaningful comparison of memberships. In addition, the KSC leadership has been reluctant to reveal details of its social composition, especially in the 1970s, making it nearly impossible to calculate the relative proportions of other groups. The absence of figures for the share of collective farmers may mask a sensitivity about dwindling support from that group, especially as they seem to have made up less than 8 per cent of candidate members since 1971. The claim that about 30 per cent of members are drawn from the intelligentsia and white-collar groups is probably an understatement. In a surprising contrast to the Polish situation in the 1970s (Woodall, 1982b), there is evidence that party 'saturation' is very high among members of the technical intelligentsia who work outside the productive sector (Wightman and Brown, 1975).

Three other dimensions of party-membership profiles require further consideration. The first is age. The age profiles of the parties are very different. The average age of the total membership is not a very helpful indicator, as it does not allow for demographic developments or period effects, when the rate of recruitment and exit from the party might have fluctuated. Contrary to expectations, the parties have been able to rejuvenate their membership (even if the same tendency could not be observed in the recruitment of their leadership!). Average ages have remained remarkably constant, although distributions have varied considerably. The major difference is between the League of Communists of Yugoslavia, in which 58 per cent were under 35 and 53 per cent under 27 in 1982 (Ferdinand, 1983), and the Czechoslovak KSC and the Hungarian HSWP parties, less than 12 per cent of whose members were under 30 in the late 1970s and as much as 25 per cent between the ages of 50 and 60.

The second dimension is national origin. This is primarily of importance in Czechoslovakia and Yugoslavia, where the balance between different ethnic groups has caused much internal tension, and has also had occasional significance in Romania. There, the massive overall recruitment of the 1960s and 1970s led to more attention to minority representation. In Yugoslavia the continuous preponderance of the Serbs (49 per cent in 1982) has been resented by the Croats (15 per cent), Slovenes (6 per cent), and other nationalities, which all have their own republican party organisation and resent their under-representation at the national level. This probably explains the great concern to ensure equal representation at the national level after the mid-1970s. Similarly, irritation has been expressed by the Slovak party, the KSS, at its under-representation at the national level. Although it has a long pre-war tradition of relative autonomy, or 'asymmetric centralism', the KSS was amalgamated with the KSC under pressure from the USSR. There was a long-standing dislike of the Novotny regime, and it was the Slovak Party that provided the nucleus of the Reform Movement of the years 1966–8, and one of their main demands was for the creation of an autonomous Slovak party organisation within a federal party structure. This was nominally achieved after 1968. None the less, the differences remain, and at one-third of the membership level of the Communist Party of Czechoslovakia (KSC), the KSS is much more strongly working class (about 66 per cent as opposed to 45 per cent).

The third dimension is gender. Since the parties' establishment, sex equality has been an official party goal. As we have seen in Chapter six, women's roles have changed since the institutionalisation of state socialist systems, but despite improved access to resources such as education and paid employment, women have not gained greater economic or political power (Lovenduski, 1986). Impressive levels of female representation in national legislatures and local politics are not accompanied by a similar presence in the Marxist–Leninist parties. In the 1960s the proportion of party membership who were women was often below 20 per cent, but during the 1970s a number of positive action campaigns raised membership levels upwards to between 20 and 30 per cent (Table 8.3). By 1983 women were said to account for 33.7 per cent of SED membership. This relative under-representation among the mass membership is influential in ensuring that women are largely absent among national party leaderships (see below). Structural features such as established recruitment patterns through the Marxist–Leninist youth organisations, the perceptions of the (again predominantly male) party personnel managers in the apparat, and the lack of 'voice' within the party, all perpetuate this pattern.

Our last point about membership patterns is related to what we have euphemistically referred to as 'period effects'. These are very much influenced by ideological developments, and, in particular, relations with the USSR. Absolute and relative membership levels have fluctuated above and below the current level. A fall can be brought about both by resignations and purges, as in the GDR after 1953, Hungary after the dissolution of the Hungarian Workers' party (HWP) in 1956, Poland in 1981–2, and Czechoslovakia in the nearly 1950s and during 1969–70, when it has been estimated that between 400,000 and 500,000 left or were expelled from the KSC (Rupnik 1981). Perhaps the most volatile membership statistics are to be found in Yugoslavia, where total numbers were reduced between 1952 and 1956, rose in 1968, and, following a purge in the 1970s, increased after 1976 to reach 1.3 million. The most rapid rate of increase of membership is for Romania, where in the 10 years after 1965 it rose from 1,518,000 to 3,370,000.

However, it is possible to over-stress the failure of Marxist–Leninist parties to represent working-class interests, gender and national minority among their leadership. For a start, party membership statistics may themselves be misleading. Only the Hungarian Party (HSWP) publishes statistics both

TABLE 8.3

Women as a percentage of total members of communist parties in the Societ Union and Eastern Europe

	USSR	Albania	Bulgaria	CSSR	GR	Hungary	Poland	Romania	Yugoslavia
1950	20.7		13.8	33.0[b]	14.0[a]	28.9	18.0[c]		18.0
1966	20.2[d]	12.5	22.4	27.4	26.5	22.9	19.1	22.4	17.8
1071	22.2	22.2	25.2		29.4[e]	24.0[d]	22.8	23.0	19.5[e]
1975	23.8	24.0[f]	27.6[g]			26.5	23.6		
1980			27.6						
1984	25.0	30.0				28.3		31.6[h]	
1985	27.6								

[a]1974; [b]1949; [c]1951; [d]1965; [f]1972; [f]1974; [g]1976.

Sources: Wolchik (1981); RFE Background Reports; Lovenduski (1986); Staar (1985).

for the social origin and current occupation of members. The distinction is very important, as membership brings benefits as well as obligations. In particular, party membership has traditionally been a source of upward social mobility. The precise extent of this is difficult to calculate with any certainty, but the Polish United Workers' Party (PUWP) membership statistics prepared for the Fifth Congress in 1968 claim that over 40 per cent of members had acquired higher education since joining, and about a quarter had received vocational or further education. It was estimated that about one in six party members were experiencing some form of social mobility from worker or peasant background to white-collar jobs and that in-service education made a significant contribution to this. But as we have seen in Chapter 6, this process cannot be carried on indefinitely.

As opportunities for social mobility decline, two possible developments can occur: either the party's role as a vehicle for social promotion declines, with a subsequent loss of incentive to join; or the manual worker or peasant members that it is recruiting are better educated and qualified than those of the preceding generation (which one would naturally expect in view of the vast improvements in education since 1945 – see Chapter 12) and they join because they perceive that party membership will enhance their chances of career advance at a time of increasing competition. The second development results from technological change. The labour process is altering dramatically in the West, with information technology in particular eradicating the need for manual mechanical labour (but creating a whole new category of operatives whose conditions of employment may have attributes of white-collar status yet little more control and remuneration than the average assembly line worker). Similarly, technological developments have had an impact upon the nature of the industrial manual working class under state socialism (see Chapter 6), both in absolute numbers and occupational skills. Thus Marxist–Leninist parties may still be justified in their claim that they represent the manual working class, because both numerically and structurally that class has changed.

In conclusion, it is clear that none of the Marxist–Leninist parties is a carbon copy of the CPSU. A number have a proportionately higher membership and their current composition does not reflect worker dominance (although the reassertion of this in the CPSU is of recent origin). It is clear that if recruitment followed 'market forces', parties would now have a numerical majority of white-collar worker and intelligentsia members. Indeed, given that these groups are still in a minority in the population at large, party 'saturation' levels are already higher among these than other social groups. Other acknowledgements of this problem followed the 1968 and 1971 events in Czechoslovakia and Poland. In the period after the Twenty-fourth Congress of the CPSU in 1971, a number of parties made a conscious effort to reverse this trend (the Czechoslovak, Hungarian, East German and Polish parties). The problem did not affect all parties with equal severity: in particular, it seems to have affected the still industrialising Balkan countries least, and even in Romania the effort to raise working-class membership started from a base level that was already quite high, and was part of a general massive increase in membership which more than doubled the absolute number of party members. Acknowledging that the vagaries of official membership statistics may well flaw our analysis, it may be surmised that only in a phase of industrial expansion will party membership among the working class be high, and that once a stage of relative industrial maturity is reached (as in the GDR, Czechoslovakia and Poland) the parties are more vulnerable to being colonised by the intelligentsia and other white-collar groups. But does this mean that these parties no longer represent working-class interests? The particular role of each party in fostering social mobility, the way in which the nature of manual labour has changed, and the way in which we choose to interpret the concept of representation could suggest the exact opposite. Finally, we should be mindful of the consequences of ill-judged recruitment strategies. Anxiety about membership densities among manual workers may have accentuated regime perceptions of legitimacy problems, and have incorporated pressures for radical change. Given that these large-scale recruitment drives were also directed towards the younger generation, it is possible to infer that disappointed aspirations about the opportunities available in a mature state socialist society rather than closer identification with the regime may have been the outcome.

The party apparatus and cadre policy

Full-time party workers and bureaucrats who belong to the party apparatus might be regarded as a membership category themselves. The number of these officials and their proportion in the total membership varies between parties and over time, as does their relative distribution between different levels of the party. Generally after 1956 an effort was made to reduce their numbers. In Poland the number of regional officials fell from 13,000 to 8200 in 1959, and to 7800 in 1963, but thereafter there was a gradual drift upwards which has been difficult to check (Cave, 1981). By 1980 they contributed 4.3 per cent of the PUWP membership. In Hungary it has been claimed that officials constitute a relatively high 14 per cent of the total membership (but whether this includes only full-time officials is not clear). In Yugoslavia the changing role of the party after 1952 brought a drastic reduction in the number of officials to 0.33 per cent of the membership, at around 1500 full-time officials. By 1981 a doubling of this proportion meant that the League of Communists of Yugoslavia (LCY) could report 5991 full-time officials (Ferdinand, 1983). The apparatus of the East German Party (SED) is very large in absolute terms, consisting of 70,000 officials in 1957, of which 2000 were employed in the Central Committee apparatus (Skilling, 1966). Although figures for the other parties are unobtainable, we know that the bulk of party officials are employed at the regional level, or mainly in large towns and cities; that there is an in-built resistance among them to the intermittent central initiatives to reduce their numbers; and that in the mid-1960s there was an effort to improve their qualification level, sometimes by in-service training (Poland), and sometimes by 'turnover', so that younger more highly qualified people were brought in (as in the GDR and, more recently, Hungary in 1985). Finally, we may note that the total size of the apparatus can have implications for the demands placed upon the *aktiv*: where the apparatus is numerically small, as in Yugoslavia, or where there have been conscious attempts to reduce its overall size, as in Poland after 1956 and 1971, the calls upon the *aktiv* have been greater, and have not always met with success (see below).

The function of the apparat is to carry out the leading role of the party. However, its numerical size precludes it from doing this alone. It needs the cooperation of party 'cadres' or prominent members in key positions in all social and economic organisations. The cadre policy of Marxist–Leninist parties is vital to the performance of their leading role. However, in all countries it appears to have been fraught with problems from an early stage, and recent developments in particular appear to threaten the party as a representative organisation. To appreciate why this is so, it is necessary to start by examining the *nomenklatura*. This refers, firstly, to the list of responsible posts and the list of eligible candidates (the 'reserve') held by the central or regional party apparatus, and, secondly, to the arrangements it has for selection, assignment and dismissal of these eligible party members. These lists are not normally available for public scrutiny, and so we have little empirical basis for comparison. Unusually, a Polish list originating from three central committee directives in 1972 was first published in France, and later appeared in English (MacShane, 1981, pp. 163–9).

It revealed that the *nomenklatura* operates on three different levels: the party central committee, regional committees, and district (town and neighbourhood committees). As the document applies to the period before the very extensive reform of Polish local government, the allocation of responsibilities between different levels has probably changed. Otherwise it confirms that under the central committee *nomenklatura* fall key figures in the central party appartaus, regional party secretaries, and key figures in the media, academia, and the major party schools. A further category included those holding high positions in the administration of the state and the economy; social organisations such as the trade unions, the youth, womens' and professional bodies; and the military. Under the responsibility of the regional party committees fall a number of personnel responsible for party bodies and propaganda, including the secretaries of district, town, and neighbourhood committees. Other notables include secretaries in higher education, the presidia of regional people's councils, the police directorate, and enterprises and combines falling under the regional committee *nomenklatura*, including all those economic units placed under central committee management. The latter are particularly important when considering central government efforts to up-grade the quality of senior management in industry, especially during a time when a policy of relentless industrial concentration was being pursued. Other *nomenklatura* posts of regional party committees include analogous posts in government bodies, regional administration, the economic apparatus, social organisations, and the mass media, publishing, and scientific institutions. Finally, the *nomenklatura* posts of district party committees include their first secretaries and staff of the BPOs; positions in government bodies, local administration, social organisations and the economic apparatus (including the directors of enterprises forming part of a combine, and the directors of factories forming part of a multi-factory enterprise – a situation which caused a number of headaches during the period of industrial concentration in the 1970s). Of itself, this is not of great interest, but in the context of policy development and the development of interest articulation, the scope of the *nomenklatura* is quite important.

Writing in the 1960s, Ionescu argued that the *nomenklatura* of the Romanian party had declined in importance. He felt that generally throughout Eastern Europe (Ionescu, 1967) parties were losing their omnipotence, and were gradually being forced into collaboration with other institutions. However, a more recent study of the effects of modernisation on local politics in Romania disputes this assertion. Far from breaking down, even in the highly personalised system of Romania, vestiges of the *nomenklatura* have survived. It remains a closed process, and the main difference is that the criteria for recruitment have changed (Nelson, 1980): more specialised people are recruited, but their greater educational and technical expertise is redressed by a greater dose of political education through the party school system. The changing background of local political leaders suggest that with the rise of the Ceausescu regime since the mid-1960s the criteria for entry to the elite have changed (see below). Thus the vital importance of personal connections in Romanian politics encourages diversity in recruitment into the political elite, about which the official *nomenklatura* conveys the superficial impression of uniformity.

As we shall see, it is doubtful whether the *nomenklatura* operates as it was initially intended to in any state socialist society. While in Romania the pattern of patron–client relations and 'bakshish' is such as to preclude the possibility of 'rational' cadre placement, the *nomenklatura* has not faced serious political challenge. Elsewhere, opposition from party rank and file members has produced a direct challenge. After the Prague Spring in 1968 the *nomenklatura* was abandoned in Czechoslovakia, and not fully reintroduced until 1970. There were strong pressures for its removal in Poland before the Ninth PUWP Congress in 1981. However, the scope of the *nomenklatura* in Yugoslavia has fluctuated considerably since the break with Moscow. Control was decentralised in the early 1950s, only to be recentralised in the late 1950s and decentralised once more, owing to pressures from republic party organisations, in the mid-1960s. After the Eighth LCY Congress in 1964, part of the responsibility for cadre placement passed out of the hands of the LCY and into the control of such other bodies as the Socialist Alliance, the communes, and workers' councils. The decentralisation of the *nomenklatura* to the regional level complemented the development of a pluralistic system in Yugoslav politics during the 1970s (Rusinow, 1985). However, after the economic reform creating Basic Organisations of Associated Labour in 1972, there was a renewed recentralisation before the LCY moved to a system of negotiated 'accords' on personnel placement with state and social organisations. Yet the LCY retained the ultimate sanction of veto over appointments, which it was only able to exercise with considerable unease. Elsewhere, the *nomenklatura* remains, apparently intact.

Two outstanding features figure in the structural problems of cadre policy. First, the expansion of educational opportunity during the last two generations, the growing professionalisation of occupations, and the greater complexity of decision-making, create an in-built tendency towards the de-professionalisation of careers in the party and mass organisations, but also towards more specialised cadre training. In Yugoslavia it was found that those who became party officials had a career pattern less and less distinct from those employed in analogous state positions (Cohen, 1983). Similar trends have been identified in Poland (Cave, 1981). The second problem relates to the accountability of cadres to the rank and file membership, and to the fact that as a group they are increasingly unrepresentative (see the discussion at the introduction to this chapter) of the party membership as a whole. Party leaderships have become quite sensitive to criticisms from the mass membership on this issue, and for this reason have introduced rotation of cadres. However, such a seemingly democratic principle has tended to have less than democratic effects. Adopted in Albania in 1965 and Romania in 1969, it was used as a means of weeding out and purging certain senior figures. In Poland measures of cadre rotation in the 1960s and 1970s were used mainly as a device to bring in greater expertise, sometimes from outside the party's ranks – a practice that flies in the face of greater accountability. In Yugoslavia new measures to increase the rotation of cadres were designed to raise the inter-apparatus mobility of personnel, and thereby minimise the development of inter-factional rivalry in the League of Communists of Yugoslavia (LCY) following on the death of Tito. A survey of regional LCY elites in 1972 and 1980 showed that about two-thirds were continuously in office throughout this period, in sharp contrast to the administrative, executive and legislative elites (Cohen, 1983).

Middle level elites have been very resistant to plans for their own removal. In Poland in the late 1960s it was reported that over 90 per cent of officials were from worker or peasant backgrounds and that the up-grading of qualifications had taken place mainly via in-service training (Cave, 1981). It was not until the 1970s that the introduction of cadre rotation measures (after the Sixth PUWP Congress) brought in a larger number of professionals at this level. There is reason to believe that the training provided through institutions run by the PUWP was neither extensive or effective. There have been frequent changes of name, organisation and senior staff in the Higher Party School attached to the PUWP Central Committee, and the regular in-service training available to both rank and file and cadres alike is very limited compared with what is available in the GDR (Starrels and Mallinckrodt, 1975). This probably accounts for the relatively high qualifications of secretaries of East German Basic Party Organisations: over two-thirds were university or technical college graduates in 1981 (Zimmerman, 1984).

The upshot is that a series of contradictory objectives are pursued by the party leaderships. In line with mass membership trends in favour of a greater recruitment from among the intelligentsia and educated white-collar group, there are pressures upon a party to recruit its senior officials from the same group. Many of these will already be well advanced along a career in another apparat. In social background terms this produces a crisis of representation. The party leaders are then forced to overlook the obstruction of such cadre recruitment policies by long-established middle-level party elites, resorting only to half-hearted in-service cadre education. Simultaneously there is an attempt to redress the imbalance in party saturation among the working class and the other under-represented social groups. The result is that neither the objective of a rational cadre policy nor accountability of officials to the mass membership are achieved.

Leadership

Political scientists look to trends in membership structure and cadre policy for signals about regime anxieties over legitimacy and the desire to incorporate key social groups into the policy-making process. However, to the novice, the most exotic aspect of Marxist–Leninist parties is their leadership structures. Even political scientists are not immune to the simple fascination with the 'great men' (and men they have always been!) who in lonely isolation guide the ship of state. Such a primordial fascination with power was encouraged by the example of the Stalin dictatorship in the USSR between 1928 and 1953. We have come to expect leadership structures within the USSR and Eastern Europe to constitute but a pale reflection of this prototype. Furthermore, the operation of democratic centralism may be understood as pushing the locus of power in the party upwards. We would thus expect the general first secretary of the party to be in a position of supreme authority. However, in the same way as it is misleading to focus upon the personal styles of Western presidents and prime ministers, it is similarly misleading to concentrate solely upon the personal basis of power of East European leaders. Institutional structures are important, and these are not always a carbon copy of the Soviet model. Also, every political 'chief' needs 'indians', and the chances are that the structure of political elites will place considerable constraint upon what the individual at the top can do, and how long he or she may stay there.

Scholars of East European politics in the post-Stalin period base their analyses of leadership upon a study of career patterns within both the party and state apparatus, and in particular within those institutions which constitute the 'high command' of the political system: the Politbureau, the Central Committee, and its Secretariat. Leadership structures are also seen as corresponding to the different stages of regime development: revolution/takeover, institutionalisation and modernisation (Beck, 1973). Some have argued that post-Stalin East Europe has undergone an irreversible transition from individual to collective leadership (Korbonski, 1976). Others (Rush, 1974) adopt a more cautious stance, seeing the emergence of only a more limited form of personal rule. All are fascinated by systems which differ most noticeably from liberal democracies in that there are no fixed rules governing incumbency and succession. MacCauley (1983) has pointed out that there are only four ways in which the Soviet Union can change its party leader: death of the incumbent, incapacitation through illness, resignation or enforced removal/ purges. However, none of these arrangements are routinised. In such a system change is both infrequent and prompted by crisis. Leadership turnover usually takes place on the death of an incumbent or at the Party Congress. However, Khrushchev, Gomulka, Gierek, Kania, Ulbricht, Novotny and Dubček were all removed from office outside of Congress sessions.

Often the best indicator of the likely successor is the person charged with the responsibility for making the funeral arrangements! More recently there has been some attempt at comparative analysis. Soviet and East European leaderships have been evaluated against their Western counterparts in terms of policy outputs. Bunce (1981), drawing heavily upon budgetary data, has argued that in both systems leadership change is related to policy change, and she also notes that leaders in both East and West enjoy most power at the beginning of their period of rule. However, analysis such as this can be very misleading, and ultimately offers little advance upon Kremlinological approaches. More mileage is to be obtained by a combination of Kremlinological and policy-output approaches, integrated with the study of political elites.

Starting with the 'supreme' leaders, nowhere has the 'cult of personality' reached the proportions it did under Stalin. However, the two leaders who were continually in office between 1945 and 1980 – Tito and Hoxha – both operated a highly personalised form of rule. Perhaps the common experience of partisan warfare and independent acquisition of power contributed to this, though inevitably leading to problems with their succession in the 1980s (see below). A ruthless system of purges and executions seems to have taken place in Albania in 1945–8, 1956, 1974–6, and 1982, when Hoxha's contemporary Mehemet Shehu 'disappeared', in order to pave the way for the succession of the younger Ramiz Alia (Artisien, 1985). In Yugoslavia, following the Croatian crisis of 1971, Tito introduced elaborate constitutional changes designed to prevent inter-republican rivalry and secession from the federation of what had become a very decentralised and pluralistic system. In contrast, the Kadar leadership in Hungary survived for 30 years with a very low personal profile on the part of its general secretary. Not so with Ceausescu, in neighbouring Romania, who in the past 20 years has built up a highly personalised system of rule in which members of his own family assume key positions. Madam Ceausescu is currently 'second in line', and son Nicu attained control of the party secretariat at an unprecedently early age in his mid-thirties (Shafir, 1985). Such 'party familialisation' has been practised to a less marked degree in the other East European states. In Bulgaria Todor Zhivkov's daughter Lyudmilla (until her death in 1981), and in the GDR Erich Honecker's wife Margot, both held prominent government positions. Elsewhere the practice has not occurred.

Such nepotism is only likely to occur in states where the leadership has been in office for a substantial length of time, or where there are pre-war traditions of familialism and clientelism. On the whole, though, the absence of regular procedures governing succession may lead to change by means of crisis, but this is not a frequent occurrence. A glance at Table 8.4 would confirm this. There have only been four changes in party leadership in Czechoslovakia since 1948, and apart from the exceptional case of Poland (six changes since 1948), elsewhere it has been even less frequent. Generally a pattern of ageing of the leadership has been apparent. The cases of the USSR (before 1984), Yugoslavia (before 1980), Albania, Bulgaria and Romania all illustrate this point.

An important factor controlling the incidence of leadership change is the state of relations with the USSR. Soviet control over the initial appointments at the end of World War Two was fairly relaxed. With the development of the Cold War and Stalinism in 1948, 'nativists' in Poland and Czechoslovakia were ousted to be replaced by pro-Soviet 'Muscovites'. Prolonged resistance to this by the Czechoslovak Party was dealt with severely. The 'nativist' first secretary Rudolf Slansky and a number of other prominent party members were ruthlessly purged in 1951. In Bulgaria, Hungary, GDR and Romania, no change was necessary. However, the USSR was relatively uninfluential in the appointment of the Yugoslav and Albanian party leaderships, and despite the grave turmoil that ensued in Hungary in 1956, Kadar was certainly not closely identified with the USSR. On the other hand, the USSR has maintained a watchful eye over leadership change in the more troublesome cases of Poland and Czechoslovakia. In the former the change of party leaders following the crises of 1956, 1970, and 1980–1 were the subject of prior Soviet endorsement. This was not obvious in the appointment of General Jaruzelski (already Minister of Defence and Prime

TABLE 8.4

Party leaders since 1945

Country	Party First/ General Secretary	Date of birth	Period of office
Albania	Hoxha	1908	1941–85
	Alia	1925	1985–
Bulgaria	Dimitrov		1945–9
	Chernenkov	1900	1950–4
	Zhivkov	1911	1954–86
Czechoslovakia	Gottwald		1929–46
			(1951–53)
	Slansky		1946–51
	Novotny		1953–68
	Dubcek		1968–9
	Husak	1913	1969–
GDR	Ulbricht	1893	1950–71
	Honecker	1912	1971–
Hungary	Rakosi		1944–56
	Gero		1956
	Kadar	1912	1956–
Poland	Gomulka	1905	1943–8
			(1956–70)
	Bierut	1892	1948–56
	Ochab		1956

Table continued overleaf

Table cont.

Country	Party First/General Secretary	Date of birth	Period of office
	Gierek	1913	1970–80
	Kania	1927	1980–1
	Jaruzelski	1923	1981–
Romania	Gheorghiu-Dej		1945–65
	Ceausescu	1918	1965–
Yugoslavia	Broz-Tito		1937–80

Post-Tito: Presidents of the Presidency of the Central Committee of the LCY

	Doronjski	1919	1980 (Vojvodina)
	Mojsov	1920	1980–1 (Macedonia)
	Dragosavac	1919	1981–2 (Croatia)
	Ribicic	1919	1982–3 (Slovenia)
	Markovic	1920	1983–4 (Serbia)
	Sukrija	1919	1984–5 (Kosovo)
	Zarkovic		1985–6

Presidents of the Presidency (Heads of State)

	Koliseviki	1914	1908 (Macedonia)
	Mijatovic	1913	1980–1 (Bosnia-Herzegovina)
	Krajger	1914	1981–2 (Slovenia)
	Stambolic	1912	1982–3 (Serbia)
	Spiljak	1916	1983–4 (Croatia)
	Djuranovic	1927	1984–5 (Montenegro)

Source: G. Skilling (1966); M. McCauley and S. Carter (1986); RFE Background Reports.

Minister) to the post of first secretary of the PUWP in October 1981. In Czechoslovakia the USSR was initially highly supportive of the replacement of the Stalinist Novotny by the Slovak Alexander Dubcek. This position was completely reversed after the summer of 1968, and in 1969 the pro-Soviet Husak replaced him. Finally, it is not always accurate to impute a malign anti-reform influenced to the USSR. In 1971 the SED leader, Walter Ulbricht, was replaced on Soviet instructions by Erich Honecker, for the purpose of ending East German obstruction towards Western 'detente' and 'Ostpolitik' initiatives (see Chapter 13). The significance of Soviet involvement in leadership selection is evident in the central *nomenklatura* of the CPSU: allegedly it includes the leaders of the GDR, Polish, Hungarian, Czechoslovak, and Bulgarian parties.

We have seen how the *nomenklatura* shapes political careers by setting pathways that lead in and out of the party and state apparatuses. Although these are more fully documented for the USSR than for Eastern Europe, the practice is little different. Aspiring leaders follow a *cursus honorem*, whereby it is recognised that if their career has passed through a number of different posts of responsibility, they will be more likely to be considered as potential leadership 'material' than if they have just worked their way upwards within the central party apparat. Thus being head of a large city or regional party organisation or in senior industrial management, as well as holding senior office in one of the central state apparats (the military, the security police, the media, education and academia, industry etc.), is crucial. A potential leader needs to choose from such a 'menu' in order to promote his leadership chances. For example, in Poland, Gierek was the party boss of one of the largest industrial regions, Silesia; Kania had a long-standing career in the PUWP secretariat before his appointment as first secretary in 1980; and Jaruzelski had been Minister of Defence since 1968 and Prime Minister between 1981 and 1985, when after the Sejm elections Messner took over. It is interesting to note that, apart from Kania, only Edward Ochab (who was first secretary for a brief period in 1956) had followed a career mainly through the central party apparat before becoming leader.

It has been remarked that while senior management experience is the avenue to leadership in the state apparatus, party cadre experience is the route to the party leadership. This is far too simplistic a statement. It ignores the effect of interlocking party and state office-holding. In the GDR Honecker had been a senior official in the FDJ youth organisation and in the security police before entering the SED apparat and serving as Ulbricht's second in command before he took over in 1971. As Central Committee Secretary in charge of organisation and cadres since 1954, Ceausescu had built up a clientele among regional first secretaries. By 1969 eleven out of the sixteen in 1965 had moved into leading party and state positions (Shafir, 1985). The *cursus honorem* followed by a particular leader may well be the reason for his success. It is also the basis by which opponents emerge. Clientelist support is needed by the potential leader, and he must be as careful as any US president or British prime minister not to alienate significant factions of the party. It was for this very reason – his hostility to reformers – that the Czechoslovak leader Antonin Novotny lost the support of his party presidium in late 1967. However, his successor, Alexander Dubcek, a Slovak like many of the reformist intelligentsia, swung in the opposite direction. The presidium and central committee set up in April 1968 were dominated by men who had personal or professional links with Dubcek. He exercised considerable patronage to counteract antipathy to reform, but this backfired as pressure mounted from within the rank and file for more radical reform (Wightman, 1986). Yet it is interesting that Dubcek was replaced by another Slovak, Gustav Husak, though one who was much more mindful of Soviet interests. The need to obtain support from Slovak members of the party was a crucial consideration in the leadership change of 1968 and 1969, both for the pro-reform and for pro-Soviet elements. However, such rapid turnover in the Politbureau and Central Committee is rare. Poland after the Ninth PUWP Congress in 1980 is the only other example. Generally the succession of a new leader is not followed immediately by rapid turnover in these positions. The process of consolidation of power and elimination of opponents usually takes a number of years. It took Zhivkov from 1954 to 1957 and Honecker from 1971 to 1973.

Both Ceausescu and Tito introduced ingenious arrangements to fend off opponents. Between 1965 and 1969 Ceausescu was mainly preoccupied with eliminating his opponents, especially the Minister of the Interior, Alexander Draghici. Yet as Shafir (1985) notes, no major personnel changes affected the topmost leadership for quite a while after Ceausescu's succession. This flies in the face of the orthodox view that political succession in Eastern Europe is accompanied by a fast turnover at the top of the party hierarchy (Korbonski, 1976). Rather, Ceausescu responded to the situation by reducing the institutional power of his colleagues. This explains the elaborate institutional innovations in the party (Shafir, 1985). At the Ninth Party Congress (1966) an executive committee of the Central Committee was set up as an intermediary with the top party leadership, and provided a means for the advancement of a number of Ceasescu's protegés who were not yet sufficiently experienced to make it to the top echelons. Further changes in the party statutes enabled the simultaneous holding of the posts of party secretary general and chairman of the Council of State after 1967; compulsory 'rotation' from 1971 onwards of senior party personnel requiring them to exchange positions in the central state and Party apparats; and the replacement of the Party's Standing Presidium by a Permanent Bureau in 1974. The latter was appointed indirectly by the Central Committee's executive committee (now called the Political Executive Committee), thus by-passing the Central Committee itself. Thus by the mid-1970s Ceausescu had managed to create the institutional basis for his highly personalised form of rule.

Tito's problem was of a completely different nature. After supressing the threat posed by the pro-centralist Serbian head of the security police, Rankovic, in 1966, and subduing the separatist moves from the Croatian Party organisation, Tito addressed his attention to ensuring that inter-republican rivalry would not erupt after his death. Again elaborate arrangements were made to prevent the rise of separatist factions in what had become a highly decentralised and pluralistic political system. Tito institutionalised a collective state presidency in 1971, headed by himself, and the 1974 constitution specified the procedures that would be invoked upon his death. His powers as president of the republic were to devolve to the collective state presidency, which would henceforth be headed by an annually rotating president of the presidency chosen according to a pre-ordained sequence of the right republics and provinces. The office of President of the League of Communists of Yugoslavia (LCY) was vacated and ceased to exist after the 1982 Congress. Instead a president of the presidency of the Central Committee now rotates annually between republics and provinces (Rusinow, 1985). One year after Tito's death the leadership consisted of the same group of men who inaugurated the changes after 1971 (Carter, 1982). As Rusinow has remarked, 'institutional permanence, stability, and primacy over individual leadership roles' are the basis of the current Yugoslav leadership structure, and all the evidence since Tito's death in 1980 points to its success.

Finally the different pathways to the post of party leader, and the different experiences of consolidating their personal power, have meant that East European leaders have not all combined party and state office in the same way. Starting with the example of Yugoslavia, Rusinow (1985) has remarked that it is distinguished from other state socialist societies by the relatively greater weight enjoyed by state organs *vis-à-vis* the party ones at all levels. From an early date Tito combined the presidency of the LCY with the post of head of state (President of the Socialist Federal Republic of Yugoslavia) and that of commander in chief of the armed forces. Although dual office holding as head of both the party and the government has been prohibited in the USSR since 1964 (largely as a reaction to Khruschev, and as an expedient to allay the rivalry between Brezhnev and Kosygin), after 1977 Brezhnev assumed the additional position as head of state. In Czechoslovakia Novotny was both First Secretary and President between 1957 and 1968, and in 1975 Husak resumed this practice. Ceausescu became President in 1974. After being appointed Prime minister in February 1981, Jaruzelski took the post of First Secretary of the PUWP in October 1981, not relinquishing the premiership until the autumn of 1985. As Sanford (1985) has observed, the normal pattern of top office holding is for party state posts to be held separately. From 1947 to 1970 (with a short break between 1952 and 1954) Jozef Cyrankiewicz held the post of Chairman of the Council of Ministers (prime minister). However, apart from Bierut, no first secretary has also occupied the presidency and, apart from Jaruzelski, none has also been prime minister. In the GDR the posts of prime minister and president were held separately until Ulbricht effectively became President through the newly created Council of State in 1960. However, his successor, Honecker, consolidated his own position by reallocating posts so that eventually by 1976 he was Secretary General of the SED, Chairman of the Council of National Defence, and Chairman of the Council of State. Only the post of prime minister was held separately by his opponent Stoph between 1964 and 1973, and again since 1976, with Sinderman as the incumbent in between. Similarly, in Bulgaria, Zhivkov is simultaneously Secretary General, President and Chairman of the National Defence Committee. Only in Hungary are the posts of state president, prime minister, and first secretary held completely separately.

To return to our original point, we cannot appreciate the exercise of political leadership to the full if we focus exclusively upon the party first/general secretaries and their immediate allies and rivals. We have to look further and consider the political and social mechanisms of elite recruitment more widely.

Political elites and party rule

Studies of political elites tell us that the political sub-system may be conceived of as stratified in much the same way as society. Those at the bottom lack nearly all the prerequisites for exercising political power, whereas those at the top possess the relevant characteristics in abundance. This is an empirically verifiable fact. All political systems are stratified in a manner which demonstrates greater or lesser gradations of power. Differences run from the small segment at the top who rule (the political elite) through increasingly larger segments who have declining degrees of influence until the largest group, that of the least powerful, is reached at the bottom of the hierarchy. The basic shape of the power distribution is the same in all societies, although it may differ in height, profile and stability.

In such respects East European political elites differ little from those which exist in other societies. But the special nature of the composition of state socialist political elites makes it imperative that they be subject to systematic study. This is not so simple as it might first seem. The logical starting point of a definition of elites is linked to the broader question of the distribution of power. The well rehearsed debate between pluralists, elite theorists, and neo-Marxists (see the work of Robert Dahl, C. Wright Mills, and Stephen Lukes) in the context of liberal democratic politics illustrates this point. We do not intend to repeat this debate here, and feel that it is only necessary to make the point that we can expect the definition of the composition of the elite and perceptions of their cohesiveness to vary according to whether we define power as a 'relation' or as a 'capacity'. These issues will be taken up later in Chapters 9, 10 and 11 in the context of our discussion of the state apparatus and of the application of the interest group model of politics to state socialist societies. In this chapter we identify elites in terms of the positions occupied and the criteria that affect eligibility and recruitment. This enables us to take some of the themes of the party–state relations developed in the previous chapter a little further. The best place to begin our examination of elite composition is by reference to membership profiles of the ruling parties. As we have seen already in this chapter, party penetration of the higher occupational strata is high through-out Eastern Europe. Those with the greater levels of income, education or status are more likely to be party members; and those in white-collar occupations consistently play a dispro-portionate role in party leadership. In Eastern Europe the occupational stratification of political elites is an important indicator of regime intentions, perhaps more so than actual patterns of social mobility. Ascent to party leadership positions reflects both the availability of particular occupational strata (e.g. technological specialists, ideologists, managers) and the socio–economic shape of the powerful.

But today's elites differ in important respects from those which were installed in the immediate post-war years. At first a contradiction existed between the two major criteria for elite eligibility: expertise and political reliability. An early Soviet objective had been the training of a generation of technically competent and ideologically sound 'red directors', with the concomitant preoccupation with specialist knowledge. This was reflected in the sharply rising educational levels of party bureaucrats and economic managers at regional and national elite levels, and characterised leadership recruitment in all the East European states. But growth in the technical and managerial training of elites has not come at the expense of experience and training within party organisations. Positions at all levels of the party leaderships have increasingly come to be held by what Putnam (1976) calls 'dual executives', who combine specialist training in a branch of the economy with long service in the party apparatus. Lane, too, remarks on the dual nature of the path to the top, pointing out that while the educational profile of party leaderships has been transformed in the generations since the war in general, the highest posts are held by those whose political credentials are also extensive (Lane, 1982, pp. 122–4).

The 'red versus expert' dichotomy has been something of a red herring in the theoretical literature on state socialist elites, with little hard evidence to suggest that such a conflict has persisted. There is no doubt of course that the leadership appropriate to the early mobilising phases may be inadequate to the consolidation periods which follow it. Numerous authors have asserted that whilst intellectuals lead revolutions, managers are better suited to organising the societies which proceed from them. Bauman (1971, p. 42) places particular emphasis on what he regards as the withdrawal of status from professional revolutionaries as they become undermined by those with more appropriate technological skills. Such contentions raise important empirical questions about elite composition in the various states, and during the 1970s a number of empirical studies of the East European elites appeared (Beck, 1973; Farrell, 1970; Ludz, 1970). However, data on elite composition, change, attitudes, and support are patchy, collected for a variety of purposes, and presented in a range of different kinds of study.

Concentrating on available data, elite studies analysed central committees and politbureaus during the 1950s, 1960s and the first few years of the 1970s. In general they reported interesting changes in the compositions of the various elites, but noted also important differences between the various countries. Cultural factors were found to be especially important, with much depending upon the size of the original communist party: the smaller parties in particular were more easily swamped. A further set of differences arose from the research strategy employed. If the elite is defined broadly to consist of the entire central committee, for example, different results are found than if the elite is more narrowly defined as consisting of the politbureau and perhaps the central committee secretariat. This point is well illustrated by the work of Beck (1973) and Ludz (1970), who have studied central committee compositions in Bulgaria, Poland, Hungary, Czechoslovakia and the GDR, and Baylis (1974), who concentrated part of his research on the Politbureau of the GDR.

Beck's study covered four sets of central committees in Poland, Hungary, Bulgaria and Czechoslovakia, beginning with those which were in office in 1948. On average the number of members who could be classified as 'revolutionary activists' fell off sharply with the passage of time. Members of mass organisations (trade unions, national fronts, anti-fascists, and partisans) were drawn into the central committees in large numbers in the first, second and third sets of committees but fell off during the fourth. Persons with positions in the party apparatus increased their representations over time, especially local 'first secretaries', who increased on average from 1 per cent in the first to 13 per cent in the fourth sets. Likewise central level functionaries increased from 19 per cent to 33 per cent. Those with domestic party education increased over the second, third and fourth sets, but those with party education in the USSR declined over the same period. Men with technical and educational careers increased their representation in all the committees Beck studied. Divergences were also found, enabling Beck to distinguish between three types of leadership profile – ranging from the revolutionary activist type which emerged in a politically stable regime such as that of Bulgaria, through the elite stagnation which was apparent in Czechoslovakia by 1966, to the Polish and Hungarian reliance upon central party officials drawn from newly educated elites for the core of their party elites. Thus leadeship profiles were linked closely to the political history of the regime but were also characterised by the increasing presence of technical specialists of various kinds.

In Ludz's study of the GDR attention is drawn to the increasing cooptation of individuals with specialised knowledge into the areas of policy where their skills are most required. Such cooptation to the central committee of the SED has changed the composition of that body, which has become increasingly populated by technical specialists. Ludz argues on this basis that an 'institutionalised counter elite' has emerged in the GDR. Baylis (1974) challenges Ludz's contention, stating that the technical intelligentsia in the GDR is an example of a stratum consciously created by the regime for the furthering of regime goals of remaking the polity. He shows that although there has been a sharp increase in the proportions of technical intelligentsia in successive central committees, the leading politbureau and other top party bodies have at no time been out of the hands of the apparatchiki and the ideologists. Baylis's conclusion is that while economic specialists have had sufficient representation to provide an input of needed expertise, they have had little influence in power terms. More recent evidence (Zimmerman, 1984) confirms this. In 1981 the SED functionaries constituted 47 per cent, and members of the state apparatus 28 per cent, of all central committee members. Direct representation of economic interests .was much lower (about 20 out of a total of 186 full members).

Several points arise here. The first and most significant is that when we speak of elite power in a political system, the way in which the elite is defined is going to affect the nature of our findings considerably. All our evidence about state social-ist decision-making indicates that final authority resides in the party politbureau and the central committee secretariats. Thus these bodies, rather than the central committees, are the ones which are significant in determining who governs.

However, questions of who influences and/or who benefits suggest a wider set of boundaries, and studies designed to answer more general questions about the stratification of political influence benefit from a wider focus. Here central committee, local executives and legislatures, and councils, as well as the patterns of access to state positions, are all appropriate objects of scrutiny. Cohen's (1983) study of Yugoslav elites is a case in point. Close analysis of the composition of Yugoslav regional elites indicated that there had been distinct phases of elite recruitment in Yugoslavia between 1945 and 1981. Cohen's data, collected from a study of Yugoslav regional elites in 1980, reveals fairly comprehen-sively the characteristics of contemporary Yugoslav elites. The picture presented is of a highly educated group within which party functionaries are most likely to have training in politics and administration or the military, whilst those with technical or economic training are concentrated in the state apparatus. A large number of younger party officials have been trained in philosophy and law. The national and middle level elites are youthful but consistently experienced. The partisan generation has now been more or less promoted out and a reasonable dispersal of age distribution exists amongst subsequent generations of officials. Efforts have also been made to achieve ethnic balance, but Serbs tend still to be over-represented in party posts (Cohen 1983, p. 128). Cohen's data suggest that the most successful of Yugoslav elite candi-dates demonstrate both political reliability and professional credentials.

On the whole, patterns of elite change are difficult to map out, largely because of the problem of access to the relevant data. For example, the Romanians publish no biographical dictionaries, hence career patterns are difficult to trace. Notwithstanding these obstacles, Fischer (1983b) identifies a generational change in the party Politbureau between 1965 and 1974 which largely saw off the Soviet element in the initial leadership but has found no similar later shift. In 1983 the Romanian Politbureau consisted mainly of post-war communists, ethnically Romanian and many bearing the name Ceausescu. The bulk were party generalists. Only between 20 and 25 per cent were specialists.

As well as over-representing the better educated and higher occupational strata, political elites have been overwhelmingly male in Eastern Europe. to some extent this simply reflects general patterns of recruitment in countries where, except in Romania, no special efforts have been made to promote women to the top of the political structures. Although East European women tend to be well, if not proportionately, represented in the state socialist legislatures by comparison to women in Western Europe, there is no equivalently high proportion of women in the vastly more important party councils. Moreover, a pattern of steadily increasing women's party membership in all the states (Lovenduski, 1986) has not been reflected in the assumption of leadership positions above the local and basic party organisation level. Women are normally less than 10 per cent of central committee members and hold just over 5 per cent of politbureau places (in effect a single 'token' post in a politbureau of less than 20). Gender inequality is characteristic of state socialist political stratification. There has been little evidence there of a correlation between levels of political participation by women and their share of top political posts. Women's party roles have not kept pace with their social and economic roles, evidence of not only undoubted legacies of sexism but also of recruitment policies aimed at achieving gender equality in political life at mass but not elite levels. East European political elites differ little from their Western counterparts in such respects.

However, in the final analysis, no one enters the ruling stratum of a party state without having been carefully selected by the party. Indeed the entire elite, broadly defined, must be approved by party gatekeepers via the *nomenklatura* system. It is the *nomenklatura* that defines the elite and provides the mechanism for recruitment and renewal. In this respect it is perhaps easier to identify the contours of political elites in state socialist societies than it is in their liberal democratic counterparts.

Conclusion

In terms of membership structures and leadership recruitment, the Marxist–Leninist parties of Eastern Europe are neither identical with one another nor with the USSR. The more extensive and developed institutions of civil society (see Chapter 9), especially in the more industrialised states, made it difficult from the start for these parties to claim to be the sole legitimate representative of working-class interests, and later of the whole working people. In particular, secular trends in the development of membership structures have taken the basis of support further away from the manual working class. This generates a legitimacy problem that recruitment strategies have been ill designed to solve. Their mode of operation also undermines legitimacy. The absence of institutionalised mechanisms for regular leadership renewal may have produced a stability that is remarkable by comparison with the West, but it also has all the hallmarks of inertia as the incumbents fail to display any immunity to a natural ageing process. However, below the level of the party leaderships, mechanisms of elite recruitment ensure a regular process of renewal. Yet, as we saw in our conclusion to the previous chapter, there are grounds to believe that the practice of the 'leading role of the party", by means of cadre policy and the *nomenklatura*, fails both to achieve its rationally intended objective, and to ensure mass control and accountability. The most abject failure in this respect is to be found in the case of Poland between the 1980 and 1981 Eighth and Ninth Congresses of the Polish United Workers' Party. By the Ninth Congress membership had fallen, 80 per cent of regional party committees were new, nearly all regional party secretaries and over half the secretaries of Basic Party Organisations had been replaced, and only 8 per cent of the old central committee were re-elected. What had been presented as a 'renewal' had clearly become an example of a collapse of authority (Lewis, 1984c; Sanford, 1983; Kolankiewicz, 1982b). To assume that the achievement of party goals on a legitimate basis is inherently simple is naive, as it is to assume that in an industrial society with an advanced division of labour experts will not use their position as a basis to acquire power. The party leaderships are aware of this, but they still prefer to pretend otherwise. Mass control and accountability are a fiction, and the basis of political power in state socialist societies lies elsewhere. We endeavour to explore this further by now turning to look more closely at institutions, political processes, and policies.

9

The State Institutions

If our analysis of East European politics is to be adequate, an understanding of the leading role of the communist parties must be accompanied by an appreciation of the state structures which they direct. When we employ the concept of the party–state, we imply that the formal governing institutions are themselves important to the structure and process of state socialist politics. The state socialist societies of Eastern Europe developed as mobilising regimes run by communist parties through sets of governing institutions. Organisationally they are both centralised and bureaucratised; their large administrative apparatuses are a function of the direct state management of the economy. The ambit of government is greater than in liberal democracies. Although both liberal democratic and state socialist systems feature highly complex states, under state socialism the nature of the state is in a large measure determined by the relation between the party and the other governing institutions. As we have shown in Chapter 8, this relation has been described both by the concept of the party–state and by Ionescu's (1967) apparat-state, in which the party is the apparat to which other apparats such as the ministries, the cultural organisations and the police are subordinate and through which party rule takes place.

So far our discussion of the ruling institutions has covered the role and characteristics of the communist party. In this chapter we extend our analysis to the institutions through which party rule takes place. Those institutions are necessarily complex, their roles and operations affected both by their relation to the party and to each other, a point which may be illustrated by applying Althusser's (1971, p. 136) distinction between the repressive and the ideological state apparatuses to state socialist systems. The repressive state apparatus consists of a variety of administrative and coercive institutions which function in conformity with the dominant political elite. Those structures are by no means unitary. Although the administrative organs do not operate independently of the ruling party, which provides both leadership and political momentum, party control cannot be complete as the very complexity of government requires a division of labour among a great variety of institutions. The sheer scale of administration and the vast detail of its coverage leads to a measure of autonomy in policy implementation, which in conjunction with the professionalisation of administration and the concentration of expertise in particular bureaucracies leads to the emergence of a set of distinctive state interests. These interests are mediated and the power of the dominant elite is assured by an ideological state apparatus of various legal, cultural and communications structures. In the state socialist systems the ideological state apparatus may be regarded as including the party itself, as well as a range of representative and mobilising structures such as the various assemblies, the trade unions and youth organisations, the media and the legal system and culture.

In short, the repressive and ideological apparatuses consist of institutions of control, inspection and persuasion designed both to operate and legitimate communist rule. But, as Lewis (1984b) reminds us, the East European governments appear to have acquired little normative power over their populations. They have experienced severe problems in surviving major tests of their systems at times of crisis. In Lewis's view the major upheavals in state socialist systems since the death of Stalin may be understood as efforts to adapt centralising institutions to new demands as society has become more complex. Thus the removal of Krushchev may be linked to his efforts to reorganise the party into agricultural and industrial sections, the better to ensure party leadership over industrial development. Party cadres, many of whom would have lost power, resisted. In Czechoslovakia the Prague Spring was a belated response of the party leadership to the demands of a stagnant economy during which it lost control over the relation between party and society. The Polish workers' revolt of 1970 demonstrated clearly the penalties of failure to confront the need for adaptation by governing institutions, while the militarisation both of the ministries and the party under Jaruzelski was an acknowledgement of that failure.

If the party–state is to function, the party–state relationship must be a dynamic one, accommodating not only the changes which characterise an industrialising society but also those which occur within the apparatuses it produces. The maintenance of party dominance means accommodation to the politics of the division of administrative labour, an accommodation whose nature varies both over time and between the states. Over the 40 years of communist rule in Eastern Europe there has been a movement from reliance upon the repressive state apparatus to reliance on the ideological state apparatuses, a process which has meant a considerable party effort to secure and maintain control over the coercive institutions which had been so powerful during the Stalin era. During that time constitutional and legal institutions have developed and changed as they have come to terms with a more sophisticated and complex society. Our understanding of East European politics requires an appreciation of those changes and of the current roles and functions of the variety of ideological and repressive institutions. Accordingly our next three chapters complete the account of the apparatuses of East European state socialism begun with the discussion of the party in Chapters 7 and 8. First, we shall outline and assess the institutions of East European law and government. After a discussion of constitutional systems we describe the legislative and executive, organs of government, the organs of local administration, the role of socialist law and the various judicial organs. In the concluding section we attempt to assess the capacities and the legitimacy of state socialist institutions.

Constitutional systems

Constitutions in state socialist society have two related functions. They provide the framework for socialist government and set the context for socialist public law. The eight East

European constitutions set out the current form of the institutions of government. Often they are programmatic documents. They have been regularly updated and tend to be relatively easy to amend. In this sense they are dissimilar to the sacrosanct constitutions which are characteristic of most liberal democratic systems, and on some definitions would not be regarded as constitutions at all.

Most of the countries enacted new constitutions within a year or so of liberation. These set out structures which combined borrowed Soviet forms with various residual domestic institutions and traditions. The particular mix in each case depended both on the degree of establishment of communist party rule and the degree of legitimacy of interwar arrangements. Thus in Czechoslovakia and Poland, for different reasons, the first post-war constitutions (of 1945 and 1947) retained most of the elements of the interwar political institutions. In Yugoslavia, Bulgaria, Romania and Albania the imprint of Soviet institutions was rather more marked in the early years.

As communist rule became established, the leading role of the party became a constitutional norm. The first constitutions were replaced to reflect changes brought about by the termination of the multi-party coalitions and most states adopted variants of the 1936 USSR constitution, although only Yugoslavia opted for a federal system. Bulgaria, Czechoslovakia (until 1969), the GDR, Hungary, Poland and Romania chose unitary forms and were characterised by a high degree of centralisation. All but the GDR and Czechoslovakia experienced similar patterns of evolution, whereby an early constitution accommodating a multi-party governing coalition was replaced during the Stalin period to assert the leading role of the communist party. Each established organs charged with carrying out the executive and judicial functions of government and each established a series of directly elected assemblies with legislative (representative) functions at local and national levels of the system.

The GDR was, for a considerable period of time, an exception to the general pattern. Legal constitutional development there was greatly affected by early ambivalence over its sovereignty. The first constitution, adopted in 1946, was modelled on the Weimar Constitution of 1919. The 1949 version was adopted in response to the enactment of the Basic Law by the Federal Republic of Germany earlier that year. At this point the status of the GDR was in some doubt. Stalin at that time regarded Soviet interests to lie with a united, non-aligned Germany, and as late as March 1952 was proposing peace negotiations to the Western Allies with such an outcome in mind. That overture was followed up in April with an offer of free elections under four-power supervision. Even after Stalin's death in 1953, contacts between Churchill and the new Soviet leadership led to rumours in the SED that the party might have to return to opposition. Only after the failure of the 1954 and 1955 Berlin and Geneva Four Powers Conferences to agree a solution to 'the German Question' and the admission of the Federal Republic to NATO in 1955 did Moscow end its equivocation and admit the GDR to the Warsaw Pact alliance as a sovereign member state (Minnerup 1982, p. 7). Finally, the building of the Berlin wall in 1961 proved to be a vital turning point, after which the belief that the GDR was a transient and partial form awaiting an inevitable reunification began to give way to the idea of a GDR nation. When the building of socialism became a declared goal, important constitutional changes were made. Federal arrangements were reformed. The traditional Laender (states) were abolished to be replaced by fourteen Bezirke (regions) and all traces of federalism were gradually removed until the Landerkammer was finally wound up in 1958. Since that time GDR government has been a highly centralised affair.

Czechoslovakia is unusual in that after some years as a unitary state it adopted a federal system. Its first post-war constitution was enacted in May 1948, before which date the 1920 constitution had been in force. The 1948 law combined Marxist principles with traditional institutions and was transitional in nature, but was not replaced until 1960, when Czechoslovakia became the first country outside the USSR to announce the achievement of socialism. The new 1960 constitution duly outlined the programme for the transition from socialism to communism. In 1968, as a result of grievances expressed by the Slovak population during the Prague Spring, a constitutional change was proposed which made the system federal. Enacted on the first of January, this reform established separate republican governments for 10 million Czechs and 4 million Slovaks under a federal authority, which maintains exclusive jurisdiction over foreign policy, national defence, natural resources and the protection of the constitution. Joint control by the federation in conjunction with the two republics is exercised over planning, currency, prices, industry, agriculture, transport, communications, the mass media, labour, wages, social policy and the police. The government is led by the vanguard Communist Party of Czechoslovakia, which ensures that the system is in practice a centralised one.

Yugoslavia has been the only East European state socialist society to introduce any extensive administrative decentralisation. The course of post-war Yugoslav governing institutions has been complex, comprising three constitutions and three sets of amendments so extensive that they might as well have been new constitutions. A 1946 Soviet-style federal constitution was followed by a 1953 domestic model which introduced workers' self-management. Self-management forms were much elaborated in the 1963 constitution, which was then substantially amended in 1967, 1968 and 1971, when alterations were made which progressively removed power from the federal centre to the six republican governments. A new constitution in 1974 restored some powers to the centre, but the balance of legal initiative remained with the republics.

Yugoslavia's experiments reflect not only the multi-national, disparate character of the state but also the Titoist attempt to forge a nationalist, non-aligned road to socialism. Pre-war Yugoslavia did not have autonomous territorial sub-units, merely administrative districts of various kinds. The three leading nations were recognised as constituting the state as expressed in the name adopted in 1918 (the Kingdom of the Serbs, Croats and Slovenes). Politically, however, the nations were represented by parties, they did not have their own designated state institutions. The new communist-led Yugoslavia was conceived at the second session of AVNOJ, the Anti-fascist Council for the National Liberation of Yugoslavia, at Jajce in November 1943. It was to be based upon a federal constitution, with territory to be divided into six republics established on both historical and ethnic considerations. Within the Republic of Serbia, two large minor nationalities were to be dealt with by the establishment of an autonomous province and an autonomous region (Kosovo-Metoija and Vojvodina). The republics quickly became power centres, with their own parties, and developed a jealous sense of their local interests, widely felt to be held together only by the immense persuasiveness of Tito. Attempts to strengthen a Yugoslav interest via the creation of a collective presidency initially met with little success, as did attempts to increase central party control. The 1971 crisis in Croatia (see below, Chapter 11) had to be resolved by Tito outside the party and state machinery, using military backing. Once the Croatian leaders were removed, things progressed more smoothly (Burg, 1983). The net result of developments up to 1971 was the establishment of a *de-facto* Republican veto, which had to be accommodated but not explicitly mentioned in the 1974 constitution. The device finally agreed to was a series of inter-republican committees within which republican governments were to bargain until agreement was reached. Such processes by-passed federal machinery, so much so that original proposals for the 1974 constitution omitted a republican chamber in the Federal Assembly. So long as acute nationality disputes were avoided, the mechanisms of party and government for regulating republican conflict had come to operate fairly smoothly, and by the late 1970s were able to function without heavy reliance on Tito, whose death in 1980 failed to precipitate the constitutional crisis expected by a number of observers.

Variations in practice and development should not obscure the fact that the state institutions of Eastern Europe have a number of common features which they also share with liberal democratic systems. In all eight countries the governing bodies established by the state socialist constitutions divide in the traditional manner into executive and administrative organs, legislatures, systems of local government and judicial structures. A formal division of labour between institutions responsible for rule-making, rule-implementation and rule-adjudication is apparent in each system. However, scholarly attention to the various East European governing bodies has been sparse and our knowledge of their operations and functions is far from complete. Enough research has been conducted, however, to enable the outline and in some cases the assessment of the institutions. Thus, despite inevitable gaps, the literature on each set of institutions is sufficient to provide important insights into state socialist government.

The institutions of government

Rule-making – the legislature

During the late 1970s and early 1980s state socialist legislatures became a topic on which considerable research energy was expended by Western scholars concerned to identify and describe their political roles. (White, 1980; Sakwa and Crouch, 1979; Cohen, 1982; Nelson and White, 1982; Nelson, 1982; Seroka, 1983) Legislatures, with their *de-jure* power to elect or appoint members of state executive organs and their law-making functions have constitutional centrality in state socialist systems. They also show signs, particularly during periods of crisis, that they have important, if not traditional, political functions. Thus they are carefully managed by communist parties, who run the front organisations responsible for organising elections, and therefore control the selection of legislative personnel. Although there has been an increasing incidence of contested elections since 1954 (see Chapter 10), ruling parties dominate legislative assemblies and are careful to ensure that their control is not threatened. Normally this takes the form of ensuring that the communist party has an absolute majority in the legislature, although in the GDR the SED settles formally for a simple plurality of deputyships. There seats are allocated by a standing agreement with the other parties and front member organisations. Bulgaria, Czechoslovakia and Poland also permit non-communist parties to operate, but the activities of these 'other' parties are closely controlled.

The fact that they are communist-party-controlled does not mean that the East European legislatures have a negligible role. Indeed the existence of a vigorous legislature may well be functional to communist party rule, providing a means of checking government performance as well as contributing to the legitimation of party policy. Legislatures are not challenges to party dominance; they are, rather, one of the means by which that dominance is exercised. It is for this reason that parties have promoted legislative activism and the expansion of assembly authority, introducing contested elections in many of the states and expanding the committee systems in Poland, the GDR and Yugoslavia. The idea that a single dominant party precludes the existence of an influential legislature on the grounds that if power lies with the party, it cannot rest elsewhere, may be mistaken. It derives, as Nelson and White (1982) remind us, not from observations of legislative behaviour, but from unsubstantiated assumptions about the nature of the party–state.

What, then, are the roles of the East European legislatures? What is their purpose and how do they behave and what does their study tell us about state socialist politics? Representative assemblies have a well established ideological pedigree. Both Marx and Lenin, while regarding parliamentarism as bourgeois, believed that representative assemblies of some kind were essential to proletarian democracy. Thus neither sought to do without representative institutions and both pointed to the Paris Commune of 1871 as an example of the sort of assembly they envisaged, i.e. one in which executive and legislative functions were fused. This vision suited ruling communist parties well. An ethos of mass participation presupposed a relationship between government and people which required institutional expression of the kind which could be found in a legislative assembly. Communist parties were able to pursue popular representation in legislatures without contradicting their dominant roles.

Today's East European legislatures function as legitimating institutions and as such as part of the ideological apparatus. They are representative in that they mirror the population in certain important respects. Deputies are selected according to occupational, language, gender and sometimes geographical criteria, although government and party officials tend to be over-represented in systems of election which enable the ruling parties to control nomination processes. Legislative representation also enables the incorporation of individuals who may not be integrated via the party hierarchy. For example, a village doctor may be a person of considerable influence in the community but no more than a nominal party member. Such individuals will often be members of people's councils or other state assemblies.

The study of communist legislatures illuminates rather more than representative capacities, however, Legislatures are a useful source of information about other things, providing data and background information on their members which tells us who receives political recognition. The topics discussed, reported or voted upon give clues about government priorities. Changes in frequency and type of formal assembly activities give indications of attitudes to participation. Elite status is often denoted by legislative membership, i.e. recruitment to the political elite is often signalled by election to a council or assembly of some kind.

Although the ruling parties are capable of constraining legislatures, they do not always do so. White, Gardner and Schopflin (1982) suggest that legislative roles vary considerably between periods of what they term weak and effective party control. They point out that the Prague Spring, the 1980–1 events in Poland and the 1963 Yugoslav constitutional reform were all accompanied by a revitalisation of parliamentary activity. This, they reason, supports a proposition that, when possible, state socialist legislatures attempt to perform their constitutional functions. But electoral practices (see below Chapter 10) lead to only a weak relation between deputies and their ostensible electorates, and deputies lack a sufficient sense of competence and legitimacy to withstand pressures to remain compliant. Nevertheless, a degree of legislative autonomy is evident, ranging from the comparative freedom experienced by the Yugoslav and Hungarian assemblies to the almost complete control exercised over the Albanian assembly, with the other systems falling somewhere in between.

The legislatures may be described by the degree of their resemblance to the USSR Supreme Soviet, where unanimity in full session is normal, meetings are short and infrequent and most of the legislative work actually takes place in committees in which drafts may be and sometimes are amended. White's (1980) study of the USSR Supreme Soviet shows that its patterns of representation and interest articulation have not led to the acquisition of significant political authority. Increasingly composed of a broad sample of social groups, the Supreme Soviet concerns itself mainly with basic socio-economic issues. It is probably not marginal to the political process, as evidence from budget debates indicates that deputies intervene to protect or to promote constituency interests, and that such intervention is often effective. There are also indications that real bargaining takes place in the commissions (committees) which rose in number from four in 1938 (8 per cent of deputies) to thirty-two in 1980 (76 per cent of deputies). The commissions cover all the main policy areas. They meet three to four times per year and generate sub-committees which meet more frequently for preparatory work. Although they have only a limited role in policy initiation, the commissions have important functions in overseeing the implementation of policy.

The East European legislatures have developed along similar lines. Commission activity has been particularly evident in the Polish Sejm, the GDR Volkskammer and the Hungarian National Assembly. Except for Yugoslavia, where legislative elections are indirect, all have representative national assemblies which are formally (that is, constitutionally) endowed with considerable legislative authority, although in practice legislative initiative tends to come from the party via the executive. Ionescu (1967) has made the point that when debate does take place in the East European assemblies, it tends to be much harder hitting than debates in the party, even though the same people may be taking part. This is explainable to a certain extent by role differentiation, but should not be overstated – many important party debates are not repeated in the assemblies. When they are repeated, however, the context is very different. Assemblies contain representatives who are not communist party members, and in several of the states include representatives of the 'other' parties. The communist party members who are selected for assembly candidacy are chosen partly on the basis of their popularity with the community as a whole and its various local groups of public opinion. This means that many of the party deputies will not necesarily be the most trusted or party-minded types in the view of those in the upper party echelons. The absence of unequivocal leadership backing in turn leads deputies to be more dependent upon their electoral base, as a result of which a 'legislators' frame of reference' emerges.

Yugoslavia has been especially prone to such tendencies. The pronounced geographic basis of representation has enhanced the 'legislators' frame of reference' and over time the Federal Assembly has gradually evolved from a typical sounding board to a body with ever growing initiative, a development given considerable early impetus by the break between Tito and Stalin. Between 1953 and 1967 the balance between the Yugoslav legislature an executive altered considerably. From a position in which vastly more measures were introduced in the Federal Executive Council (1373) than in the assembly (254), the ratio altered in favour of the Assembly (to 686 to 782). Parallel developments included a measurable increase in the activities of the deputies and of the legislature as a whole. The number of interpellations to the cabinet increased dramatically from fifty-eight in the 1953–7 session to 475 in the 1963–8 parliament. But as the legislature became more important as a decision-making arena, it became less representative of the population as a whole. Not surprisingly, as it became a real centre of power, it attracted real holders of power. In personnel terms two trends were apparent: a sharp fall in the proportion of deputies whose professional base was the League of Communists or one of the mass organisations and a rise in the presence of managerial personnel. Such trends became the focus of considerable debate as the League of Communists launched an attack on nationalism, technocracy and liberalism during 1971. The 1974 constitution was designed partly to reverse trends of legislative professionalisation, providing for rotation in office, limitations on consecutive terms and bans on dual party and state office holding by deputies (Denitch, 1976, pp. 132–8).

Committee structures are often better developed in Eastern Europe than they are in the USSR, although this may vary considerably with changes in the political climate. During period of weakened party control in Poland, the Sejm has been the site of a considerable articulation of interests, especially in its committees. In the immediate aftermath of regime establishment the Sejm, which dates from 1505, had a relatively limited and apparently cosmetic function. But after the upheavals of 1956 its various permanent committees, which were organised along functional lines, began to develop a fuller role. Their number increased from eleven to nineteen committees, which paralleled important ministries. Most deputies who were not Sejm officials, including those from the 'other' parties and the church-based organisations, took part. Although Sejm deputyship is a part-time occupation, its committee chairs are full-time posts. The chairs are divided proportionately by party, although the PUWP takes care to ensure that it retains the chairs of the Defence and the Economic Planning and Regulations Committees. Sejm committees meet at will and become a locus of continuity, both because they meet between sessions and because their chairpersons tend to experience lower rates of turnover than other deputies. They may generate sub-committees and conduct investigations into the activities of administrative departments and economic enterprises. They play a significant role in the legislative process, possessing powers of amendment as well as limited capacities of initiation. The thrust of their work has been to protect citizen rights. For example, bills on criminal law have been amended to eliminate single-member courts and to allow the disqualification of jurors. They also have important scrutiny functions and pay particular attention to the ministerial implementation of delegated legislation. During the upheavals attending the rise of Solidarity and the subsequent imposition of military rule in Poland, the Sejm played an active role. Its 'legislators' frame of reference' was apparent in that it exhibited an evident concern to retain popular respect, opposing constitutional changes and policy measures proposed first by the discredited Kania and later the military administration (see White *et al.*, 1982; Olson and Simon, 1982; Sanford, 1985).

The cases for which we have evidence appear to support Nelson's (1982, p. 11) argument that the state socialist legislatures have a mediating function and are an organic connection between government and the governed. Ruling parties utilise them to bring about integration, which is defined as the acceptance of party hegemony, the supremacy of central over local concerns and needs, the dominance of the plan in decisions regarding resource allocation and the primacy of collective over individual goals and interests. Thus their significance does not rest simply on an ability to formulate, debate and consider bills or enact laws or their minor role in policy formulation, a marginality shared with West European legislatures. It has to do also with their contribution to system integration and their role in structuring political conflict.

Rule-implementation: national government

At national level, government in Eastern Europe is managed by political executives or cabinets, normally the Council of Ministers, which is formally responsible to the legislature. Bridging the ideological and repressive state apparats, the executives have responsibility for the conduct of administration. Each country has a cabinet (normally the Council of Ministers) as well as a Presidency or State Council which undertakes the functions of head of state (Table 9.1). State socialist cabinets may be regarded as the executive arm of the party, fulfilling the bureacratic and administrative functions of government. Cabinets are often extremely large, paralleling the various components of the economy for which it is responsible. When a government is directly responsible for the management of the economy, a considerable and differentiated administrative apparatus is an operating necessity. As the highest organs of state administration, councils of ministers normally include the head of the economic planning agency as well as the various administrative and economic ministers.

Councils of ministers are formally appointed by legislatures to whom they are responsible for state administration. In practice their membership is a party matter, for clearly ministerial office will form part of the *nomenklatura*! In the mid-1980s the Hungarian Council of Ministers consisted of a premier, four deputy premiers, the heads of fourteen ministries and one agency (the National Planning Office). Although the constitution made provision for twenty-six

TABLE 9.1
Main constitutional state organs

Country	Head of state	Cabinet	National legislature	No. of legislators
Albania	Presidium	Council of Ministers	People's Assembly	250
Bulgaria	State Council	Council of Ministers	National Assembly	400
Czechoslovakia	Presidium	Federal Cabinet	Federal Assembly of:	
			Chamber of the People	200
			Chamber of Nations	150
GDR	State Council	Council of Ministers	Peoples Chamber (Volkskammer)	500
Hungary	Presidential Council	Council of Ministers	National Assembly	353
Poland	Council of State	Council of Ministers	Sejm	460
Romania	State Council	Council of Ministers	Grand National Assembly	369
Yugoslavia	State presidency	Federal Executive Council	Federal Assembly of:	
			Federal Chamber	220
			Chamber of Republics and Provinces	88

ministries, the number had been gradually reduced in a process of executive streamlining. At the same time the Bulgarian and Polish Councils of Ministers consisted of twenty-five and over forty members respectively. In 1985 Jaruszelski was known to be attempting to streamline the Polish body, largely by amalgamating economic ministries. The Romanian Council of Ministers was also large, accommodating the aggrandizement of the Ceausescu family by providing large numbers of posts in which its members practice their unique form of dynastic socialism. Czechoslovakia, the GDR and Yugoslavia all differ from the normal pattern. The Czechoslovak presidency has always been an office of great prestige, having acquired stature both under Masaryk and Benes. The office itself is a valuable political asset, with successive presidents eager to occupy it and party general secretaries keen to have it under control. The president has the constitutional power to appoint and recall the cabinet, whose premiership carries less political weight than the presidency.

In the GDR changes in the balance of power within the political elite have been reflected in the changing roles and relations of the State Council and the Council of Ministers. Today the Council of Ministers is the pre-eminent institution. Throughout the 1960s the functions of the State Council increased, but when Ulbricht lost the general secretaryship of the SED in May 1971, he retained his chairpersonship of the State Council. To minimise his influence, laws were passed to curtail the powers of the State Council, which until that time had been the dominant state organ. After Ulbricht's death, constitutional amendments restored the balance between the two bodies. Hence the State Council now performs mainly head of state roles while the Council of Ministers is the government. The Council of Ministers undergoes frequent changes and reshuffles, largely reflecting developments in the economy. It includes a number of specialised economic ministries as well as the State Planning Commission, and in 1985 had forty-five members.

In Yugoslavia the executive consists of the Presidency and the Federal Executive Council. Tito held the office of President until his death in 1980, when the position was abolished as an individual office and replaced by a collective presidency. There are nine members of the State Presidency – one from each of the constituent republics, one each from Vojvodina and Kosovo and one *ex-officio* member. The office rotates annually among the eight full members, who may serve up to two consecutive 5-year terms. The collective presidency was some years in development and reflects the multi-national and federal character of Yugoslav politics. It is paralleled by a similarly constructed body in the League of Yugoslav Communists. The President of the State Presidency is the head of state, and the vice-presidency is the second most important state position. The Federal Executive Council is the cabinet in the sense of being the executive source of legislative proposals. It consists of a president, five vice-presidents and twenty-three members. The devolution of many administrative responsibilities, particularly those to do with the economy, to the republics means that the Yugoslav cabinet plays less of an executive and administrative role than its East European counterparts.

Neither the executive nor the administrative operations of East European governments have received much attention from scholars, who have preferred to concentrate on top politicians in their party roles, and have regarded government members without top party positions as senior administrators rather than political leaders. While there is much to be said in favour of such a view, it has meant that we know less than we might about the detail of East European government at national level. The problem is compounded by the fact that, as with all national governments, much of the deliberation and decision-making of the councils of ministers, presidencies and councils of state are secret. Moreover, our knowledge of central administration is also sparse. Such information as is available indicates that ministries in state socialist systems tend to be run by specialist administrators and executives rather than politicians. Personnel turnover is relatively low and individuals may, during their resultant long period in office, build up a considerable personal power base. White *et al.* (1982, p. 102) have noted that low turnover in office has led to high levels of prestige for long-serving individual government members, and refer to party efforts to prevent this by introducing rotation of personnel. They cite the example of the GDR Minister of State Security, Erich Mielke, in post since 1957, who is regarded as having become so well entrenched in office that he is 'irremovable' – an East European equivalent of J. Edgar Hoover! In practice a recognised need for ruling parties to allow governments some room for manoeuvre tends to give way to party efforts to regain control. Occasionally cabinets will include individuals who are not members of the ruling party, but such representation tends to be small. Four of the forty-five members of the GDR Council of Ministers in 1985 were not members of the SED. Ruling parties prefer to supervise governments closely and there is normally a significant degree of politbureau-cabinet overlap (Staar,1984, *passim*).

The administrative apparatuses which the cabinets lead are nowadays largely staffed by professional bureaucrats who have made their careers in state or enterprise management. Party membership is normally an essential prerequisite to a successful career in the state bureaucracy, but, over time, professional qualifications have also come to have considerable importance. In Yugoslavia before the reforms of the 1970s administrators were the most professional of all of the political elites, frequently spending their entire careers in state administration. Even where initially recruited by the party, their time in the civil service gradually gave them expertise in a single area, a pattern which contrasted sharply with the generalist orientations typical of the party leadership. Administrators also came from higher social stratum than other members of the elite. Administrative professionalisation was regarded as anti-democratic and reforms were designed to reverse the pattern. Election to top posts and rotation in office became requirements in the civil service as well as in political posts. But difficulties were encountered in replacing senior administrators. Qualified personnel were few in number and many of those who were qualified preferred higher status occupations than those which were available in the civil service. High levels of specialisation meant that many senior administrators were non-transferable. The pool of eligibles was small, a factor compounded by the unwillingness of non-Serbs to go to work in Belgrade (Zukin, 1984, pp. 267–9). Thus limitations arising from the requirements of skill, specialism and nationality mean that Yugoslav senior administrative positions tend to be held by virtually the only available capable people. The resulting closed nature of the Yugoslav bureaucracy is not dissimilar to that which is to be found in civil services throughout the world.

Our sparse knowledge of their functioning permits little in the way of generalisation about the roles of the national level of East European executive bodies. They may have legitimating functions in the sense that some regard is paid to due process and parties appear to be unwilling to rule without the mediation of constitutionally established structures of government. A striking example is provided by the case of Poland under military rule. Although the Military Council for National Salvation (WRON) took over the functions of government in Poland between 1980 and 1981, not only the legislature but also the executive was retained, and WRON directives were issued via a somewhat militarised cabinet. But executive roles are contradictory. As managers of the administrative apparatus, which normally included the institutions of state security, the executives are part of the repressive state apparatus. As bodies which are responsible to elected representative assemblies, they are also part of the ideological state apparatus. Parties need the additional avenues of communication which state structures provide as well as the expertise which government officials supply. The results of enhancing dominance to the point of hegemony may be a schlerotic structure incapable not only of responding to crisis but also of normal administration. This danger becomes more apparent when we extend our discussion of government administration to the local level. Many of the syndromes that may be present at national level are much more apparent at local, district and regional levels of administration

Rule-implementation: local government
Local, district and regional institutions are also important components of the party state. Nelson (1980, pp. 1–2) provides three reasons for giving sub-national government consideration in studies of state socialist systems. Firstly, he

writes, it is in the local arena that state and citizen are most likely to meet. It is here that officials are approached by citizens with particular demands, where preferences and values are articulated through citizen participation and where officials, both elected and appointed, are recruited. It would therefore be a serious error to regard local authorities simply as local extensions of superior governments. Secondly, the study of local politics affords us opportunities to gain new insights into national politics as we examine grass-roots-level cleavages, issues and administration. Finally, and more pro-saically, it has been easier for Western researchers to gain the necessary access to do field research on local than national politics. Community studies are regarded as less sensitive by officials and there are often local scholars in place willing to cooperate with Western researchers.

Characteristically, the network of governing and judicial institutions which runs between commune and capital in Eastern Europe is built around a hierarchy of assemblies normally called people's councils. Originally these were modelled on the system of soviets which developed during the Russian Revolutions of 1905 and 1917 and were institutional-ised in the Soviet Union during the 1920s and 1930s. Appro-priate adaptations were made to take account of the unitary nature of most of the East European systems of government. Except in Yugoslavia, the organisational keynote of the first post-war decade was centralisation. Politically, this reflected the imperatives of consolidating the party state. Economi-cally, centralisation was necessary to ensure that industrial development proceeded as uniformly as possible, and that initial regional discrepancies did not solidify into important and lasting patterns of geographically determined inequali-ties. Only in the already industrial GDR was centralisation delayed until 1958, when the five traditional Laender in-herited from Weimar were replaced by fourteen regions (Bezirke). The Bezirke are named after their respective capi-tals (Halle, Magdeburg etc.). Each has its own assembly, which is elected on the same day as the Volkskammer. Bezirketage elect a council from amongst their numbers. Its functions are limited to carrying out centrally determined policy through their commissions, which cover such areas as planning, coordination, budget and finance, supervising the local supply economy and so forth. The Bezirke are divided into districts or Kreise. There are twenty-eight urban districts (Stadtkreise) and 191 rural districts (Landkreise). Each Kreis has its assembly or Kreistag, elected from a list of candidates approved by the National Front. Kreise are divided into municipalities or communes of which there are 7620. At any given time about 190,000 GDR citizens are members of their various local or regional assemblies, which, despite having little room for manoeuvre in policy-making, have been an important voice for local grievances of a non-controversial nature, such as complaints about poor amenities (Childs, 1983, pp. 134–5). In the GDR tight economic control is accompanied by tight political control.

Elsewhere in the region a decade of centralisation was followed by reforms during the 1960s and 1970s which had a decentralisation motif; the most far-reaching took place in Yugoslavia. These were necessary accompaniments to the economic reforms of the same era. Economic and political reforms had parallel fates. Resulting from economic imperatives, changes commonly featured a reduction in specific dictates from above and a corresponding widening of the decision-taking role of the enterprise, which was now more responsive to market forces. The reform of local government was thus an accompaniment to a gradual dismantling of parts of the command apparatus. But, in general, local authorities were not given the sort of control over resource allocation which was necessary for a genuine political decentralisation to take place. Only in Poland did local budgeting (unexpectedly) escape central control, with disastrous results. In Yugoslavia, where decentralisation went furthest, central government struggled to keep the process sufficiently under control that long-standing wealth differences between its localities did not become greater. The hope there that commune level budgetary initiatives would promote greater equality was not fulfilled (Nelson, 1980, p. 217). Elsewhere, control of local authorities is achieved both politically through party mechanisms and through democratic centralist principles of organisation, and financially through central direction of resources, a strategy well tried in liberal democracies. Elites are uncomfortable with political decentralisation and have been reluctant to condone the kind of political reforms necessary to make economic reforms work. But there has been some experimentation, resulting in appreciable differences in central local relations in the various states. These differences may be illustrated by a more detailed account of the Czechoslovakian, Hungarian, Romanian, Yugoslav and Polish systems.

Despite its federal nature since 1969, the Czechoslovak system of local government remains highly centralised. The Czech and Slovak Republics each have their own assemblies and governments, which are responsible for running the state administration. These are further sub-divided into eleven regions, over 100 districts and about 14,000 local units. Each tier is organised around a 'national' committee consisting of anywhere from eleven to 130 members. An executive council, chosen by each committee, includes a chairperson, deputies, a secretary and varying numbers of members. The committees and their executives are subordinate to republican-level governments. They issue some decrees and ordinances but have no policy-making authority. The local authorities were extensively restaffed during the purges which followed the 1968 Warsaw Pact invasion. Since that time they have gradually increased their administrative authority but remain subject to democratic centralist principles, which in practice have tended to be more centralist than democratic. As in most of the other states, the leadership is cool to any manifestations of regionalism, and planning remains highly centralised. Nevertheless, the federal system has been used to take a genuine account of Czech and Slovak differences, a result of which has been a visible increase in Slovak commitment to the nation (Staar, 1982, pp. 68–9; Gitelman, 1981).

Romanian and Hungarian local administrations are based upon similar networks of assemblies and executives. These are hierarchically subordinate and have agencies of centralisation in both systems. But in each case economic reforms have led to an increase in the responsibilities of the local authorities. In Romania the enactment of the New Economic and Financial Mechanism began to be implemented in 1979. Late in 1980 legal changes required people's councils to manage their own labour and material resources, taking into account the unified plan of economic development. In practice this meant that the people's councils were to be held responsible for the implementation of plan directives and for recruitment of resources. A classic example of responsibility without power, the changes have not given the councils a greater say in their own planning processes (Shafir, 1985, pp. 106–7).

In Hungary the introduction of the New Economic Mechanism meant that previous 'central agency' functions of local government were no longer adequate. The authorities were gradually transformed into more autonomous units and given important budgetary and planning functions. They were able to generate local revenue as well as being given responsibility for a range of local economic, welfare and cultural tasks. Specifically an act of 1971 arranged a new basis for the election and operation of the councils. This act made three changes. Firstly, local responsibilities and resources were increased. Secondly, the population was to take a greater part in the planning and control of local operations, so was provided with a more adequate forum. Thirdly, the increased responsibilities and independence of the local councils were accompanied by increased efficiency and control in central administration, which was to assume a general guidance role and provide partial long-term finance. Electoral mechanisms had already been altered to provide for the indirect election of city, territorial and regional councils by lower level assemblies. Certain council revenues were linked to the performance of enterprises under local jurisdiction (Kovrig, 1979, p. 386). The thrust of the reform was to redefine the position of the local councils in the system from being simply part of the states' representative and administrative apparatus to being organs of local representation and self-administration. Alterations in electoral procedures separated national and local elections in 1973, enabling the fuller expression of local interests in elections. But despite all this, municipal councils continue to be denied budgetary control, although they may obtain special investment funds for certain purposes. Without budgetary autonomy they are weak political bodies and likely to remain so (Huber and Heinrich, 1981).

More radical, but somewhat contrasting, reforms have been attempted in Yugoslavia and Poland. Both economic and cultural considerations were important in shaping the organisation of local administration in Yugoslavia, where, uniquely in Eastern Europe, the localities have considerable influence and authority over policy. There local authorities are closely concerned in the system of self-management which has been developing since the 1953 constitutional reform. Officially described as a self-managing socio-political community, the local commune is the basic unit of local government. Larger cities have district status and smaller ones are governed by special town councils. Districts have jurisdiction over broad political matters such as law enforcement and elections. Communes have several primary concerns, including planning, investment and internal trade. They also provide municipal services and social management (that is, citizen control over public activities). The economic management system parallels the system of social management. In a state of continuous evolution since the first modifications of the command structure in the 1950s, the self-management system has encouraged local enterprise initiative and afforded a wide degree of workers' control. In 1953 self-management was given legal weight by the transfer of enterprise ownership from the state to employees in workers' councils. Further changes during the 1960s added to the responsibilities of the workers' councils and continued a progressive down-grading of the command apparatus. Republics were given greater roles, taking responsibility for banking and investment. The system of economic chambers incorporated into government was developed at federal, republic and district levels. The most recent manifestation of this development is to be found in the tricameral organisation of functional representation. Three institutional zones of locality, economy and political action are designated as the basis of representation in political organs, which are divided into economic, community and political chambers. Representatives to the three chambers are chosen via a system of delegates selected at the lowest level by directly elected self-managing councils of the three basic types. Entry into the political arena in Yugoslavia may legitimately take place only through one of the three designated areas of activity. For example, journals may be established or broadcasts made only with the approval of one of the legally constituted organisations within one of the areas. The state retains the right to 'defend self-management', giving it the authority to exclude initiatives of which it disapproves (Zukin, 1984). Party control remains strong and is most manifest at the republican levels. Nevertheless, real decentralisation has taken place in Yugoslavia, and local organs have meaningful functions of representation and self-management.

Poland's political reforms have been as ill fated as the economic reforms they accompanied. As elsewhere, both political and economic motivations were behind the reforms of the 1970s. Structural reform between 1972 and 1975 had three aims: (1) to centralise on a local plane the system of state administration and party supervision in the countryside, (2) to strengthen party leadership over people's councils, which had hitherto combined self-management and administration tasks, and (3) to streamline the structures of party and state by transforming the three-tier administrative apparatus into a two-tier structure. By contrast to reforms elsewhere, the Polish initiative had the effect of making government less local. From the standpoint of local elites, it was a centralising reform. Extensive reorganisation changed the three-layer system of communes, counties and provinces to a two-level structure of townships and provinces. The size of provinces was reduced and their number increased from twenty-two to forty-nine. The aim was that these should be compact and self-sufficient units, reflecting what were often different local historical traditions (Nelson, 1980, pp. 6–7). The changes were part of a general process of reform publicised in the early 1970s and covering various areas of Polish social life, including industrial production, the economic administration, industrial relations and closer party links with the workforce (Lewis, 1982a,b, p. 84). The emphasis was on the separation of party and state activities in order to strengthen party control over state organs, thus enhancing party leadership. The changes introduced a strict division between legislative and executive organs, whereby the executive presidium previously elected by local councils was replaced by professional managers nominated by the central government. Within the council the first secretary of the local PUWP branch became (by custom) the chairperson of the county's presidium, allocating additional and direct control to the party over the local council. Such changes destroyed the power of the large provinces, previously run by important state and party bosses. Direct control from the centre increased and the provinces were eliminated as generators of potential future rivals to Warsaw (Nelson, 1980, p. 7).

The reorganisation introduced considerable confusion into the general state administration. Moreover, insufficient attention was paid to the economy and the structure of local economic administration. While the number and powers of the Large Economic Organisations were increased, necessary alterations to ministerial powers and organisation were not made. In the event the reforms as they were enacted weakened party control and overburdened the state executive. Combined with the availability of increased investment funds allocated by central ministries and at the disposal of agents of the centre, this served to bolster the relative position of plant directors and the economic advisers, increasing their autonomy *vis-à-vis* local party authorities. Such managerial autonomy led to widespread corruption as well as to inefficient use of investment funds, resulting in considerable popular disaffection. Although the new structure took account of the geographical distribution of industry, it did not harmonise well with the network of economic administration. The enterprise autonomy which had developed under Gierek led, for example, to production plans being altered by enterprise or association directors with no reference to the provincial authorities responsible for the coordination of economic activities (Lewis, 1982a,b, p. 84).

The failure of the Polish reform to achieve its aims illustrates the problems of the government-managed economies of the party–state. The Polish measures aimed to strengthen party leadership by specifying more precisely the persons and offices with responsibility for state administration and by reducing the size of major administrative units in order to enhance social and economic coordination. But improvements in local planning and coordination did not result. The excessive powers of plant directors, the dominance of economic specialists over party organisation, as well as the formalism of local government, all undermined the reform. Although present there in an extreme form, such eventualities have by no means been unique to Poland. The problems are structural and organisational ones to do with the operation of large enterprises. But the Polish reforms were particularly ill conceived in that they reduced the size of the province, thus reducing the status of provincial leaders in a period when directors and managers had their autonomy enhanced by a relatively free flow of funds. Instead of increasing its control over the managers, the party experienced a loss of control over them. The problem was compounded as the situation led party cadres with responsibility over managers to form alliances with them in order to enhance their shaky power bases. Cross-pressuring and the absence of the necessary administrative apparatus to perform their roles resulted in the inability of party cadres to provide a lead as the loss of coherence became more acute.

Ultimately the survival of the PUWP itself was placed in jeopardy. Reduced levels of authority and cohesion proved impossible to correct in the face of the rise of Solidarity. The Kania leadership which replaced Gierek faced an increase in such problems. High levels of turnover in party personnel took place in 1980 and 1981, but proved insufficient to reinstate the party's authority (Lewis, 1984a). The Polish reform may be characterised as one which reduced the dual mechanisms which underpinned the party–state. The failure of the reform suggests strongly that to some minimal extent party–state dualism must be institutionalised and organisationally maintained throughout the system. In short, both the parallelism of party and government structures and their structural integrity are essential components of the party–state.

Socialist law

Legal structures in the East European systems reflect both the particular culture in which they have evolved and the determining principles of socialist law. The law itself is regarded as explicitly political and is adjudicated according to principles of political justice rather than abstract concepts. It is important when discussing such structures to distinguish between the content of the law and its application. Our agreement or disagreement with its content should not impede our ability to assess the nature of its implementation. Far from being lawless, state socialist societies have been increasingly consistent in the application of their laws. But the principles which underlie the substance of the laws differ substantially from those which prevail in states based upon the Anglo-Saxon legal tradition. The political trials which receive so much publicity in the West are normally conducted by prosecutors and judges following strictly defined legal procedures, reflecting the development of a communist *Rechstaat*, or rule of public law, in Eastern Europe (see Fisk, 1969–70).

As our discussion of the East European constitutions implied, that *Rechstaat* is set in a framework of socialist law. The primary purpose of socialist law is mobilisation for social involvement, and its most distinctive features are its educative function and its capacities for social integration. Socialist law is a form of public law, the cornerstone concept of which is state ownership of the means of production, although, in fact, private ownership, of the land, for example, exists on a wide scale. Another important element is the law of planning, which produces a specialised administrative apparatus for the preparation and implementation of economic plans. State economic enterprises are legal entities able to make contracts with each other in conformity with the plan and systems of tribunals that exist to settle disputes between them. There also exists a corpus of family, inheritance, tort and (individually owned) property law in what is regarded as a structure of private law. Private law varies considerably from system to system, but public law is basically similar in the USSR and seven of the eight East European states. Yugoslavia, where public law accommodates the highly developed system of self-management, is an exception in this regard.

The concepts of socialist public law have probably been most fully developed in the GDR, where a long-standing legalism forms part of the political culture and where the role and function of socialist law has been extensively debated. In common with other state socialist systems, law in the GDR is regarded as utilitarian in character and subject both in interpretation and implementation to political influence. Thus a council of state rather than a legal body has the task of interpreting the constitution. Socialist law is not a system conceived primarily for the preservation of individual interests; rather, it is social law. It is a legal system for the community and exists to serve the general interest while at the same time enabling the individual to find an appropriate place in the community. In practice GDR law follows the general European tradition of code law, but with considerable flexibility of application in the interests of preserving the state (Scharf, 1984, pp. 136–7).

Sontheimer and Bleek (1975) provide what is perhaps the most accessible introductory account of socialist law in the GDR, an account which may readily be applied to the other states. It is thus worth rehearsing in some detail. They point out that legal statutes are frequently of the framework variety, given shape only by orders issued by the executive. The equivalent liberal democratic device is the practice of delegated legislation. Use, too, is made of indefinite legal concepts, allowing the maximum scope for interpretation. The preambles of laws always contain a mass of general socialist precepts intended to suggest modes of interpretation.

Basic rights are not rights *vis-à-vis* the state, for they do not guarantee a private, protected sphere for the individual. Rather, they act in an integrating capacity, ensuring that the individual participates in the various areas of social life. Accordingly the right of codetermination and collaboration is a fundamental socialist right. Rights are accompanied in socialist public law by a strong emphasis on complementary basic duties. The right of participation is in fact the right and duty of social and political participation. Work is an overriding duty as well as a right. Only by work may human potential be realised. The right of education, which enables individuals to participate in the general cultural process, is also a duty – to develop the intellectual capacities which will enable people to give of their best within the process of social production. Concepts of basic rights are integrating mechanisms which guarantee social welfare and protection.

Officially GDR socialist public law has two imperatives. Firstly, the legal system must be seen and interpreted from the standpoint of developed socialism. It is the expression of the political will of the working class and regulates therefore, in a legally binding way, the basic social relations of the citizenry, between citizen and community and between these and the state. Secondly, socialist law requires the participation of both citizen and community in the administration of law. This participation is both a significant way of exercising power and a means of social self-education of the working class. Thus socialist law is not the restrictive, limiting law of Western bourgeois systems, in which once law has been codified, it is transferred from the political system to the judiciary, where it often develops a logic which is separate from that intended by its creators.

Rule-adjudication: courts and the administration of justice
A pattern of a hierarchical set of courts, a state prosecutor's office of some kind, and a state security apparatus is repeated in each East European country, although the precise division of jurisdiction between civil and military courts may vary and the mixture of professional and lay judges also differs. As in Western liberal democracies, the judiciary and the police are supervised by ministers with cabinet status. Most of the countries have systems of regular courts complemented by people's or community courts modelled on the comrade's courts of the Soviet Union. Federal Yugoslavia and Czechoslovakia also have constitutional courts which decide on the conformity of laws and other regulations with the constitution as well as dealing with inter-republican and other federal types of dispute. Widespread participation of the community in the processes of law derives from the theories of socialist law outlined above and reflects a conviction that many of the conflicts and disputes of bourgeois society disappear under socialism. Society disarms its opposition as it progresses, a development which will be reflected in a gradual decrease in the need for a state-run system of justice. Over time, law will

come to have only a sort of confirmatory function and will recede into the background as a means of settling conflicts and deciding sentences. It will be replaced by agreements, a process already evident in the work of the various people's and community courts.

The East European court systems were radically reorganised after World War Two, when systems which paralleled those of Stalin's USSR were inaugurated. The Hungarian system is a fairly typical one. There the first steps were taken under Soviet occupation, when, on 25 January 1946, people's courts were established to prosecute citizens who had supported German and Hungarian fascists. The people's court system was then reorganised several times until the present system was introduced by the constitution of 1949. The judicial structure as described by Toma and Volgyes (1977, pp. 78–80) is hierarchical, with different levels corresponding to the different tiers of government. At the bottom of the hierarchy are district and municipal courts, which are the courts of first instance and have authority over all violations not statutorily assigned to other courts. The county courts and the Budapest capital court are appellate courts as well as courts of original jurisdiction in matters of homicide, major theft and other important cases. The Supreme Court is the highest judicial body. It has original jurisdiction over specific cases and matters referred to it by the chief public prosecutor. As well as being the appellate court for the county and capital courts, the Supreme Court judges the constitutionality of laws and the decisions of the lower courts. It is responsible for establishing the theoretical principles of law and legal guidelines which bind all lower courts. The Supreme Court is divided into civil and criminal branches and has nominal authority over the military tribunal or Collegium.

The Hungarian system resembles the Soviet one in many respects. Each sub-division is headed by a president or presiding judge and all lower courts consist of councils composed of three persons – one professional judge and two lay assessors – whose opinions rank equally under the law. Judges at subnational level are selected for 3 years by the competent organs of state power at the relevant level. The Supreme Court president, professional judges and law assessors are chosen by the National Assembly for periods of 5 years. In practice such selections are made by the Ministry of Justice. Procedures for the recall of serving judges exist, but these have not been used. Lay assessors are provided from a pool of individuals, who may only serve for 1 month per year, for which service to the community their place of employment must release them with pay.

Bridging the Hungarian security and judicial apparatus is the Chief Public Prosecutor, who has constitutional responsibility for ensuring the legality of government actions, acting as public defender, prosecuring those charged with crimes and defending the state. Analogous to the Soviet Procuracy, the Hungarian Chief Public Prosecutor exerts some measure of control over most aspects of public life. Separate from the judiciary, the office is accountable only to the highest political organs. Legal sanctions are limited to the right of the National Assembly to recall the incumbent. The Chief Public Prosecutor is elected by the National Assembly for a 6-year period and appoints all the public prosecutors who serve in the geographically and hierarchically organised offices under his or her control. There are both military and civil branches of the office, which has supervisory responsibility over four separate types of legality: general legality, the legality of criminal investigations, the legality of court procedures and the legality of punishment.

Significantly the Chief Public Prosecutor prosecutes anyone suspected of endangering the social order or the security or independence of the country, and also may undertake preventive detention. Such wide powers enable the office to be used as an instrument of terror, a capacity which was used during Rakosi's rule in Hungary. Equivalent bodies implemented Stalinist terror in the other states. But in 1959 Kadar amended the powers of the Hungarian body and during the 1960s the office began to develop a new role as a public defender, since which time it has demonstrated a capacity to investigate in the public interest, even in such sensitive matters as corruption among party officials. Its new professionalism has not yet led to the development of the ombudsman potential of the office, but its evolution has been one of significant liberalisation.

Liberalisation of the Public Prosecutor's Office has been more limited in the other East European states, but in other respects judicial administration is similar. Development of the courts has been characterised by an increasing juridical professionalism since the death of Stalin, a pattern which is most apparent in the less controversial areas of judicial decision-making. The systems of prosecutor's offices are an important link between courts and the police, whose work is closely coordinated.

Rule-enforcement: the police

Although traditional interest in rule adjudication by social scientists has led to the production of a steady stream of research on the East European courts, relatively little empirical research has been conducted into the security apparatuses which are responsible for law enforcement. Thus an up-to-date knowledge of the workings of the courts is not accompanied by a similar availability of information about the police. Clearly most police work in Eastern Europe as elsewhere is routine and not particularly politically interesting. But the police, along with the military (to be discussed in Chapter 10), are the main source of coercive power, and have in the past been the linchpins of the repressive state apparatuses. In their political roles, as guardians of state security, the police played a considerable role in establishing the post-war regimes. But no equivalent to the substantial body of theory which informs the work of state socialist courts appears to inform their use of police terror. Hence neither Marxist canon nor solid empirical research enhance our knowledge of the state socialist security apparatuses. A 'secret police', by its very nature, is not amenable to scholarly scrutiny, whatever the nature of the political system in which it operates.

The information available comes from a range of sources and is patchy and incomplete. It should be treated with considerable caution, but does enable a few low-level generalisations. Stalin's apparatus of police control and his use of police terror to enforce his dictatorship are well documented, and a number of accounts illustrate the role of the East European secret police before de-Stalinisation (see Adelman, 1984). McCauley and Carter (1986, *passim*) have shown that many of the most important post-Stalin power struggles in Eastern Europe were those in which party leaders sought to gain control of their own security apparatuses. Such struggles seem to resurface during periods of crisis, and periodic arrests of dissidents remind us of the continuing existence of internal security forces. Bromke (1967, p. 163) has shown how the Polish security apparatus was brought under party control and considerably curtailed at the same time as it underwent an extensive purge of personnel after Gomulka's ascent to power in 1956. It is well known that the secret police were an important target of those who demanded reform during the Prague Spring, and that the Yugoslav police force was decentralised, its control devolved to the republics, after Rankovic fell from favour in 1966 (allegedly for placing the top party leadership, including Tito and Kardelj, under electronic surveillance). But it is important to remember that the security forces were controlled, they were not abolished. Recent reminders of the political role of the police include the harassment of members of the Czechoslovak dissident group, Charter 77, and the use of Yugoslav paramilitary forces to put down the Albanian riots in Kosovo during 1981. In Poland in 1984 the Popieluszko affair, in which four members of the security services were charged and convicted of the unauthorised murder of a dissident priest, led to a leadership clampdown on the Interior Ministry. Party General Secretary Jaruzelski assumed direct responsibility for the politbureau supervision of party work in the ministry, displacing Miroslaw Milewski, the central committee secretary and politbureau member who previously held that responsibility. Milewski resigned from all his party posts in 1985, and other senior members of the Interior Ministry were suspended from office (Lewis, 1985). The reasons for these manoeuvres are not known but it seems likely that Jarulzelski was taking further steps to ensure his control of the security forces at his disposal.

The changing role of the Hungarian police provides a useful example of the way in which East European elites have sought to reduce the autonomy of their political police. The Hungarian secret police had its powers curtailed during the 1960s. Originally the secret police grew from the political section of the state police. In March 1946 they were detached from the main police force and placed under the authority of the Ministry of the Interior. In December 1949 they were severed from the Ministry and made into a special department, the AVH (Allamvedelmi Hivatal or State Security Authority). The AVH cooperated closely with the Soviet MCD, which operated within Hungary until its occupied status ended. At the apogee of AVH power (from 1950 to 1952) it had official responsibility for the frontier police as well as internal security guards. By 1950 there were seventeen clerical divisions in AVH central offices handling everything from the surveillance of foreigners to the supervision of youth, social and cultural associations as well as espionage and counter-espionage. The AVH also ran the political prisons. Both the secret police and the state police assisted the Soviets after their invasion to suppress the 1956 Hungarian Revolution. Both forces were significant targets of attack during the uprising, a measure of their unpopularity with the citizenry (Adelman, 1984, pp. 175–6). From the time of Kadar's installation the force lost ground politically, but only in 1970 did a direct challenge to its power take place. In January that year Interior Minister Andras Benkei complained that the police were often inappropriately used as arbiters of disputes which did not involve illegality. He announced administrative decisions aimed at checking such proceedings and asked for a clear codification of his ministry's duties *vis-à-vis* those of other government ministries. On 25 October 1974 the Presidential Council issued a decree law on state public security which supplied a framework for the regulation of activities of the Ministry of the Interior. This was followed by a Council of Ministers' decree. The law now defines the tasks which are associated with state security in a set of extremely detailed regulations. The regulations were not sent to the National Assembly for approval, hence public discussion was avoided, but they are none the less evidence of a genuine control over the security forces by other agencies of government.

The available information on the political status of the East European 'secret police' indicates that a significant decline in power was experienced by security forces during de-Stalinisation, after which a modest recovery was made. Security officials appear to ensure their status through cohesiveness within the party rather than the state institutions, but police ministries (interior ministries) are no longer necessarily held by party politbureau members or central committee secretaries. the likelihood is that communist party leaders, mindful of the independent potential of a secret police force, share an interest in keeping the state security apparatus under the same close and careful control as their counterparts have established in other types of regime.

Institutional legitimation

So intertwined are the various apparatuses of the party–state and so overlapping are their functions that it is difficult to sustain analytical distinctions, which refer in the main to output. While Althusser's notions of the repressive and ideological state apparatuses point up the scope and complexity of the socialist state, they are less useful in distinguishing the functions of different state and party institutions. That distinction is better.illustrated by the concepts of the apparat--state and party–state. Clearly all three ideas enhance our understanding of state socialist institutions. Ultimately, however, it is difficult to determine with any certainty whether the institutions themselves rather than their policies have achieved any measure of legitimacy. Our discussion of the imposition of Stalinism and the subsequent development of the party–state has demonstrated the persistence, though with some modification, of structures whose contours were formed during the period of regime mobilisation. Perhaps the mere longevity of those structures, now 40 years old, has assisted their legitimation. Yet the capacity for survival of such institutions should not be confused with their effectiveness. Particular enhancing events and policies, such as the independent nationalistic stance adopted by the Romanian leadership or the successful economic strategies of the Kadar and Honecker regimes, have been important in securing popular support. But effectiveness alone is a precarious basis for a regime. The absence, except in Yugoslavia and Albania, of authentically national revolution inhibited, but normally did not preclude many of the cultural processes of legitimation which were available to the USSR, and which enabled institutions there to achieve a measure of popular regard. While pre-regime history may enhance the standing of a legislature, and national tradition may give credibility to the cabinet and the army, the institutionalisation of the party–state itself has been a more recent process.

The debate over the legitimacy of the state socialist systems is a complex and interesting one which we will take up in more detail in our concluding chapter. At this stage we would simply point out that those who would argue that the party–state in Eastern Europe has pacified rather than convinced its citizenry are dismissive of legitimacy based upon economic success and social provision. They point to the crises which often follow economic failure as evidence of their case. They probably underestimate the adaptive capacities of the party – state institutions and ignore the fact that not all economic difficulties have led to crisis. Most of the East European states were sufficiently well established to weather the considerable impact of the recession of the late 1970s with relatively little if any political upheaval. The party–state has a proven capacity to persist. Legitimation may come with time and will depend as much upon the standing of the party as on that of the state institutions.

10

Political Participation and Interest Articulation

It has been shown repeatedly in this text that there is no single model of politics which has the capacity to explain or predict all the important features of state socialist society. Our solution to the problems this presents has been to draw upon a variety of different models, on each occasion choosing those which are best suited to illuminate the processes and institutions we wish to describe and analyse. Accordingly we will begin the discussions of political participation and interest articulation in this chapter with a brief account of the relevant analytical models and the manner in which they may be applied. These accounts will be supplemented by a number of examples in an attempt to provide a thumbnail sketch of modes of participation and interest articulation in the various institutions which have been established for such purposes. It will become apparent that not all participation and interest articulation takes place in the relevant formal legal channels, and that a considerable amount of bargaining and negotiation may take place elsewhere. Often such spillover is accommodated by institutional adaptation of various kinds, but sometimes it goes beyond the boundaries of elite tolerance, taking the form of opposition to some aspect of the regime or its policies. Thus no discussion of participatory processes under state socialism will be complete without a consideration of its limitations, and we might best conceive of participation as part of a continuum which includes legal and non-legal activities alike.

Clearly in a study of eight different regimes over a 40-year period it will be difficult to make hard and fast distinctions about some activities. Legal activity shades into non-legal activity at different points in different countries at different times and it is difficult to draw the boundary between the two, even in a single country at a single point in time. This is an analytical problem in many studies of political action and we do not claim to have solved it here. Rather, we have opted first to discuss what are the mainly legitimate activities which have either been regime-directed or have arisen from the development and adaptations of various institutions. The main arena of participation, the communist party, has already been described in detail in Chapters 7 and 8, so here we take up the other arenas. Thus in Chapter 10 we cover the formal participatory arena, including elections, the mass organisations, and the media. This will accompany an outline of avenues of interest articulation and the various institutional groups. In Chapter 11 we extend our coverage to include more informal participation, political opposition and dissent.

Political participation

Important problems of studying political participation in Eastern Europe arise from the fact that the term is often defined in such a way that the political activity of individuals in state socialist society does not qualify as participation. The term participation is itself a controversial one, which is usually defined for the purpose of analysing liberal democracies. When state socialist systems are also considered, a wide definitional continuum becomes apparent. On one side there is the traditional Western notion of participation as action resulting in control over political leaders by the rational, informed activities of citizens who have considered the major policy alternatives. On the other there are images of totalitarian participation in which the citizenry are said to be manipulated and coerced into hyperactive support of policies formulated by self-opinionated, malevolent leaders who are impervious to public opinion. There also exists a more usable third median model lying somewhere along the continuum, which describes participation as real and psychologically satisfying to those who are engaged in it, but which is known by the cognoscenti (and the model-makers) to be based on a myth or self-delusion that such activity influences government (Little, 1976, p. 437).

Neither the citizen control nor the manipulated citizen model accurately describes political processes anywhere, but they do point up differences in the orientations of scholars specialising in the different types of political systems. A persistent idea in the literature on political participation is that the type which obtains in the liberal democracies is fundamentally different from that which is to be found under state socialism, and that the liberal democratic variant is somehow superior. That idea has been challenged, however. D. Richard Little (1976), in a comparison of political participation in the USA and the USSR, has argued that if mass rather than elite participation is the focus of study, different patterns emerge. He finds that the Soviet citizen participates more extensively in terms of the types of activities in which citizens engage, the conditions under which those activities take place and the significance they have for the system as a whole. He therefore takes up the claim that the participation of the Soviet citizen is somehow not genuine and assesses the insistence by many scholars that there are qualitative as well as quantitative dimensions to participation which are absent in the Soviet Union. The quality of state socialist participation is most often challenged by an assertion that there is a real difference between participation and mobilisation. Often related to such assertions is the statement that participation is significant only when it affects the 'input' side of politics, i.e. when it has a direct effect upon decision-making and policy-formulation. This is contrasted to 'output' side participation, which is regarded as obedient or mobilised participation.

In Little's view these distinctions are misconceived when mass rather than elite engagement is considered. He points out that, in practical terms, mobilising the Soviet masses differs little from Western public relations. The distinction between mobilisation and participation is a made up one which is both difficult to determine and difficult to sustain. Moreover, it diverts attention from what may be much more important questions about citizen activism in both types of system. There is a great deal of individual volition by Soviet citizens who choose whether or not to join the party, to be active, to seek political careers and so forth. The difference between the liberal democratic and state socialist systems is not to be found in the presence or absence of choice, but in the level of significance of such choices. Moreover, the complex and evolutionary nature of the real world of policy-making does not allow it to be understood by over simple and dichotomous formulations such as the input/output distinction, particularly given that the implementation process (output) is known to be an important defining stage. Finally, the view that competent citizen participation characterises the USA whilst subject participation predominates in the USSR does not square with what we know about American participation, which almost all of the available evidence suggests is engagement of a subject kind.

Little's arguments show that existing definitions of political participation carry ideological baggage which makes them less powerful as analytical tools than they might be. They do not assist the production of accurate descriptions of political processes because they assume that participation necessarily means an influence upon policy formulation. But that is to conflate two different phenomena. What is needed is a definition which separates acts of political participation from effects of influencing policy formulation. Such a definition enables both a comparison of participation in different political systems and a test of the impact of participation upon policy-making, as a separate next step in an analysis of participation and policy-making. Accordingly, political participation might be defined as the association of individuals in various types of political activities. Little's argument, which is clearly applicable to other political systems as well, is an important one, not only because it points out an area of discipline myopia but also because the resulting definition allows us to proceed in a fairly straightforward fashion with a description of East European participation. His assumptions may equally pre-determine our findings, in that they are postulated upon existing patterns of participation. Nevertheless, his approach is valuable in that it offers a different perspective and a sympathetic counterweight to more traditional approaches.

East European political participation varies in quantity by state, but takes a similar qualitative form throughout the region. The most important activities are, as we have seen, those which are to be found within the communist parties, which encompass between 8 and 17 per cent of all adult citizens. Membership is no longer confined to elite vanguards but encompasses many ordinary citizens. Activities around the various state and party mass organisations such as the Young Communists, the trade unions, the women's associations and the 'other' parties which exist in many of the countries, encompass millions more. One way and another political participation is extremely widespread. But it is by no means equal. Evident stratification patterns exist whereby socio-economic status is a correlate of political activity and party activity is a predictor of activity in other fora. Party membership is a precondition for rising in posts of responsibility, and gender, nationality, and ethnicity are also correlates of political activism (Bunce, 1983, p. 39).

The regimes aim to encourage and channel political participation, which carries a considerable amount of information regarded as important by elites, who have come to recognise the political importance of social diversity. There is recognition that various demands might be made by distinct social groups and interests. Divergences arising from non-antagonistic occupational differences are regarded as best revealed and resolved. They are not a problem for regimes which have increasingly sought to develop participatory mechanisms. Stephen White (1986) has noted these changes and outlines four means by which state socialist regimes have sought to strengthen their political structures, each of which is based on the development of participatory channels. Here we adapt his scheme to order our discussion of the processes of political participation and interest articulation. The participation of important groups has been accommodated in four ways: (1) political incorporation through membership of the ruling party, (2) the increased use of electoral mechanisms, and (3) the development of institutional intermediation via the emergence of various 'institutional' groups and the increased role of the associational groups, particularly the trade unions. Finally, there is the greater use of such generalised channels of citizen communication as letters to the press and the consultation of state officials. We have already considered the effects of developments within the communist parties in Eastern Europe, but each of White's other three 'mechanisms of adaption' has also been in use and merits discussion.

Elections

In common with all political systems which claim to be democratic, elections in state socialist Eastern Europe are an important arena of citizen activism. The elections feature large turnouts and considerable citizen participation, but they have not been designed to produce changes in government. Rather they have symbolic and educational importance, they are tangible demonstrations of popular unity and support for the regimes and they are an opportunity to put policies across and to celebrate achievements. But elections have more prosaic functions as well. They are, for example, an important part of information and communication networks. The electoral campaign brings a considerable number of persons together in organisational activity (over 25 per cent of the adult population in the USSR). Not only is this a means for the party to observe the activity of its members and candidate members, but also the widespread canvassing provides considerable information about complaints, discontents, and sources of irritation generally within the communities (see Zaslavsky and Brym, 1978). Moreover, elections are probably the most efficient possible mechanism for selecting the numerous deputies who represent local and national constituencies, and they also allow deputies to report back to their electorates. Such practical considerations are probably at least as important as educative and symbolic functions.

The East European elected assemblies have not been totally dominated numerically by the communist parties. 'Other' parties exist in Bulgaria (1), Czechoslovakia (4), the GDR (4) and Poland (2), and other organisations have nominating rights. Only in Romania has the communist party held every single seat in the national legislature and then only at first. Elsewhere seats are allocated to a variety of participating groups, associations and political parties. In contrast to the Soviet Union, the GDR, Hungary, Poland, Romania and Yugoslavia all allow for choice between candidates at certain stages of the electoral process, and Bulgaria and Czechoslovakia have also modified their electoral law to allow for multiple candidacies. The growing incidence of multiple candidacy is a process which White (1986) sees both as part of regime strategies to enhance the political aspects of their legitimacy and to increase the willingness of their citizens to accept unpopular decisions via an apparently greater influence over the choice of those who make them.

That being said, candidate selection demands considerable care, and attention is paid to achieving a balance between various types of candidate. Usually a National Front of the organisations and parties permitted to nominate candidates is responsible for running the elections. Key organisations as well as the 'other' parties and the mass associations are included in the fronts. In Poland three Catholic groupings are virtually guaranteed a presence in the Sejm.

In the GDR, for example, the National Front consists of the political parties – the Democratic Peasants Party (DBD), the Liberal Democratic Party (LDPD), the National Democratic Party of Germany (NDPD), the Christian Democratic Union (CDU) and the ruling SED – as well as the main mass associations of youth (FDJ), women (DFD), culture (KB) and trade unions (FDGB). Volkskammer elections are held every 5 years. Open meetings are held in each electoral district, at which delegates from various designated and other organisations propose candidates. These are then screened by the National Front, which selects lists of qualified candidates that are presented to additional public meetings. Candidates are normally listed in a preferred order, and there are usually a few more candidates than seats. The public meetings may, but rarely do, alter the initial ordering of candidates. Electors vote either by dropping an unmarked paper into the ballot box, in which case the top names are deemed to be selected, or by striking unwanted names from the list. The top names are elected unless deleted by a majority of voters, in which case the next name on the list is elected. Urban voters have rejected approved candidates, but such occurrences are rare. Volkskammer seats are allocated by agreement, and electoral lists are presented accordingly. Since 1963 the 500 seats have been divided as follows: SED 127, DBD 52, LDPD 52, DFD 35, NDPD 52, FDGB 68, FDJ 40, KB 22 (Childs, 1983, pp. 130–2; Scharf, 1984). The mass association candidates are often also SED members. The various 'other' parties have what are essentially interest group functions, allowing individuals who are not Marxist–Leninists to express their loyalty to the system. They are relatively small, but enable the representation of agricultural, professional and Christian interests.

The Hungarian example illustrates well the participatory capacities of East European elections. Large numbers of people are engaged in them, often for protracted periods of time. As in the GDR, individuals discuss and bargain over various kinds of specific and important, but essentially non-controversial and usually local, issues. Hungary has only one political party but also casts a wide net in the candidate selection and screening process. Nominations have been accepted from the floor of public meetings since 1971. Candidates need not be communists but must support the programme of the Patriotic People's Front (PPF), which organises national and local elections. Through its network of 4000 committees and over 110,000 members, it is also busy with such matters as organising special national minority conferences, providing fora for the discussion of local problems and mobilising individual and group action in support of national and local official policies. The PPF is an important institutional symbol of Kadar's alliance policy and its electoral centrality gives it a vital communications function. In 1983 a new electoral law required that at least two candidates had to be selected to run for 352 of 387 parliamentary seats, a culmination of efforts to democratise elections which had been in train since the 1960s. The organisation of the relevant meetings for the 1985 elections proved complex, straining the capacities of the PPF. The law (Article 38, Law 12) also required that at least two nomination meetings be held in each constituency. In 1985 there were an extra 400,000 participants in the nominating process and about 1.5 million people (of 7.8 million eligible voters) participated in 42,500 local council and 719 parliamentary nominating meetings, up from a total of 1.1 million in 1980. Of the 352 contested parliamentary seats, 298 had two candidates, 50 had three and 4 had four. In the local council elections four candidates stood in eighty-seven of the 42,500 districts, three in 2554 and two in each of the remainder. At the various nominating and other electoral meetings a variety of political issues were raised, ranging from specific community concerns over road conditions, water supply and transportation to general interest subjects such as the situation of the elderly and the problems of young people. Seventy candidates were nominated from the floor of meetings, nineteen of whom replaced original PPF nominees. Twenty-five National Assembly seats were won by independents (see Radio Free Europe Research, RAD Background Report/51 [Hungary], 5 June 1985).

Similar activity may be observed in the multi-stage, mainly indirect Yugoslav elections. There citizens approach voting in a threefold capacity: (1) as direct producers who elect delegates from among colleagues in enterprises, state institutions and the armed forces to Chambers of Associated Labour in the communal assemblies, (2) as consumers who (regardless of where they work) elect delegates to Chambers of Local Communities (10,000 local communities elect such delegates to 501 communes, hence many are combined for this purpose), and (3) as members of various mass political organisations (the LYC, the Socialist Alliance, and the unions) selecting delegates to the Socio-political Chambers of the communal assemblies. The tripartite divisions of councils is repeated at provincial and republican levels, where councils are elected by the corresponding lower bodies. The electoral process is a lengthy one, and in 1974, 1978 and 1982 took place in four phases, each of which lasted about a month. The first phase is the candidate selection process. Next comes the first level of election, in which 3,000,000 delegates are chosen to decide who will be selected for the higher bodies. In the third phase 100,000 of the delegates are selected for communal, provincial and republican assemblies, and, finally, each level of assembly meets to choose its executive.

Clearly if such elections do not resolve questions of political succession, they nevertheless permit a measure of popular participation in politics and are the site of at least some preliminary political bargaining. A number of scholars have argued that elections have been important political barometers in post-war Eastern Europe (Sakwa and Crouch, 1979; White *et al.*, 1982; Sanford, 1985) but their case remains unproven, as regimes have avoided holding elections during periods of weakened party control (Hungary 1956, Czechoslovakia 1968, Poland 1981–2), making it difficult to determine how far such capacities might be developed. Arguably local elections in Poland in 1984 and national elections in 1985 were useful indicators to a regime intent on normalisation policies. The local elections, although a modest success, were the site of some expressions of discontent and met with fairly low turnouts, indicating that considerable progress had to be made before the party could be confident that popular support would be forthcoming for Sejm elections in the Autumn of 1985. Held in October 1985, the Sejm electoral campaign was a sustained competition between the government's desire to demonstrate political stabilisation via a high turnout and the campaign run by underground Solidarity activists to demonstrate opposition strength and government unpopularity with a boycott of the ballot. Officially 78.86 per cent of the eligible electorate voted, which the government regarded as satisfactory but which was a marked contrast to the 1980 figure of 98.77 per cent. Solidarity leaders disputed the official figures and claimed turnout to be as low as 66 per cent. Official figures were higher by 4 per cent than the 1984 local turnout, hence were read by the government as an indicator of a growth in support. The figures remained in dispute, providing comfort for both sides (Radio Free Europe Research, Situation Report/18 [Poland], 8 November 1985).

Institutional intermediation

While elections are the most widely dispersed opportunities for adult participation, they are notoriously imprecise in the messages they are able to carry. In the absence of either leadership or policy alternatives their functions might best be described as participatory and informatory, but only minimally influential. Thus between the two major participatory structures of communist party and elections there exists a considerable intermediate area. On this terrain a considerable amount of interest aggregation takes place. Rarely will interests which are not directly represented by the party or effectively expressed in elections disappear, and party leaders recognise this. Each system contains a number of organisations designed to cover the various social, cultural and political interests deemed to be legitimate. As we have seen, these may include political parties other than the communist party. They also include trade unions, women's organisations and the youth movements. In some systems the churches play a more or less active and legitimate social role. Often regarded as mere transmission belts existing only to deliver policy decisions, the mass associations have from time to time played a more independent role. Moreover, recognisable 'interest groups' have also emerged within the state and party apparatuses.

The idea that the identification and analysis of political groups might be a useful approach to the study of state socialist systems was recognised in communist studies by the end of the Khrushchev era, but initial formulations were rather timid. Totalitarian theory was at first revised in various ways to produce such conceptualisations as 'totalitarianism without terror' or 'partialtarianism'. But as political change became more apparent in Khrushchev's USSR and evidence of political bargaining became more widely available, it became clear that totalitarian theory had been stretched to, if not beyond, its limits. Thus Skilling and Griffith's 1971 publication of *Interest Groups in Soviet Politics* struck a responsive chord in a discipline starved of methodological innovation.

Early interest studies were focused mainly upon the USSR, but two scholars, Gordon Skilling and Ghiţa Ionescu, gave their attention to events, processes and formations in East European society. Both based their arguments on the observation that no industrial society was free of plural groupings. Ionescu (1967) argued that the complexity of group formations in a society varied directly with the level of social development. The question was not one of whether or not groups existed, but of whether it was useful to regard them as political interest groups. In the course of a complex argument on the nature of plural checks in Eastern Europe, he outlined a classification scheme which focused upon possible sources of group activity. The model had four parts of which the first, the party-central apparat was the primary grouping. Other groups were classified according to the extent to which they might check the party. Thus the three remaining categories of Ionescu's scheme were the 'other' apparats, the socio-economic classes and groups and the legislature and the judicial organs, the information media and the cultural organisations. This model has the advantage of underlining the party's upper hand while recognising that it is subject to an increasing variety of influences. The 'other' apparats, such as the army, the security forces, the unions, the state and local administration, often have some constitutional power, their own 'esprit de corps' and, administratively, may be the rivals of the party. The socio-economic classes and groups are less cohesive than the apparats, but potentially dispose of a great deal of bargaining power. In the role of producers the workers have the added cachet of the status, if not all of the trappings, of a privileged political class. Finally, the constitutional and cultural bodies may also have a distinguishable interest, as might the press. Often ex-manifest, in the sense of having a pre-communist political experience, such structures may sometimes become centres of debate, and expressers of interests.

Brunner and Kaschkat (1979) also contend that a variety of interests operate within and across the institutions of state socialism. The most important and influential are those based upon functional considerations, which they divide into three categories: the power elite, the intelligentsia and the mass organisations, each of which may be further sub-divided. The power elite divides along the lines of the political sub-system and consists of four main sections: party officials, state officials, the military establishment and security officials. Of these, party officials are the most important group, but do not comprise a homogeneous interest – the ideologists tend to be

somewhat conservative while the organisers are more pragmatic and welcoming of change. Less significant but still very
important are the state officials, who are more specialised and
disparate than party officials. Their activities include economic, cultural, judicial and foreign service functions. Rather
less influential, but still having a role are members of the
military establishment. This, as we will show below, is a
relatively closed group whose members share common career
patterns and vested interests, although there are differences
between political and professional officers. Finally, security
officials tend also to be a cohesive group, but exchange
personnel with the party.

Brunner and Kaschkat's intelligentsia is divided into those
whose functions are technical–economic or scientific–
cultural. The technical–economic intelligentsia is differentiated by industrial sector and by type of training. Striking
differences occur between production-oriented engineers and
economics-trained managers (see above, Chapter 5). Both
these groups depend upon the state bureaucracy to assert
their interests while the scientific–cultural intelligentsia is
accommodated by a range of professional and cultural associations which vary from country to country in their willingness to express a group interest.

The various social organisations are attached to one or
other groups of officials. Thus youth and propaganda organisations rely upon party officials, paramilitary bodies are
associated with the army, and economically orientated and
sports associations rely on state officials in the relevant
services to express their interests. Analytically, the most
intractable problems are posed by the trade unions, which are
connected to the party, the state social and labour administrative apparatuses and the working class. Trade unions in
Eastern Europe follow the Soviet pattern of organisation
along industrial/production lines to act as transmission belts
between the workforce and the central administration. Each
country has a single trade union 'peak' organisation which
combines the various industrial unions (Table 10.1). In
common with the other socio-political organisations, the
unions operate according to the principles of democratic
centralism and their senior officials come under the *nomenkla-*

TABLE 10.1

Trade union 'peak' organisations in 1984

Country	Name	Membership	Chair
Albania	Trade Union Federation of Albania	610,000	Sotir Kocallari
Bulgaria	Central Council of Trade Unions	c.4,000,000	Petur Djulgerov
Czechoslovakia	Revolutionary Trade Union Movement		
GDR	Free German Trade Union Federation (FDGB)	9,100,000	Tisch
Hungary	National Council of Trade Unions	9,500,000	Lajos Mehes
Poland	National Trade Union Accord	4,900,000	
Romania	General Union of Romanian Trade Unions	7,000,000	Lina Ciobanu
Yugoslavia	Confederation of Trade Unions of Yugoslavia	5,500,000*	

* 1981 figure.

Source: Staar (1984, 1985).

tura of the party. Such constraints limit the unions' capacities to represent the workforce. Pravda (1983, p. 246) emphasises the impotence of the official unions, pointing out that they rarely possess information that the government wants, and that they have nothing of substance to offer in return for concessions. If at shopfloor level veiled threats of non-cooperation may persuade management, no such tactics are available to senior union officials. For them the only available strategies are to influence the general climate of government opinion and to try to gain party support where their views conflict with those of the ministry. Nevertheless, between 90 and 95 per cent of the economically active population belong to trade unions. The reason is that the cost of non-membership is high. Besides managing labour on behalf of the enterprise director, trade unions in state socialist societies distribute social welfare benefits as well as fringe benefits of various kinds. They also perform much the same functions as trade unions in liberal democracies in the representation of workers in disciplinary cases and sometimes in grievance cases brought against management.

The union structure in the GDR typifies most of the East European states. The FDGB federates sixteen component unions and includes about 97 per cent of all employed persons. Some 80 per cent of trade unionists do not belong to a political party. Elsewhere, a similar pattern is followed. Since the 1970s, however, there have been a number of indications that mass trade unionism has outlived its usefulness in Eastern Europe, and that such organisations are insufficiently flexible to cope with the demands of enterprise politics as they are presently conducted. Union officials have tended to make their careers by playing down conflicts of interest in the workplace, a strategy better designed to secure their own advancement than to promote members' interests. Pliability and experience in the party administration or management are more likely to lead to appointments to union positions than trade-union experience. Their limited scope and power and detailed supervision by the party mean that union careers are not sought by the most able and ambitious, a fact which further reduces the role of unions as interest organisations (Pravda, 1983). Although more resourceful at the workplace than at national level, trade unions have on several occasions proved deaf to workforce pressures. Nowhere was this more evident than Poland. In 1956 there was a movement for democratically elected workers' councils, in 1970 for unofficial factory committees and after 1976 for free trade unions, a development which culminated in the birth of Solidarity in 1980. Solidarity was a trade union of a type new to state socialist Eastern Europe. It was organised on the basis of inter-factory strike committees, its operations extended beyond the workplace and it did not confine itself to 'economistic' issues. Its innovative horizontal forms of organisation were a direct response to worker experience of the official, vertically organised unions, Ultimately Solidarity became more akin to a nationwide social movement than a trade union, posing a political threat to the regime, which made its suppression inevitable. By contrast, in Hungary the regime itself initiated modifications to union practices during the 1970s and 1980s. In both systems the problem was one of ensuring an adequate arena for the expression of working-class interests. This is an issue we take up in more detail in Chapter 11. Here we simply note that it appears that the transmission belt model may no longer be the appropriate union form.

Although evidence from the different countries indicates that mass trade unionism finds less favour than once it did in Eastern Europe, the utility of the mass association form for other social groups is still highly regarded. Both the mass and the professional organisations are associational groups in that they consist of individuals who already have something in common. Groups such as these are strictly controlled through systems of state licensing which are imposed on all organisations from the state-run mass associations to cultural societies. All groups must register, but the range of permitted associations is wide, and genuine services and facilities are provided by them. They are therefore supported by their target populations. Outside Poland there is practically no evidence that organised youth, for example, is seeking alternative structures. Youth movements are country-wide social organisations which usually contain student and pioneer organisations. Along with the schools, the youth organisations are the major public instrument for socialising children into regime values. Membership is voluntary. Pioneer organisations tend to include nearly all children but youth leagues are less embracing (Table 10.2). Members are offered all sorts of activities, from art clubs to holiday camps, from football teams to orchestras, in fact the same range which would normally be provided by the voluntary sector in Western Europe. In Eastern Europe, as in Canada, the USA and Australia, such activities are provided by a body organised around the school.

The senior level of party youth is more overtly political. The youth leagues are organisations for older adolescents and young adults (up to almost 30 years old). With the exception of Poland between 1956 and 1973, these were modelled on the Soviet Komsomol. They are unitary organisations which cover the range of youth activities for senior school pupils, students in higher education, young workers, farmers and

TABLE 10.2

East European communist youth organisations in 1984

Country	Youth organisation	Membership	Leader
Albania	Union of Labour Youth of Albania (ULYA)	—	Mehmet Elezi
Bulgaria	Dimitrov Communist Youth League	1,500,000	Stanka Shopova
Czechoslovakia	Socialist Youth Union		
GDR	Free German Youth (FDJ)	2,300,000	Eberard Aurich
Hungary	Communist Youth League	874,000	György Fejti
Poland*			
Romania	Union of Communist Youth (UTC)	5,200,000	Nicu Ceausescu
Yugoslavia	League of Socialist Youth of Yugoslavia	3,800,000	

*See text pp. 300–1.
Source: Staar (1985).

members of the armed forces. Although mass organisations, they are also the main 'feeder' associations for the communist parties and often play a role in national politics. In the GDR for example, the Free German Youth League has recruited about 75 per cent of the eligible population. Organised along democratic centralist and territorial production lines, the FDJ has 30,000 deputies in local government bodies at various levels and forty deputies in the Volkskammer. Although the question of 'youth' has exercised the regimes at various times (see Chapter 12), widespread demands to alter the youth movements to become genuine articulators of interest have been rare. But within particular institutions they have a role to play, and they offer members the possibility of activity on a national scale. The leagues play an important part in school life and are particularly active in higher education. Here they usually have representatives on the college or factory councils and sit on committees dealing with the admission of students and the payment of grants. Their role as the official channel of communication between students and staff, their political connections and their place in the administrative machinery all enhance their power in higher education institutions. From such positions students became integral parts of the reform movements in Poland and Hungary in 1956, in Czechoslovakia after 1963 and in Poland in 1968 and 1980/81. The inability of student branches of youth organisations to contain the demand for reform generated a variety of breakaway groups, many of which achieved considerability. Indeed in Poland in 1980-1 the official Union of Polish Socialist Youth ceased to be regarded as the legitimate representative of Polish youth. In Czechoslovakia, where students played an important role in the reform movement, in 1968 there were moves to sub-divide the youth movement into its functional components and to federalise the organisation. After the Warsaw Pact invasion these changes were reversed. In Poland the youth organisation has been in a state of flux since martial law was declared in 1981. The small communist Union of Polish Youth, which had never been officially recognised, was disbanded in December of 1982. At the time of writing a variety of organisations are permitted to organise young people, including the Polish Socialist Youth Union, the Rural

Youth Union, the Polish Scouts Union and the Socialist Union of Polish Students. These have all signed a joint declaration of Principles on the Cooperation of Socialist Youth.

The remarkable quiescence of the various youth movements may be due simply to the fact that an organisation so widely conceived subsumes rather than expresses the interests of what must be a highly stratified and diverse membership. The component sections are likely to pursue their interests in other channels. Thus student demands may be channelled through institutional structures in their educational establishments, e.g. in the faculty or college councils on which they have representation. Student dissent, where it has existed, has tended to be part of intellectual dissent rather than representative of youth discontent. Similarly, young workers have expressed their interests within class rather than generation-based structures. The youth organisations may have important mobilising functions in that they organise social and political activities for large numbers of young adults, including millions who are unlikely ever to become party members, but their role as interest mediators has yet to be demonstrated.

Women's organisations have also been poor articulators of their members' interests and may have been unsuccessful mobilising organisations, as women are generally less politically active than men. In Albania, Czechoslovakia, the GDR and Yugoslavia a mass women's association is structured along territorial lines and closely supervised by party cadres. In Poland, Hungary, Bulgaria and Romania the mass women's associations were disbanded in the 1950s and replaced by national committees of prominent women who are called upon to give advice on women's questions. The mass organisations of women which still operate act as a form of pressure group with fairly limited power and are social and educational institutions of a traditional women's kind. These organisations tend to be quite hostile to Western feminist movements. Indeed the prevailing conception of organisation in Eastern Europe, whereby all institutions have as their stated purpose the execution of party policy and the mobilisation of their constituencies for the fulfilment of party goals, precludes the inclusion of officially unrecognised interests. Feminism is not officially approved, having definitively fallen out of favour in the USSR in the 1920s and never having been ideologically reinstated. Early Soviet policies on the political organisation of women set a pattern which was later followed by other state socialist systems. An independent women's movement was regarded as inadmissible and feminism was seen as divisive. Hence women's organisations were created in the standard mass association transmission belt image, although over the years some variations in format have occurred, particularly in countries experiencing labour shortages and acute fertility decline. Such phenomena may explain why women's issues appear to be taken more seriously by elites in the 1970s and the 1980s. In both Romania and Bulgaria chairpersons of national women's committees were appointed to politbureaux in the 1970s. Women's committees are attached to the trade unions in all the states and in the GDR, uniquely, a women's party organisation exists. Elsewhere, however, a separate women's interest is not officially recognised within the party, women's interests are neither well articulated nor well represented.

In the absence of evidence to the contrary, we must assume the mass associations adequately perform interest articulation functions only where the relevant issues are non-controversial, where there is no conflict between official and group definitions of an interest. As mechanisms they appear to be poorly designed to forestall discontent or to collect information. Their vertical channels work mainly downwards. This is not to say that their structures are not used by strategic groups seeking to advance an interest; the associations may often be used for such strategies. But their power is severely limited by their lack of independence.

The mass associations are only one institutional form of interest intermediation. Another, possibly more important, form is to be found in the emergence of informal groups within institutions, examples of which include various groups of professionals or experts distributed throughout the state and party bureaucracies. Two such examples, those of the managers and the planners, have been illustrated in the discussion of economic reform in Chapter 5. In a party–state an interest wishing to press its claims requires party support if it is to be successful. Indeed support from party officials is a necessary if not a sufficient condition for an interest to prevail. The party seeks to contain and control various possible interests, as a result of which alliances undoubtedly form between the party officials with the relevant supervisory tasks and the group they seek to control. Personnel overlap has an effect in that functions become integrated. Partial fusion of this kind is widespread in modern bureaucracies, but perhaps best developed in the party–state.

Pre-eminence within the bureaucracy is not sufficient, however, to make the parties confident of their control over all groups, and considerable care has been taken to ensure controls over the security forces (see Chapter 9) and the military. Interesting both as an example of a strategic group in state socialist systems and in its own right, the politics of the East European military warrant detailed attention here. As a structure with professional interests, an institutional identity and capacity for armed warfare, the military are at least potential rivals for political power. The capacities of the armed forces have been controlled by political monitoring, by socialisation and by benefits and positive inducements. There is a strong encouragement for officers to join the communist party, membership of which is a prerequisite to promotion above a certain level. Ninety-eight per cent of GDR and 85 per cent of Polish and Bulgarian military officers are party members. Once in the party, an officer's private and political activities are more easily monitored. He or she is subject to party discipline, and party meetings have a socialisation function. Military matters are controlled by a central committee department in each country and all military political matters are controlled by the main political directorate or its equivalent (the central committee department responsible for promotion and personnel matters). The main political directorate supervises the work of party organisations at each level of the military command. An extensive political education programme in the military aims at sponsoring both socialist patriotism and socialist internationalism. Finally, clandestine security operatives are believed to have a considerable presence in the forces (Kramer, 1985).

Socialist internationalism is in fact an important political inhibition to the East European officer corps, which has not been nearly as engaged in military related policy formulation as have officers in the USSR, largely as a result of Soviet domination of Warsaw Pact decision-making in military matters (see Chapter 13). Decisions on defence expenditure are a subject for Soviet political leaders and the leadership of the country concerned. Lobbying by East European military staff will include attempts to influence their Soviet colleagues. The upshot of all of this is that there is a significantly lower presence of military representatives on high level decision-making bodies in Eastern Europe than in the USSR (Herspring and Volgyes, 1980).

In general, the East European officer corps is characterised by high morale resulting from high prestige (except in Hungary) and significant fringe benefits and remuneration. Only in Czechoslovakia have these instrumental inducements been insufficient to maintain morale, a product of Warsaw Pact military occupation. Salaries for officers are well above those for ordinary citizens and priority access to housing, health care and fringe benefits number among the inducements to a military career. The armed forces are also a significant channel of upward social mobility, all of which enhances loyalty to the party (Kramer, 1985).

Interestingly, East European armed forces have consistently failed to support regimes when confronted with serious internal disturbances. In Pilsen in 1953 the army refused to put down riots. In East Berlin in 1953 some soldiers refused to leave their barracks to march on demonstrators. In Poznan in 1956 the army refused to disperse rioters and in some cases joined them. In Budapest in 1956 the armed forces refused to support a regime faced by armed attacks on police headquarters and 80 per cent of Hungarian officers initially refused to sign pledges of support for the Kadar regime after Soviet intervention. In Czechoslovakia in 1969 58 per cent of officers under 30 left the army at their own request after the 1968 invasion. The Polish army strongly resisted the task of putting down the 1970 Gdansk riots and then defence minister Jaruzelski is reported to have declared in 1976 that Polish soldiers would not fire on Polish workers who were demonstrating in Lodz and Warsaw (Herspring and Volgyes, 1980).

Before the 1981 military takeover in Poland there were only a few potentially significant instances of military intervention in East European politics, none of which amounted to a planned military coup. Thus, while the military's loyalty is apparently conditional, it does not have political ambitions (see Herspring and Volgyes, 1977, 1980). Its interests are professional ones, hence its political roles are specific. Nevertheless, the martial law experience in Poland followed the growing political role of the army during 1981. Basically the military became increasingly politically engaged as official responses to the challenge of Soldarity became more manifestly inadequate. The Polish army was acting in accordance with party wishes and the initial martial crackdown was carried out by the security forces rather than the army. However, the year of formal military rule was directed by the military command. It was a year during which formal military powers replaced the Communist Party as the supreme political authority in the country. The army was the only regime pillar which retained its cohesion and ability to act in a crisis during which most official institutions were collapsing. But its role ultimately was to act in such a way that those institutions might be restored.

The army also has a special role in Yugoslavia, which has one of the largest land forces in Europe and where an all-people's populist defence system has been in place since 1968. Each unit is under an army chief, but the structure is based upon the home-guard type of guerrilla organisation which was used during the wartime resistance movement. The military is represented politically in the Chambers of Associated Labour. In ethnic terms, although the army contains a disproportionate number of Serbian and Montenegrin officers, it is, and sees itself as, a genuine all Yugoslav institution, a guarantor of the country's integrity in the face of fissiparous local nationalisms. As a respected institution, the army draws considerable strength from its origin as a partisan force during the Second World War (Zaninovich, 1983).

The militarisation of GDR society has been a political issue in a country which perceives a constant military threat. The SED is the only GDR political party allowed to operate in the

GDR army, whose character as a responsive force is also enhanced by its position in the Warsaw Pact. Strategically important, the GDR has engaged recently in a considerable militarisation of its educational system, which has chrystalised religious dissent there (Holmes, 1981; Mushaben, 1984; and see Chapter 11).

Growing professionalisation, modernisation, the rise and fall of 'detente', variations in the perceived level of threat from the West, as well as the tensions between socialist internationalism and national feeling, all mediate party control of the military. Career advancement rests both upon technical skill and political reliability. Officer classes have since 1956 been indigenous, although most have received some training in the Soviet Union. Variations between states reflect both cultural differences and political circumstances. A strong Polish military tradition has given the army there considerable pride and prestige, but has made it more of an autonomous force, although its experiences of direct rule may have undermined both its prestige and its *esprit de corps*. A careful party control over the GDR army defends an artificially constructed state. In post-invasion Czechoslovakia the army is politically isolated, while, slowly, the Hungarian armed forces have ceased to be regarded with suspicion by a government mindful of their unsupportive role in 1956. Today Hungary has what is probably the least politically significant military of any state socialist society. In Romania the military has been at odds with the regime over its deviations from Warsaw Pact policies. However, the political role of the East European military has been considerably reduced since the interwar period. In the mid-1980s it is a well established but well controlled strategic group whose compliance is ensured by a strong affinity of interests among top party officials and military elites (Kramer, 1985).

The military is an institutional interest in that its organisations have explicit purposes other than pressing group claims upon political leaders or bringing together individuals with a common characteristic or concern. Much weaker are the groups which arise from territorial and national divisions that might form in the central, regional and local levels of administration, each of which is a political sub-system with a small degree of autonomy. Local interests clearly exist but local administrators are also part of their vertical administrative and professional hierarchies, i.e. the party, the planning apparatus and so forth, which cross-cut horizontal allegiances. Nevertheless the weight of territory may be important in the larger countries, and national considerations play an important part in the interest politics of multi-national states. Another type of interest group which sometimes emerges is based on personnel considerations. These are rather more *ad hoc*, deriving their cohesion from the fact that their members have gone through important stages of their lives together. In the Soviet Union, for example, a large proportion of the Brezhnev group came from around Dnepropetrovsk, where Brezhnev grew up and received his training. Three such groups in Eastern Europe were the 'Muskovites', so-called because they returned at liberation with the Red Army; the 'illegals', who had stayed put and worked underground in the resistance; and those who had spent the war years in the West. A notable and distinctive group were the Titoist partisans of Yugoslavia, but a modern example is the group around Honecker in the GDR, whose members began their political careers in the youth organisation where Honecker was first secretary from 1946 to 1955 (Brunner and Kaschkat, 1979).

Although the outline structure of a group system may be discerned without too much difficulty, there are problems with demonstrating that the groups have an influence. Brunner and Kaschkat (1979) take an institutional approach to this question, identifying four main methods of influence: (1) contact with power-wielding agents, (2) the use of advisory roles, (3) representative activity in power, and (4) public expressions of opinion. Their different methods of influence are specific to particular groups. Contact with power-wielding agents best suits members of the power elite who have access to the top organs of the party and the state. Top security and military advisers are likely to have direct access, while the intelligentsia's access may be indirect via the appropriate department, ministry or academy. As in the West, only at the very top will there be an overlap of direct and indirect, formal and informal and personal contact, and it is at this level that group activities will be most effective but most difficult to demonstrate.

Making use of advisory roles is a strategy most available to the intelligentsia, whose knowledge is required by the party and the state leadership. Such processes normally take place in specialist committees, which are partly *ad hoc*, partly institutionalised into the party and state. Representation on power-wielding bodies is an important basis for exercising influence and is well documented by students of communist politics, who have carefully counted the differential presence of party and state officials and functionaries of various kinds in the politbureaux, the central committee secretariats, the central committees and their auditing commissions. In each case it is the party officials who have the upper hand, but other groups also have a consistent presence, including the trade unions, the military, the security officials and, at central committee level, the intelligentsia. Access to the apparatus of power is a privilege enjoyed by certain groups and not by others, indicating a stratified interest structure.

The Brunner and Kaschkat model is useful in its clarity and detail. In effect their approach highlights a continuum of proximity to the policy-making centre, citing differing degrees of institutional penetration as group resources. It is in many respects similar to Ionescu's model of plural checks, with its focus on the party central apparat. Ultimately Brunner and Kaschkat assume but do not demonstrate that the represented groups have preferences and that these are expressed in the course of their official duties. The failure to demonstrate a group effect is an important problem in the application of group theory to East European politics, and we return to it in the conclusions of this chapter. First, however, we must describe the more generalised channels of citizen participation and mobilisation.

Mass communication, participation and mobilisation

Stephen White (1986, pp. 226–8) reminds us that as elections take place infrequently, as party members represent only a small proportion of the population, and even trade union membership represents only the employed workforce, there is still a need for mechanisms of access for the whole population. Here he refers not only to the encouragement of letters to party and state officials, but above all to the press, describing a variety of examples of 'espistolatory democracy' whereby the press have opened complaints columns which are well used by the citizenry and which are known to be closely followed by officialdom.

White regards such trends as an indication of institutional adaptation in that they increase the possibilities for effective participation. But considerable control is maintained over newsprint and printing presses and over the actual content of what is published. Publications are subject to systems of approval or licensing. In addition, the size of print run for each publication is controlled, a practice which may be regarded as a form of state management of information flow, if not actual censorship. Some exceptions are made for religious groups, which often have their own presses and may issue their own journals, but within well defined guidelines. The strongest controls are exercised over media and journalism of all kinds. Journalists themselves are privileged members of society. They are well aware of the limitations of acceptable reporting; hence most of the states rely upon the kinds of pressures they can exert on journalists and editors to control the news rather than on overt censorship. By 1982 only Poland and Czechoslovakia still had systems of pre-publication review (Curry, 1982). But not everything goes the party's way. A recent report in *The Guardian* (21 July 1986) on the unofficial press in post-Solidarity Poland asserted that the underground's published material was so well organised that anyone could get hold of a copy of an underground newspaper if he or she wanted it badly enough. By contrast, some of the best informed state publications could not be had two days after publication, as their limited print runs meant they were sold out almost immediately. The press role varies somewhat between the countries, and it may have an ombudsman function whereby individual grievances are highlighted and publicised, but this rarely extends to general criticism, and criticism of the system itself is never acceptable. The

Western press is not permitted to circulate, but the regimes have been unable to prevent the transmission and receipt of Western broadcasting services. In the GDR most of the population is able to receive Federal Republic television transmission. Access varies both over time and by group. On occasion issues are thrown open for public discussion, and they receive encouragement from the official press. Group expression is probably greatest in Hungary, where the media are relatively loosely controlled.

In fact the East European media have long been part of the participatory apparatus, recent developments having simply made them more open. Public expressions of opinion are clearly a form of indirect access to decisionmakers. But in the absence of a guaranteed freedom of speech, the game is rather different from that in liberal democratic systems. Mass media under state socialism are partly controlled, giving party and state officials the most leeway. Trade unions are also in a favoured position, possessing their own daily newspapers. The army, too, has its own media, but, except in the Soviet Union, ministries of defence do not and neither do the security organs. The techno-economic intelligentsia is dependent on party and government media but has some recourse to specialist technical and professional journals, as does the scientific–cultural intelligentsia. Thus there is considerable variation in the extent to which different groups may find expression in the media, an observation which strengthens the case that a stratified hierarchy of interests obtains in Eastern Europe.

Summary and discussion

This chapter has shown that a variety of forms of participation exist in the East European countries and that some of these may be more effective than others. In particular, elite participation has more effect on policy that has mass participation. We would be surprised if it were otherwise. We have also shown that there are a number of important unsolved problems attending the study of interest group politics in Eastern Europe, and that the original promise of applying interest group theory to state socialist systems has yet to be fulfilled. All the concepts used in the study of state socialist interest articulation were developed for the study of liberal democracies and borrowed, modified and applied to other types of systems. Ideally such innovation enhances the comparability of studies of different types of political system, but there are limits to how far a concept may be stretched yet retain its analytical core. In general, the differences between studies of liberal democratic and state socialist systems have been of degree rather than kind. Politics at the top, where most decisions are made, is highly secret in all systems, and researchers' problems of access have been considerable everywhere. Proof that much could be learned about groups in Eastern Europe came in the form of detailed studies of them (for example, Lane and Kolankiewicz, 1973) but, as Holmes (1981, pp. 22–3) reminds us, these tended to stop short at the point of showing evidence of actual group influence. A consistent difficulty in the literature has been in specifying the activities and issues over which groups have intervened. Although considerable attention was given to the part played by social organisations, professional groupings and movements in state socialist systems, the continuing preponderance of the party was proof that the pluralist model was ultimately inapplicable and scholars continued to search for alternatives to totalitarian theory.

One body of scholarship recognises the elements of truth in both totalitarian and plural theory and has sought to devise an intermediate model which takes these into account. The bureaucratic or administrative politics model has been extremely influential since the mid-1970s and appears in a variety of guises (for example Hough's 'institutional pluralism' and Rigby's 'administered society). Its core idea is that bureaucratic organisations are not simply a means for achieving collectively agreed ends, they also protect divergent individual or group interests. Plans and rules are thus simultaneously instruments for coordinating activity and shields with which bureaucrats protect their freedom of action. Thus administrative structures, apparats, bureaucracies or whatever we choose to term them are contradictory phenomena. They contain individuals and groups competing for advantage. Such competitors learn skills which enable them to secure private or group privileges. Those skills include the capacity to manipulate the organisational apparatus, the highest avowed purpose of which is to promote the public interest. While there is no single logic of bureaucratic action, a universal struggle to reconcile private advantage and public collective purpose exists in bureaucratic politics. Hence a bureaucracy may be treated analytically as a structure (though one with a distinctive history) and bureaucratic politics as a framework for a system of bargaining which takes place within that structure.

Bureaucratic politics exist in a variety of political systems and are not exclusive to Eastern Europe in particular or state socialist systems in general. But the party–state generates its own kind of bureaucratic politics. Its particular ideological and functional imperatives give rise to three defining characteristics, each of which has important political implications: (1) the explicit claim that the state socialist system is superior to other systems, which gives rise to the measurement of achievement in economic terms; (2) the party monopoly over planning, which gives it too much stake in that process, leading to the over-institutionalisation of planning mechanisms and structures; and (3) the claim that political control rests with the working class, which requires credible substantiation of some kind (Sabel and Stark, 1982). Each of these characteristics also has implications for the articulation of interests: the supremacy of the party is underlined, the critical position of the working class is highlighted and enterprise politics are emphasised. At the enterprise level it is possible to demonstrate a clear group influence (see Chapter 11).

One of the problems of analysing East European interest politics is its changing nature. Group activity has varied in degree, intensity and scope, both over time and by country. It has been substantial in Poland, Yugoslavia and Czechoslovakia at different times and risen to unprecedented expression in Poland and Czechoslovakia during periods of radical reform. Both examples show that when groups become radical and their activity becomes continuous it is supressed, and its original more modest forms may also be suppressed. Thus, except in periods of radical reform, interest politics in Eastern

Europe never meets the minimum criteria of Western pluralism (neither, as it happens, does much of Western interest activity). Hence it has been argued that the study of interest groups is inappropriate to state socialist systems, that the relevant concepts do not stretch as far as they need to go (see Skilling, 1984). The parameters on debate and the central role of the party keep numerous alternatives off the political agenda. Many issues never get discussed, and interests, where evident, do not so much demand as request (Holmes, 1981, pp. 268–9). But this does not mean that interest politics should be ignored; it means rather that the modest incidence of such politics should be recognised. The advantage of the bureaucratic politics model is that it does precisely that. It does not conflate interest articulation with pluralism. It hypothesises a modest degree of extra-party political bargaining. It enables the recognition both of the centrality of the party and the constraints within which party leaderships operate, elements which seem to us to be essential requirements of any usable model of East European politics.

11

Political Accommodation: Interests, Opposition and Dissent

The arrangements for political participation and interest articulation which we described in Chapter 10 are essentially devices for the management of political demand. Directed at key social categories and important strategic groups, these extra-party channels tend to be over-controlled and are, in practice, often incapable of processing unanticipated demands, especially those that are radical or innovative. In such circumstances patterns of opposition and dissent may emerge, often as an overspill of demand from legitimate channels. Under state socialism interests are likely to have coalesced in all of the institutional structures from which demands might be made. As we have seen, specialist interests have outlets within the party and, less satisfactorily, the state structures. But while such groups as the military and branches of the bureaucracy are well integrated with the party, other groups have more pronounced 'outsider' status and the articulation of their interests is therefore more likely, when it occurs, to rely on political protest and/or dissent. Some of this has been episodic (for example Solidarity in Poland or the widespread group challenges which characterised the Prague Spring). Other interests have been more persistent and have become a regular, if less than welcome, feature of the East European political landscape. Examples here are the churches and the nationalities. Human rights groups such as Charter 77 and

various protests by intellectuals have also been, if not persistent, then recurrent features of the East European political
scene. Each of these will be discussed in this chapter.

First, however, we shall consider the protest potential of a
more central group. Amongst 'insiders' in Eastern Europe the
white-collar strata are well catered for by the party and
possess, in addition, their various professional organisations.
But it has, ironically, been the working class whose participation and representation has most exercised the regimes.
Although the party is its theoretical and political vanguard,
the working class is also represented by the mass trade-union
movements in each system. Central to regime legitimating
ideology and officially possessed of a considerable organisational arsenal, East European industrial workers have an
ostensible political advantage. Consideration of how (or if)
that advantage is used must therefore be a major part of any
discussion of East European interest politics.

Working-class politics

An appreciation of the political place of the East European
industrial working classes will turn on two related questions.
We must ask, firstly, if there is such an analytically distinct
entity as a working-class interest and, secondly, what evidence
is there that a particular working class recognises such an
interest? The answer to the first question is not so obvious as it
might seem. The regime's ideological base in the working class
makes it extremely difficult for the party to recognise workers'
interests which are additional to and not coincidental with
official goals. Hence their articulation is a problem, particularly given that the trade unions are not normally in a position
to play such a role. Our answers may be complicated by the
fact that the classes differ from state to state. Manual workers
are the largest social group in all the countries except Yugoslavia and Albania, but their cohesiveness varies both between
and within countries, as it is affected both by differences in
composition and internal gradients of skill. In general manual
workers experience income disadvantages by comparison to
non-manual groups and are also disadvantaged in social

consumption in Hungary, Poland and Yugoslavia. Class identification is apparently high, however, and attitude data indicate that most workers feel themselves to be short of political influence. According to Alex Pravda (1981), the East European working class has a concept of socialism which centres on full employment, a relatively easy day's work for steady pay, reasonable and stable living standards and the minimisation of pay differentials. Johnson (1981) also sees the 1970s East European working class as quiescent and conformist. This, he argues, was due to the effective abolition of material insecurity in ridding the economies of the threat of cyclical unemployment, high rates of upward social mobility, which enabled the majority to evaluate their situation as having been improved, and regime effectiveness at socialisation through mobilisation. Here, then, is the implicit social compact upon which working-class political quiescence is said to be based. In that social compact is an answer to both our questions. It entails both a clear class interest and its recognition.

But what happens when that social compact is threatened? By the end of the 1970s it had become clear that regimes could not always meet their side of the bargain. Moreover, the compacts as they were understood made systems difficult to reform because preferred strategies might cause short-term unemployment for some groups and rising prices for some goods. Rising expectations aggravated matters and reform packages which depended on pay differentials as a part of incentive schemes proved difficult to sell to a class which was increasingly self-recruiting and self-interested (Pravda, 1981; Johnson, 1981).

To assess the working-class responses to such perceived threats we need first to outline its political role. Aggregate national indicators are not that revealing. For example, Czechoslovak, Hungarian and Polish survey research shows that about three-quarters of workers claim to be interested in politics. About one-quarter are highly interested, just under half are mildly interested and the remainder are indifferent. But avowed interest is not matched by high levels of political knowledge. A Hungarian survey during the 1960s revealed that a majority of blue-collar workers could not name the ruling party and, more recently, two respondents thought that Khrushchev was president of the United States (incidentally, by international comparison, such results are respectable). In general, such surveys indicate that working-class political knowledge and interest, especially in national politics, is stratified along occupational lines. Politicians are not highly regarded and a certain disdain for politics is apparent. But interest is higher in local and particularly in enterprise matters, where it is conceived of not only in instrumental and material terms but also involves a high valuation of equality (Pravda, 1981, pp. 45–6).

Working-class political activity may take place on several levels. Common participation in occasional official mass demonstrations and voting in elections has been so inclusive that its analysis has little to offer an understanding of class activity. But other forms of activism are more important. Participation in social and political organisations such as the communist party and the unions engages about two-thirds of the workforce in minimal and about one-quarter to one-fifth in moderate activity. One in ten workers is highly active. But workers are significantly under-represented amongst political activists as a whole. Moreover, there is a significant positive correlation between levels of skill and activism within the class. Within the communist party the most active continue to be the technical intelligentsia. There are a number of reasons for this. Firstly, party recruitment policies are implemented in an environment of different propensities to activism by manual and non-manual workers. The demands of party membership are better coped with by white-collar individuals, whose life styles and educational advantages are political resources. Secondly, party membership is more beneficial to the white-collar stratum. It enhances their promotion prospects. But amongst manual workers, and especially amongst the unskilled, such advantages do not obtain. For them the political clout which party membership brings may be offset by the demands of party activity (Pravda, 1981).

The East European regimes have enhanced the political roles of their industrial workforces by comparison to liberal democratic systems, but have by no means achieved either the working-class parity, or indeed the dominance, the official ideology decrees. The major political arena, the communist party, although theoretically receptive to a large working-class presence, is not characterised by a high level of working-class activism. But what of less traditional fora? In the absence of private ownership, the management and direction of industrial enterprises is a state function. Systems of worker participation in management are part of the institutional apparatus of state socialism. What role do manual workers play in these?

Formal workplace politics have been institutionalised in a series of committees, conferences and councils established to ensure worker participation in management. As well as manifesting the philosophical commitment Marxist–Leninists have traditionally made to workers' control, participation in management ideally pre-empts collective dissent by workers. Moreover, their direct voice in decision-making is held to integrate workers into the enterprise. In practice, however, enterprise politics are part of the party–state both locally and nationally. The enterprise power structure includes both the unions and the communist parties as major institutional links between the factory and the wider political system. Formally, both mobilise and educate the workforce, supervise management, ensure policy implementation and reconcile interests within the enterprise. Unions have a special brief to protect workers' legal rights and play a coordinating role over the various forms of worker participation in management. But their performance is not highly regarded by workers. The communist party also plays a dual role, on the one hand helping management to fulfil production plans, on the other expected to articulate worker's interests. But the latter function is vitiated by a strong identification with management, even where workers look to the party for representation at enterprise level. Thus party officials come to be seen as directors' men and are often mistrusted by non-communists, although skilled-worker communists may make good use of their party position. The enterprise level committees are seen as even less adequate. They are viewed by workforces as operating mainly in the interests of the technical intelligentsia. In general, available data indicate that participation in factory affairs is stratified both by skill levels and by the political commitment of employees. Party members play a larger part than the rest. Factory committee members tend to be the administrators; production conferences are dominated by technical issues, so that specialists dominate meetings. Membership of the committees is disproportionately white-collar (Bielasiak, 1981).

The formally established structures for enterprise politics have not, then, been guarantors of an equitable working-class representation. But patterns have differed considerably by country and over time. Regimes have exhibited varying levels of commitment to workers' self-management and participatory arrangements have taken a variety of forms, ranging from extensive and innovatory arrangements in Yugoslavia to desultory and pro-forma arrangements in Czechoslovakia and the GDR. Yugoslavia was the first East European country officially to adopt workers' councils as part of a dual form of representation of workforce interests. Starting in 1950, a series of laws were passed to promote the autonomy of the firm and the decentralisation of management within it. They have aimed also to increase opportunities for the direct and indirect participation of the workers themselves. Several revisions to the original law have not removed the workers' council as the principal institution of self-management. The council is charged with the formal responsibility for enacting policies on production, personnel, wages and investment. Varying in size from thirteen to 120 members (a figure which is a function of the size of the organisation), the councils are directly elected by the entire workforce in the relevant organisation. Once elected, the council selects a management board. The period of office is restricted to a maximum of 2 years and, in common with many other Yugoslav state institutions, there are restrictions on reselection.

The Yugoslav workers' councils have attracted considerable academic interest and are well researched by scholars. Most studies tend to focus on the scope for workforce participation and point to patterns of under-representation of the unskilled and of manual workers in general and the over-representation of technicians and lower management personnel. Workers are also disadvantaged in certain decision areas, and find it easier to influence wages and personnel policy than, say, investment decisions. Councils have also found it difficult to cope with the ever-increasing size of enterprises, which grew to an average of over 17,000 employees in the 1970s.

Today the basic level workers' councils correspond to subdivisions of the firm and are known as Basic Organisations of Associated Labour. These first appeared in the late 1960s and were officially recognised in the Associated Labour Act of 1976. Taken by Shabad (1980) to reflect a trend toward increasing decentralisation in the Yugoslav economy, the BOALs have not similarly impressed other analysts (Sacks, 1983). The extent to which workers' councils exert real influence over enterprise decisions compared to the enterprise directors and their staffs varies both by type of enterprise and by issue. Most commentaries indicate that the influence of the manual workforce at enterprise level is far from a predominant one. Yugoslav enterprise politics turn around two parallel structures: the self-management system itself and the firm's organisational hierarchy. One is a political entity, the other is conditioned by economic forces. The sovereign of the self-management structure is the entire workforce, the sovereign of the firm is top management. Officially management merely implements self-management decisions and self-management decisions are taken in an apparatus implicitly dominated by workers. But in practice the organisational superiors have the dominant influence in the self-management structures. In short, the firms' executives dominate both structures. We should therefore note Shabad's point that structural contradictions in the workplace do not altogether impede the ability of a workers' council to articulate a working-class interest. But we should give more credence to findings by Comisso (1981) and Shabad's suggestion elsewhere (Verba and Shabad, 1978) that Yugoslav workers' councils open channels mainly for a more technocratically oriented participation in which, once again, it is the white-collar citizen who is most likely to be active.

However, Yugoslav workers' councils are part of a society-wide system of self-management which has been integrated with the system of political representation since 1974. Workers' councils are organically related both to commune and republican chambers of associated labour and feed into the system of political representation. There also exists a system for regulating relations between economic organisations and social services, known as the Self-Management Associations of Interest, and a system of Social Compacts and Self-management Agreements. The social compacts are agreements between government, economic chambers, and trade unions over such matters as pricing policy, incomes, employment and planning. Self-management agreements regulate relations between work organisations (on such issues as cooperation over production, mergers and foreign investment in the firm) (IDE, 1981). Whatever their limitations, Yugoslav institutions of self-management are central to the political system.

Such integration is unusual. Elsewhere in Eastern Europe the appearance of workers' councils has been confined to industrial enterprises and has tended to occur only during times of crisis (Poland), ambitious economic reform (Czechoslovakia) or efforts at leadership consolidation (Romania). In no case have they been a forum exclusively for the representation of manual working class interests. Kolankiewicz (1973a) has observed that in Poland, where workers' self-management has been a political issue since 1956; when councils were established spontaneously in a number of enterprises, the early councils were in practice a forum used by lower management to protest at mismanagement by their superiors. Polish legislation in 1958 neutralised the original councils, but demands for their reactivation appeared again during the unrest of the 1970s and in 1980–81. During the 1970s the councils were management discussion clubs, except briefly following periods of unrest, when efforts were made to bring in more blue-collar members. By December 1978, i.e. just before the beginnings of the Solidarity movement, only one-tenth of the 1956 councils were still in existence. These were engaged in similar patterns of collusion between the enterprise director, the chair of the factory trade-union branch and the party to those which have been described in Yugoslavia (Kolankiewicz, 1973a, 1982a). In Poland the inadequacies of the surviving councils became a considerable irritant to an increasingly disgruntled working class.

Nor did workers' councils elsewhere serve to soothe working-class discontent. Czechoslovak workers were initially only lukewarm in their responses to the Prague Spring and proposals of workers' councils (Pravda, 1963). In Romania workers' councils established in 1971 were government-sponsored. In the form of Consiliilor Oamenilor Muncii (COM), these were promoted by Ceausescu as the key mechanism for worker participation in making and implementing decisions. But not until after the Jiu valley miners' strikes of 1977 were they accorded a prominent profile. Then, in the face of growing labour unrest, a considerable effort was made to upgrade the COMs. Each has between nine and twenty-five members and the total membership is around 153,000 managers and workers. But the majority are non-elected members, primarily higher managerial or technical personnel. Workers are elected from the factory floor but are most often foremen. They play only a minor role in discussions and debates, which are dominated by the statutory members. The result has been a general lack of interest in the councils. Twice-yearly meetings of enterprise general assemblies apparently attract more interest and participation, but these are dominated by the party, hence are not in practice an extra-party participatory institution (Nelson, 1981a).

At the time of writing, a variety of mechanisms for the conduct of enterprise participation exists. The workers' councils which emerged as a response to political disturbances either did not last (in Poland they were reformed by 1958 and replaced by Soviet-style production conferences in 1978) or were given little scope (in Romania their agendas were determined by enterprise management). In Czechoslovakia, Bulgaria and the GDR production conferences are the normal form of 'self-management'. Their decision-making scope tends to be limited to very narrow technical issues, wages and welfare, excluding broader matters of production and business strategy. The problem is one of structural incompatibility. Genuine workers' councils cannot operate without considerable decentralisation, which is inconsistent with centralised economic mechanisms. Hence there is little evidence that the self-management fora have been democratic participatory instruments in Eastern Europe. Even in decentralised

Yugoslavia the pattern is one of managerial predominance, the hierarchic stratification of participation and a predominant influence by the already advantaged.

Nor have official trade unions met working-class participatory needs. East European trade unions, as reconstituted after World War Two, were modelled on those in the Soviet Union, which had been established on the 'transmission belt' principle. The idea was that, organisationally, unions were to be two-way transmission belts, expanding working-class consciousness from the most advanced sectors to the new recruits and communicating workers' interests. In practice the role of the Soviet trade unions in instilling labour discipline soon came to mean that what was transmitted was limited to party, state and managerial demands. Under Stalin the unions also became vehicles for exercising political control over the workforce. They enforced production norms, prevented labour turnover and took responsibility for labour allocation and personnel selection. Ultimately they became merged organisationally with labour departments of the state apparatus. After Stalin's death USSR unions assumed a more benevolent form, taking on the administration of various welfare programmes, but continuing to bear responsibility for labour discipline (see Zukin, 1981). Similarly in Eastern Europe, the transmission-belt union has been little loved by the workforce and its operation has tended to deteriorate to a form of party–union collusion and union managerialism. It has nevertheless been adhered to, except in Hungary, where, within the framework of the regime's alliance policy, there has been some attempt to experiment with trade-union structures. However, increased workforce participation has been made contingent on increases in labour productivity and the Hungarian regime was a fervent critic of free trade unions, firmly suppressing sporadic initiatives of this kind after 1980.

There are major contradictions in the unions' roles, however. In each system the unions have a legal responsibility to protect worker interests even though they are consistently urged to mobilise workers to fulfil production plans. A tension between production responsibilities and workforce representation tends to be resolved in favour of the former, so that unions have become agencies of labour management rather than participation. Backing for strikes is exceptional and the position of unions in the factories is generally weak. Polish, Hungarian and Yugoslav workers have all been highly critical of their unions.

Unions are potentially channels of communication between workers and management. Calls for independent unions or for reforms of the existing ones indicate that attachment to the ideals of unionism is present. Where unions have actually supported working-class interests, they are believed to have helped forestall protests. Alex Pravda believes that the reforms of the Hungarian unions inspired by the NEM led to the observable decline in strikes there during the 1970s. The Hungarian reforms gave unions more power to defend workers' interests, enabling a union veto over certain management moves. At national level Hungarian union leaders played an important part in reform negotiations, presenting reform proposals to workers in modified and palatable forms. They aggregated and articulated demands from the shopfloor and were able to modify some potentially unpopular aspects of NEM, thus enhancing their blue collar support (Pravda, 1982a).

In Yugoslavia developments appear to be taking the opposite direction. Officially autonomous of party and state, Yugoslav unions are supposed to act as a watchdog over the organs of workers' self-management, a counterforce to bureaucratic inertia and a check on the powers of technocracy. Organisationally they reconcile workers' control with managerial state power. Union federations correspond structurally both to major industrial branches and to the federal system. The constitutional reforms of 1974 gave them direct representation in the organs of state, but in the socio-political channels rather than in the self-management system. They have become increasingly close to the party and have acquired increasing management functions as their representative capacities have been overshadowed by the workers' councils. Since 1974 Yugoslav unions have been legally partners in the self-management system, have planning responsibilities and have a formal role in the detail of everyday management. They may propose laws to the cabinet and initiate work in social-service areas. Their central representative task is to obtain for workers as much as possible of the income realised in each enterprise. This places them in an ambivalent position, as the size of the pie to be distributed will, to some extent, depend on productivity. Yugoslav workers are not satisfied with their unions, which they regard as identifying with management but as having less power than enterprise directors. Unions tend not to support workers in dispute with management or the party and are regarded as insufficiently representative. They do not possess the institutional identity necessary for workers to regard them as defenders of their interests (Zukin, 1981).

The dangers arising from the failure of official unions to protect working-class interests have been most apparent in Poland, where their representational role has always been especially weak. The effects of that weakness were exacerbated by a managerial stratum which was more powerful but less able and flexible than its equivalent elsewhere. Polish unions in the 1970s tended to be unwilling to support even those of their members who took management to court; and, save for the 1958 legislation, the erosion of Polish workers' councils was carried out solely by directives of the Central Council of the Trade Unions, the peak organisation until 1981. Union organisation was until 1980 governed by a Stalinist statute enacted in 1949. Twenty-three branches covered all the major industries and services under the direction of a central council. Forty-nine regional and 30,000 factory councils, divided into 240,000 groups or sections, completed the structure, which engaged 1.5 million people in the full- or part-time services of its bureaucracy. Interlocked with economic and government organs, the unions confined activities mainly to workplace social or welfare activities. A lack of autonomy meant that functions of looking after workers rights were neglected. At the end of the 1970s 60 per cent of factory council chairpersons were party members discredited by association with both organisations, and a generation gap between younger workers and older functionaries was evident. By this time union leaders were aware of the shortcomings of the system and in the June 1980 elections raised a number of issues of union reform. As events were soon to prove, the large, party-controlled, centralised unions had outlived their time. They could no longer cope with the diversified nature and conditions of the working class (Kolankiewicz, 1981, pp. 146–7).

The free-trade-union movement which grew so rapidly after 1979 was a manifestation of the need of the Polish working class for more autonomy from and control over the administrative apparatus. They required an organisation capable of expressing the needs of an increasingly differentiated class, and one which could defend its interests against those of other groups. The demand for free trade unions was a highly political one. Insofar as free unions exist alongside official ones, they legitimate the notion that there is more than one working-class interest. The new unions themselves were prepared to take strong stands where they perceived worker interests to be threatened and, while pledging loyalty to the constitution, they were more reluctant than official unions to subordinate themselves to the leading role of the party in either formal or practical terms (Pravda, 1981).

The foundation of Solidarity marked a departure from a more usual, less well defined form of worker protest in Eastern Europe. Alex Pravda, who has written extensively about informal working class activity in the region, draws attention to a general avoidance of political demands and a general economism which is characteristic of worker protests. Four kinds of activity are characteristic. Firstly, there are large-scale violent protests against regime policies which threaten welfare concepts of socialism. Such outbursts are relatively rare, with Poland the only country to have experienced more than one by 1986. Second are strikes, which are more frequent than mass demonstrations but are relatively few by Western standards. When they occur, strikes tend to be defensive and specific in character. They rarely cover more than one factory and are normally settled by local management within a few hours. The third form of worker protests are slowdowns and partial stoppages directed at extracting gains from management rather than protesting about specific measures. Finally, disciplinary infringements and job changes may be expressions of dissatisfaction with conditions (Pravda, 1981, 1982a).

In general, blue-collar workers believe that they have little influence over policy and see themselves as having less influence than non-manual groups. But survey data indicate that they are not resigned to powerlessness, and that younger, better educated workers may be more desirous of political influence (Pravda, 1981). Such findings may augur an important change. During the 1950s and the 1960s workers proved generally sceptical of political ferment and were interested mainly in the limited demands which we may interpret as a defence of their 'social compacts' with the regimes. Mobilisation around reform policies in Poland in 1956, in Hungary the same year, and in Czechoslovakia in 1968, are interpreted by Pravda (1982a) as resulting from the crystallisation of emotionally based nationalism and the threat of outside intervention. Only in Hungary were workers at the centre of armed resistance, and there invasion was combined with an intense dislike of the USSR. By the end of the 1970s, however, there were signs of a growing class consciousness and some signs of worker cooperation with other social groups in political protest. This, it has been suggested, marks a significant change in East European working-class politics.

In Poland, and to a lesser extent elsewhere, poor economic conditions and perceived violations of official promises about conditions (for example, sudden price increases, revisions of work norms and confiscatory currency reform) have triggered protest in the past. But before 1980 abstract system demands were conspicuous by their absence (Montias, 1980). The 1970 Baltic uprisings occurred as a result of worsening living standards, which were especially evident amongst poorer groups of workers. The Polish coastal towns had some special characteristics, including the structural conditions which make for class cohesiveness. The combination of a large population of youngish rural immigrants, a high proportion of shipyard workers living in employee hostels and a considerable tourist industry had the effect of underlining social inequalities. The availability of expensive amenities to wealthy tourists provided popular talking points, and tourists became a reference group against which workers could compare their own living standards. A sense of relative deprivation was important to a socially compact working class (Lane, 1973b). In December 1970 the breakdown of regular food supplies, rising prices, growing unemployment and suspicion of imminent changes in the system of material incentives triggered a series of strikes and riots. Their suppression officially tolled forty-five dead and 1165 injured, and was followed by strikes in other parts of Poland, the downfall of Gomulka and the installation of Gierek as party secretary. The immediate result was a withdrawal of the offending price rises.

Under Gierek a considerable effort was made to increase worker presence in the party and to foster blue-collar support for party policies. But a stress on education and expertise tended to enhance the advantage of white-collar groups, who also dominated enterprise participation. Workers' opportunities for participation proved insufficient in both quantity and quality to enable the defence of their interests through official channels (Bielasiak, 1983, pp. 240–2). Frustration mounted and finally workers formed their own, independent organisation.

The independent trade-union movement thus established achieved an eventual membership of 10 million. Solidarity mobilised numerous previously non-active workers, peasants and young people. More a social movement than a trade union, it was young, with regional officials tending to be in their twenties and national officials in their thirties. Its programme included not only economic demands but also concern for civil liberties. Catholicism proved to be an important link between some reform-minded intellectuals and workers. Intellectuals organised in the dissident KSS/KOR (Committee for Social Self-Defence/Committee for the Defence of Workers), which built up a record of support for blue collar rights KSS/KOR are believed to have inspired the Solidarity demands for the release of all political prisoners and for full constitutional civil liberties.

With its centre in Gdansk, Solidarity drew upon the experiences gained during the various protest movements of the 1970s as well as on input from intellectual supports. Staniszkis (1981) illustrates this point. She writes that experience taught Gdansk negotiators that deals agreed at enterprise level lacked guarantees, hence central negotiations took place on major issues. Local negotiations undertaken by less experienced workers attended to more specific points. In her view the links between Solidarity and the Catholic church (see below for a discussion of this from the viewpoint of the church) prevented a more fruitful alliance with the anti-bureaucratic movement within the party. Moreover, overt demands for rights for an institutionalised Catholic movement made at Gdansk undermined the movement's chances of survival. An implication of her argument is that the 1970s experience of the Polish working class might, had the class not been so religious, have encouraged an important split within the party apparatus. From such a split would have come significant support for independent unionists. Other observers limit themselves to commenting on the incremental nature of post-1970 Polish working-class protests, and all agree that the presence of political demands in 1980 represented a qualitative change (Kolankiewicz, 1981; Nuti, 1981; Pravda, 1981, 1982b; Bielasiak, 1983).

Solidarity was outlawed in 1982, since when it has made a considerable but flagging effort to maintain an underground existence. Unofficial Polish sources and western press reports during 1986 indicated that a considerable underground organisation persisted, able to mobilise large, if diminishing, numbers of individuals and to produce an impressive output of Samizdat. The Polish government faces the unenviable task of creating a new trade union structure. The 1982 law banning Solidarity also sanctioned new unions to be established from the bottom upwards. Starting in individual factories and branches, by 1985 there were 129 branch federations incorporating 20,000 factory level organisations and including, reputedly, 5 million people. During 1984 moves toward more central control were begun, with the integration of the new unions into a central representative council. Inducements to join included easier access to housing, holidays and bonuses. Even so, many young people were disinclined to join the new unions and membership was particularly low in the very largest enterprises (Radio Free Europe, Polish Situation Report No. 5, March 1985).

Although the appearance of free trade unions in a number

of East European countries at the end of the 1970s was reported in the underground press, nowhere did these approximate the strength of Solidarity, and none disrupted systems of industrial relations. At the time of writing it seems unlikely that the Polish events will be duplicated in the rest of Eastern Europe. It is, however, worth remembering that evidence of similar problems in the other countries exists. Workers in Hungary, Czechoslovakia and the GDR have shown an interest in finding an independent voice. Such wishes are backed by political resources. Sabel and Stark (1982) argue that the planned economies, by their very nature, create the preconditions for shopfloor power in that they generate permanently tight labour markets. In their view struggles within the party apparatus over economic matters become intertwined with limited workplace struggles, allowing workers an indirect but significant voice in economic strategy, with an occasional veto over important economic decisions. Their model of a planned economy is one in which efforts by industrial managers to protect and expand their local power bases against the impositions of central planners lead to the hoarding of labour by factories. An unintended result of this is that workers achieve an advantageous bargaining position.

Alex Pravda also stresses the significance of enterprise politics. He suggests (1981, pp. 58–9) the existence of a core of working class activists who are well informed about enterprise politics and skilled at gaining concessions by covert bargaining means. These tend to be skilled men in their thirties and forties who know how to apply pressure on management and have some contact with establishment elites. Their numbers may include brigade leaders and unionists, but not enterprise officials. Kemeny (1979) sees such activities as leading to a system of dual power at enterprise level, consisting of a set of official rules operating alongside a parallel set of informal rules. Dual power takes the political pressure out of enterprise conflict and provides an outlet for narrow, specific grievances.

Other commentators make similar points, which, taken together, provide considerable evidence that, far from being merely 'adaptive', the East European workforce pursues its interests as and when it may. Forms of industrial action range

from strikes to more discreet manoeuvres. There were 3000
strikes in Yugoslavia between 1958 and 1980 (Shabad, 1980).
These differed from the better publicised strikes in the West in
that they tended to be spontaneous, of only a single day's
duration, and confined to a single enterprise. Officially they
were tolerated. More common are 'white' strikes, based on
absenteeism, working to rule, small-scale sabotage and
obstruction of the production process. All are indicators that
important tensions exist at enterprise level and that the
sources of the Polish events were not unique.

But a relatively more favourable economic climate combined with greater levels of management flexibility and union
and party acuity have so far enabled the other East European
systems to cope. Mishandling often exacerbated Polish tensions, which might have been eased by more able leaders,
especially at enterprise level. Elsewhere, signs of worker
protest are sporadic but recurrent, especially in Romania,
where coalminers have been consistently restive. The opportunities for social mobility provided by strategies of
industrialisation have largely been exhausted as industrial
patterns have become established. Further improvements
must come through increases in productivity, and these in
turn require worker cooperation. Increasing not only the
quantity but also the quality of worker participation may be
the key here, as the associated feelings of efficacy are known
to increase job satisfaction and to lead to greater social
integration.

To return to the questions with which we began this
discussion, we may now state with some confidence that the
East European working class preceives itself as having interests which are distinct from, although not necessarily in
conflict with, those which are expressed by the communist
party. This perception varies in strength, distinctiveness and
precision, and is not necessarily accompanied by a desire by
workers to alter the party's role. But difficulties in articulating
blue-collar interests are widely recognised within the class. A
persisting attachment to the ideas of unionism indicates that
the preferred solution may be the development of more
representative trade unions. The vertically organised transmission-belt mass trade-union model is generally felt to be

inadequate, and other models capable of expressing a more diversified, specific and complex set of class interests must be devised. An important conclusion that may be drawn from the Polish experience is that there is a more or less urgent need to devise forms of public participation which are both effective and reasonably open. A political role must be found for a new generation of reasonably well educated workers who have capacities for political activity but no real outlet. In short, it is in the interests of the East European regimes to evolve new participatory forms for its workers and in particular to attend to the reform of their union apparatuses (see Woodall, 1981; Wiatr, 1984).

Religion and the churches

Some flexibility in the management of working-class political demands is to be expected in regimes where official ideology requires the prioritisation of the working class. But the atheism of Marxism–Leninism makes it less easy to comprehend policies which accommodate religious organisations and the expressions of religious interests. Nevertheless, the churches are perhaps the most interesting example of a persistent non-communist institutional interest in Eastern Europe.

Except in Poland, religious observance and affiliation has declined since World War Two but is none the less considerable in the states for which data are available (Table 11.1). Substantial variations in religious freedom vary from an outright ban on observance in Albania to the relative autonomy of the churches in the GDR and especially in Poland.

Patterns of regime accommodation with religious organisation vary by the type of religion in question. In general, Orthodox churches have proved less problematic for ruling communist parties than have Catholic, Protestant or Muslim denominations. This may be because Orthodox hierarchies tend to be co-terminous with national boundaries, so that the profession of Orthodox beliefs does not implicate the believer in extra-system loyalty (see Sanders, 1982). But even where Orthodox faiths are practised, there are important differ-

TABLE 11.1

Religious affiliation in Eastern Europe in 1983 as a percentage of the population

	Catholic		Protestant	Orthodox	Muslim
Poland	95				
Czechoslovakia	70		10		
Yugoslavia	31			40	16
Hungary	56	Calvinist	19		
		Other	5		
Romania	10			70	
Bulgaria	1			70	10
GDR	7		46		

Source: Adapted from *The Economist*, 10 September 1983, pp. 63–4.

ences between church and state, and systems have varied in the way these have been accommodated. In general, the areas of difference between church and state have been religious education, the appointment of higher clergy and the provision of places of worship. These have been the subject of negotiation with the Vatican and have resulted in a variety of working arrangements for Catholic congregations (see Dunn, 1982–3). Arrangements by other denominations have been made on a national basis.

The political role of the churches is a contradictory one. They must submit to a certain amount of state control if their are to survive, but such submission may cause disaffection in their congregations. The balance which has been achieved is in most cases a fine one, with only the Polish Catholic and the GDR Evangelical Churches having moved beyond well defined limits to some measure of autonomy.

Elsewhere churches are well controlled by the state. Religious believers are everywhere excluded from important political positions, but in some cases this has extended to other areas of endeavour as well. In Albania, where religious practice is illegal, little evidence of worship exists, although there have been reports that consumption in canteens has been down 70 per cent during the Ramadan fast (White *et al.*, 1982). Policies in the Orthodox countries vary. Yugoslav authorities have endorsed religious freedom, subject to state approval, since 1946. There, highish levels of official tolerance of religious sentiment are occasionally strained by the close links between religious and ethnic divisions. In Bulgaria the churches are kept under political control, but the regime appears to be disinterested in people's religious observance, believing that this will disappear over time (Sanders, 1982). By contrast, in Romania the regime has aimed to ensure dominance over all religious denominations. It packs the Orthodox hierarchy with reliable nominees able to control the lower clergy, and prohibits relations between the Romanian Orthodox Church and foreign chapters outside the Soviet orbit. The Orthodox church accepts this high degree of control, which includes state determination of its budget. The Catholic church has not permitted such interference and as a result has not been approved under the 1948 General Regulations for Religious Cults, and is without the benefit of legal status.

The fortunes of Christian churches have altered significantly over the post-war period. The Hungarian Catholic Church was at first subjected to considerable repression, culminating in a life sentence for Primate Cardinal Jozsef Mindszenty in 1956. During the 1960s, however, church and state began to accommodate each other in Hungary. As a result, the Catholic Church was allowed to receive Vatican support, its organisational structure was re-established, and congregations became active. Numerous fields of common church–state concern were acknowledged. The state expects the church to control its membership, which proved difficult in the early 1980s, when thousands of small prayer and meditation groups sprang up. These were usually breakaway groups from church organisations who were in dispute with the church hierarchy and who were often exercised over the issue of conscientious objection to bearing arms. Disputes often divided younger and older clergy. Czechoslovakia, on the other hand, has been consistently repressive of its churches, refusing to approve the appointment of sufficient clergy and denying the children of religious observers access to many careers if they have received religious education. Congregations have been bitterly opposed to the concessions demanded from the senior clergy by the state, making it difficult for the church establishment to negotiate more favourable circumstances during the rare (and brief) periods when the state has shown signs of relaxing its vigilance (Ramet, 1982).

In most of Eastern Europe church activity has been very much a rearguard defence of whatever privileges religious groups have been able to preserve. Only the Polish and German churches have been able to defend a more widely defined political interest. These two cases merit detailed description. The East German Evangelical Church perceives its role as that of the church under socialism. With a (falling) membership of 46 per cent of the population in 1983, it is the sole GDR membership organisation which is free from direct SED control. Significantly, it was part of an all-German Evangelical hierarchy until 1969. Initially, opposition to the establishment of an East German state led to the severe curtailment of Evangelical activities. Restrictions eased considerably during the 1960s, a process which culminated in the establishment in June 1969 of the GDR Federation of Evangelical Churches. The federation embraced eight GDR regions. In 1978 a growing church–state rapprochement was sealed by a meeting in March between SED secretary Honecker and Bishop Schoenherr. The meeting resulted in church retention of its right to criticise regime policies as well as its receipt of important concessions over the building of new churches, limited access to state-controlled media, state support in organising large-scale events and official recognition of its extensive role in areas of health care and social welfare.

The aim of the SED is to pacify the church, then recruit its followers, a strategy which may in the long run prove effective. In the short and medium term, however, the church has considerable strength. That strength derives in part from a willingness to take up certain extra-religious issues. Military matters have been most likely to draw the church from a narrowly defined defence of religion. A notable case is Evangelical support for the principle of conscientious objection. Since conscription was introduced in 1962, the church has supported the cause of conscientious objectors, gaining some concessions for them in 1964. Conscientious objectors may do construction work during their military terms, but are discriminated against after their service, something which the church has been unable to prevent.

Peace has also been a central issue in church opposition to SED policy. Real differences over this issue began in 1978, when the regime introduced obligatory military training for the 14-year-old age group. In 1981 the provision of military education was further extended. Both moves were vociferously opposed by the church. The issue of conscientious objection was once again to the fore. Church members demanded social (that is, non-military) service as an alternative. Eventually the issue was taken up by the church hierarchy (Bowers, 1982). Peace is a sensitive issue for a regime which regards itself as a peace movement. Official, quasi-official and quasi-legal peace organisations operate side by side. Four different peace organisations exist. The GDR Peace Council has the task of popularising official peace policy. There is also an unofficial but regime-approved Christian Peace Conference of 500 members whose views are close to that of the official Peace Council. Peace seminars are organised within the basic communities of the Evangelical Church. Finally, a spontaneous independent peace movement is closely associated with the church. This has no organisational structure but has between 200 and 5000 activists who may have a further 30,000 to 50,000 supporters (Ramet, 1984). Thus three of four component parts of the peace movement are in some way linked to the church. Evangelical stances on peace matters attracted increasing numbers of youthful supporters at the beginning of the 1980s, which was worrying for the SED. Ecclesiastical caution over some issues has, however, dismayed lower clergy and tempered peace-movement support. Notably the May 1982 withdrawal by the church of its 'Swords into Ploughshares' badge caused alarm at a time of growing harassment of unofficial peace-movement supporters.

The GDR Evangelical Federation has more autonomy than any other East European church except the Polish Catholic

Church. SED policy has been ambivalent in its toleration of a church political role, but has been increasingly permissive of its religious functions. Church administration *per se* is not interfered with. The appointment of bishops does not require state approval. Since 1978, 325 churches have been built with West German financing. West German money has also re-modelled a further 302 churches and reconstructed twenty-five. (Religion brings in hard currency.) The existence of a West German counterpart undoubtedly strengthens the posi-tion of the Federation, but domestic state support has been forthcoming. The government provides 12 million marks annually for administration and clerical salaries and allows the church limited production of its own media, including the publication of two weeklies (Dunn, 1982–3). But discrimina-tion against Christians in education and employment con-tinues. During the 1970s there was considerable pressure within the church to stiffen resistance to regime policies. The self-immolation of Pastor Oskar Brusewitz in front of his church in Zeitz in August 1976 was part of this pressure. Open letters to Honecker objecting to the state distribution of war toys were issued by some clergy. The church dissociated itself from those episodes, earning accusations that it had compromised needlessly with the regime (Ramet, 1984). Perhaps in response to such criticisms the church streng-thened its complaints, objecting not only to discrimination against Christians but also to manifestations of regime into-lerance of criticism, to hostile characterisations of the West in the media and later to hostile press coverage of the Polish workers' movement. In the mid-1980s the GDR Federation of Evangelical Churches faces evident problems of incorpora-tion. Reluctant to endanger a relatively propitious *modus vivendi* with the state, it seeks to occupy the narrow space between opposition and opportunism (Ramet, 1984).

Problems of incorporation may also exist for the Polish Catholic Church, although its identity as an international force backed by the Vatican is more distinctive than that which a Federal Republic counterpart can provide the GDR Evangelical Federation. By standards of international com-parison the Polish Catholic Church is a successful religious institution. Ninety-three per cent of the Polish population are baptised Catholics, the number of clergy has doubled since 1945 and vocations increased during the 1980s. Some of its success may be attributed to its leadership. For over 35 years Polish Catholicism had the benefit of a talented head in Cardinal Wyszynski, who from 1956 onward was an able negotiator with the regime. Nowak (1982) outlines three phases of church–state relations in Poland. Between 1948 and 1956 the Catholic church fought attempts by the government to destroy it as an independent institution. The years between 1956 and 1970 were marked by the success of resistance to government efforts to circumvent religious and educational activities. From 1970 onwards the church insisted on unhindered religious rights and became, as a result, a rallying point for supporters of human rights.

Until the 1960s the church conceived its role narrowly, limiting its interests to cultural, spiritual and moral issues. A broadening of its concerns reflected changes in international Catholicism. The Second Vatican Council (1962–5) encouraged attempts to define a proper relation between church and society. This led in turn to a gradual take-up of human rights issues, with Wyszynski taking care to demonstrate an even-handed approach. After the workers' protests of 1976, the church declared support for KOR (Committee for the Defence of Workers), an organisation established to support workers in the strike movement. This extended to turning over one Sunday's church collection to the KOR to help the families of arrested workers. Support for victimised workers led to some rapprochement between the church and the left. This occurred largely as a result of KOR leader Adam Michnik's 1977 essay on the history of opposition in contemporary Poland, in which it was concluded that divisions between the church and the left had caused debilitating weaknesses. A growing propensity for the church to defend human rights provided a basis for cooperation between left-wing intellectuals and Catholic activists (Hruby, 1982–3).

The Catholic church has a special position in Poland, where it is strongly associated with the idea of nation and well established in the country's culture. Strengthened by the selection of a Polish Pope in 1979, it may have been weakened by the death of Wyszynski in 1981 and his replacement by the less able Archbishop Glemp as national primate. Before the formation of Solidarity the church was the only organised force cutting across all social groups which was prepared to confront the government when civil rights were abused. Hence the emergence of Solidarity transformed the role of the church from that of a major adversary of the regime to one of mediator between the state and an independent social movement. The religious feelings of striking workers were strong, manifested in demands for church access to the media and in the use of religious emblems. Widespread working-class support has always been a strength of Polish Catholicism. Initially its new mediating role created misunderstandings, but gradually the usefulness of the church's negotiating skills became apparent. Under martial law the church's role was enhanced, especially after the suppression of Solidarity, when it functioned as a vital communications network between internment camps (Nowak, 1982; Hruby, 1982–3). But the church has been careful to preserve a stance of official neutrality and remained steadfastly neutral in the competition between the party and underground Solidarity during the 1985 Sejm elections.

Legally the church is a political actor. Political Catholicism includes the PAX and Znak groups, which have representation in the Sejm. Znak takes its name from a monthly journal founded in Cracow in the immediate post-war period, which was suppressed and then revived after 1956. Its editors and contributors evolved into a close knit intellectual community which in its parliamentary manifestation serves as a channel for conveying the sentiments of Polish Catholics to the authorities. The group has several major centres and enjoys esteem amongst Catholics (Bromke, 1975). PAX, on the other hand, is a communist-party-backed organisation founded by pre-war fascist leader Boleslaw Piasecki as an official Catholic movement. It enjoys rather less support than the independent Znak. In addition to a parliamentary presence, the Polish Catholic church controls more than twenty publishing ventures, prints eighty-nine papers and periodicals with a combined circulation of 1.4 million and produces twenty-six internal church bulletins. Sunday masses have been transmitted by radio from Warsaw since 1980, and a number of worker and rural pastoral communities have been in operation since the middle of 1980. A new church–state Concordat, highly favourable to the church, was under negotiation during 1985 (see Stehle, 1985). At the time of writing its position as a powerful institutional interest appears assured. However, its strategy of moderation makes the Polish church vulnerable to charges of compromising with the authorities and betraying the cause of Polish human rights. Its position features the expected ironies of a rigidly hierarchical organisation possessed of a conservative social doctrine which has come to encourage democratising tendencies. The chief mission of the Catholic church is a conservative one, but a liberal input has been necessary to the maintenance of a society-wide base in Poland.

Opposition and dissent

Before discussing the various manifestations of dissent in Eastern Europe, we should first treat the question of why we are interested in it and of how much weight should be given to it in a text such as this. There are, in our view, two reasons for being interested in East European dissent; one is analytical, the other ethical. The analytical argument is that dissent may disrupt the regimes and its potential must therefore be assessed in any overview of East European politics. The ethical argument is that internal dissidents offer a moral challenge to state socialist regimes, whose response to that challenge may be an important part of our evaluation of them. Both arguments are valid and present problems only when they become conflated. We propose here to confine ourselves, as far as sources allow, to the analytical questions. But a major problem in studying dissent in Eastern Europe arises from the way it is viewed in the West and from the sources provided by both domestic and exiled dissidents. Western press coverage has often exaggerated the incidence and support for dissident movements, and of course official sources are far from illuminating. Many Western commentators and most dissidents believe that dissent is the only form of politics in Eastern Europe, and that all else is repression, a view which has no more to offer analytically than totalitarian theory, and which is misleading in that contemporary dissident groups tend mainly to be small groups of highly committed intellectuals who are prevented from forming links with broadly based social groups.

But the expression of and type of dissent has varied throughout the region. In Poland, as we have seen, opposition tends to emanate from intellectuals, industrial workers and, to a lesser extent, the church. Only lately have the three groups been inclined to cooperate. There, mirroring the regime itself, any protest movement will have to come to terms with the church if it is to gain wide and sustained support. In Hungary, Kadar's 'live and let live' Alliance policy has generated an ideological opposition, consisting of the new left followers of Lukacs such as Hegedus, Heller, Kemeny, Markus, Bence, Kis and others who are critical of the social and economic consequences of reform. As we have seen in Chapter 6, they are particularly concerned about the rise of bureaucracy, but they also concern themselves with what they see as the immoral use of consumerism to manipulate public opinion. Most of the leading lights of the Hungarian new left have emigrated, leaving behind them an amorphous oppositional entity mainly based in the arts (Tökes, 1984). The GDR also hosts an arts and humanities based intellectual opposition which has adopted a new left political stance. Dissidents such as Havemann, Lubbe and Bahro harnessed Marxism to argue that the GDR is not an adequate socialist forum (Ramet, 1985). The 'new left' tone of dissident intellectuals marks a change from opposition movements in the past. Connor (1982) has noted three marked shifts from previous patterns. Firstly, the basis of the political critique has broadened. Marxist perspectives have been expanded to include liberal civil rights ideologies. Secondly, emphasis has been placed on the mobilisation of reformist social forces outside the ruling party, rather than on change within it. Finally, there has been a growing appreciation of the need for a linkage between dissident intellectuals and the working class. Outside Poland, where there were a considerable number of intellectuals in Solidarity, the activity of the dissident intellectuals has concentrated on constructing wide-

ranging critiques of contemporary state socialism (real existing socialism). These critiques have been valuable sources for
Western scholars, but it cannot be stated with any certainty
that they posed any significant threat to the regimes. Of the
other major social groups, the peasantry, although potentially
oppositional as a site of religious and nationalist feelings has
been quiescent since the end of the 1960s; but the working
class, as we have seen, has considerable oppositional potential.

Human rights have been a particular preoccupation of
dissident intellectuals, who have objected to their limited
scope in Eastern Europe. Limitations on human rights and
civil liberties are rooted in the state socialist conception of
democracy, which stresses substantive equality and collective
over individual goods. The party of course determines the
collective interest. Such a view of democracy limits individual
rights in important ways, a circumscription which is reinforced by the fact that the idea that justice is independent of
political considerations is not held in Eastern Europe. There
has nevertheless been a general trend toward the recognition
of human rights where these do not conflict with official state
interests. But important constraints on freedom of speech are
widely operated, freedom of association is limited and organisation for the purpose of criticising the state or breaching the
state monopoly on information leads to severe harassment or
worse. The law recognises some political infringements as
crimes, and dissidents are often imprisoned.

The best known of the human rights groups is the Czechoslovak Charter 77, which issued its original declaration in
January 1977, with 241 signatures, a figure which had risen to
1200 by 1985. Charter 77 has no aspirations to become a mass
movement, but wishes rather to publicise its objectives. Its
political goals are twofold. Firstly, it wishes to breach the
party monopoly of information, signalling that society has the
right to engage in horizontal communication without interference from the state. Pooling information leads to greater
social awareness of regime injustice. Secondly, Charter 77 has
sought to persuade the authorities to engage in a dialogue
with society which would impel the party to redefine its
leading role. In this it has largely failed (White *et al.*, 1982,
p. 244).

Based mainly in Prague and Brno, Charter 77 consists mostly of intellectuals but contains some workers. It has a collection of spokespersons, originally prominent figures, latterly less so, as harassment has discouraged involvement. Its principal activity has been issuing Samizdat materials (illegally produced documents), which are passed to relevant government departments and international organisations as well as being distributed to members. It is closely associated with the separately organised Czechoslovak League for Human Rights, which issues numbered communiqués noting imprisonments, arrests and investigations as well as cases of extra-juridical repression. Widely publicised in the West, both groups are poorly supported. But Charter 77 in particular has become a stable political reality, although it is narrowly based and has been described as a ghetto by its own members (Skilling, 1985).

Activity within the nationalities, particularly in Yugoslavia, has been another form of recurrent political protest. The distinction between individual and group rights is crucial in the nationalities issue, which cover language, culture and sometimes religion, all of which require unrestricted activity in a group or community. Individual members of the minor national communities often regard autonomy in the sense of insulation from outside influences and the preservation of the special interaction of the national group as a prerequisite to individual rights. Yugoslavia is the state which has done the most for its component nationalities. Its decentralised federal structure was devised to ensure that all national voices are heard. But national unrest is a hardy perennial there. Croatia was the site of considerable unrest in 1971 and in the 1980s the Albanians in Kosovo staged violent anti-regime demonstrations. The regularised articulation of nationalities' interests has not ensured either their satisfaction or diminution, and evidence of assimilation is sparse at best (see Shoup, 1968; Meier, 1983; Baskin, 1983). Nationality rights are collective rights, so that the protection of the individual depends upon the recognition of the collectivity. Centralised regimes such as Romania deny group rights of this kind (Fischer, 1983a). The thrust of this rather convoluted argument is that the preservation of nationalities, an essential demand of such groups, requires that additional rights should be conferred on the national group. Most of the East European states are reluctant to provide such additional rights, and as a result their minor nationalities are slowly becoming assimilated. But a core of each is likely to continue for some generations to come.

Other forms of dissidence have been more sporadic. Samizdat activity has been episodic, normally following protest movements and becoming more prevalent when these are widespread. It has been estimated that in Poland in 1980 around forty publications were appearing regularly. Such activity has been less apparent in the GDR, where access to the West German media reduces dependence upon illegal documents. The relative liberalism of the Yugoslav regime means that far more information is available anyway. In Hungary Samizdat consists mainly of left-wing criticism of the regime.

Analysing East European dissent is a difficult task. Not only are there gaps in our information but the limits of official toleration have varied and definitions of dissent have changed. As we have seen, the line between legitimate and illegal activity is often a fine one, which shifts with changes in the political climate and varies from country to country. Writing about opposition in Eastern Europe, Skilling attempted to conceptualise the status and position of various groups during the 1960s. He identified four characteristic types of opposition: 'integral', which was anti-system opposition normally carried out by anti-communist forces and included some alienated behaviour as well as anti-system violence or other illegal demonstrations; 'factional' opposition, which referred to rivalries between leaders; 'fundamental' opposition, which was undertaken by key groups inside or outside the party who wanted to resist or change party policy; and 'specific' opposition, which was also policy-orientated but did not reject the regime. In 1968 Skilling wrote of a decline of integral opposition, the tempering of factional opposition, the persistence of fundamental opposition and the rise of specific opposition. He regarded official toleration of specific opposition as having increased, and felt that parties had come to recognise that some groups were bound to characterise a developed society and that some differences of opinion were acceptable. Skilling's conclusions were a product of their time and it is unlikely that he would be so optimistic today. However, his point that the nature of opposition and the way in which dissent is treated has changed is probably valid.

But one should not confuse changes in official definitions of dissent with changes in practice. Toward the end of the Stalin era, for example, numerous 'Titoists' were purged from the East European parties as a result of the Yugoslav defection. As it is likely that Stalin's plans for party consolidation required purges at that time and that 'Titoism' was merely a convenient label, it is difficult to say with any accuracy whether any or some of those so purged actually advocated the banned strategy of national independence.

The problem for regimes is twofold. They must on the one hand establish the limits within which interest expression may be tolerated and on the other gain insights into both popular feelings and the wishes of strategic groups. When, for whatever reason, control over discussion is loosened, numerous interests appear to be ready to make their presence felt. Such emergence may take place over a prolonged period. The 1968 Prague Spring is held to have begun with a 1963 discussion document written by four young economists in a party working group created for the purpose of preparing a blueprint for a much needed reform. Splits occurred between those favouring and opposing reform and those seeking a compromise solution. Increasing numbers of interests entered the debate, which soon became part of a wider discussion of the role of the party and the state. Reform groups as well as conservatives were well established in the party, but the debate spilled over, engaging an increasingly large number of people. A continuing political struggle between various interests characterised the whole period, ending in 'victory' for conservative forces only with the Warsaw Pact invasion of August 1968. Provoked by the threat of economic failure, the Prague Spring resulted from the disillusion of various social groups, notably writers, intellectuals, social scientists, journalists and students. It illustrates well the group forces at work in

East European politics (Brown, 1969; Golan, 1971; Korbonski, 1971; Skilling, 1971; Dawisha, 1984) Its occurrence serves as a warning to regimes that such forces exist and must be given room to manoeuvre if they are not to flood legitimate channels. Its suppression serves as a warning to those who would make such forces too overt.

12

From Ability to Need: Social Welfare and Educational Policy

Economic and social policy

For the majority of the population, regime legitimacy rests not so much on general macro-economic or sectoral performance as upon the more tangible outputs of social policy. From its inception, the Leninist model of transition to a socialist society has included three criteria which have considerable implications for the role of social policy. First, the transfer into public ownership of the means of production and distribution would serve to abolish social-class domination. Second, although people would be paid according to their work in the transitional stage of socialism, economic policy would reduce income differentials substantially, with the gradual displacement of economic incentives by moral and non-material incentives. There would also be a shift in the basis of distribution of economic rewards toward the principle of need rather than desert, and upon the parity of esteem between mental and manual labour. Finally, the transitional phase of the dictatorship of the proletariat would gradually give way to a participatory self-managing society as all vestiges of the state as an oppressive apparatus withered away (George and Manning, 1980, p. 3). Here non-material needs would take precedence over more material concerns (Heller, 1976). Thus social policy is central to the ideological criteria for the creation of a socialist society, and has indeed

347

been elevated to a higher status in much of the debate in the 1960s and 1970s on the new 'stage' of Developed Socialism and the Scientific Technological Revolution (see Chapter 7).

For a period of about 25 years, after 1936, official Soviet thinking held that social needs should correspond to a given level of development of the forces of production. In war-torn Eastern Europe the broken fragments of educational and social policy were soon reassembled according to this principle in the late 1940s. Economic reconstruction and growth rendered social policies almost entirely contingent upon the economy, in a way that was not in line with the original Leninist criteria.

Any examination of social policy in Eastern Europe implies that there are dimensions of social inequality over which social policy is to have a redistributive effect, but more important here is a consideration of the scope of social policy and its relation to the centrally planned economy. Just as in Western industrial society social welfare policies can be either comprehensive or restricted in scope, work-related or need-related, a positive instrument of social change or take on a residual role (Titmus, 1974, pp. 23–32), so they can also vary within and between state socialist societies. As many writers on western social policy point out, it is not wise to assume that social policy will be necessarily benevolent or welfare-oriented; authoritarian regimes as well as liberal democracies can adopt social policy. Neo-Marxist writers have argued that Western welfare policies may be both functional to the maintenance of the capitalist mode of production, and serve to legitimate its social order (Gough, 1979; Offe, 1982). Similarly, state socialist social policies can fall far short of socialist let alone communist criteria (Deacon, 1983).

It has been argued that, in comparison with Western capitalist society, the expanded role of the state in state socialist societies is similar but that the attendant social conflict in the 'sphere of consumption' has been largely overlooked. Politicisation and conflict arise because of the socialisation of consumption and the substitution of the plan and bureaucratic principles of resource allocation and distribution for those of the market. This is also underpinned by ideological considerations such that real social needs are presented as corresponding to a given level of development of the forces of production. It is this that is used to determine the rationing of housing, education and health facilities (Pahl, 1977, pp. 153–77). The political nature of social policy has been acknowledged in the discussion linking consumption to human needs and aspirations (Heller, 1976; Feher, Heller and Markus, 1983), and in debate about material incentives. If consumption is to be directly linked to production by means of incentive schemes, then this implies an important role for personal as well as social consumption.

The allocation and control of consumption facilities may thus lead to considerable tension between the value of free-dom and the value of equality of outcome. Different societies facing similar tensions may produce very different outcomes, but the expansion of the state through the socialisation of the means of consumption is a phenomenon common to all advanced industrial societies. Yet we should be wary of assuming that an expanded role of the state is necessarily a powerful instrument of egalitarianism. Szelenyi has argued that there is ample evidence that the administrative allocation of goods and services favours the well-to-do at the expense of the poorer:

> Under state socialism, the state will redistribute surplus that was never accumulated in personal incomes, but which was concentrated in the budget, and reallocated according to centrally defined goals and values (Szelenyi, 1979, p. 75).

Thus, in the cases of housing, education and non-cash bene-fits, social inequalities are greater than before redistribution took place! The whole process is designated 'rational', and the underlying principles of redistribution are endorsed as legiti-mate, despite the fact that such a defence of social needs masks the maintenance of privilege. Yet, paradoxically, the introduction of market-regulated prices by means of econ-omic reform can go a long way towards meeting working-class interests (Szelenyi, 1979, p. 64).

But, returning to the differences between state socialist and capitalist social policies, the Hungarian sociologist Zsusza Ferge refers to 'societal policy' in preference to the term social policy. The latter is ingrained with the paternalistic traditions and values of capitalism: 'the main task of societal policy is to create conditions for the emergence of relations of production of a socialist type' (quoted in George and Manning, 1980, pp. 165–6). Social policy thus tends to be seen in very broad terms – to help satisfy the needs of the population, to eliminate social inequalities and to help create a classless society. It covers not only education, health and social security, but housing and subsidies for holidays, transport and food. Moreover, social policy is a government responsibility to a far greater extent than in any capitalist society. The contribution of the individual is minimised, but that of the workplace is more extensive. Following this logic, socialist social policies must be seen in a broad perspective. In addition, like capitalist welfare policies, they will vary from one state-socialist country to another according to the country's economic development and its cultural traditions.

It is, however, incorrect simply to assume that in a centrally planned economy economic policy decisions alone will determine the shape of social policy. It is a two-way relation, and the type and level of social provision has tremendous significance for the achievement of economic objectives. For example, the output of highly educated and trained people, the level of urban housing and transport, and the criteria of eligibility and level of payment for pensions etc., can be crucial to the success of general labour market policy and regional economic development. Social policy is developed and implemented within the framework of particular models of planning, usually as part of the annual budgetary process. Each government ministry responsible for housing and urban development, education, health, and so forth, will be engaged in a process of annual budgetary planning for all the establishments, personnel and resources they require to implement services. The same mechanisms come into play as in the case of industrial planning in general. Budgetary planning is a highly fragmented activity, which features poor coordination between institutions and services, an in-built tendency towards incrementalism and little regard to criteria of efficiency or effectiveness, and an in-built antipathy to innovation.

It was not until the late 1960s that the East European countries started to elevate social policy to the status of an integrated set of services amenable to systematic investigation. Before then it was subsumed under the heading of 'consumption' in plan and budgetary documents. Thus if we wish to know what priority is given to social policy considerations, we have to examine this item. At this point it is helpful to clear up a number of semantic difficulties. In the West, consumption has connotations of private choice followed by individual action. Economic literature makes frequent reference to consumer sovereignty, and although the collective consumption of goods and services provided by the state has been analysed by neo-Marxists, the impression remains that consumption is something that is best decided by private individuals. Such preconceptions infect the Western analysis of state socialist societies, with the consequent over-attention to the absolute and relative volume of 'consumption' in national income, and little attention to its distribution between personal consumption (understood as wages, fringe benefits and other sources of income), social consumption (understood in terms of services and benefits provided by state agencies or through the place of work), and collective consumption, defined to include defence, administration and the services of local authorities (comprising housing, urban transport, water and sanitation, roads and parks).

As if this confusion were not enough, a further analytical problem is the extent to which consumer prices are centrally fixed or left to the market. The latter accounts for up to one-third of all such prices in Yugoslavia, about one-quarter in Hungary and from 10 to 20 per cent elsewhere. A further complication arises in Yugoslavia, where both federal and republican governments administer consumption funds, and since 1965 Self-Management Associations of Interest also collect and distribute revenue on social services. To acquire a true picture of the scope of social policy, all possible sources of social expenditure must be considered. While it is possible to isolate the social consumption funds in the budget, caution is needed in interpreting the statistics, as funds for redistribution on social consumption include part directed towards production and capital expenditure. Also, social consumption is not entirely funded out of the central state budget: social security and health insurance expenditures are to quite a large extent paid through social insurance contributions in which state, employer and employee participate through various funds. Clearly, it is not wise to draw conclusions about level of provision purely from per capita indicators of social provision. What is required is a comparative analysis of the development of each individual service in terms of the comprehensiveness of cover, the extent of entitlement, and the method of finance and provision.

To summarise, many of the expenditures regarded as social consumption in the broad sense do not contribute to the standard of living, but represent costs of government or enterprise administration, or even capital expenditure. In this text our definition is somewhat narrower, but none the less we attempt to cover the labour market, education, housing and urbanisation, social security and pensions, health, and family policy.

The labour market

There are three good reasons for starting with a discussion of employment policy. First, in principle, remuneration initially rests upon labour inputs, with social need as a secondary criterion to be officially determined according to the specific stage of social development. Secondly, employment record and status are determining factors for a range of benefits. Finally, labour-market requirements are the main legitimate technical criterion for education policy. It might seem odd to write of a labour market in a centrally planed economy, as the direction of labour is designed to fulfil the requirements of the national plan and includes the development of skills, full employment, and efficient utilisation of labour. The main instrument of planning is the 'labour balance', whose function is to coordinate available labour resources with the requirements for labour. This is calculated from statistical data and the planned level of output and labour productivity, usually by a central agency responsible for employment, wages, and prices. Centralised labour-market planning is difficult to achieve. There are only four instruments available: control over the total numbers of highly qualified manpower (especially doctors and teachers) in terms of training and first destination in employment, regulation of the total size of an enterprise workforce, restrictions on the number of clerical and administrative employees relative to manual workers employed in an enterprise, and limited local authority powers to reduce labour turnover. In practice, all four are difficult to achieve. Tight control over the direction of labour conflicts with the objectives of economic decentralisation and the introduction of market mechanisms, as illustrated in the cases of Yugoslavia and Hungary.

The economic system is low in labour productivity because, despite high investment ratios, production is labour-intensive. Thus the fulfilment of the social objective of full employment creates economic underemployment in the industrial sector, something which in the past had been confined to agriculture. This is aggravated by a long working week (as high as 48 hours in Romania), a high retirement age and a pension system that encourages the continuation of work after retirement. Labour participation rates are also high. The employed as a percentage of the population has grown since the late 1940s (except in Yugoslavia, where it fell from 49 per cent in 1946 to 43 per cent in 1975), and in most countries is currently just below 60 per cent. But the most striking development is in female rates of employment. In the 1970s these were highest in Czechoslovakia and the GDR, with 86.5 per cent, followed by Hungary (69 per cent) and Poland (Michalsky, 1982; Ferge, 1978; Adam, 1982), with the lowest rate of all in the Balkan countries. In Yugoslavia, for example, women are 35 per cent of all state-sector and 45 per cent of all private-sector employees, with considerable variations between republics. Yet it may be that the greater proportion of the population employed in agriculture disguises the true female economic activity rate in the Balkan states.

Most of Eastern Europe faces a relative labour shortage, compared with the West. The notable exception is Yugoslavia. Since 1965 unemployment there has averaged between 8 and 10 per cent, with a high regional variation (Macedonia 29 per cent, Serbia 21 per cent, and Slovenia 1.5 per cent)

(Dyker, 1983). In the early 1980s there were over 800,000 registered unemployed, but this probably understates the true figures as non-registration in rural areas is common (Singleton and Carter, 1982). There is also evidence of high youth unemployment, especially in Kosovo in 1971, where it reached 50 per cent (a contributory factor to the political unrest of that year). Until the recession of the late 1970s emigration to the West was high.

Such large-scale unemployment has not been manifest elsewhere in state socialist Eastern Europe, but demographic development, technical change, and the effects of educational policies have worsened opportunities for youth. In Hungary a saturated labour market has brought about downward occupational mobility, long-distance daily commuting, and a growing inequality of earnings (Szalai, 1984). Outside Yugoslavia unemployment is not officially acknowledged. All state socialist citizens are obliged to work, and if they do not, they are vulnerable to charges of parasitism. Hungary has experimented with job-sharing and part-time work, and Romania has had some difficulty in sustaining full employment. The age profile of the Polish population demands a steady new flow of jobs. As unemployment is not officially admitted, state programmes of unemployment benefit do not exist, except in Hungary, where benefits exist but are difficult to claim as so many jobs are available. Elsewhere, the firm which discharges a worker has responsibility for his or her maintenance until new employment is found – a practice which does not encourage the most efficient allocation of the workforce. None the less, mismatch in the labour market cannot be atributed to such practices alone. Educational policy is also an important contributory factor.

Education

Education can be examined from at least three points of view: as an important instrument of political socialisation, as a means of social consumption or 'societal' policy to ensure the widening or redistribution of social opportunity, and as an essential factor in the production process to ensure that the labour market is supplied with the essential skills.

Political socialisation

Along with its partner concept, political culture, political socialisation emerged as a subject of study during the behavioural revolution in the social sciences in the late 1950s. Its existence was seen as essential to the establishment and maintenance of a political system, and was used to denote a process of acculturation whereby the population is introduced to societal procedures, institutions, and values. However, because of such an all-embracing scope, and because of a somewhat mechanistic and linear basis of explaining its effects, political socialisation has come under considerable criticism (Marsh, 1971; Fiszman, 1977). Furthermore, the quantitative techniques used to measure attitudes do not lend themselves easily to the situation in state socialist societies, and a variety of very different sources of evidence are resorted to. Analysis distinguishes between informal/primary structures of socialisation and formal/secondary structures (Volgyes, 1975). Included in the former were family, the church and peer groups, while the latter included the dominant Marxist–Leninist party and its associated youth groups, schools, trade unions and the military. The role of the media was also seen as very important (including television, radio, the press, books, films, theatre and the performing arts), because political socialisation is the conscious intention of the regime, and hence the media is the major instrument of implementing regime intentions. This focuses attention upon the practices of various social and political institutions, but does not enable us to measure their effect, which must be inferred.

We must look elsewhere therefore for explanations of why a particular structure of socialisation is important in one country and not in another. For example, why are the school systems and youth organisations seen to be of greater influence in the GDR (Hanhardt, 1975), but the media and the party in Czechoslovakia? Or, why do similar efforts by the party organisations in the GDR and Hungary result in considerable apparent success in the GDR, whilst little success in instilling the high moral standards of a socialist society has been achieved in Hungary? A variety of studies indicate that a revolutionary transformation of values has not taken place since 1945. Conscious attempts by the regime to direct the processes of political socialisation come up against the obstacle of the continued existence of institution values, norms and styles which have survived the political changeover (Fiszman, 1975, p. 133). So, in the case of Poland, the continued presence of the Roman Catholic church and the persistence of historical memories of Russian intervention remain important components of the culture. Thus in People's Poland the individual finds him/herself cross-pressured by conflicting demands and expectations from the formal agencies of socialisation, and from the formal and informal institutions representing the community and/or traditional culture (for example, the church, the family, the peer group, the youth sub-culture, the apolitical culture clubs and circles). While Polish educational institutions have been effective in breaking down social barriers, at the same time Poles seem to maintain with considerable enthusiasm traditional cultural attachments to the Roman Catholic church, to historic nationalism and to conventional family patterns and values. Yet the family has an ambivalent status – it is not the militant upholder of traditional nationalist values, as it can equally be a force for political restraint (Fiszman, 1975).

Political socialisation as a conscious process is focused mainly on youth. Hence the school and youth organisations are the main instruments for instilling the desired values of 'building socialism', 'socialist morality', 'patriotism' etc. While the latter two values are inculcated from the start of formal education via the normal curricula, in much the same way as moral education is imparted to primary school children in the West, there is little attempt to engage in direct indoctrination of Marxist–Leninist principles before the age of at least 12 years. In the words of Nigel Grant (1969), 'there is nothing at this level that would not be heartily endorsed by the YMCA, the Headmasters' Conference, or the late Lord Baden Powell'! It is only at the level of upper-secondary and higher education that the classical texts of Marxism–Leninism are perused, and then for no more than a few hours per week.

Emphasis of the socialisation effort upon youth denotes an anxiety about its effectiveness. There is not a single Marxist-–Leninist party in the region that has not voiced its misgivings

about the anti-socialist nature of modern youth culture, with
its hooliganism etc., and not called periodically for a more
intensive campaign among youth. In Romania this cost the
Communist Youth Union control over many responsibilities,
which were transferred to educational and cultural organs
(Heath, 1980, pp. 51–2).

But in all countries of Eastern Europe the attempt to create
a 'Socialist man' who unselfishly works for the common good
has met with only limited success. The inculcation and
internalisation of such values and symbols is at best partial.
There is considerable evidence that corruption, absenteeism,
waste and insufficient application of skills exist to a greater or
lesser extent in all East European countries. However, we do
not have the means to assess this with any precision, nor, for
that matter, to make the claim that it is definitively greater
than in Western capitalist societies.

Education and social opportunity
As well as socialising the citizenry of Eastern Europe into
acceptance of the legitimacy of the regimes, the structure and
operation of the education systems themselves is an important
guarantor of a legitimacy that made upward social mobility
an imperative of the system. Before 1945 only Czechoslovakia
and the GDR boasted a well developed system of primary,
secondary, vocational, and higher education commensurate
with the needs of an industrial society. Standards were not
universally low, but opportunities were unequal. For a few,
entry into lycée or grammar-school-type education provided
the passport for entry into higher education. The Christian
churches, both Catholic (especially in Poland) and Protestant, were major providers of education at all levels, but the
vast majority of the population were excluded. A measure of
such exclusion is the illiteracy rate. Although negligible in
Czechoslovakia, and under 9 per cent in Hungary, in Poland
and Romania it was around 25 per cent in 1939, 37 per cent in
Bulgaria, 46 per cent in Yugoslavia, and about 80 per cent in
Albania (Grant, 1969, pp. 17–18, 73). In the 41 years since
1945 illiteracy has largely been eradicated, and the right to
equal educational opportunity has been guaranteed in all
constitutional documents during this period. 'Sovietisation' of

the education systems took place in the post-1948 period, and the systems have undergone the transition from selective to mass systems to a greater extent than has been true of Western Europe. Conscious moves in the direction of unification, comprehensivisation, expansion, and emphasis upon vocational part-time and adult education all testify to this.

The first measures of transformation came in the late 1940s, with the 'Sovietisation' of the existing system. The central features can be summarised as including a strong ideological bent, which stresses that schools should serve society and be a means of transmitting socialist values and of creating the 'socialist man'; strong centralised control over institutions, curricula and the recruitment and training of teachers; the rejection of streaming according to ability in favour of universal comprehensive education freely available to all; a close relation between school and working life to ensure the 'unity of theory and practice'; a strong emphasis upon adult education; an expansionist approach to higher education; and a high priority to science and technology. Unlike Western systems, which still (despite the effects of growing youth unemployment since the 1970s) place considerable emphasis upon liberal principles such as freedom of choice and personal fulfilment, the major reference point is the collective need of society defined principally in terms of labour-market requirements.

The original model of school organisation was the unified 10-year school, taking pupils from the age of 7 to 17. While most pupils completed only the shorter version, the 7-year school (7–14), many followed general or vocational part-time courses afterward. This was modified after the 'Khrushchev' reforms of 1958, when the basic 8-year school (7–15) was inaugurated. These reforms also provided the model of what became known as 'polytechnical' education at a secondary level in three different types of institution. This attempt to bring education closer to real working life was intended to help overcome what was perceived as a growing gap between the masses and the educated elite, and the need to take greater advantage of the benefits of science and technology. The so-called 'Scientific Technological Revolution' brought about a second phase of development in Eastern Europe, but one

FIGURE 12.1

Patterns of schooling in Eastern Europe: the typical system

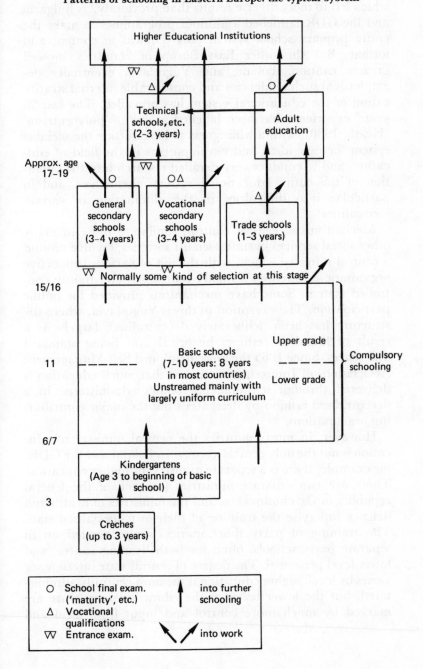

which led to more diverse results than previously, as Bulgaria and the GDR launched ambitious programmes to make the entire primary school system polytechnical in content and format. But the other East European countries showed greater caution. Poland and Yugoslavia eventually de-emphasised such tendencies and considerable internal stratification of the educational system has prevailed. The last 20 years' experience has been labelled as one of 'polycentrism' (Heath, 1980), with a willingness to look outside the socialist system for new ideas and developments in the field of education, and to conduct very detailed research into the operation of the entire educational systems themselves, and in particular into difficulties in the elimination of certain inequalities.

Mechanisms of central control, similar to those in many other social services in state socialist societies, revolve around a central ministry which, with the aid of various supportive organisations, operates a highly centralised and tightly controlled system. Some have mechanisms provided for public participation. The exception to this is Yugoslavia, where the structure has been deliberately decentralised, largely as a result of linguistic, ethnic, historical and living standard differences. Since 1865 the aforementioned Self-Management Associations of Interest, have meant that much education is delivered through self-financing bodies administered in a decentralised fashion by delegates from the major contributing organisations.

However, in most countries the central ministry of education is not the only central agency. In Poland and the GDR, for example, there is a separate ministry for higher education. There are two separate ministries for each of the federal republics in Czechoslovakia, and the ministries of health and defence supervise the training of their own specialised staff. The training of party functionaries is also carried on in separate party schools, often for both 'leading cadres' and lower level personnel. The degree of central state interference varies by level: higher education is the most centrally administered, but the lower levels of the educational structure are marked by much more control and input from local and regional authorities and interests. For example, in Czechoslovakia pre-primary schools are run by the lowest local authorities, while secondary schools are managed at the regional level, and the universities are run directly by the central ministry of education. In Bulgaria there is a mechanism to ensure local accountability through the district people's councils, and the GDR and Romania have elaborate systems to ensure parental and popular participation in school affairs in the locality. In many ways there is a strong similarity to arrangements in the UK and the USA. The control and administration of education in most East European countries conforms to the pattern in Figure 12.2 (Grant, 1969, p. 151).

Pre-school education
The provision of pre-school education is determined more by labour-market considerations than by concern with widening opportunities for women or with the implementation of child-centred theories of education. The introduction of prolonged maternity leave in a number of countries in the late 1960s, besides being of benefit to individual women, was also designed to cut down on the rates of absenteeism among female employees and ease the pressure for expansion of nursery facilities. Only Poland was without a child-rearing allowance until 1981. Labour shortages encouraged more generous arrangements to be adopted after the late 1960s, to encourage maximum female labour market participation. While generous by the standards of many Western industrialised countries, nurseries (which usually accommodate children up to about the age of 3) and kindergartens (which take children from 3 or 4 to school entrance age – usually 6 or 7) are neither compulsory, comprehensive, nor completely free. Priority is usually given to children of working mothers or those in poor health. In a large number of such establishments funded and controlled through the workplace, mothers' employment record, status, seniority and even sheer clout can be the primary determinants of access to places. Thus attendance by the eligible age group can vary from approximately 10 per cent in Yugoslavia, less than 20 per cent in Albania, through 25 per cent in Poland, to a high of 67 per cent in

FIGURE 12.2

Diagrammatic representation of control and administration of education in Eastern European countries

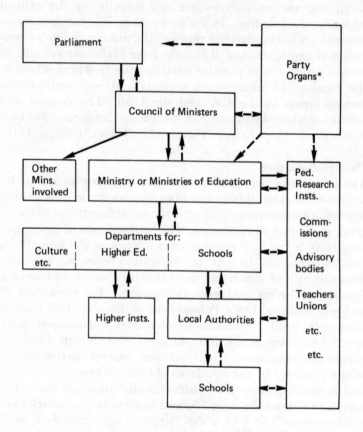

→ Formal authority
--→ Influence

*Lower Party Organs concern themselves with
the running of the system at all levels

Czechoslovakia and 92 per cent in the GDR. The number of places tends to reflect the level of industrialisation of particular countries (Heath, 1980, p. 231; Edwards, 1985).

Primary education

Although compulsory, primary schooling varies both in

duration and age range. Countries also vary in the extent to which they reflect Soviet patterns. Thus while polytechnical education was introduced at the secondary level in the GDR in the late 1950s, it was not diffused through the entire educational system until the Law on the Integrated Educational System of 1965. Then the primary schools were converted into 10-year polytechnical schools, with a strong emphasis upon science and applied studies. No other country has implemented this principle to the same extent, although Bulgaria comes the closest. Other innovations include the appearance of all-day primary schools in Czechoslovakia and the GDR, reforms to liberalise the curriculum in Hungary in 1978, and a tendency in both Yugoslavia and Romania for educational developments to echo the independence pursued in other areas of policy. In Yugoslavia the persisting problems of illiteracy and disparity of achievement between the federal republics and autonomous regions also affect the standards of provision.

Secondary education

There are three basic types of secondary school in Eastern Europe: a general secondary school of 4–5 years oriented towards the university, technological secondary schools of 4–5 years that train technicians and industrial managers, and vocational training schools of 2–3 years aimed at producing skilled workers. There are also systems of work-based learning such as apprenticeship schemes, especially in Poland and Czechoslovakia. Thus the emphasis is both upon diversity and narrow specialisation, reflected in the changing pattern from a short period of primary education followed by a longer period of secondary education to the reverse. In all countries there has been a concern to expand the vocational stream relative to the others, and also to increase the numbers going on to secondary education. Such increases are illustrated in the GDR, where 16 per cent of primary-school graduates proceeded to the ninth and tenth grade in 1952. The figure rose to 73 per cent in 1965, and 88 per cent in 1972 (Heath, 1980, p. 238). By the early 1980s around 80 per cent were then going on to a further 2 years of vocational training: 5 per cent were preparing for 'abitur' (the qualifying examination for entry into higher education) in vocationally orientated studies, and 12 per cent continued in the extended polytechnical secondary school to prepare for entrance to university.

A similar expansion was attempted in Poland in the 1970s and in Czechoslovakia in 1968. In Poland in 1979 a new type of polytechnical school with a course that lasted as long as the academic stream for university entrance was introduced. Since then the model has spread to the rest of Eastern Europe, although only recently to Yugoslavia, where in the mid-1970s educational reform eliminated selection at the secondary level and introduced a common curriculum and work experience for 2 years. Despite concerns with better manpower planning, this was construed as a threat to social privilege and parents resorted to personal contacts to get round the reform. However, the drive towards vocationalism has encountered obstacles which have their parallel in developments in the West. For a start, the prestige associated with a general secondary education persists, and is reflected in a restratification of the secondary education system whereby the political and social elite is able to operate a form of social closure (see below) that enhances the life chances of its own progeny. This has been particularly in evidence in Poland and Hungary. However, it may be that in the 1980s vocational training has been made more attractive and that higher education is facing hitherto unforeseen problems in recruitment. Also a growth in credentialism has fostered a growing demand for secondary education. The demand is met in two ways. The first comprises measures such as the aforementioned developments in Poland and Czechoslovakia which facilitate curricular reform, allowing students to transfer from one type of school to another. This is often designed to facilitate the expansion of the vocational element. The other de-emphasises the vocational element. A final observation concerns proposals to lengthen the period of schooling. In contrast to developments in the industrial West, which have tended to delay entry on to the labour market by lengthening the period of schooling to include 'initial training', the endemic labour shortage in most East European countries means that such an option is not considered, and the result, if anything, tends to towards an earlier start to schooling.

Higher education

Despite initial redirection of the expansion of places in the immediate post-1945 period (mainly for the rapid training of graduate engineers to solve the serious shortage of managerial manpower in industry – especially in Poland, the GDR, and Czechoslovakia), in most of Eastern Europe the transition from elite to mass higher education has not yet taken place. Higher education is provided in a variety of institutions (not all of them universities) and courses last between 3 and 6 years. With respect to manpower planning requirements, the functions of training and selection normally take precedence over the objectives of general intellectual training or personal fulfilment. Thus there are more places available in the applied sciences than in the humanities or the social sciences (even training in economics was relatively neglected until the 1970s). However, until the mid-1950s higher education planning tended to be *ad hoc*. The consequence was a mismatch of skills to labour market needs, or a dilution of entry requirements and standards, which later had repercussions for the quality of the calibre of staff in senior positions throughout the economy and society. Only in the GDR has manpower planning been an early and important influence.

Access to higher education is surprisingly similar to that which prevails in the West. For example, a common school matriculation examination and an entrance examination are normally taken, followed in some cases by further institutional selection and interviews. As the supply of places is determined by estimates of labour-market demand, chances of a successful place can depend very much on the subject chosen and the year of entry. Furthermore, in all countries except Hungary, there is a system of positive discrimination in favour of children of workers or peasants, to help them compete against children from a relatively more affluent or culturally endowed background. In Poland this was introduced in 1963–4 and further reinforced in 1967, and in 1973, following the abortive school-reform programme. In contrast, in Hungary this points system was abolished in the early 1970s, aggravating already existing inequalities of access (see below). Another factor which determines patterns of access is the mode of attendance. Although age participation rates of full-time attenders are notoriously unreliable indicators of access to higher education, they are useful for comparative purposes. They indicate a considerable variation. In the early 1980s the participation rate of the eligible age group ranged between 28 per cent in the GDR to 15 per cent in Poland, 11 per cent in Hungary, and 8 per cent in Romania – again a reflection of relative levels of industrialisation (Fulton *et al.*, 1982, pp. 9–10). Expansion to these levels took place fastest in the first half of the 1960s, but in Poland was concentrated in the period 1971–7. However, not all who graduated during this period were full-time students. In Poland a growing number were taking courses on a part-time basis or by correspondence – something which was much more pronounced than elsewhere (over the same period the number of part-time students fell in the GDR, and, if anything, was displaced by the growing number enrolled in on-the-job vocational training (Glaessner, 1984, p. 205). Finally, there are variations in the financial support students receive both within and between countries. Not all students receive financial aid, and those who do may receive differential amounts according to the subject of study, to whether they are sponsored by an enterprise for whom they are pledged to work, and according to their social background. Even then the possibility of study may be restricted by the difficulties of finding accommodation, especially for students from rural family backgrounds (a particular problem in Poland in the 1970s). Inequalities in modes of access and sources of financial support are reflected in the social class basis of recruitment.

Education, manpower planning, social inequality and politics

As may be seen, education policy is more than a mechanism to redistribute social life chances, it is also responsive to labour-market requirements. Nowhere is this more obvious than in higher education, which is best seen as the culmination of a process of social 'filtering' that tends to over-represent the sons (and to a lesser extent, the daughters) of the intelligentsia. Only in the privately run theological colleges in Poland do youth of peasant and working-class backgrounds overshadow those from the intelligentsia (Fiszman, 1975, pp. 91–2) – possibly a factor of importance in explaining the role of the church in the 1980–1 events. Inequalities also arise from urban–rural differences, so that in all but the primarily agrarian Balkan countries children from peasant background are more disadvantaged than those from working-class families. These inequalities also repeat themselves in the type of study: students of working-class and peasant backgrounds and from provincial towns are disproportionately represented among those studying part-time. They are also over-represented among those studying for highly vocational subjects such as engineering, teaching or agronomy, rather than medicine, humanities or pure sciences. Despite the points system to compensate for social background, it is difficult to operate with such general terms as 'working class' or 'peasant', which can conceal such wide social differences (see Chapter 6). Possibly for this reason the points system was abandoned in Hungary and it appears to be a source of considerable resentment in the GDR and Poland (Glaessner, 1984, p. 201; Tomiak, 1982, pp. 159–60). Neither do developments after entry to higher education counteract the effects of background in the intelligentsia (although there is a 50 per cent chance of entry): an average of 20 per cent of students drop out after the first year, again mainly of peasant and working-class backgrounds. Finally, the obligatory government-controlled job-placement service ensures that after graduation those from intelligentsia family background have better opportunities for well paid jobs with good prospects.

This latter phenomenon became very marked during the 1970s, when the graduate job market became saturated. Ineffective manpower planning, for example, the belated realisation that the Romanian economy needed agronomists as well as engineers (Gilberg, 1979), was one reason. The massive increase in enrolment of students during the late 1960s and early 1970s in line with demographic trends, and the persistence of traditional predispositions towards humanistic and away from vocational education were further causes. While about 30 per cent of graduates enter jobs which are unrelated to their qualifications (higher than one would expect in a centrally planned economy, but much lower than in the West), aspirations for higher education far outstrip the capacity of the labour market to meet expectations. The result is comparative underemployment, with some graduates entering jobs where hitherto higher education was not an entry requirement (such as factory foreman or chargehand). Also apparent is a tendency whereby those of 'lower' social background acquire the least popular placements, and a general growing resentment among more recent graduates towards a system where less qualified people from the immediate post-war generation are in senior positions. Such a situation goes a long way towards explaining the growing social support for dissident movements in Czechoslovakia and the GDR (Skilling, 1976; Zimmerman, 1978), and of course the growth of a movement like Solidarity in Poland (Woodall, 1981). Here the central issues in Polish higher education in the 1970s were university autonomy, selection principles, balance in the curriculum, and student welfare, jobs and placements (Tomiak, 1982, p. 158).

Finally, it is important not to restrict an explanation of social inequality in education to developments at the level of university entrance, as 'the social class composition in the institutions of secondary (and, subsequently, of higher) education reflect the unequal quality of the pre-secondary school education available to the various classes' (Fiszman, 1975, p. 89; Gazso, 1978, pp. 252–3, 256). In a system where other forms of inheritance are severely curtailed, education becomes an important instrument of social mobility, and hence a means by which those already well endowed with its benefits can transmit such 'cultural capital' to their offspring in a manner that primary and secondary schools are ill-equipped to counteract (Ferge, 1978). The continued insistence upon the formal principle of merit is a means by which (in the absence of effective compensatory education) the more socially advantaged can operate a system of social closure (Lane, 1982) in their own favour. This is very similar to the mechanism seen to operate in favour of middle-class children in Western primary schools. Yet is does not rest upon 'cultural capital' alone – the system of resource allocation is also at fault. In Poland, Czechoslovakia, and Yugoslavia in particular, the economically poor provinces and rural areas get left behind because a great deal of the responsibility for providing educational facilities is left to local initiatives and resources. Thus much within the system, the manner in which it functions, and much within the cultural tradition and heritage is stacked against those of lower class background and against the rural areas in general (Fiszman, 1975, p. 108). It is, however, precisely from among these groups that the system seeks its support and on behalf of whose interests it legitimises its rule, and whose youth it professes to favour.

Housing and urbanisation

Eastern European countries face a chronic housing shortage. The deficits are largest in Poland and Bulgaria, with a slightly better situation in the GDR, Hungary, and Czechoslovakia. The shortage has persisted, despite a large increase in the number of dwellings constructed since 1965, largely because of the cumulative effect of neglect since 1945 and changing needs. Housing policy achievements can only make sense when seen in the context of family policy and manpo..er policy. Thus shortage may inhibit marriage rates. It is also a major cause of the high divorce rates in this part of the world. Multi-household units are still the East European norm. Often two or three generations are living in three-roomed flat, and newlyweds have to wait as long as 15 years for a one-room flat. As for single people, unless they have come from a rural area to work in industry, they stand little chance. Even then accommodation will normally consist of a bunk bed in a crowded dormitory. Thus it is not surprising that as many as 40 per cent of those who live in rural areas work outside agriculture and that in Poland, Bulgaria and Hungary there are large numbers of 'peasant–workers' who make various arrangements for commuting into work in the towns but who also return periodically to work on the land (see Chapter 6). Thus an urban housing shortage affects labour mobility, and, indirectly, economic performance.

Housing has been seen by two Hungarian sociologists as the second most important component of basic consumption policy next to education (Hegedus and Markus, 1969). They argue that society must determine a basic level of consumption which is ensured for all its members, and, because of this, commodities which constitute this basic level should be removed from the arena where forces are in operation. The market should be allowed to become effective only over and above this level in 'differentiated consumption'. However, Szelenyi disagrees. His research in the late 1960s demonstrated that higher status groups, and the better qualified with a higher than average income, were heavily over-represented in post-war housing built and run by the state. The working class had to buy or build in the market (Szelenyi, 1979). Initially a strong supporter of the introduction of market forces as a means of social levelling, he later modified his views. Szelenyi's arguments apply not only to Hungary but equally to all other state socialist societies where the state assumes a managerial as opposed to a regulatory role in the housing market (Morton, 1979). Here the state has the means to distribute differential rewards to social groups, but it may not necessarily possess the means to redress inequalities effectively.

Housing policy is affected by the pre-1945 patterns of urbanisation and the pre-1945 structure of history. Rates of growth of employment in industry have been faster than the rate of urbanisation throughout East Europe. But regional inequalities seem to be least where a high degree of industrialisation has been achieved, such as in Czechoslovakia and the GDR. Also where there are a large number of dispersed industrial locations, a greater symmetry in access to social services is achieved. This is not the case in Poland, Yugoslavia and Romania (Musil, 1980). So there are great differences in settlement patterns, with the GDR the most urbanised (it has the highest concentration of population in large cities of all Eastern Europe), followed by Czechoslovakia, where well over half the population live in the numerous small and medium-size towns. Poland is more complex in that despite a doubling of the urban population since 1965, there has also been a long-term increase of the rural population not working in agriculture and there are pronounced regional inequalities of industrial development and associated economic and social infrastructure. In Poland the post-war economic development strategy encouraged over-industrialisation but under-urbanisation. By 1978 the number of households exceeded the number of dwellings by 1.8 million (Misztal and Misztal, 1984). Hungary is an oddity, in that well over 40 per cent live in rural areas, there are very few medium-sized towns, and one enormous conurbation, Budapest. Romania and Bulgaria have undergone the most rapid rate of urbanisation since 1945, but problems of rural settlement continue to create problems for industrial location. However, regional differences are greatest in Yugoslavia: the north-western republics are more densely populated than the south and east; Croatia and Serbia are the most urbanised, but the growth of the urban population has been restrained by the slow rate of house-building. By 1985 rates of urbanisation were as follows: Albania 39 per cent, Yugoslavia 46 per cent, Romania 64 per cent, Hungary 57 per cent, Poland 59 per cent, Bulgaria 68 per cent, Czechoslovakia 66 per cent, and the GDR 78 per cent (WHO, 1985). The number of households per housing unit was lowest in the GDR, followed by Hungary, Czechoslovakia and Poland. But when we consider the annual number of marriages and the annual number of new units built, we find few indications of long-term improvement. Between 1965 and 1975 in no Eastern Europe country did the rate of new units built consistently exceed the number of marriages (except for odd years in Czechoslovakia and Romania). Only Czechoslovakia managed to construct more dwellings than the number of marriages between 1971 and 1975, and the GDR, which had the greatest increase in housing units, still could not keep pace with the number of marriages. By the mid-1970s the deficit was worst in Poland, followed by the GDR and Bulgaria, and least in Hungary, Romania, and Czechoslovakia. In Poland the pledge to 'build a second Poland' after 1972 was still unable to reduce the shortfall, and cuts in investment for construction after 1977 had the effect of further lowering popular confidence in the government.

Governments are not the major providers of housing. Rather they exercise their managerial function by their monopoly over capital investment priorities, the planned rate of financial investment in housing, the production and utilisation of building materials, the number of multi-dwelling units to be built by state agencies, and the amount of credit available to cooperative and private builders. Although housing investment increased between 1960 and 1976, especially in Hungary, Bulgaria and Poland, the percentage share of housing in total capital investment outlays in the economy declined significantly in all except Czechoslovakia, where it remained unchanged, and Hungary, which was the only one to record an increase. Indeed Hungary was the only country to spend more on consumer development during this period (Morton, 1979). Thus central government preferences with respect to socio-economic development in general determine the volume and type of housing provision.

Housing construction is financed in three basic ways: by the state, by housing construction cooperatives, and privately. The first category is concentrated in the building of apartment blocks in towns, while the second is financed from a variety of sources: down payments by shareholders (anything from 6 to 40 per cent), credits from the state bank, and state subsidies. Private housing construction is largely funded by individual credits and loans. The relative balance between these three types of provision varies across countries and over time. In the more industrialised countries, such as Poland, Czechoslovakia, and the GDR, state finance was dominant from the start, while cooperative and privately financed construction was more extensive in Bulgaria, Hungary, and Romania, and after the 1960s had become more pervasive elsewhere. Indeed by the mid-1970s there had been such a dramatic shift that in Poland less than 20 per cent of all new housing was state-financed and one-third was privately owned in the GDR (Edwards, 1985, p. 45). In Hungary two-thirds of new housing built in Budapest in the 1980s were privately owned dwellings. Furthermore, private purchase was stressed to the extent that in Bulgaria, Czechoslovakia, •Poland and Romania, those employed in the state sector elite were encouraged to buy their own homes – long before the sale of council houses in the UK was considered! Thus the relative balance between the various sectors of provision, plus the general degree of shortage, can affect public access to housing. It is clear that housing is not supplied free of charge as of right, and that the 'consumer' is having to foot an increasing share of the bill – especially the less affluent 'consumer'. Shifting the onus to the consumer may have been very useful to the macro-economic objectives of the state, in that it relieved pressure on the government as the major provider of investment, and reduced available consumer spending power that otherwise would have had an inflationary effect, chasing other goods and services in short supply, but it also encourages the persistence and creation of inequalities. Given the administrative nature of the housing allocation process, a mechanism exists for governments to reward certain groups with superior accommodation, at a lower rent and after a shorter waiting time. The state sector can be a very useful way of subsidising elite groups, with the cooperative and private sectors performing a residual function (Szelenyi, 1983). Not only is this the exact obverse of the pattern in the West, but it constitutes a negation of the legitimating principle of providing housing free of charge as a social service that gives priority to need first and labour input second.

Social security and pensions

Even under a system which guarantees the right to work, some form of income maintenance for the non-working population is required. State socialist societies provide a wide (if not totally comprehensive) range of services in this respect. Old-age pensions, health insurance and survivors benefits exist in a similar form to that which prevails in the West. The only exception to this is unemployment benefit, which apart from Yugoslavia rarely takes more than the form of a one-off payment.

Pensions
The distribution of pensions recognises both the universality of needs and the reward of effort. No country operates a completely flat-rate system, but the degree to which payments are earnings-related varies. Pensions arrangements vary according to the general level of earnings and income differentials, the system in operation during the inter-war period,

occupational category, and source of finance and method of administration. Entitlement is fixed at age 60 for men and between the ages of 53 and 57 for women in most countries (although this was reduced from 65 to 60 in Poland as late as 1978). As a percentage of the national average wage, most pension systems offer replacement rates of between 50 and 70 per cent, but higher rates are offered to those doing arduous or dangerous work. The systems in Bulgaria, Romania and Poland are strongly earnings-related, but in contrast Czechoslovakia has a fixed basic pension rate for each category of work up to a maximum ceiling. Hungary introduced a uniform pension rate in 1975 which is related to years of service. The GDR is the exception in combining a flat-rate sum with an earnings-related increase for every year of insurance. It is interesting to observe that while the wealthiest countries (the GDR, Czechoslovakia and the USSR) have the lowest replacement rates, the poorest countries (Bulgaria and Romania) have the highest ones (Porkett, 1979). However, the relation between income levels and pensions is not that clear-cut. Generally, since the early 1960s average nominal old age pensions have risen everywhere, but the gap between them and average wages was not decreased everywhere. Just as the average worker in state socialist societies is worse off than his/her counterpart in the West, so is the average pensioner. Also it should be obvious that some pensioners are better off than others. Even in 1981, 15 per cent of those of pensionable age were ineligible in Hungary (Deacon, 1983). This is partly due to the fact that pensions are mainly earnings-related, but also to the absence (with the exception of Poland since 1986) of automatic adjustment to rising price and wage levels, and the possibility of continuing work after retirement. If a worker remains economically active after retirement age, then he or she may be offered a higher pension on retirement (Hungary, Bulgaria and Czechoslovakia), the possibility for the pension to be protected if he or she takes up work (GDR) or to be suspended either wholly or partially during periods of gainful employment (Hungary, Bulgaria and Poland). However, the pension rights may not be affected at all if employment is under a number of hours, or in a specified occupation (i.e. not a white-collar post). It is difficult to acquire an accurate picture of the proportion of employed pensioners; it is probably somewhere between 20 and 30 per cent, with the highest rate in Hungary, as would be expected in view of the labour shortage there and the scale of the second economy.

The assumption that all workers are in the same position is mistaken, though. Occupational differences are very important. Inequalities in the wage system are reflected in wage-related and work-conditioned benefits (Deacon, 1983). Much of this is due to the pre-1945 arrangements. All countries except Albania had schemes for both white- and blue-collar workers (Albania did not introduce any scheme before 1947), and these were taken over and transformed by the new state socialist governments in the late 1940s. In the GDR, and to some extent in Poland, elements of the pre-existing schemes were retained. Obviously the initial emphasis was upon arrangements for manual workers, and it was not until later that farmers employed on cooperative and collective farms were included. Their inclusion has reflected closely the ease with which governments have been able to exert control over the agricultural sector. Thus the relative ease of collectivis-ation in Czechoslovakia was accompanied by compulsory insurance for old age in 1952; in Hungary it was first introduced in 1958 and after 1967 pensions for farmers were on the same basis as state sector employees (Adam, 1983). Not until the 1970s did Yugoslav and Polish peasants get access to such pensions. The resistance of the private farmers in Poland to collectivisation delayed their inclusion in the scheme. Since 1962 the state had been offering private farmers a pension in exchange for their land, but it was not until 1978 that old-age insurance was made compulsory. However, the terms were less favourable than those for the state sector: entitlement was at age 65 for men, and 60 for women. The qualifying condition included a record of regular sales of produce to the state above a minimum value and over a period of 25 years (thereby excluding the peasant–workers with pensions from non-agricultural employment); and high levels of contribu-tion relative to other employees – 18 per cent as opposed to 5 per cent) (Lukianenko, 1978; Porkett, 1981). At the other end of the scale come members of the repressive state elite, such as the military, police, and certain government and party officials, who receive preferential treatment. This is particularly evident in Czechoslovakia and Poland, but less so in Hungary. Some other categories of employee also receive better pensions: railwaymen and miners in Poland; and lawyers, ministers of religion, and career members of the armed forces in Romania. Supplementary pensions have been available for members of the intelligentsia in scientific, artistic, educational and medical institutions in the GDR since the 1970s (Porkett, 1979; Michalsky, 1984).

The finance and administration of pension schemes is not wholly under central state control. As we have already pointed out, the finance of social policy measures is drawn from social consumption funds, based upon allocations from the state budget, and from the resources of enterprises and social organisations. The specific funds for social security are drawn from the resources of enterprises, state administration, and collective farms, and from state budgetary credits, plus modest contributions from certain categories of the population. They are planned within the framework of the state budget. The relative proportions of contributions vary between countries and between different sectors of economic activity, but there is a noticeable trend towards increased allocations from the state budget. So in Bulgaria contributions by the employee are not made but they are in Poland and Hungary (but even here they are a relatively small proportion – 5 per cent and 3 per cent respectively).

Health insurance
In state socialist countries social security is defined in a broad sense to compensate for loss of income as a result of risks to which the individual is exposed, and to create living conditions that will meet special needs. It consists of cash benefits (pensions, and allowances), health care, social services, rehabilitation, maintenance of children, and other benefits in cash and kind. In most countries it is administered by state agencies working jointly with the trade unions and other social organisations (as in Poland, Romania and the USSR), but in Hungary and Bulgaria it is run wholly by the trade unions. In the GDR since 1950 85 per cent have been in a

scheme run by the FDGB. State budget expenditure directly finances health protection (including medical care for the elderly and the disabled), institutional care and vocational and social rehabilitation of the disabled, care for pre-school children; allowances for single parents (female only) and military and other special pensions. In Poland, as in Hungary and the USSR, pensions are administered and paid at the insured person's place of work or residence. Among the public organisations responsible are the Ministry of Labour, Wages and Social Affairs, which develops and implements social policy, including social insurance. The latter has been administered by the Social Insurance Institute since 1960. It has branches in each voivodship (fifty-four since 1976), 136 inspectorates and 200 information offices, which liaise with each place of work. The Ministry of Health and Social Protection is responsible for health care and rehabilitation. At the voivodship level the planning of services takes place along with the coordination of specialised agencies, while the actual delivery of services is through the lowest level of local government, the commune. In Hungary, however, since 1965, the development, administration, supervision and control of social security have been the responsibility of the Central Council of Hungarian Trade Unions – the culmination of gradual developments since 1950. A Central Social Security Council with representation from several interested associations, and a general directorate of social security, oversee the details of policy and administration. These operate within a decentralised framework so that over 90 per cent of all employees are paid their allowance directly by the social security fund of the enterprise where they work. Indeed, in Hungary, firms which employ over 1000 people are financially responsible for the payment of contributions and benefits, and social security at the workplace is run by various bodies elected by the workers – the trade union committee, the Social Security Council, and sub-committees for such matters as health and pensions (Lukianenko, 1978).

Health

Theoretically, socialist health policy is predicated upon the assumption that capitalism is the major cause of ill-health in the way in which it exploits working people by making them work long hours in unhealthy and dangerous conditions for little money, and then sends them home to live in an unhealthy house in a poor environment on a poor diet. Thus a socialist health policy would be concerned primarily to prevent avoidable illness. Secondly, it would do so in a manner that aimed to redistribute access to health resources between social classes. It would also overcome the pre-existing medical division of labour, which entrusted too much power to doctors and encouraged over-specialisation in certain forms of acute medicine at the expense of prevention and care. It would ensure that the service was run in a manner that guaranteed maximum accountability to the needs of the population it was designed to serve. In order to evaluate the progress of the state socialist societies in these respects, we shall now look at the historical development of national health services, their finance and administration, the way in which health needs have been met by the medical division of labour, redistributive measures, and, finally, the accountability of the health services and their contribution to regime legitimacy.

The creation of national health services and the pre-1945 situation

Despite commitment to improvements in health, the creation of a universal public health service did not take place immediately after 1945. Not only scarcity of resources but the level and scope of pre-existing services were important in determining the scope and timing of the new arrangements. Thus where these were fairly comprehensive such as in the GDR, they were revived, and a large number of autonomous sickness and pension funds continued to exist in Czechoslovakia after the 1948 National Insurance Act, although in Hungary such autonomous funds were amalgamated into a central fund in 1945. In countries which had experienced boundary changes, like Poland, insurance cover was more comprehensive in the former German territories, but on the whole, like the rest of the non-Balkan countries, most of the urban salaried middle class and skilled and manual working class were covered. However, it may come as some surprise to discover that a large part of the Polish peasantry were covered by sickness insurance in the interwar period. The same applied to the interwar Romanian peasantry. For most countries legislation founding a national health service was passed in the late 1940s and early 1950s, and the right to health was guaranteed in the constitutions from an early date.

Finance
Health services are not all financed directly out of taxation, nor are they entirely free of charge. For a start, the principle of social insurance is widespread, with contributions coming from taxation revenue, employers and employees, in varying amounts. While taxation is the major source of finance in the USSR and Bulgaria, it contributes less than 50 per cent in the GDR and Hungary. Social insurance costs are borne entirely by the government and the employer in all countries, except for the GDR. Treatment is not always provided free of charge, especially for prescriptions, where a sliding scale of charges operates (except for Czechoslovakia, where since 1966 all treatment has been free). Nor is all treatment confined to the public sector. Private practice has survived in the GDR, Romania and is most extensive in Hungary, both legitimately and as part of the second economy (dental treatment and something approaching 'pay-beds' exist here). However, in Poland and Bulgaria since 1972 it is officially banned. Private hospitals are usually run by religious foundations, such as in the GDR and Poland. The relatively limited role of private practice is held to be important in keeping the cost of providing health care down. Taking into account the problems of statistical comparability, Kaser (1976) calculated in the early 1970s that health expenditure as a proportion of GNP was much lower in Eastern Europe than among industrialised Western states. It ranged from between 2.4 to 2.8 per cent in the USSR, Bulgaria and Romania, to 4.8 to 5.1 per cent in Czechoslovakia, Poland and Hungary. The GDR was the highest spender at 5.8 per cent.

Administration
Two patterns are common. The first is a central ministry of health and social services, with coordination at the regional level, where the major teaching hospitals are controlled (such

as in the GDR and Czechoslovakia). The other is a structure decentralised to the district or area level (Hungary, Poland since 1973, and Romania since the early 1970s). However, the central ministry of health (two for each of the republics in Czechoslovakia after 1968) is not the sole provider of health care. There are a number of other agencies, such as the school medical service, run by the ministries of education, the factory health service run by management or the trade unions and also a specialist occupational service, often with separate treatment facilities, for the political, military, state security and academic elite. Thus considerable organisational fragmentation exists both at the central and local level. In times of cuts in government expenditure, as in Poland after 1975, such fragmentation may heighten inequalities, which a politically weak ministry of health is unable to counteract, and can contribute to considerable waste of resources (Millard, 1982). In particular, the size of the factory health service differs from being fairly narrow in scope in Hungary but more significant in Poland, where institutions of workforce representation control access to a number of rest and holiday homes and sanatoria owned by the trade unions.

Demographic developments and health needs
Like other elements of social policy such as education, housing, and pensions, health needs are very much affected by demographic developments. Despite the loss of life during the war, in all countries except the GDR population has tended to increase. A major cause is the decline in infant mortality rtes to between 20 and 30 per cent of the 1940 level, and the increase in life expectancy by about 20 years in all countries except the GDR and Czechoslovakia. In family policy (see below) government policies have inadvertently encouraged a fall in the birthrate (except for Czechoslovakia in the 1970s) and it would appear that maternity services are not uniformly of a high standard (especially in Poland in the 1970s). The growing need is for health care for the elderly, who now constitute about 20 per cent of the population – a rise of nearly 100 per cent – in most countries. Health needs have also changed, as can be seen from statistics on epidemiology. While the diseases of poverty (such as tuberculosis, rickets

and pellagra) have largely disappeared, the diseases of civilisation such as cancer and circulatory diseases are on the
increase, especially in the more industrial states, such as the
GDR and Czechoslovakia. A disturbing development is the
increasing mortality rate among all male cohorts over the age
of 19, especially in Poland, Hungary, and the USSR (WHO,
1985). Thus the central issue becomes whether the medical
division of labour is able to meet these needs.

The medical division of labour
Compared to the West the ratios of physicians to the population are generally much higher, but salaries are comparatively lower in relation to other professional groups such as
factory managers, and lowest of all in Bulgaria. The composition of the profession reflects the immediate post-war
shortage of personnel, as many emigrated to the West. The
subsequent exodus of further numbers (until 1961 in the
GDR, and after 1968 in Czechoslovakia), and the subsequent
need for rapid training meant there was a shortage of doctors.
As in the USSR, the medical profession is highly feminised,
but, as might be expected, with female under-representation
in senior positions. In Poland, which had the fastest rate of
increase in the number of new doctors trained throughout the
whole of the CMEA between 1960 and 1973, 63 per cent of
the new doctors were women. The division of labour is very
similar to that of the West, the major exception being the
category of *feldsher*, a kind of highly qualified medical auxiliary found in the former territories of the Russian empire,
most of whom are attached to health centres or 'polyclinics',
and dispense primary care. The balance between types of care
is much more hospital-oriented in Eastern Europe, with a
large out-patient facility dealing with primary care. Even
general medical doctors are usually attached to a clinic, and
Hungary is somewhat of an exception in permitting patient
choice of doctor. There is nothing directly analogous to the
British general practitioner. However, the prestige that ac-
crues to medical specialisms is very similar – cardio-vascular
surgery, in particular, has high status, but paediatrics, and,
surprisingly, gynaecology are of lower status, and geriatrics
and care for the mentally handicapped are at the bottom of

the pile. What is distinctive about the 'Cinderella' services is that they appear to be in an even less favourable situation than in the West. This is reflected in the generally very low priority given to caring and social work. No East European country has the battery of social workers that are found in the West. Social services that do exist mobilise an army of largely voluntary welfare workers, as in Poland (Noron, 1983). As a result, despite government statements to the contrary, increased emphasis upon an effective integrated delivery of primary care has not borne fruit. Nor has preventive medicine been a resounding success. Starved of resources (except for the GDR in the 1970s), it has usually received the lowest priority. Reports from Poland before and during the crisis of 1980 to 1981 confirm this observation (DIP, 1981).

Redistributive measures

Since the creation of national health services in the post-war period, cover has been extended beyond the urban salaried middle class and skilled manual workers. However, inequalities persist. Most notorious is the case of the peasantry in Poland, although less favourable treatment is also the lot of workers on cooperative farms and the self-employed elsewhere. It was not until 1972 that the Polish peasant was brought under the cover of health insurance and had access to free treatment. By this time the 'rot' had set in, with most younger people choosing to leave the land to work in industry, so that by the late 1970s one-third of heads of household in private agriculture were over the age of 60 and most were without an heir to take over their farm. This is an example of how social policy can have a very deleterious effect upon the economy. We have already seen how members of the state apparatus enjoy more privileged treatment. There are also certain categories of blue-collar worker (especially in transport and mining) and members of the intelligentsia who have privileged access to health facilities (especially in the GDR). However, putting the different facilities aside, universally throughout Eastern Europe social indicators suggest that members of the intelligentsia enjoy better health and are more likely to consult their doctor at an early stage of illness. Overlying the class division in access to health care is the urban–rural divide. In Romania and Hungary there is an over-concentration of doctors in the capital cities that manpower policies have not been able to redress, and because of the discriminatory policy towards the Polish peasantry until 1972, the demand for doctors was lower in rural areas. After that date further problems were created by the failure to deploy more medical personnel to meet the rising demand for care.

Accountability and legitimacy

The lack of public accountability in the Polish health service became a central issue in the 1980–1 crisis, but nowhere has there been any concern to change the social relations of medical practice. As in the USSR, medicine remains technical, urban, specialised and curative (Navarro, 1977) throughout Eastern Europe. Again the Polish case is illustrative of the marginal importance attached to health. Public expenditure cuts in Poland after 1975 immediately focused on investment and imports, with disastrous implications for hospital construction and the supply of medicines. However, the low priority given to health policy does not rest simply upon its position *vis-à-vis* the 'productive' sector of the economy, but also in the organisational weakness of the ministries of health. The ministries do not exert complete control over the planning and distribution of health resources, and are particularly vulnerable to the pressures of doctors, planners and industrial interests. Popular influence is largely absent (even in Yugoslavia), and is most likely to be felt at the level of the industrial enterprise. Finally, on a broader level, if, as in Poland during the late 1970s, social indicators show falling standards and a rise in all mortality rates, the claim that state socialist governments take better care of their citizens than their capitalist counterparts appears to be totally without foundation.

Family policy

This is a relatively new area of concern in the West, dating largely from the 1960s and 1970s (although in some countries, such as France and Sweden, its origins come earlier in the post-1945 period). Hitherto, largely taken for granted in debates on social policy, the family has now become a key issue. But family policy itself is a rather amorphous concept, susceptible to both narrow and broad definition. It can be both explicit and implicit; both a means of providing support and a vehicle for shaping the lives of children and of women. The term may denote both the description of a field of interest and a conscious instrument of change. It can refer to both a cluster of policies and a vehicle to transmit social values (Kamerman and Kahn, 1978). The growing interest in family policy can be attributed to changes in the structure, composition and function of the family, and a wider anxiety about population policy. From very early on the Bolsheviks were concerned with the question of what a 'socialist' family and personal relations would entail. Also central to this was the thorny problem of the 'Woman Question'. Indeed, the frequent changes in official attitudes towards the family immediately after 1917, 1921, 1936 and again after 1956, were influential in shaping the family policies of the East European state socialist societies.

In Eastern Europe family policies usually concern themselves with the following issues: entry into marriage, divorce, birthrates and family size, abortion and contraception, the provision of child-care facilities and the organisation of domestic labour. Generally, the average age of marriage has fallen since 1945 from the late to the early twenties. However, this does not necessarily denote the creation of entirely new households, because of the constraints of the housing shortage (see above). Also, even though there have been improvements in access to housing, this has not stopped the divorce rate from soaring. Although calculated differently, this tends to have risen to around 40 per cent of all marriages, with evidence that the majority of petitions came from women (David, 1982; Edwards, 1985). Only in Romania has access to divorce been restricted since the mid-1960s. Elsewhere it has been made easier. Birthrates and family sizes have fluctuated, with a general tendency to fall in the 1960s, since when there has been an incomplete recovery. Family structure and regime employment policy have been important influences. The tremendous shift from agriculture to industry, and from rural to urban environment in a situation of acute housing shortage, has accelerated the breakdown of the extended family and the three and four generation household – especially in the less industrialised states. Also, the acute labour shortage and subsequent encouragement of women to enter the labour market have contributed to a falling birthrate, which is now below the replacement rate. This is especially the case in Hungary and the GDR, although the birthrate appears to have recovered somewhat in Romania, and Poland, and outstandingly in Albania (David, 1982).

Fertility has also been affected by the availability of abortion and contraception. All the state socialist societies of Eastern Europe, except Albania, eventually followed the lead of the USSR in 1955 in abolishing the 1936 restrictions on abortion. The liberalisation process began in Hungary, and abortion on demand was legalised there in 1956. Bulgaria and Poland also passed liberal legislation in 1956, followed by Romania and Czechoslovakia in 1957, and Yugoslavia in 1960, usually restricting abortion on 'social' grounds to the first 3 months of pregnancy, and on medical grounds up to 6 months. However, the GDR deviated from the trend in following up a period of relative liberalisation with restrictive legislation in 1950, and only a slightly more liberal interpretation in 1965. Abortion on request did not come until 1972. But, by the early 1960s, governments were becoming anxious about the decline in birthrates. Restrictions upon the availability of abortion came first in Romania in 1966, in Bulgaria in 1968, and in Czechoslovakia and Hungary in 1973 and 1974. Surprisingly, in view of the strength of the Catholic church, restrictive legislation did not appear in Poland. It is interesting to note that abortion also constituted a form of contraception. The withdrawal method appears to have been the most widely used, followed by IUDs and condoms, rather than the contraceptive pill. Only in the GDR did a domestically manufactured oral contraceptive become widely available in the 1970s.

The growing restrictions upon abortion were part of a wave of pro-natalist policy measures designed to increase fertility rates and family sizes during the late 1960s and 1970s. Most countries introduced or raised such cash incentives as lump sum birth grants, paid maternity leave, monthly family and child-care allowances, and even low-interest loans for newlyweds. Other measures included subsidies for nurseries, kindergartens, school meals, and children's transportation and rent rebates. Thus official population policy became pro-natalist (except in Albania and Yugoslavia, where a combi-nation of federal and national diversity, and a constitutional guarantee of individual self-determination over childbirth in 1974, complicated policy). The level of the benefits was highest in the GDR, Czechoslovakia and Hungary, and lowest in Albania and Yugoslavia, but there is general doubt about their long-term effect upon fertility (David, 1982), and agreement that they probably only have an impact upon the timing of births. The major determinants appear to be the availability of child care and the division of domestic labour. Time budget analysis for the GDR, Poland and Hungary reinforces the impression that women bear a double or even a treble burden in that besides waged work, the bulk of the child care, food preparation, cleaning, laundry and shopping fall to them (in conditions where the labour-saving tech-nology and infrastructure of domestic services and convenient shopping facilities are largely absent). In conclusion, it can be said that government attempts to influence private repro-ductive behaviour and family policy will only be of limited success so long as living conditions are such as to discourage women from having more than one or two children (David, 1982).

Conclusion: social policy and inequality

We have seen how the state socialist societies adopt social policies in much the same way as do Western industrialised states. We have also shown that while in some instances there is a similarity in service organisation and entitlement, this is not the case for others, and indeed not for all aspects of a particular service. Whether this leads to a more egalitarian society is doubtful. Social structure and the structure of political power impinge upon this. On the whole the regimes of Eastern Europe have viewed inequalities in objective terms: that is, they believed that they would disappear with the development of the forces of production. However, the effects of advanced industrialisation, with the attendant increase in skill and educational levels, have tended to increase and not reduce inequalities. There has been a tendency for social consumption to benefit those with higher incomes, especially in the case of access to education and housing. In addition, with many benefits tied to income level (social security and pensions), the existing division of labour is an important determinant of access to social consumption (Lane, 1982, p. 66). But as Frank Parkin has observed, it is not income alone that determines access, but rather occupation. The white-collar intelligentsia is able to transmit its 'cultural capital' to the following generation, and is also to operate a mechanism of 'social closure', understood as the 'process by which a wide range of social groups (class occupational, gender, racial, religious) seek to maximise their own rewards and to exclude access from "subordinate outsiders" to resources and opportunities' (Parkin, 1979). For this reason, the debates between Szelenyi and Ferge in Hungary are particularly relevant, in that they point to the futility of expecting redistributive policies to reduce inequalities if they rest solely on the formal guarantee of equal opportunity and bureaucratic methods of allocation.

13

The External Relations of the East European Socialist States

So far, our discussion of the political process and policy-making in Eastern Europe has placed as much emphasis upon the distinctiveness as the close similarities of these societies to the USSR. However, when examining their relations with the outside world, we come up against the inescapable fact that the prime determinant is the USSR itself, and that any distinctive foreign policy 'line' is the product of a bold decision taken by brave political leaderships. The constraints of 'bloc' politics mean that in military, diplomatic, economic and ideological aspects, Eastern Europe comes under the Soviet 'umbrella'. A number of international organisations exist to underpin this Soviet hegemony, but that should not delude us – complete uniformity of interest, conformity to Soviet interests, and persistent continuity of line since 1945, are absent. East European interests and behaviour diverge, and sometimes maverick stances are adopted.

The Warsaw Pact provides the basic military framework of the alliance, in terms of its position in Euope, but not all East European states are members. Nor are members altogether acquiescent to the lead from the Soviet military. This divergence extends further into the world role of these countries. Some have managed to wriggle under the perimeter fence of the Soviet Bloc and embrace non-alignment as a negotiating position. Others have seen new possibilities in closer ties with the world's 'third force' – the People's Republic of China – and have consequently arrived at a strange destination in international diplomacy. Nor are these countries merely the cipher for Soviet involvement in the Third World. Again there is considerable divergence from the Soviet position in terms of aid to the less developed countries and support for liberation movements. In economic terms, the Council for Mutual Economic Assistance (CMEA or Comecon) provides a weak measure of integration, and at certain stages of its development there was reason to speculate about its advantage to the USSR. There were expectations that the era of 'detente' would prise these countries away from close economic ties with the USSR, and bring them into greater economic dependence on the West. Ultimately ideological somersaults are needed for this to occur, but again ideological unity is under attack.

A recent threat arose from outside Eastern Europe, although in the past the reverse was true. This time the Marxist–Leninist parties in Western Europe were the cause. So-called Euro-Communism steadily infected the communist parties of Italy, Spain, and to a lesser extent France and Great Britain after 1976. Certain central tenets of the Leninist theory of party organisation and the nature of the transition to socialism came under attack. This was not entirely unprecedented (indeed, many of the East European countries had flirted with similar ideas in the past) and Euro-Communism has waned since 1979. But, coming as it did during the full-flowering of 'detente', and after the Helsinki Accords of 1975, it provided a legitimate encouragement for the growth of dissident movements in East European countries. Their significance for domestic politics and the cohesion of the international socialist commonwealth was considerable, as illustrated by the events in Poland during 1980–1. If nothing else, such developments surely illustrate the link between domestic and international policy-making arenas, and that East European regimes are not obedient puppets which dance only to a tune played from Moscow. In this chapter we shall try to convey an impression of the distinctiveness of East European foreign and trading relations. Before doing so, we shall give some attention to the overriding military and strategic framework of bloc politics.

Bloc politics: the development of a framework

To return to our earlier point, it is important not to focus on what is exceptional about Eastern Europe to the exclusion of what it has in common with the USSR. It should not be forgotten that none of the Marxist–Leninist regimes, with the exception of Yugoslavia and Albania, came to power as the result of partisan struggle alone. In some way or other, all were dependent upon Soviet assistance either in assuming or in retaining power. The geopolitical map of 1945 is important in explaining the reasons for Soviet 'assistance'. The Red Army had borne the worst of the fighting against the Nazis on the Eastern Front and the USSR had lost 25 million war dead. Furthermore, the previously isolationist USA had been elevated to the status of a great power in Europe, and her newly acquired nuclear capability had implications for Soviet security interests there. These are the factors that explain the Soviet strategy towards the East European countries that it was 'liberating' in 1945. A concern to protect its territorial integrity and sphere of influence arose as much out of defensiveness as out of chauvinistic design. From the blockade of Berlin in 1948 to the invasion of Afghanistan in 1979, Soviet actions along its borders have been motivated by a feeling of vulnerability to Western interests.

The geopolitical map of Central Europe may not have changed much since the late 1940s, but the contours of super-power relations have not remained static. This has implications for East Europe in terms of the strategic balance between East and West, and the period 1947 to the present can be divided into four. The first is marked by the onset of the Cold War during 1947–8, when an 'Iron Curtain' descended between East and West Europe, and meaningful diplomatic relations broke down. From 1953 until 1969 there were a series of initiatives on both sides directed at the reduction of confrontation, but these were ineffective because of the impact of other forces and tensions upon the East–West conflict (for example, the Suez Crisis, the Cuban Missile Crisis of 1962, increased US intervention in Vietnam in 1965, and the Arab–Israeli conflict of 1967). The year 1969 marked the beginning of an era of 'detente' associated with the arrival in office of President Nixon and US Secretary of State Kissinger. However, the 'anti-Atlanticism' of the Gaullist party in France, and the 'Ostpolitik' of the West German Social Democrats towards the GDR, brought the arena of East–West relations firmly back to Europe. The Helsinki Conference on European Security and Cooperation offered extensive trading relations with the West to the sagging economies of Eastern Europe, in exchange for concessions on human rights. The two SALT Treaties of 1972 and 1979 provided the framework within which the arms race could slow down. However, a renewed bellicosity towards the USSR coincided with the beginning of the Reagan presidency, and the USSR took an intransigent stance on disarmament. Soviet intervention in Afghanistan in 1979, and the events leading to martial law in Poland in 1981, inaugurated what has been termed the 'Second Cold War' (Halliday, 1983). This time, however, the rattling of sabres is accompanied by a continued participation in international negotiations by both major protagonists.

It is within this context that the East European countries are international actors in Europe. The context may be further elaborated by a discussion of developments in the strategic military balance. The diversification of the nuclear arsenal of both super-powers has made calculations about parity extremely complex and we are unable to do justice to an explanation in this text. To summarise, the late acquisition of a nuclear capability in 1953, and the debacle of the Cuban Missile Crisis in 1962, stimulated the USSR into improving its missile delivery systems (Baylis and Segal, 1981). A US superiority in warheads, but a Soviet lead in delivery vehicles, was the context in which the SALT Treaties were negotiated. The USA was still able to maintain its lead in warheads and introduce innovations which slipped through the loopholes in the SALT agreements. But the USSR did not significantly reduce its numbers of delivery vehicles. Furthermore, the possibility of deploying the new generation of intermediate range weapons (Cruise and Pershing II) in Western Europe was designed to enhance US superiority. Ostensibly in response to the Soviet stationing of SS20 intermediate weapons capable of striking West European targets, the US, supported by prominent NATO members, has deployed these weapons. In fact, the USSR deployment of the SS20s is not the recent act of provocation it is made out to be. It was already underway in the mid-1970s. In this light, the refusal of the USA to renounce 'first use' of nuclear weapons, and the 'offer' to the USSR of the 'Zero Option' – the promise not to station Cruise and Pershing in return for the Soviet withdrawal of all of its SS20s and some earlier generation missiles – can only be seen as a tactic designed to enhance US superiority. This change in the strategic military balance thus leaves the USSR on the defensive – a position that the diplomatic initiatives of the Soviet leader Mikhail Gorbachev have gone some way to change.

Outside the purely strategic military issues, the changing world role of the two super-powers has increased tension between them. During the 1950s the USSR did not take an active part in World politics. Even after the end of that decade, Cuba apart, it did not directly aid independence movements and radical regimes. However, between 1974 and 1980 there were fourteen revolutionary upheavals in the Third World (Halliday, 1983, p. 92), and the USSR became drawn into support for liberation movements in Africa, Central America and South East Asia. This was not always without complications, as is illustrated by the fate of Soviet initiatives in the Middle East, Ethiopia, and Afghanistan. In most countries the revolutionary movements had originated because of domestic factors rather than Soviet intervention, and where the USSR was drawn in to provide support, this was not always in favour of liberation movements or progressive governments. Often the motive was to pre-empt or to counteract the influence of the USA. In this context political disturbances in Eastern Europe are an obstacle to the Soviet pursuit of a World role.

In the light of our discussion of international relations between the two super-powers and their respective military alliances after 1945, we can see that geographical incorporation of Eastern Europe into the Soviet sphere of influence became less central to the cause of East–West tension over time. Until the advent of the Second Cold War, the Middle East, South East Asia and later Black Africa and Central America became the loci of dispute. Even the characteristic attempt of the 'detente' era to seduce East European regimes with the promise of economic prosperity was only designed to destabilise the membership of the Warsaw Pact in order to prosecute US international advantage elsewhere. Moreover, the strategic focus of the Second Cold War is upon Western and not Eastern Europe, which is implicitly viewed by NATO as an extended launching platform for Soviet missiles. But is this how the East Europeans see themselves, and are they content with such a role? To answer this we shall start with an examination of the East European role within the Warsaw Pact.

The Warsaw Treaty Organisation

The Warsaw Pact, or to give it the correct title, the Warsaw Treaty Organisation (WTO), has been described as 'an institutional means for conducting intra-bloc relations, relations whose dimensions and intensity are determined to a great extent by the Soviet Union (Cason, 1983, p. 221). However, it is not an alliance system originally designed to execute joint military operations in wartime. In this respect it is not the mirror image of NATO. Rather, the Warsaw Pact was formed in May 1945 to provide a system of collective security for the USSR, Albania, Czechoslovakia, Hungary, Bulgaria, Romania, and Poland (the GDR joined in 1956, Albania left in 1961, and Yugoslavia, for reasons of ideological difference with the USSR, remained outside). On one level it can be seen as a diplomatic ploy in response to the admission of the Federal Republic of Germany (FRG) into NATO, as a means to provide a legal basis for the presence of Soviet troops on Hungarian and Romanian territory following the signing of the Austrian State Treaty in 1955, and as a means of international collective representation for the 1955 Geneva talks. However, the prime reason for its creation was to provide a system of collective security for what the USSR had come to define as its 'sphere of influence'. That is, it was there to protect the ideological integrity of Marxist–Leninist regimes and use the threat of physical force, if necessary, to dissuade opposition towards the Moscow leadership.

The organisational structure within which this was to be achieved reflects both the political and military roles of the WTO. At the centre is the Political Consultative Committee (PCC), on which top party and government officials of the member states are represented. Although meetings of this body were infrequent during the first 10 years of its existence, it has since become the clearing house for all the foreign policy declarations of the WTO. However, in 1969 the PCC meeting in Budapest permitted the creation of three new consultative bodies, including a military council, a committee of defence ministers and a technical committee. Since 1976 these have been supplemented by a WTO Council of Foreign Ministers during the interim between PCC sessions (Erikson, 1981). The military organisation is headed by a Joint Command. Although the command of each national army rests with the party leadership of each member state (except for the GDR, whose military are directly controlled by the WTO Joint Command), the Commander-in-Chief is a senior Soviet military official (Marshal Kulikov in 1986), and the Chief of Staff of the Joint Command is usually a Russian General. Despite its title, the full-time staff of the WTO is located in Moscow. Control over the system of officer education (most have passed through local military colleges, but those aspiring to senior command receive their advanced training in Soviet military academies); an integrated network of political administrations which enables Soviet monitoring of the application in member states of the common military doctrine, operations and tactics; and the Joint Command, which assigns detachments from each individual military service to joint exercises, training and other operations; all enable Soviet control over the promotion of officers to the senior command posts of the East European armed forces (Jones, 1981).

During its first 5 years of existence the WTO was politically inactive and slow to respond to the effects of de-Stalinisation. When change came, it was because of technical and economic considerations. In 1960 Khrushchev dismissed Marshal

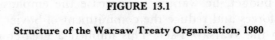

FIGURE 13.1

Structure of the Warsaw Treaty Organisation, 1980

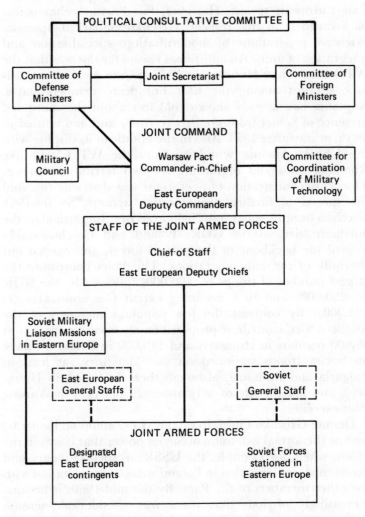

Zhukov and replaced him with Marshal Grechko as Commander-in-Chief. This was in line with Khrushchev's defence strategy: intoxicated with the rapid Soviet advances in nuclear and space technology and anxious to cut the Soviet defence budget, he wanted to increase the emphasis upon nuclear forces and reduce the commitment of Soviet ground forces to the Warsaw Pact. This implied a greater role for East European troops. However, faced with technological backwardness in this respect, Grechko embarked upon an extensive programme of modernisation, specialisation and integration of units. An additional reason for this was that the WTO invasion of Hungary in 1956 did not awaken enthusiastic support among the East European members states. Romania had already shown cold feet about the continued presence of Soviet troops on her territory and had refused to let them stay after 1958. Also in the middle of its dispute with the USSR, Albania withdrew from the WTO, and like Romania set about organising its own territorial defence. Thus closer integration of operations was desirable to avoid the spread of further disintegrative actions. So in 1961 Grechko began regular joint field exercises. In particular, the northern 'tier' of the GDR, Poland and Czechoslovakia formed the backbone of the ground forces, and carried out the bulk of the joint operations. The Poles contribute the largest number of troops (c. 400,000) followed by the GDR (c. 250,000) and to a declining extent Czechoslovakia (c. 195,000). By contrast the less populous members of the southern 'tier' contribute proportionately fewer troops (about 93,000 regulars in Hungary, and 149,000 in Bulgaria), have no Soviet troops stationed on their territory (at least in Bulgaria and Romania, although there are a few in Hungary), and are the site of only about 20 per cent of Warsaw Pact exercises.

Despite Grechko's initiatives, the WTO could no longer be seen as the formal extension of Soviet power that it was in the 1950s, when, for example, the USSR invaded Hungary and threatened similar action in Poland without consultation with the other members of the Pact. By the mid-1960s it became increasingly obvious that there was considerable tension between the aim of military cohesiveness and the growing political diversity of the members states. Obviously, the best known example of this was the intervention in Czechoslovakia in August 1968 and the proclamation of the Brezhnev Doctrine. However, as we have already noted, there was already evidence of a desire for greater independence from the integrated military command in Albania and Romania. While Albania left the WTO in 1961, from the late 1950s onwards, Romania began to copy the earlier example of Yugoslavia and establish its own territorial defence system. Protesting at the absence of East European representation in WTO policy-making bodies, Romania refused to participate in the joint manoeuvres, and in particular refused to join the WTO invasion of Czechoslovakia. Indeed Soviet forces led this act of intervention. Romanian resistance to closer integration of the Warsaw Pact command was repeated in 1974. In 1978 the Romanian response to Soviet demands for increased defence expenditure and closer military integration was even more intransigent. It received limited logistical support from Yugoslavia, China and the West, and so was able to continue to operate a nationally based concept of defence. Mainly because it is part of the less significant souther 'tier', Romania's stance is grudingly tolerated by the USSR.

Tension between WTO membership continued in the 1970s. Even the GDR expressed irritation at the Soviet willingness to supply more advanced weaponry to Egypt in the 1973 Arab–Israeli war than was available to the WTO. After the 1978 Political Consultative Committee meeting in Moscow, further integration and modernisation was urged upon member states. Yet the issue of 'burden-sharing' was more urgently pursued. The financial commitment to WTO defence expenditure varied from 11 to 13 per cent of the GNP for the USSR, to 6.3 per cent for the GDR, and between 2 and 3 per cent for the other members (with the exception of Romania). But in 1979 the USSR had called for an across-the-board increase of 5 per cent. Although prompted by similar developments within NATO, this demand was not welcomed by the East European states, most of whom were facing economic difficulties at that time (Moreton, 1981). Tensions have continued into the 1980s, when the USSR became increasingly reliant upon the East European military as it got more globally engaged, especially in Black Africa and Central America. In addition, defending its borders against Chinese incursions and supporting the costly invasion of Afghanistan were major preoccupations. Existing divisions between the East European members of the WTO and the USSR in foreign affairs over issues such as the 1967 and 1973 Arab–Israeli wars, diplomatic relations with the People's Republic of China, the 1968 invasion of Czechoslovakia, the 1981 military coup in Poland, and 'fraternal' relations with the West European 'Eurocommunist' parties, all affected willingness to make further commitments to the Warsaw Pact (see below).

It would not be possible to conclude an evaluation of the East European role within the Warsaw Pact without consideration of the time when WTO troops were used to intervene in member states. As Ross Johnson (1984) has pointed out, the USSR either threatened or used military force to intervene in Eastern Europe numerous times between 1945 and 1981: it supported the communist party takeovers of power between 1945–7, it engineered the Czechoslovak party coup of 1948, it exerted pressure on Yugoslavia 1949–52, it intervened in the GDR to help suppress the 1953 Berlin uprising, it intervened in Hungary in 1956, sought to influence Albania during 1961–2, coordinated a joint WTO invasion of Czechoslovakia in 1968, and put pressure upon the Polish military to declare martial law in 1980–1.

The best known justification of the right of the WTO to intervene among its member states is the Brezhnev Doctrine, spelled out after the invasion of Czechoslovakia in 1968 in an article in *Pravda*, and in Brezhnev's speech to the Fifth Congress of the Polish United Workers Party. Summerscale (1981) has argued that it was not an ex-post rationalisation of events, as the underlying principles were the indivisibility of the socialist commonwealth, the primacy of its interests over the sovereignty of an individual socialist country, and the legitimacy of military assistance to a fraternal country where 'the overt actions of enemies of socialism within the country and beyond its boundaries ... create a threat to the common interests of the socialist camp' (Summerscale, 1981). He also notes that such views were aired at meetings of the WTO and party leaderships before the event. It should be obvious that what was at stake was not so much variations in national communist ideology, which had been accorded recognition in the Belgrade Declaration of 1955 (see below), nor economic reform along the lines of market socialism, which was also being proposed for Hungary (see Chapter 5), but rather the integrity of the Marxist–Leninist principles observed by the ruling parties. Unlike events in Hungary in 1956, and later developments in Poland in 1981, the authority of the communist party had not collapsed.

Interestingly, the Brezhnev Doctrine has never subsequently been reiterated, even in the case of the 1979 invasion of Afghanistan (on the grounds that the latter was not a 'socialist' state). In that case it was a specifically Soviet action, not the WTO's, even though there were consequences for the role of the other members in the defence of Eastern Europe. Since 1968, then, there has been no formal statement of the rules of the game. Evidently the implications of the Helsinki Final Act signed in August 1975 made it imprudent to reassert the Brezhnev Doctrine. The Declaration of Principles pledged the signatories to mutual recognition of sovereign equality, renunciation of the threat or use of force against one another, and non-intervention in internal affairs. Coming as they did at the high point of the period of 'detente', the Helsinki Accords provided sufficient allure in terms of trade and technology to guarantee that individual WTO members accepted these terms and that there was tacit (overt in the case of Romania) rejection of the Brezhnev Doctrine.

Where does this leave the WTO? The multilateralism of the Pact does serve wider purposes, such as negotiation on arms control, disarmament and security, but the fundamental basis of the military structure is 'bilateralism strictly enforced and assiduously nurtured by the USSR' (Erikson 1981, p. 169).

East European foreign policy initiatives

Are the East European states miniature alter egos of the USSR? To the extent that the USSR is only satisfied if it sees a reasonable facsimile of itself reflected back seems at first glance to be a particularly appropriate principle governing the foreign policy of East European states. However, in recent years analysts have come to the conclusion that each of the East European states without exception has an autonomously defined foreign policy interest, based upon nationally deter-mined priorities and concerns that may or may not coincide with those of Moscow or with each other (Moreton, 1981; Kanet, 1983; Gati, 1976). Indeed, concern with foreign policy development has reflected the fact that an alliance such as the WTO, held together as it is by Soviet military power, can be more of a liability than an asset (Moreton, 1981; Johnson, 1976). The problem of engineering consensus in that organisation depends upon imposing some unity of foreign relations in a wider sense. Diverging economic, diplomatic and political relations with the outside world can create different perspectives on military and security interests. Representation in international organisations follows a different pattern from the USSR. At first, tensions within the wider socialist international community created different alignments. In particular, the breakaway of Yugoslavia in 1948 and the Sino-Soviet dispute after the late 1950s had reverberations for Albanian and Romanian loyalty to the Soviet 'line'. Also, since the mid-1960s attitudes to relations with West Europe have diverged. Finally, beginning in the mid-1960s and more markedly in the 1970s, a variety of diplomatic and trading relations have developed with the Third World.

Commencing with the international representation of Eastern Europe, not until after 1956 was there any evidence of an international role and status distinct from that of the USSR. An examination of their participation in international agencies associated with the United Nations reveals a growing membership profile since 1965, especially on the part of Yugoslavia and Romania. As would be expected, this applies least to Albania. Indeed, the East European states are members of organisations in which the USSR itself is without representation, such as the FAO (only Albania is not a member), and GATT (Czechoslovakia since 1948, Poland since 1967, Romania since 1971, Hungary since 1973, and Yugoslavia are members, and Bulgaria has observer status). Only the GDR and the USSR are not participants. Romania and Yugoslavia are affiliated to the International Monetary Fund. Although Hungary was admitted in 1982, Poland's application in 1981 was rejected. Membership of the IMF and the IBRD give access to an important source of short- and long-term credit. This is particularly useful where a country has balance of payments problems. However, membership means obligations to supply information on foreign trade, currency, and general economic policy. Generally speaking, the more integrated an East European state is within any of the Soviet bloc groupings, such as the WTO or the CMEA, the less likely it is to take an independent role in such organisations (Aspaturian, 1984, p. 28). The foreign policies of the East European states may be analytically described by a three part typology:

1. Those whose activity is coordinated with Moscow's policies and interests (GDR, Czechoslovakia, and Bulgaria).
2. Those whose activity is independent of Soviet policy and behaviour (Romania and Yugoslavia).
3. Those who have not developed any significant involvement with the Third World (Poland and Hungary) (Aspaturian, 1984, p. 24).

Thus there is a core of five states whose foreign-policy development is relatively closely coordinated with the USSR, while the remaining three are renowned for their maverick positions (Yugoslavia, Romania and Albania), even though one state, Romania, is a member of the WTO. However, our categorisation contains a measure of over-simplification which may be corrected only by an examination of the individual countries.

For example, more recent evidence suggests the development of a Balkan security sub-system that spans both East and West Europe. Yugoslavia, Romania, Bulgaria, and also Greece have rediscovered close interests in common (Brown, 1983). Yugoslavia stands out because it has taken a leading role in the movement of non-aligned countries. This was provoked by the state of affairs following the denunciation of Tito by the Cominform in 1948, the mounting of an economic blockade by the rest of Eastern Europe, and the stationing of Soviet troops near the Yugoslav borders. Although substantial economic aid was forthcoming from the West, Yugoslavia was still to all intents and purposes a Stalinist system, and so this precluded overly close relations. Until 1955 relations with the USSR remained hostile. However, pursuing domestic political advantage, Khrushchev engineered a reconciliation with Tito and visited Belgrade in 1955. Yugoslavia wanted to acquire economic and technical aid without becoming dependent upon the USSR, and without becoming constrained to endorse the Soviet position on all matters. Yet the invasion of Hungary in 1956, for which the Yugoslavs initially criticised the USSR, the Berlin crises of 1958 and 1961, and the developing Sino-Soviet split of the late 1950s, were signals that such a position would be extremely difficult to maintain. This was the context in which Tito, Nehru, and the new President of Egypt, Nasser, convened the first conference of non-aligned nations in 1958. It did not signify complete opposition to the USSR. However, by 1965 the Yugoslav economic reform, which included considerable decentralisation and an opening of vastly expanded trading relations with the West, made it more difficult for Yugoslavia to adopt parallel policies to those of the USSR. Forced to condemn the invasion of Czechoslovakia because this act implicity condemned market socialism, Yugoslavia adopted the view that in international affairs the USSR was the principal military threat. This was translated into Yugoslav hostility towards such events as Soviet support for the Vietnamese invasion of Kampuchea, and the Soviet invasion of Afghanistan (Zimmerman, 1981). However, the growth of a trade imbalance with the West during the 1970s, and a subsequent reliance upon Soviet aid, did temper this position.

To understand the Yugoslav position within the non-aligned movement, it is helpful to begin with a brief description of how this movement developed and also of the changing Soviet attitude towards the less developed countries. After World War Two, independence movements and their subsequent governments were dismissed as the 'lackeys of capitalism' by the USSR. However, in the late-1950s Khrushchev's espousal of the doctrine of 'Peaceful Co-existence' directed attention away from Europe as an ideological battleground to demonstrate the superiority of socialism over capitalism. Intervention in the Third World became more attractive as a measure of ideological success. Thus Soviet aid was directed to India, Egypt, Indonesia and Burma, as well as to the Arab Middle East, but in all cases it was not destined to support independence movements so much as the 'national bourgeoisies' of these states (only Algeria was radical). As already mentioned, some of these countries played leading parts in the non-alignment movement (Kanet, 1983) which was founded at the Bandung Conference. During the Brezhnev era there was little change until 1965. However, the overthrow of the Algerian government in 1965, followed by similar developments in Indonesia, Ghana, Mali, and, after 1970, the Sudan and Egypt, forced the USSR into a position where it would have to support more radical successor governments if it was to retain influence. At the same time, bloc politics were undergoing a considerable change: the USA became heavily committed in Vietnam after 1965, the Sino-Soviet dispute hardened and began to assume an importance in the battle for Third World influence, a growing rapprochement between the USA and China made this all the more urgent, and the USA gained greater influence in the Middle East, especially with Egypt. As we observed above, the 1970s was a time when many revolutionary governments seized power (Halliday, 1983, pp. 66, 92). What was distinctive about these was that such takeovers of power were not due to direct Soviet intervention so much as domestic political change and the emergence of indigenous liberation movements, not all of whom were sympathetic to the USSR. In these circumstances, the USSR assumed what can only be described as 'flexible diplomacy' (Radvanyi, 1981), supporting the new radical elements plus military assistance to local communist parties where they successfully came into power. As illustrated by the cases of Ethiopia and Afghanistan, 'flexible diplomacy' often generated anomalous and burdensome commitments.

Thus up until 1966 the USSR was supporting countries with influence in the non-aligned movement, but by 1974 changes in Third World and bloc polities meant that it had reconsidered its position. The non-aligned movement itself underwent considerable change after its foundation in 1961. The Belgrade Declaration of that year set out the following principles: non-interference in the affairs of members, rejection of the external imposition by force of social or political systems, peaceful coexistence among states with different social systems, a call for disarmament and a ban on nuclear tests, and a call for a changed basis for economic aid (Milenkovitch, 1981, p. 282). Yet during the ensuing period five further conferences were held and the total number of participants rose from twenty-five in 1961 to reach ninety-two in 1979. The movement itself also went through three stages: until 1970 the main objective was to ease Cold War tension and maintain neutrality; from then until the sixth conference in 1979, there were efforts to reconcile the growing discord within the movement by following the twin objectives of upholding sovereign independence of states and promoting increased inter-bloc cooperation; finally, after 1979 (and possibly with Soviet encouragement) Cuba became the leading force in the non-aligned movement. Previous support for sovereign independence has been abandoned, and states have become polarised over the issue of neutrality. Support for the USSR has increased, while there has been a growing hostility towards the West. Thus, in this context, Yugoslavia has shifted from being at the centre of the stage of non-alignment to being increasingly constrained by others. This may account for the stronger Marxist bias adopted by Yugoslavia after 1979. The non-aligned movement strongly condemned the West for supporting South Africa, Israeli expansionism on the West Bank, and increasing US interference in Puerto Rico, Cuba and the rest of Central America. The Chilean Junta was condemned but the Argentinian claim to the Falkland islands was upheld! Despite the growing hostility between non-aligned members (for example, Vietnam and Kampuchea; Ethiopia and Somalia), Yugoslavia has continued to participate. Her main trade may be with the CMEA and the EEC (especially the FRG), but she is still heavily reliant upon the Third World for oil imports. In 1980 the EEC signed a generous trade agreement with Yugoslavia.

The other East European state which takes an international stance that is relatively independent of the USSR is Romania. This is usually attributed to the idiosyncracies of the Ceausescu dynasty after it came to office in 1965. However, the original move predates Ceasescu's rule. As a means to cope with the effects of the Sino-Soviet split, the previous party leader, Gheorghiu-Dej, started to adopt a more open position. Between 1960 and 1968 the Romanian position within the Eastern bloc was reassessed. Its role within the Warsaw Pact and the degree of integration within the CMEA as well as diplomatic relations with the West and the Third World all came into question. During the 1960s the rapprochement with the West culminated in the visit of President De Gaulle of France in 1968, and the establishment of diplomatic relations with the FRG in 1967 (long before relations between the Eastern Bloc and the FRG were 'normalised' in the 1970s). The breach with the Soviet Union was more marked in 1967 and 1968. In 1967 Romania maintained diplomatic relations with Israel after the Arab–Israeli War, when the rest of Eastern Europe followed the USSR and broke off relations; and in 1968 Romania refused to attend the 1968 Conference of Communist Parties at Karlovy Vary, later refusing to participate in the invasion of Czechoslovakia. During the 1970s Romania continued to maintain both these stances on the Middle East and called for greater ideological unity among the Communist Movement. Like Yugoslavia it did not support the Soviet invasion of Afghanistan, and endorsed the principle of the Helsinki Accords in expressing its disapproval of the military takeover in Poland in December 1981.

Romania does differ from Yugoslavia in that it has not become so heavily engaged in the politics of non-alignment. It has become an observer at non-alignment movement meetings, a full member of the Group of 77, and a member of such international organisations as GATT, the IMF and the World Bank. Romania has been particularly active within the UN and its associated organisations. This has produced some anomalous positions, such as support for the Khmer Rouge in 1978 and abstention at the UN vote condemning the invasion of Afghanistan, but close support for Mugabe in Rhodesia and support for the Eritreans and the Polisario liberation movements (Radu, 1981). The key to an understanding of such behaviour lies in the self-image of the Romanian government. While the rest of Eastern Europe was debating the implications of entering a phase of 'Developed Socialism' in the early 1970s (see Chapter 7), in 1972 Romania declared itself to be a 'socialist developing country', i.e. implying that with the lowest per capita GNP, apart from Albania, it had in some respects more in common with the developing world than with other state socialist societies. This marked the beginning of a series of visits by Ceasescu to developing countries, which were extended to include improved relations with China and Yugoslavia. There was also an economic motivation. Whereas in 1970 Romania was self-sufficient in fuel oils, by 1978 it was importing up to 50 per cent of its needs. It thus turned to the Third World (especially Brazil, Liberia, and India) and OPEC for supplies and became the biggest trader in Eastern Europe with such nations (about 20 to 30 per cent of its annual trade balance). Thus it is not surprising that at UNCTAD and Group of 77 meetings Romania actively supported calls for a New Industrial and Economic Order. It has pioneered a number of joint investment projects with Third World countries, mainly in the Middle East. Besides bringing an economic return through the supply of raw material, such ventures also provide an indirect means to enter other world markets, such as the EEC, as many of the countries are members of the African, Caribbean and Pacific (ACP) states. What is distinctive about Romania is that it has a widespread presence in nearly all developing countries, but apart from providing training for technical personnel it does not provide military advisers, and refuses to become involved in conflict. So whereas Yugoslavia has been particularly influential within the politics of non-alignment, and the GDR has concentrated upon military and security arrangements with a limited number of radical developing regimes, Romania has chosen to enlarge its scope of influence across a broad range of developing countries.

It would be mistaken to portray Romania and Yugoslavia as the only two East European countries with connections in the Third World. The other East European countries followed suit in the mid-1970s, not so much out of support for social revolution as from an awareness that the failure of 'detente' and of trading relations with the West would have to be remedied by other measures. East European countries were interested in a potential role for the Third World in providing stable long-term agreements on the supply of products and raw materials in return for the 'dumping' of East European manufactures, with the ultimate objective of strengthening CMEA members, rather than improving the position of the Third World itself. Up until the 1960s Czechoslovakia was the primary source of development aid (because of arms sales) to these countries. Yet, on average, between 1955 and 1981 nearly 90 per cent of such sales came from the USSR, reflecting the growing Soviet involvement in this activity. By the end of the Brezhnev era two-thirds of Eastern Europe's aid to the Third World was provided by the GDR, followed by Romania. Czechoslovakia, Hungary, Poland, and Bulgaria kept their commitments low (Aspaturian, 1984). Usually aid took the form of technical assistance and training, credits to purchase goods, and joint economic ventures, with the capital provided by the East European state and labour and raw materials provided by the developing country (such as the aforementioned projects operated by Romania). East European trade with the Third World has increased in absolute terms because total trade turnover rose nine times between 1960 and 1977, but this only represents a slow rise relative to their total volume of trade. As we shall see below, the Eastern European states still trade mainly with each other and the USSR. Whether they desire this or not, they are constrained by the structure of the CMEA.

However, before moving on to a consideration of the CMEA, it is necessary to make some further remarks about the external relations of the GDR. As we noticed above, the GDR has been extremely active in diplomatic relations with the Third World. This arises from its peculiar international status and absence of diplomatic recognition by Western powers, who refused to countenance the legitimacy of the GDR as a government of the German people alongside the FRG. Although the Federal Republic of Germany acquired full sovereignty in 1956, the GDR had to wait until the 1970s. Consequently, the GDR could receive diplomatic representation only through the intermediation of the USSR. Western refusal to recognise the GDR and Soviet Bloc refusal to recognise the FRG (with the exception of Romania after 1967) was a considerable barrier to trading relations. Moreover, because of its high diplomatic reliance upon the USSR, and because of its strategic location on the border with the West, the GDR has clung very tenaciously to ideological orthodoxy. So much was this so that when the FRG officially broached the issue of normalisation of relations between the two Germanies, the GDR was cool. Poland and the USSR were particularly enthusiastic at the prospect of anticipated trade benefits, as were Czechoslovakia and Hungary to a less marked extent. Forthright objection came from the Ulbricht government: acceptance of the FRG by members of the WTO was an ideological threat, as the main aim was to ensure that Bonn did not acquire any political influence in Moscow or any of the other East European capitals. Thus the GDR persistently blocked Soviet initiatives during 1970 and 1971, which could only be resolved by a major leadership change in the GDR party–state. The hardline Ulbricht was replaced by the more accommodating Honecker. Eventually the treaties of Moscow and Warsaw were signed in 1971 and 1972, and only in West Germany was there parliamentary delay over their ratification.

The whole issue of normalisation of relations between East and West Germany illustrates the variety of positions taken by individual East European countries. It also illustrates the potential for autonomous foreign policy activity, especially on the part of the GDR. Until normalisation, the GDR aimed to acquire diplomatic recognition from as many states as possible. However, the non-aligned world would not cooperate on this matter, and it was only after 1969 that Iraq, Cambodia, Syria, South Yemen and Egypt became the first non-communist countries to give the GDR diplomatic recognition. Ten years later the GDR had diplomatic relations with 130 states, and was able to reverse its former dependence upon the USSR. This time the latter became dependent upon the GDR as an intermediary for economic and military aid to Latin America, Black Africa and the Middle East. The international role of the GDR had changed from supplicant for diplomatic recognition to surrogate for Soviet intervention (Sodaro, 1983).

Finally, normalisation between East and West Germany did not stop at diplomatic recognition. The whole issue has a human dimension. Better arrangements for transit traffic between West Berlin and the FRG, the citizenship status of West Berliners, the citizenship and pension rights of refugees from the East, better telephone and postal links between the two states; greater access for journalists, greater ease in family visits, and the possibility for GDR families to receive hard currency remittances from relatives in the West are all part of the relationship. The result has been that the people in the GDR and FDR now make considerable contact. This brings problems as well as benefits. The black market in Deutsch Marks has expanded rather than declined, and increased access to the Western media has been used to advantage by dissident groups. However, in return, trade between the two states is regarded by the FRG as 'intra-German trade'. There are no customs or excise duties on imports from the GDR, there are no import quotas, and the FRG grants a considerable amount of interest free credit to the GDR (Wettig, 1984). Thus even if it is unwilling to accept special status in political and diplomatic relations, the GDR is only too willing to accept these economic concessions. At a time of economic recession, when most of its neighbours have accumulated large debts to Western governments with little optimism of redeeming them in the medium run, such favourable terms of trade are advantageous to the GDR. The situation has thus been reversed. Whereas in 1969 it was the other members of the Warsaw Pact who perceived an advantage in 'normalisation', the GDR leadership has become extremely anxious to avert inner-German confrontation. With the emergence of the second cold war, the GDR has come to realise that far from being an ally, the USSR could damage its interests. At the same time, the GDR is wary of any measures that will lead to greater political and ideological links with the West, which could potentially undermine its control over its population.

In summary, we can see that those who would argue that there is no such thing as independent foreign policy-making for the East European states are very wide of the mark. Not only the more ideologically unorthodox countries such as Yugoslavia and Romania, but also the ideologically loyal such as the GDR, adopt a stance distinct from the USSR. What is interesting to observe is that states which have embarked upon radical economic and social change are not at the forefront of diplomatic initiatives. Yugoslavia apart, it is those countries which have maintained a tight control over economic and social affairs that have been the diplomatic leaders. Finally, while these developments antedate the 10 years of 'detente', they received a considerable boost during those years, and in the context of the new cold war show little signs of reversal. In other words, this autonomy in foreign policy appears to have a dynamic of its own.

East European trading relations

The trading relations of the East European countries with each other, the USSR, and the West, have been constrained more by ideological and inter-bloc politics than by economic interest. The onset of the first cold war meant that after 1948 a general pattern of autarchy (economic self-sufficiency), collectivisation of agriculture and diversification of industry, provided less incentive to trade with each other than was the case in the pre-1939 period. Furthermore, until the mid-1950s, trade with the West was minimal, and the major trading partner of each country was the USSR. This marked a radical shift for such countries as the GDR, Czechoslovakia, and Poland. As a result, many Western observers portrayed East European as a colony of the Soviet 'empire', saying that socialist internationalism was a one-way relationship. Nowhere was this seen as more evident than in the institutional framework of Comecon (the Council for Mutual Economic Assistance or CMEA). Comecon ws regarded as a means for the USSR to exercise tight control over East European trading relations and for trading relations themselves principally to serve Soviet interests. This is, of course, an oversimplification. It is also inaccurate in that much changed after the death of Stalin.

Changes in inter-bloc politics have their parallel in changing East–West economic relations; the degree of economic integration within Comecon has never been highly developed, is obstructed by differing national economic interests, and by no means always serves Soviet purposes. Despite international events since 1979, it is unlikely that Eastern Europe will revert to the trading practices of the Stalin era. Furthermore, the changing trading patterns in the 1970s have blurred the distinction between what is traditionally seen as foreign policy and trade policy. The substance of foreign affairs has changed, with many issues of 'low politics' such as currency, finance, agriculture and oil supplies, being catapulted into the arena of 'high politics'.

If we begin with an examination of trading relations with the West, we can see the effect of cold war. By 1949 most Western states had withdrawn 'most-favoured-nation' (MFN) status from the East European states making them vulnerable to any and all tariffs, quotas and other trading restrictions that the Western states chose to apply. Furthermore, COCOM, a coordinating committee of trading states set up in 1949, including the whole of the NATO membership and Japan, placed a ban on trade in specific items with these countries. The banned items involved technologically advanced products and manufactures that might be advantageous to the Soviet defence programme – so great was the level of anxiety infecting East–West relations during the cold war. COCOM was an example of US legislation in peace time designed for trading with potential enemies. This situation was changing by the mid-1960s. Although the USA granted most favoured nation status only to Poland, Romania and Hungary (and withdrew it from the former after the 1981 events in Poland), the rest of Western Europe proved to be much more responsive. Many East European states developed bilateral trade agreements with individual European Community (EEC) countries. The existence of a Common Agricultural Policy made a general agreement between Eastern Europe and the EEC all the more desirable from the point of view of the former, as along with raw materials, food products were a principal export item. However, the adoption of a Common Commercial Policy by the EEC brought a degree of uniformity to hitherto *ad hoc* arrangements, and only Yugoslavia and Romania had any formal trading agreement with the EEC (see below). Some developments in agricultural and textile trade agreements have taken place. None the less, a declining

US influence in COCOM permitted a more flexible trading relationship with Western Europe, particularly for industrial products.

Flexibility was enhanced during the 10 years of 'detente' after 1969. The 1972 SALT treaty between the USA and USSR and the subsequent agreements about trade, shipping and credit, and the 'normalisation' of relations between East and West Germany, brought about a profound change in the balance of East–West Trade. During the first half of the 1970s East European imports from the West grew faster than their exports to this area. A variety of mechanisms were in operation. Because national East European currencies are only convertible with the USSR rouble, payments to the West had to be in hard currency. An earlier trade surplus with the West had led these countries to take advantage of so-called euro-dollar purchases to meet this payment. In the recession-hit 1970s this was clearly not enough to cover the import bill. As a means to get round these constraints, the devices of counter trade, compensation and counter-purchase agreements were used. Essentially they were a development of the principle of barter (Bornstein, 1981). Industrial Cooperation Agreements (ICAs), and the borrowing of credit from Western financial institutions, governments and consortia, were a particularly important development of the 1970s. ICAs were based on a variety of measures: the pooling of assets and the coordination of their use, licensing, franchising, and subcontracting arrangements; the sale of equipment, co-production, co-marketing, specialisation etc. By 1976 about 1,200 ICAs had been signed (Bornstein, 1981) but it was difficult to assess their total value, and their share of the volume of trade is probably still small (less than 10 per cent) and varies by product and country (Hill, 1983).

To the Western observer of the East European trading scene, the most notable development of the mid-1970s was the rapid increase in hard currency credit from the West. In the case of Poland this has been advanced as a cause of the profound economic and political destabilisation of 1980. Although the total size of the debt owed to Western financial institutions was highest in Poland, East Germany, Hungary and Romania also owed sizeable sums. What varied, however, was the size of the debt-service ratio (the sum of annual interest and debt principal repayments as a percentage of the value of annual exports of merchandise in convertible currency). The problem was that in Poland in the late 1970s, the debt service ratio exceeded 100 per cent! Other countries did not face such problems, either because they had a healthier balance of trade (in the case of the GDR this was greatly aided by the favourable conditions operating with respect to 'inner-German relations') or because they were more prudent managers of their hard currency debts, avoiding the 'front-loading' that was a feature of Polish policy. Although in the 1980s Western financial institutions have been more circumspect in their operations in Eastern Europe, they have no option but to continue them, even if this means a continuous process of debt rescheduling.

It should not be forgotten that despite all that has occurred in East–West trade, the USSR remains the dominant trading partner. Fifty per cent of Bulgarian trade and about 30 per cent of Polish, Hungarian, Czechoslovak and GDR trade are with the USSR. The general pattern consists of the export of finished manufactured and food products to the USSR in return for fuel and raw materials. Most of Eastern Europe, with the exception of Poland and the GDR, faces an energy shortage, and until the 1970s the USSR was their principal supplier of oil. The popular impression is that the terms of trade are greatly to the benefit of the USSR. This was the case until the early 1960s. From then to the mid-1970s, the reverse was true. In the mid-1970s it was believed that Eastern Europe was a liability rather than an asset to the USSR in economic and military terms. The complexity of this issue can only be understood by examining the mechanism of the CMEA, and its development after 1949.

The CMEA has been described as an 'international protection system' that is distinctive from an international trade system such as the EEC (Sobell, 1984). The concept of economic integration is much narrower, and has rarely meant more than the coordination of national plans (Bornstein, 1981). Like many other international organisations, its supreme policy-making body is a council consisting of heads of state, and occasionally the party leaders of member states, which normally meets once every year. An executive commit-tee composed of the permanent representatives of CMEA countries oversees the work of the council committees and full-time secretariat, along with the many other consultative bodies and specialised agencies (see Figure 13.2). Originally membership was confined to the USSR and the East Euro-pean countries, with the exception of Yugoslavia (Albania withdrew in 1961). However, in the early 1970s Cuba became a member, and special agreements were made with Iraq, Finland and Mexico. In 1978 Vietnam joined.

FIGURE 13.2

Structure of the Council for Mutual Economic Assistance

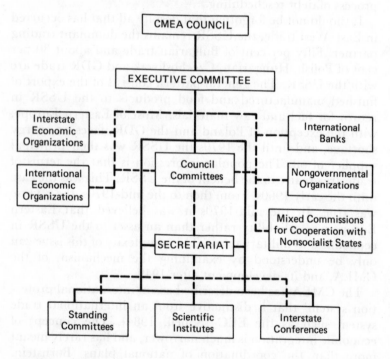

LEGEND:

───── Hierarchical relationship
- - - - Advisory relationship

The level and degree of economic integration has changed during the period of its history. Until 1954 it took a back seat in the coordination of economic trade, except for the coordination of military production during the Korean War. However, the events following the Twentieth CPSU Congress in 1956, which suggested the possibility of 'national roads to socialism' at least in terms of economic development, brought about changes. The recognition that an international division of labour could legitimately support economic specialisation on the part of the member states led to the establishment of twelve standing commissions to organise direct cooperation in specific areas. Further cooperation and more advanced specialisation (in the construction of an oil pipeline and in chemicals and agriculture) were endorsed at the 1958 Conference of Communist Parties in Moscow. However, the years 1962–9 were a time of intense disagreement. Khrushchev called for a move to supra-national planning, but in 1963 Romania led the East European opposition to this. The only significant achievement of the period was the creation of the 'transferable rouble' in 1964 and the International Bank of Economic Cooperation to administer its issue and exchanges against national currencies. Romanian intransigence in 1970 over the proposed creation of an International Investment Bank to facilitate joint long-term development programmes limited the scope of integration, but the years 1969 to 1974 were a time of fruitful cooperation. Most important was the 1971 Comprehensive Programme agreed between the CMEA member states. Hitherto cooperation had been limited to 1-year binding agreements, 5-year trade agreements, some jointly run industrial enterprises, and tentative measures to coordinate production on an international scale. However, the 1971 Comprehensive Programme proposed a much greater degree of integration through the coordination of national plans and 'joint sectoral planning', with the aim of specifying target programmes. Although this meant that all national planning bureaucracies now had special CMEA departments, and the Planning Commission Chairmen took a greater part in CMEA discussion, a greater degree of integration was not achieved in practice. In truth, it was apparent that not all CMEA members had similar interests: the USSR was a net exporter of raw materials, while the rest were net importers. Their economic performance also varied considerably. Thus world market price changes were viewed differently.

These differences were masked by new developments in the mid-1970s. Detente made more permanent trading bloc links with the EEC ever more desirable and possible. The changes in world commodity prices in the early 1970s were particularly significant for the cohesion of the CMEA. Although in the 1950s low world prices for energy relative to the CMEA were advantageous for the USSR, up to the mid-1970s the USSR was in effect subsidising the other members, as it was supplying them with 'hard' commodities below world prices. After 1973 this price differential was closed, highlighting the problems of an Eastern Europe increasingly indebted to the West, where recession reduced demand for East European imports. Large quantities of technological expertise were being imported, for which East European states were committed to future payment. The USSR (because of its own problems of economic growth, difficulties with oil production, and agriculture, plus its commitments to subsidising Mongolia, Vietnam and Cuba) was no longer able to shore up the East European economies. There was now an incentive to pass on the responsibility for the contribution of resources to CMEA cooperative efforts to the East Europeans themselves. This was the aim of the so-called long-term target programmes begun in the mid-1970s. In these changed circumstances it proved possible to generate greater enthusiasm for cooperation among the East Europeans. Even Romania conceded the need for a more closely integrated energy programme!

But what in the last analysis have been the achievements of economic integration in Eastern Europe? Despite the strong Soviet control over developments during the early years, the level of integration is at a relatively low level. Trading relations between the East Europeans themselves, as well as with the USSR, have remained mainly on a bilateral basis. Far from discouraging bilateralism, the mechanisms of the CMEA reinforce it. The fact that national governments and authorities set exchange rates at an arbitrary level, and the lack of currency convertibility save through the medium of the convertible rouble, both serve to underpin bilateralism.

It must not be forgotten, however, that not all of the countries under study here are members of the CMEA. Albania's economy has been run on autarchic lines since the early 1960s. Aid from China replaced that from the USSR, but was withdrawn after 1975. Yugoslavia never became a member of the CMEA. As a result, its trade with the developed West grew at an earlier date. By the mid-1960s Western nations (and the FRG in particular) were its major trading partners. In addition, since that time it has concluded a number of cooperation agreements with foreign firms, permitting shareholding and the operation of foreign controlled marketing and sales divisions. Unlike the other countries, foreign trade is not subject to tight central controls, and since 1965 Yugoslavia has been a member of GATT. This does not denote free trade, as illustrated by the number of restrictions upon imports that still prevail (Singleton and Carter, 1982). Furthermore, the value of exports has rarely exceeded imports. The threat that this constitutes to the dinar has been warded off only by running a surplus on invisible earnings from tourism, by the remittances of Yugoslav workers living abroad, and by borrowing. The recession since 1973 has caused this deficit to widen. Furthermore, the pattern of trade has changed. Between 1971 and 1975 the CMEA area displaced the West as the major trading partner, and by the end of the 1970s the value of trade with the developing world had reached half of that with the West. The major provider of trade and aid to the Yugoslav economy is the USSR.

Ideological developments

A neglected aspect of the external relations of the East European states are those between the Marxist–Leninist parties, both within the region and with the rest of Europe. Ideological cohesion is maintained by the USSR not just by means of the threat of force or economic sanction. As we have seen in the discussion of ideological developments within the individual parties, the USSR has taken the lead. However, in 1948, 1956, 1968, and 1980, it faced a challenge to some of the basic tenets of Marxism–Leninism. 'National Roads to Socialism' have been counteracted with reassertions of ideological unity by the holding of international conferences of communist parties. However, in the 1970s the ideological threat came from outside Eastern Europe, on the one hand from the People's Republic of China, which gradually took on a world role after 1972, and on the other, between 1975 and 1977, from the parties in Italy, France and Spain, which all underwent major doctrinal revisions. In March 1977 they met in Madrid and issued a declaration that suggested a collective modification of the basic principles of Marxism–Leninism. The label 'Euro-Communism' (originally coined by the Yugoslavs in 1975) was used to denote the doctrinal changes in the strategy for revolutionary transformation of advanced capitalist societies into socialist ones. This involved a commitment to uphold the autonomy and independence of Marxist–Leninist parties and regimes, the renunciation of violent revolution, the dictatorship of the proletariat, the irreversibility of communist power, a permanent commitment to the values of Western humanism and representative democracy, and a belief that such change will come about most effectively from within a national framework rather than being imposed from without (Aspaturian, 1980).

While there was much in such a programme that was common with ideas expressed in the East European countries in 1946–8, 1956, and 1968, it caused considerable disquiet within the USSR and Eastern Europe. In 1969 the World Communist Party Conference had stated a position of non-interference and 'no leading centre'. At the June 1976 Conference of European Communist parties the USSR called for loyalty to a 'single centre'. This was repudiated by Yugoslavia and Romania, both of which had not supported the WTO invasion of Czechoslovakia. Yet the Euro-communist support for the dissident groups in Eastern Europe, such as Charter 77 and KOR, made the regimes that were the focus of their dissent very nervous (Triska, 1980). While Yugoslavia was positively encouraging, Romania and Hungary favoured a more conciliatory attitude, Czechoslovakia, Bulgaria and the

GDR were hostile to such 'revisionism', and Poland was possibly more enthusiastic than she appeared.

All in all, Euro-communism was perceived as destabilising to Soviet hegemony in Eastern Europe. It was made all the more so by its appearance during the period of detente. The Helsinki Final Act meant that detente, dissent and Euro-communism appeared simultaneously (Tökes, 1978). However, Euro-communism waned as quickly as it had grown. The Spanish and French Communist Parties achieved disappointing electoral results in 1979 and 1981. The promise of a 'historic compromise' that had brought the Italian communists into parliamentary abstention in order to shore up the Christian Democrat coalition government in 1976 lasted only until January 1979, when the PCI withdrew its agreement. Although there was not a complete recantation by these Western communist party leaderships, their arguments lost much of their legitimacy, as the anticipated groundswell of popular support did not materialise. Euro-communism was obviously a significant rent in the fabric of Marxist–Leninist unity, but it was not the first. Even though the Second Cold War has called a halt to further movement in this direction, it is unlikely that such views have forever disappeared. Ironically, they seem to have been sustained among the East European dissident movement.

Summary and conclusion

The current hardening of East–West relations does not give much hope for a return to 'detente'. However, Eastern Europe has not returned to the position of Soviet tutelage to which it was submitted during the Stalinist years. Far from the obedient, perennially downtrodden satellite of the USSR, Eastern Europe has been able to assert its own identity in the international arena. Obviously Romania and Yugoslavia have been the most successful, but even the orthodox GDR has developed interests in its external relations that are distinct from those of the USSR. None the less, a distinctive identity is not the same as diplomatic autonomy. Eastern Europe remains firmly within the Soviet sphere of military, diplomatic and economic influence. The prospects for it to break away are about the same as those of West European countries with respect to their international commitments in NATO, the EEC and the IMF.

14

Conclusions: Legitimating State Socialism in Eastern Europe

This book has been structured around two main themes: (1) that East European politics may be understood only in the economic and social context in which they are set, and (2) that the general conceptual armoury of comparative politics, properly applied in the study of those politics, produces valuable insights. Important to the first theme is the perception that the economic and social context of East European politics is not 'given' but at least in part a product of political choice. However, economic policies have been constrained by political and social goals and the structures responsible for industrialisation have proved difficult to reform. The interdependence of economic and political factors is illustrated by the emergence of a cycle whereby political barriers have impeded the full implementation of economic reforms but political crises have provided the impetus for economic as well as political reform. As elsewhere, reform success depends to some extent upon the line-up of its opponents and supporters, a line-up which, as we have seen, cross-cuts status hierarchies and may divide elites. But success is often vital to political stability, for, as elsewhere, economic performance is an important component of regime legitimacy.

But it is not the only component. The ideology of Marxism–Leninism also specifies a commitment to goals of social equality. We have argued here that the social transformation

421

in Eastern Europe since 1945 has not only been economically determined, it has also been socialist-inspired. It has been predicated upon harnessing political and economic forces to achieve acceptable levels of social welfare. This conjunction of the necessity for a credible economic performance and a visible progress toward social equality is critical to the understanding of state socialist society. Such a configuration was present in the liberal democracies during the post-war years, but commitment to social equality goals was not uniformly strong. During the 1980s Britain, France, West Germany and the United States have all prioritised goals of economic growth and stability, sacrificing, even at the level of rhetoric, previously held commitments to full employment. East European governments were and are far less free to pursue such strategies, an observation which might lead us to question why ostensibly strong and less representative regimes have less room for manoeuvre than apparently more representative governments.

It is in attempting to answer such questions that the importance of our second theme becomes evident. When we compare state socialist systems with each other, and particularly when we compare them to liberal democratic regimes, it is vital to ensure that our assumptions are stated and that our concepts are applied in the same or equivalent ways. Otherwise, as we have shown in our discussion of the literature on political participation, where definitions have often been changed halfway through the comparisons, comparable and contrasting features are obscured rather than illuminated. It is to avoid these and more fundamental distortions that our discussions of methodology have rested upon the assumption that to comprehend a social phenomena we must be explicitly aware of the manner in which we understand it. Thus we have spelled out in detail our approaches to the subject matter, we have elaborated carefully the theories, models and concepts used to analyse the subject at hand, regarding these as themselves worthy objects of study.

Accordingly, we conclude the text with a discussion of the applicability of the concept of legitimacy to the East European political systems. This has been one of the most recent additions to the conceptual arsenal of students of comparative state socialist politics, but, predictably, has undergone some redefinition as it has been used. Traditional scholarship has held that an important constraint on East European governments is their relative lack of legitimacy by comparison to liberal democratic systems. The failure of large numbers of liberal democratic regimes over the twentieth century suggests that such a perception may be somewhat superficial, that there is no one set of political arrangements suitable for all purposes. Thus rather than assessing whether different types of system are more or less legitimate, we may argue (less contentiously) that state socialist and liberal democratic systems pursue different strategies of legitimisation. The point here is that in adopting, accepting or submitting to a political system grounded in the ideology of Marxism–Leninism, the countries of Eastern Europe have been directed toward particular strategies of development and legitimation.

Here we might usefully pause to discuss what we mean by regime legitimacy. Too often legitimacy is considered only in its apparent absence. The withdrawal or breakdown of political legitimacy which attends crisis attracts attention from a range of commentators concerned to pinpoint the causes of that breakdown. More complex, and probably more important, is the question of how legitimacy is constructed and sustained by a regime in the first place. Recently scholars have begun to consider the implications of such questions for the political systems of Eastern Europe. Borrowing from similar discussions about liberal democratic systems, both Western and Eastern European dissident social scientists have taken up the problems attending East European political legitimation. Many of their points have been rehearsed in the course of this text in discussions which both detail and assess their critiques (see Chapters 6, 9 and 11). Here we are concerned with the more general point of the way in which the concept is most usefully employed.

Baldly stated, the legitimacy of a regime is its entitlement to rule. Making use of Weberian theories of authority, scholars and critics alike have tended to postulate legitimacy in terms of institutions. Popular or representative institutions are assumed to command legitimacy, their entitlement deriving from theories of popular consent. Liberal democratic institutions are therefore definitionally legitimate. But by such criteria state socialist systems are not so fortunate. Their legitimacy is held to be tenuous, the result of immediate policy output rather than regard for institutions. Their popular support is held to be limited and shallow, their entitlement to rule is regarded as conditional. It is in this light that the Polish crises of 1970, 1976, and 1980–1 are often viewed.

The contemporary political systems of Eastern Europe have experienced rapid and traumatic social change. Forged in the two great wars of the twentieth century they are now ruled by elites who have inherited the institutions which undermined local traditions and implemented sweeping social and political changes. The post World War Two regimes had two key objectives: the industrialisation of the economy and the establishment of socialist societies. Both objectives required far-reaching changes in popular values. The aim, as we have seen, was to create a new socialist individual who was collectivist in outlook and egalitarian in perspective. Such individuals were to mould an innovative, productive industrial economy characterised by its planned, and therefore rational, nature. In practice, things were more complicated than that. The new economy had to be developed upon a base devastated by war, and the potentially socialist individual had to be acclimatised to industrialism. Fortunately the values of Marxism–Leninism and the values which suit industrialism are compatible in that both are change-orientated. Moreover, war had displaced traditional elites, facilitating the dispersal of traditional values. The new regimes were able to structure themselves and their value systems around an official ideology which gave centrality to the working class. In accordance with the goals of social equality, literacy, health care, elementary education, and basic housing were added to the menu of post-war reconstruction. The new communist party elites were therefore able to offer a potent cocktail to a range of social groups.

As the ruling parties consolidated, a process of mobilisation which aimed at rapid industrialisation was set in train. This was targeted mainly at the working class, a group which was simultaneously being recruited from the peasantry. The peasantry, once the largest social formation in the region, experienced a progressive and massive shrinkage as the working class grew. At the same time the demands of industrialism and the progress of education expanded the intelligentsia, a process which incorporated large sections of the emerging working class.

State-led, rapid industrialisation allows only for limited democratisation. In Eastern Europe, where the state was the creature of a single and highly centralised political party, democratic manifestations were even less likely. But even those few manifestations of democracy were subsumed by Stalinisation. In Eastern Europe Stalinisation had implications not only for relations with the USSR but also for internal party structures, for party recruitment and for party ideology. Only in Yugoslavia did resistance to Stalinism find indigenous alternatives. Elsewhere, 'independent' communists were purged and party apparatuses came to be instruments of rule rather than representation. Although, ideologically, Stalinism did not justify an elite/mass dichotomy, a gulf separating leaders and led, its organisational implication was a unified elite directing a compliant mass. Political structures became bureaucratised and, inevitably, a stratum of officials with a vital stake in Stalinist techniques built up party apparatuses. In other words, a group of individuals achieved power as a result of Stalinisation. Thus the threat of de-Stalinisation sent shock waves through that stratum. Their values, their policies, indeed their very positions were threatened. They were forced either to abdicate or to develop new strategies of rule. In many of the systems the shock of de-Stalinisation produced a major crisis, as regimes came to terms with the problems of producing strategies to legitimise institutions as well as material outputs.

As we have seen in Chapters 7 and 8, the search for such strategies continues. As industrialism took hold, the pace of social mobility slowed and new economic and social policies were required. As the apparatus of coercion was partly dismantled, structures of persuasion were devised. Institutions were reorganised and channels of mass communication were opened. After the late 1950s the emergence of a local political arena, the growth of political associations and a remodelling of workplace democracy occurred in most countries. Through all this, however, three key components of the system have been retained. These are the official (ideological) centrality of the working class, the sanctity of central planning and the leading role of the communist party. These three imperatives imposed important constraints on legitimation strategies. Nevertheless, a number of successes were achieved as the regimes gained in confidence and experience. After recovering from the trauma of invasion in 1956, Hungarian elites remodelled the economy and later introduced incipient representative institutions. In most countries a steady increase in material prosperity was evident, as was an expansion of the welfare state. Full employment was highly valued by the populations. But, for many observers, the central dilemma of East European state socialism continues to be that of legitimising the system itself. They point to intermittent crises and upheaval as evidence for their case, and supplement this by references to the regimes' low toleration of dissent.

East European regime legitimation problems became particularly acute in the immediate post-Stalin period, which coincided with the completion of initial industrial development programmes and basic post-war reconstruction. Once industrial mechanisms were in place and the party had to face its first major processes of change, flaws in the party state organisation became evident. Ideally parties aimed to take power, secure it and then rely on control and inspection capacities to keep the state in line. In practice such a strategy proved difficult and complex, presenting the party with considerable adaptation problems. The immediate consequence was often a major crisis. These occurred first in the GDR in 1953, then in Poland and Hungary in 1956, then in Czechoslovakia in 1968 and, most recently, in Poland in 1970, 1976 and 1980. In Poland repeated crises stemmed ultimately from the fact that the party was unable to master, let alone control or change, state administration.

Paul Lewis regards the Polish events of the early 1980s as a legitimation crisis of a large order, with roots deep in the party and the state. Using the concept of over-institutionalisation (borrowed from Kesselman's work on France), he argues that important questions concerning the nature of Polish institutions challenged the party and its associated structures. Traditional legitimation theory would hold that these had failed to acquire value and stability, that they were insufficiently institutionalised. But, argues Lewis, the problem is really one of over-institutionalisation. In a developed party–state a high degree of organisational complexity and bureaucratic development obtain. So a critical problem will be that of whether older established organisations are able to accommodate themselves to the new requirements which are continually being placed on their operation and functioning. The capacity to adapt is at least as significant to a system's institutional stability and legitimation as is its capacity to generate new institutions (Lewis, 1984a, p. 212).

The concept of over-institutionalisation is a useful one. A considerable body of evidence suggests that the political structures responsible for industrialism will persist. Critically, industrialising elites are able to insulate organisations and procedures established in the course of industrialisation, particularly those of the party (see Martin, 1977). But the evidently inadequate legitimation processes so apparent in Poland should not be assumed to characterise the politics of the other East European states, where parties have shown a great willingness to adapt, suggesting that what requires institutionalisation is not so much the party as the party–state relationship itself.

What the Polish case does show is that there are important cultural and historical components in a state's affinity to particular kinds of regime. That cultural receptivity, which varies considerably in Eastern Europe, has a determining effect on elite legitimation strategies. And important events may alter the course of such strategies significantly. The innovative nature of the arguably well legitimised Yugoslav state was in a large part determined by the strategic choices made as a result of Stalin's break with Tito. At that point the only two state forms which Yugoslavia had known (the interwar monarchy and the Soviet-style command system) were jettisoned in favour of what is officially regarded as a progressive de-étatisation which began as early as the People's Liberation Committees of World War Two and has continued, with only a few stumbles along the way, ever since (Zukin, 1984, pp. 250–2). Undoubtedly such a strategy was possible only because of the great prestige of Tito and the state's origins in an authentic national liberation movement. Such antecedents are good examples of the cultural and historical determinants of system receptivity.

The GDR presented rather different problems to communist elites. There the severed nature of the state was a critical inhibition to the establishment of new institutions, as elite use of long-standing and deeply felt German nationalism to engender support for new institutions was inhibited. Nevertheless, ideologues have tried to manage and harness national feelings with attempts to differentiate between revolutionary and repressive strands in German history. The very existence of the Federal Republic was a problem. Throughout the 1950s the GDR was undoubtedly threatened by the lure of Federal Germany's relative prosperity, which attracted hundreds of thousands of GDR citizens each year. The migration of a total of 2.6 million people between August 1949 and August 1961 to the Federal Republic placed intolerable strains on a state with a population of only 17 million and a chronic labour shortage. On 13 August 1961 East Berlin was placed under military occupation, the frontier with West Berlin was sealed off and a wall was built between the Soviet and Western sectors of the city, stemming the flow of refugees and forcing citizens on both sides to come to terms with the permanence of the two states. The 1960s were years of consolidation and economic development during which stable growth rates led to rises in living standards and the construction of one of the most comprehensive welfare systems in the world. With little alternative, the GDR leadership has based its claims to legitimacy not on state institutions themselves but on their output. Achievements of economic prosperity and social policy underpin the political stability of the GDR.

It is fair to state that legitimacy problems in Eastern Europe have been greater than for many liberal democratic systems and for the Soviet Union. In the absence of indigenous national revolutions, all the states except Yugoslavia and Albania were reliant on Soviet inspiration and sometimes support for the implementation of their political transformations. But in some of the countries Soviet symbols were historically unpopular (Hungary, Poland and Germany) whilst in others local political traditions were particularly insistent (Czechoslovakia). In such systems it was difficult for communist party leaders to harness national sentiment or pride to the institutions they created. This was a problem which was doubly difficult for the GDR. Without internationally recognised, independent statehood until the 1970s, and with the ever-evident prosperity of the FRG, a positive self-image was difficult to create and sustain.

Everywhere legitimation strategies were limited to the possibilities afforded by the constraints of party hegemony, working class centrality, and central planning. Those imperatives turned out to have contradictory implications. Major upheavals occurred in the GDR in 1953, Poland and Hungary in 1956, Czechoslovakia in 1968 and Poland in 1970, 1976 and 1980–1. The diverse demands made during these crises were the demands of an industrialised society. Ironically, the success of forced industrialisation threatened the leading role of the party. The need for adaptation was strong and recognised by party leaders, who initiated efforts to stimulate party organisation and facilitate the performance of its leading role, which had to become less supervisory, more strategic and more responsive. Such transformations met resistance from party hardliners, whose entrenched interests were threatened not only by the need for strategic change but also by the implications of engaging in a social dialogue. The same process brought proposals for marketisation, which threatened central planning mechanisms. At the same time most indicators suggested that the technical and scientific intelligentsia, rather than the working class, were central to regime objectives. In short, important obstacles to legitimation were built into the system.

Considerable controversy attends discussions of the degree to which state socialism has been legitimated in Eastern Europe. Best developed in the GDR, strategies of consumer satisfaction have been important in most of the East European states, which have sought to base their political authority on a range of social groups. But the argument that their growing social and economic effectiveness has meant that regimes have acquired legitimacy as they have governed, even where coercion was used to achieve initial compliance, has been disputed by a number of critics. Hungary under Kadar is a case in point. Widely considered the most legitimate of any of the systems, Hungarian state socialism is seen to be based on a considerable degree of popular consent. But critics such as Ken Anderson, Istvan Lovas, Ferenc Feher and Agnes Heller have argued that legitimation should not be confused with pacification; that Hungary is pacified, but that its basis was terrorism and is now the memory of terrorism. Lomax (1984) retorts that such critics base their assessments of what comprises legitimacy on questions of rights rather than on facts. They have strongly held views about who morally has a right to rule, views which mean they are only prepared to recognise the legitimacy which occurs in institutionally guaranteed pluralist systems. For them the question of state socialist legitimacy cannot arise.

Such views have the benefit of enhancing liberal democratic systems by damning state socialist systems, but they do not adequately describe a complex state socialist reality. Thus no explanation is offered for why crises have repeatedly broken out in Poland, but the GDR, with its own special problems, has been relatively trouble-free since 1953. While it is true that the East European regimes seek public support on the basis of their policy output, it is also rooted in the official ideology and to a certain extent in central institutions. The developments in the organisation, ideology and membership recruitment of the SED are eloquent testimony to this. Thus all the regimes except Poland were able to weather the economic depressions of the late 1970s and early 1980s. That may have been in part due to the successful establishment of socialist ideals. A considerable body of evidence suggests that egalitarian values have taken hold in Eastern Europe and that they receive widespread popular support. Such values provide a framework for legitimation. They are a basis of support for the institutions which direct the relevant policies. Although this argument has considerable application, it does not mean that the progress of value change will solve all problems of legitimation. Regimes have, paradoxically, instituted values which produce demands they cannot always meet. Indeed, the Polish crises of the last 15 years may be interpreted in part as resulting from frustrations with regime inability to produce the achievements that the framework of equality demands. Upheavals have resulted from regime failures to deliver promised social equality, from widespread observations of both privilege and corruption. Ironically, even the least successful regimes may have begun to achieve the value change which is a precondition for the attainment of popular consent for communist ideology.

A further point about the analytical use of the concept of legitimacy is that its application in the contemporary literature is a new and perhaps mistaken one. Legitimacy, as understood by Weber, was not necessarily predicated upon democratic forms. When he wrote about legitimacy and authority, Weber was referring, not to the relations between regime and population, but to those between rulers and their executive staff. He regarded the masses as unimportant. What was at issue was the credibility a ruler or a leadership had with its executive (Pakulski, 1986). In such a view it is the interrelationships between the party elite and the various strategic groups which are the key to the legitimation of the party–state. This in fact received early recognition in the GDR, but was neglected in Czechoslovakia and Poland. Legitimacy is not in the gift of the masses, but of the intelligentsia and the apparats which it inhabits. By implication, then, the most appropriate elite legitimating strategies will be those which institutionalise and protect those relationships. Thus when crises occur, the immediate response tends to be one of institutional modification. Commissions of inquiry, Committees of National Salvation, rotating presidencies and other elite deliberative fora appear. The 'normalisation' of political life in Poland after martial law and the provisions for the political succession in Yugoslavia after 1980 are nothing short of skilful legitimating strategies. However, such strategies have dangers which arise from popular feelings. Repeated institutional change encourages popular cynicism and exacerbates the continuing tension between the official centrality of the working class and the privileged socio-political position of the intelligentsia. Arguably the very concept of deliberate legitimation generates intractable problems. As Pakulski reminds us 'the "invisible hand" of market and tradition has been replaced by the "visible hand" of party agencies' (Pakulski, 1986, p. 54). Certain legitimating strategies are therefore precluded at the same time as elite responsibilities have been dramatically increased. In effect, matters which were once automatically resolved, now demand explicit legitimation. When administrative planning replaces the market, the implication is that outcomes may be predetermined. As a result elites are held to be responsible for all outcomes. Any outcome may be scrutinised and have to be justified. An elaborate structure for such justifications must be forged, and must itself be legitimated. Even where everything works as it should, the resulting tasks overload elites. When, as is invariably the case, not all outcomes have been planned, and not all planned outcomes are achieved, the resulting effects may be so unsettling as to undermine the institutions which produce them. In short, the real legitimacy problem for contemporary Eastern European governments may arise not so much from the failure of institutions to adapt, or their overconstrained representative capacities, but from the sheer scope of their responsibilities.

Whatever its outcome, we note with approval that the scholarly debate over state socialist legitimation is wide-ranging, embracing many of the issues we have raised in this text. The application of the concept of legitimacy to the analysis of the East European states sheds light on a range of political problems as well as raising new questions and opening new lines of enquiry. This has generated debate by specialists on the accomplishments of the regimes, which has led to new assessments of their possibilities and achievements. We therefore feel confident in concluding that the benefits of the incorporation of the concept of legitimacy into East European studies are apparent. Potentially it enables us to consider and compare the advantages and disadvantages of actual regime strategies and to avoid making judgements simply on the basis of preferences about regime types. This particular example of borrowing illustrates well our case that the concepts developed for the study of liberal democracies have much to offer our understanding of state socialism.

Bibliography

Adam, Jan (1976) 'Housing Policy in European Socialist Countries: the Czechoslovak Experience', *Jarhbuch der Wirtschaft Osteurapas*, vol. 6.

Adam, Jan (1981) 'Labor Shortages in Hungary and Their Treatment', *Osteuropa Wirtschaft*, vol. 26, no. 1, March.

Adam, Jan (ed.) (1982) *Employment Policies in the Soviet Union and Eastern Europe* (London: Macmillan).

Adam, Jan (1983) 'The Old Age Pension System in Eastern Europe: a case study of Czechoslovak and Hungarian Experience', *Osteuropa–Wirtschaft*, vol. 28, no. 4.

Adam, Jan (1984) 'Regulation of Labour Supply in Poland, Czechoslovakia and Hungary', *Soviet Studies*, vol. XXXVI, no. 1, January.

Adelman, Jonathan R. (ed.) (1984) *Terror and Communist Politics: The Role of The Secret Police in Communist States* (Boulder and London: Westview Press).

Althusser, Louis (1971) *Lenin and Philosophy and Other Essays* (London: New Left Books).

Artisien, P. F. R. (1985) 'Albania in the post-Hoxha era', *World Today*, vol. 41, no. 6.

Ash, Timothy Garton (1983) *The Polish Revolution: Solidarity 1980–82* (London: Jonathan Cape).

Aspaturian, Vernon (1984) 'Eastern Europe in World Perspective', in T. Rakowska-Harmstone (ed.), *Communism in Eastern Europe*, Second Edition (Manchester: University Press).

Aspaturian, Vernon V., Valenta, Jiri and Burke, David P. (1980) *Eurocommunism between East and West* (Bloomington: Indiana University Press).

Bahro, Rudolf (1977) 'The Alternative in Eastern Europe', *New Left Review*.

Bahro, Rudolf (1978) *The Alternative in Eastern Europe* (translated by David Fernbach) (London: New Left Books).

Bahry, Donna (1980) 'Measuring Communist Priorities. Budgets, Investments and the problems of Equivalence', *Comparative Political Studies*, vol. 13, no. 3, October.

Bahry, Donna (1983), 'Politics, Succession and Public Policy in Communist Systems: A Review Article', *Soviet Studies*, vol. 35, April.

433

Baskin, Mark (1983) 'Crisis in Kosovo', *Problems of Communism*, March–April.

Bauman, Z. (1971) 'Social Dissent in the East European Political System', *European Journal of Sociology*, vol. 12.

Bauman, Z. (1979) 'Clientelism: Eastern Europe', *Studies in Comparative Communism*, vol. 12, no. 2–3.

Baylis, John and Segal, Gerald (eds) (1981) *Soviet Strategy* (London: Croom Helm).

Baylis, Thomas A. (1974) *The Technical Intelligentsia and the East German Elite* (London: University of California Press).

Beck, Carl (1973) 'Leadership Attributes in Eastern Europe: The Effect of Country and Time', in Beck *et al.* (eds), *Comparative Communist Political Leadership* (New York: David McKay Co.).

Beck, Carl *et al.* (1973) *Comparative Communist Political Leadership* (New York: McKay).

Bellis, Paul (1979) *Marxism and the USSR: The Theory of Proletarian Dictatorship and the Marxist Analysis of Soviet Society* (London and Basingstoke: Macmillan).

Berman, Harold J. (1971) 'What Makes "Socialist Law" Socialist?', *Problems of Communism*, September–October.

Bertsch, Gary K. (1982) *Power and Policy in Communist Systems*, Second Edition (New York: John Wiley and Sons).

Beyme, Klaus von (1982) *Economics and Politics Within Socialist Systems: A Comparative and Developmental Approach* (New York: Praeger).

Beyme, Klaus von and Zimmerman, Hartmut (1984) *Policy Making in the GDR* (Aldershot: Gower).

Bicanic, R. (1973) *Economic Policy in Socialist Yugoslavia* (Cambridge: Cambridge University Press).

Bielasiak, Jack (1981) 'Workers and Mass Participation in "Socialist Democracy"', in Triska and Gati (eds) *op. cit.*

Bielasiak, Jack (1983) 'Inequalities and the Politicisation of the Polish Working Class' in Nelson (ed.), *op. cit.*

Birch, A. H. (1972) *Representation* (London: Macmillan).

Blazyca, G. (1980) 'Industrial structure and the economic problems of industry in a centrally planned economy: the Polish case', *The Journal of Industrial Economics*, vol. XXVIII, no. 3, March.

Blazyca, George (1985) 'The Polish Economy under Martial Law – a dissenting view', *Soviet Studies*, vol. XXXVII, no. 3, July.

Boot, Pieter (1983) 'Continuity and Change in the Planning System of the GDR', *Soviet Studies*, vol. XXXV, no. 3, July.

Bornstein, M. (ed.) (1973) *Plan and Market Economic Reform in Eastern Europe* (New Haven and London: Yale University Press).

Bornstein, Morris (1981) 'Issues in East–West Economic Relations', in M. Bornstein, Z. Gitelman and W. Zimerman (eds), *op. cit.*

Bornstein, Morris, Gitelman, Zvi and Zimmermann, W. (eds) (1981) *East–West relations and the Future of Eastern Europe: Politics and Economics* (London: George Allen and Unwin).

Bowers, Stephen (1982) 'Private Institutions in Service to the State: The Geman Democratic Republic's Church in Socialism', *East European Quarterly*, vol. XVI, no. 1.

Bromke, Adam (1967) *Poland's Politics: Idealism vs. Realism* (Cambridge, Massachusetts: Harvard University).

Bromke, Adam (1975) 'Catholic Social Thought in Communist Poland', *Problems of Communism*, July–August.

Brown, Aurel (1983) *Small State Security in the Balkans* (London: Macmillan).

Brown, A. H. (1969) 'Political Change in Czechoslovakia', *Government and Opposition*, Spring.

Brunner, Georg and Kaschkat, Hannes (1979) 'Party, State and Groups in Eastern Europe' in Jack Hayward and R. N. Berki (eds), *State and Society in Contemporary Europe* (Oxford: Martin Robertson).

Brus, Wlodimierz (1972) *The Market in a Socialist Economy* (London: Routledge and Kegan Paul).

Brus, Wlodimierz (1977) 'Stalinism and the "People's Democracies"', in Tucker (ed.), *op. cit.*

Brus, W. (1975) *Socialist Ownership and Political Systems* (London: Routledge and Kegan Paul).

Brus, W. (1979) 'The East European reforms: What Happened to Them?', *Soviet Studies*, vol. XXXI, no. 2, April.

Brus, W. (1982) 'Aims, methods and practical determinants of the Economic policy of Poland 1970–80', in A. Nove, H. H. Höhmann and F. Seidenstecher, *op. cit.*

Bryant, Christopher G. A. (1980) 'Worker Advancement and Political Order in a State Socialist Society: A Case Study of Poland', *Sociological Review*, vol. 28.

Bunce, Valerie (1981) *Do New Leaders make a Difference? Executive Succession and Public Policy Under Capitalism and Socialism* (Princeton, NJ: Princeton University Press).

Bunce, Valerie J. (1983) 'Neither Equality nor Efficiency: International and Domestic Inequalities in the Soviet Bloc', in Nelson (ed.), *op. cit.*

Burg, Steven L. (1983) *Conflict and Cohesion in Socialist Yugoslavia: Decision Making Since 1966* (Princeton: Princeton University Press).

Burks, R. V. (1964) 'Eastern Europe', in L. Cohen and J. Shapiro (eds), *Communist Systems in Comparative Perspective* (New York: Anchor).

Bush, K. (1977) 'Indicators of Living Standards in the USSR and Eastern Europe', in NATO Economic Affairs Directorate, *'COMECON: Progress and Prospects'* (Brussels: NATO).

Carr, E. H. (1964) *Socialism in One Country 1924–1926* (Harmondsworth, Middlesex: Penguin Books).

Carr, E. H. (1964) *A History of Soviet Russia: 7 – Socialism in One Country 1924–1926*, vol. III, part I (London: Macmillan).

Carter, April (1982) *Democratic Reform in Yugoslavia: The Changing role of the Party* (London: Frances Pinter).

Cason, Thomas (1983) 'The Warsaw Pact', in MJ. Sodaro and S. L. Wolchik (eds), *Foreign and Domestic Policy Development in Eastern Europe in the 1980s. Trends and Prospects* (London: Macmillan).

Cave, Jane (1981) 'Local Officials of the Polish United Workers' Party 1950–75', *Soviet Studies*, vol. XXXIII, no. 1, January.

Cave, Martin and Hare, Paul (1981) *Alternative Approaches to Economic Planning* (London: Macmillan).

Childs, David (1983) *The G.D.R.: Moscow's German Ally* (London: George Allen and Unwin).

Chrypinski, V. D. (1966) 'Legislative Committees in Polish Lawmaking', *Slavic Review*, 25.

Cieplak, Tadeusz N. (1979) 'Private Farming and the Status of the Polish Peasantry since World War II', in Volgyes (ed.), *op. cit.*

Clark, Cal (1983) 'Regional Inequality in Communist Nations: A Comparative Appraisal', in Nelson (ed.) *op. cit.*

Cohen, Lenard J. (1982) 'Politics as an Avocation: Legislative Professionalisation and Participation in Yugoslavia', in Nelson and White (eds), *op. cit.*

Cohen, Lenard (1983) 'Regional Elites in Socialist Yugoslavia: Changing Patterns of Recruitment and Composition', in T. H. Rigby and Bohdan Harasymiw (eds), *Leadership Selection and Patron-Client Relations in the USSR and Yugoslavia* (London: George Allen and Unwin).

Comisso, Ellen (1979) *Workers' Control Under Plan and Market: Implications of Yugoslav Self-Management* (New York: Yale University Press).

Comisso, Ellen (1981) 'Can a Party of the Working Class be a Working-Class party?, in Triska and Gati (eds), *op. cit.*

Connor, Walter D. (1977) 'Social Change and Stability in Eastern Europe', *Problems of Communism*, November–December.

Connor, W. D. (1979) *Socialism, Politics and Equality, Hierarchy and Change in Eastern Europe and the USSR* (New York: Columbia University Press).

Connor, Walter D. (1982) 'Varieties of East European Dissent', *Studies in Comparative Communism*, vol. XV, no. 4, Winter.

Curry, Jane Leftwich (1982) 'Media Control in Eastern Europe: Holding The Time on Opposition', in Jane Leftwich Curry and Joan R. Dassin (eds), *Press Control Around the World* (New York: Praeger Special Studies).

David, Henry P. (1982) 'Eastern Europe: Pro-natalist Policies and Private Behaviour', *Population Bulletin*, vol. 36, no. 6, February.

Dawisha, Karen (1984) *The Kremlin and the Prague Spring* (London: University of California Press).

Dawisha, Karen and Hanson, Philip (eds) (1981) *Soviet–East European Dilemmas: Coercion, Competition and Consent* (London: Heinemann).

Deacon, Bob (1983) *Social Policy and Socialism: the Struggle for Socialist Relations of Welfare* (London: Pluto)

Deacon, Bob (1984) 'Medical Care and Health under State Socialism', *International Journal of Health Services*, vol. 14, no. 3.

Deacon, Bob (1985–6) 'Strategies for Welfare: East and West Europe', *Critical Social Policy*, Issue no. 14, Winter.

Deak, Istvan (1966) 'Hungary', in Rogger, H. and Weber, M. (eds), *The European Right: A Historical Profile* (Berkeley and Los Angeles: University of California Press).

Denitch, Bogdan Denis (1976) *The Legitimation of a Revolution* (New Haven and London: Yale University Press).

Denitch, Bogdan (1981) 'Yugoslav Exceptionalism' in Triska and Gati (eds), *op. cit.*

DIP (1981) *Poland: the State of the Republic* (London: Pluto Press).

Djilas, M. (1966) *The New Class: An Analysis of the Communist System* (London: Allen and Unwin).

Douglas, Dorothy (1953) *Transitional Economic Systems: The Polish–Czech Example* (London).

Dunn, Dennis J. (1982–3) 'The Vatican's Ostpolitik: Past and Present', *Journal of International Affairs*, vol. 36.

Duverger, M. (1962) *Political Parties: their Organisation and Activity in the Modern State* (London: Methuen).

Dyker, D. A. (1983) 'The Crisis in Yugoslav Self-Management', *The Contemporary Review*, vol. 242, pp. 7–14.

Dziewanowski, M. K. (1959) *The Communist Party of Poland* (Cambridge: Cambridge University Press).

Dziewanowski, M. K. (1976) *The Communist Party of Poland*, Second Edition (Cambridge, Mass: Harvard University Press).

Dziewanowski, M. K. (1979) 'The Communist Party of Poland', in Stephen Fischer-Galati (ed.) *The Communist Parties of Eastern Europe* (New York: Columbia University Press).

Echols, John M., III (1981a) 'Does Socialism Mean Greater Equality? A Comparison of East and West along Several Major Dimensions', *American Journal of Political Science*, vol. 25, no. 1.

Echols, John M., III (1981b) 'Racial and Ethnic Inequality: The Comparative Impact of Socialism', *Comparative Political Studies*, vol. 13, no. 4.

Economist Intelligence Unit (1985) *EIU Regional Review: Eastern Europe and the USSR 1985* (London: EIU).

Edwards, G. E. (1985) *GDR Society and Social Institutions: Facts and Figures* (London and Basingstoke: Macmillan).

Ehrlich, Alexander (1960) *The Soviet Industrialisation Debate 1924–28* (Cambridge, Mass: Harvard University Press).

Elek, Peter S. (1979) 'Agro Mass Production and the Private Sector in Hungary' in Volgyes (ed.), *op. cit.*

Erikson, John (1981) 'The Warsaw Pact – the Shape of Things to Come?', in K. Dawisha and P. Hanson (eds), *Soviet–East European Dilemmas: Coercion, Competition and Consent* (London: Heinemann).

Erikson, John (1983) *The Road to Berlin: Stalin's War with Germany*, vol. 2 (London: Weidenfeld and Nicolson).

Estrin, Saul (1982) 'The Effects of Self-Management on Yugoslav Industrial Growth', *Soviet Studies*, vol. XXXIV, no. 1, January.

Faber, Bernard Lewis (ed.) (1976) *The Social Structure of Eastern Europe* (New York: Praeger).

Fallenbuchl, Z. M. (1970) 'The Communist Pattern of Industrialisation', *Soviet Studies*, vol. XXI.

Fallenbuchl, A. (1984) 'The Polish Economy under Martial Law', *Soviet Studies*, vol. XXXVI, no. 4, October.

Farrell, R. Barry (1970) *Political Leadership in Eastern Europe and the Soviet Union* (Chicago: Aldine Publishing Company).

Feher, Ferenc, and Heller, Agnes (1983) *Hungary 1956 Revisted* (London: George Allen and Unwin).

Feher, Ferenc, Heller, Agnes and György Markus (1983) *Dictatorship over Needs: An Analysis of Soviet Societies* (Oxford: Basil Blackwell).

Feiwel, G. R. (1982) *Economic Development and Planning in Bulgaria in the 1970s* (London: Butterworths).

Ferdinand, Peter (1983) 'The Twelfth Congress of the League of Yugoslav Communists', in *Documents in Communist Affairs*, vol. 2, no. 1.

Ferge, Zsusza (1978) 'Societal Policy and the Types of Centralised Redistribution', in Tibor Huszar, Kalman Kulesav, and Sandor Szalai (eds), *Hungarian Society and Marxist Sociology in the 1970s* (Budapest: Corvina Press).

Ferge, Zsusza (1979) *A Society in the Making: Hungarian Social and Societal Policy 1945–75* (London: Penguin).

Fischer, Mary Ellen (1983a) 'The Politics of National Inequality in Romania', in Nelson (ed.), *op. cit.*

Fischer, Mary Ellen (1983b) 'The Romanian Political Elite: Circulation or Change?', Paper prepared for the Annual Meeting of the American Political Science Association, Chicago, September.

Fischer-Galati, Stephen (ed.) (1979) *The Communist Parties of Eastern Europe* (New York: Columbia University Press).

Fischer-Galati Stephen (ed.) (1980) *Eastern Europe in the 1980s* (London: Croom Helm).

Fisk, Winston M. (1969–70) 'A Communist Rechtsstaat? – The Case of Yugoslav Constitutionalism', *Government and Opposition*, Winter.

Fiszera, V. (1977) 'The Workers' Councils: the Second Prague Spring', *New Left Review*, no. 105, pp. 83–91.

Fiszera, V. (ed.) (1978) *Workers' Councils in Czechoslovakia 1968–9* (London: Allison and Busby).

Fiszman, Joseph R. (1972) *Revolution and Tradition in People's Poland: Education and Socialisation* (Princeton, NJ: Princeton University Press).

Fiszman, J. R. (1975) 'Education and Social Mobility in People's Poland', in Ivan Volgyes (ed.), *Political Socialisation in Eastern Europe: A Comparative Framework* (New York: Praeger).

Fiszman, Joseph R. (1977) 'Child Socialisation: Comments from a Polish Perspective', *Studies in Comparative Communism*, vol. 3.

Friedrich, Carl J. and Brzezinski, Z. K. (1956) *Totalitarian Dictatorship and Autocracy* (New York: Praeger).

Fulton, O., Gordon, A. and Williams, G. (1982) *Higher Education and Manpower Planning* (Geneva: ILO/UNESCO).

Furtak, Robert K. (1974) 'Interessenpluralismus in den politschen Systemen Osteuropas', *Osteuropa*, 24.

Furtak, Robert K. (1983) *The Political Systems of the Socialist States: an Introduction to Marxist-Leninist Regimes* (Harvester).

Gati, Charles (ed.) (1976) *The International Politics of Eastern Europe* (New York: Praeger).

Gazso, Ferenc (1978) 'Social Mobility and the School', in Tibor Huszav, Kalman Kulesav and Sandor Szalai (eds), *op. cit.*

Gella, A. (1971) 'The Life and Death of the Old Polish Intelligentsia', *Slavic Review*, vol. XXX, no. 1.

George, V. and Manning, N. (1980) *Socialism, Social Welfare and the Soviet Union* (London: Routledge and Kegan Paul).

Gilberg, Trond (1975) *Modernisation in Romania since World War II* (New York: Praeger).

Gilberg, Trond (1979a) 'The Communist Party of Romania', in Stephen Fischer-Galati (ed.), *op. cit.*

Gilberg, Trond (1979b) 'Rural Transformation in Romania' in Volgyes (ed.), *op. cit.*

Gitelman, Zvi (1981) 'The Politics of Socialist Restoration in Hungary and Czechoslovakia', *Comparative Politics*, January.

Glaessner, Gert-Joachim (1984) 'The education system and society', in Klaus von Beyme and Hartmut Zimmerman (eds), *op. cit.*

Gomori, George (1973) 'The Cultural Intelligentsia: The Writers', in Lane and Kolankiewicz (eds), *op. cit.*

Golan, Galia (1971) *The Czechoslovak Reform Movement: Communism in Crisis: 1962–1968* (Cambridge: Cambridge University Press).

Golan, Galia (1973) *Reform Rule in Czechoslovakia: The Dubcek Era* (Cambridge: Cambridge University Press).

Gough, Ian (1979) *The Political Economy of the Welfare State* (London: Macmillan).

Granick, David (1975) *Enterprise Guidance in Eastern Europe* (Princeton: Princeton University Press).

Grant, Nigel (1969) *Society, Schools and Progress in Eastern Europe* (Oxford: Pergamon Press).

Gregory, Mary (1973) 'Regional Development in Yugoslavia', *Soviet Studies*, October.

Gripp, Richard C. (1973) *The Political Option* (Nelson).

Grote, Manfred (1979) 'The Socialist Unity Party of Germany', in Stephen Fischer-Galati (ed.), *op. cit.*

Hajda, Jan (ed.) (1955) *A Study of Contemporary Czechoslovakia* (Chicago: University of Chicago Press).

Halliday, Fred (1983) *The Making of the New Cold War* (London: Verso).

Hammond, T. (ed.) (1975) *The Anatomy of Communist Takeovers* (New Haven: Yale University Press).

Hanson, Philip (1981) *Trade and Technology in Soviet-Western Relations* (London: Macmillan).

Hanson, Philip (1981) 'Soviet Trade with Eastern Europe', in K. Dawisha and P. Hanson (eds), *op. cit.*

Harding, Neil (ed.) (1984) *The State in Socialist Society* (London and Basingstoke: Macmillan).

Hare, P. G. (1981) 'Introduction', in P. G. Hare *et al.*, *Hungary: a decade of Economic Reform, op. cit.*

Hare, P. G. (1983) 'The beginnings of institutional reform in Hungary', *Soviet Studies*, vol. XXXV, no. 3, July.

Hare, P. G., Radice, H. K. and Swain, N. (eds) (1981) *Hungary: a Decade of Economic Reform* (London: George Allen and Unwin).

Hare, P. G. and Wanless, P. T. (1981) 'Polish and Hungarian Economic Reforms – a Comparison', *Soviet Studies*, vol. XXXIII, no. 4, October.

Havel, Vaclav, *et al.* (1985) *On Freedom and Power: Essays on independent, civil initiatives in Eastern Europe* (London: Hutchinson Education).

Heath, Anthony (1981) *Social Mobility* (Glasgow: Fontana Paperbacks).

Heath, Roy E. (1980) 'Education', in Stephen Fischer-Galati (ed.), *op. cit.*

Hegedus András and Markus, Mária (1969) 'Altconativa és étélkválasztás az elosztés és fogyasztás távlati tervezésében', *Közgazdasági Szemk*, no. 9. pp. 1048–61 as quoted in Istvan Szeleny, *Urban Inequalities under State Socialism* (Oxford: Oxford University Press).

Heller, Agnes (1976) *The Theory of Need in Karl Marx* (London: Allison and Busby).

Herspring, Dale R. (1978) 'Civil-Military Relations in Communist Countries', *Studies in Comparative Communism*, vol. XI, no. 3, Autumn.

Herspring, Dale and Volgyes, Ivan (1977) 'The Military as an Agent of Political Socialization in Eastern Europe: A Comparative Framework', *Armed Forces and Society*, vol. 3.

Herspring, Dale and Volgyes, Ivan (1980) 'Political Reliability in Eastern Europe Warsaw Pact Armies', *Armed Forces*, vol. 6.

Hertz, Alexander (1942) 'The Social Background of the Pre-War Polish Political Structure', *Journal of Central European Affairs*, vol. II, no. 2.

Hertz, A. (1951) 'The Case of an Eastern European Intelligentsia', *Journal of Central European Affairs*, vol. XI, no. 1.

Hill, Malcolm R. (1978) *The Export Marketing of Capital Goods to the Socialist Countries of Eastern Europe* (Aldershot: Gower).

Hill, Malcolm R. (1983) *East–West Trade, Industrial Cooperation and Technology Transfer* (Aldershot: Gower).

Hirsowicz, M. (1978) 'Intelligentsia versus Bureaucracy? The Revival of a Myth in Poland', *Soviet Studies*, vol. XXX, no. 3.

Hirsowicz, Maria (1980) *The Bureaucratic Leviathan: A Study in the Sociology of Communism* (Oxford: Martin Robertson).

Hiscocks, Richard (1963) *Poland: Bridge for the Abyss? An Interpretation of Developments in Post-War Poland* (London: Oxford University Press).

Höhmann, H. H. 'Economic Reform in the 1970s – policy with no alternatives', in Alec Nove, H. H. Höhmann, and G. Seidenstecher *The East European Economies in the 1970s* (London: Butterworths).

Höhmann, H. H., Kaser, M. C. and Thalheim, K. (eds) (1975) *The New Economic Systems of Eastern Europe* (London: C. Hurst and Co.).

Holmes, Leslie (1981) *The Policy Process in Communist States: Politics and Industrial Administration* (London: Sage Publications).

Holmes, Leslie (ed.) (1981) *The Withering Away of the State? Party and State under Communism* (London: Sage).

Holmes, Leslie (1981) 'The GDR: Real Socialism or Computer Stalinism' in Holmes (ed.), *op. cit.*

Holmes, Leslie (1986) *Politics In The Communist World* (Oxford: Clarendon Press).

Horvat, Branco (1977) *The Yugoslav Economic System* (new York: IASP).

Hough, Jerry (1969) *The Soviet Prefects: Local Party Organs in Industrial Decision-Making* (Cambridge, Mass: Harvard University Press).

Hough, Jerry F. (1977) *The Soviet Union and Social Science Theory* (Cambridge, Mass: Harvard University Press).

Hruby, Suzanne (1982–3) 'The Church in Poland and its Political Influence', *Journal of International Affairs*, vol. 36, pt 2.

Huber, Maria and Heinrich, Hans-Georg (1981) 'Hungary – Quiet Progress' in Holmes (ed.), *op. cit.*

Huszav, Tibor (1978) 'White-Collar Workers, Intellectuals, Graduates in Hungary', in Tibor Huszav, Kalman Kulesav, Sandor Szalai (eds), *op. cit.*

Huszav, Tibor, Kulcsav, Kalman and Szalai, Sandor (eds) (1978) *Hungarian Society and Marxist Sociology in the 1970s* (Budapest: Corvina Press).

Hutchings, Robert L. (1983) *Soviet–East European Relations: Consolidation and Conflict 1968–80* (Wisconsin: University of Wisconsin Press).

Industrial Democracy in Europe (IDE) International Research Group (1981) *European Industrial Relations* (Oxford: Clarendon Press).

Ionescu, Ghiţa (1964) *Communism in Rumania: 1944–1962* (London: Oxford University Press).

Ionescu, Ghiţa (1965) *The Break-up of the Soviet Empire in Eastern Europe* (Harmondsworth: Penguin Books).

Ionescu, Ghiţa (1967) *The Politics of the European Communist States* (London: Weidenfeld and Nicolson).

Ionescu, Ghiţa (1982) *Comparative Communist Politics* (London: Macmillan).

Jancar, Barbara Wolfe (1978) *Women under Communism* (Baltimore and London: Johns Hopkins University Press).

Jeffries, I. (ed.) (1981) *The Industrial Enterprise in Eastern Europe* (New York: Praeger).

Johnson, A. Ross (1976) 'Has Eastern Europe become a liability to the Soviet Union?', in Charles Gati (ed.), *op. cit.*

Johnson, A. Ross (1984) 'The Warsaw Pact: Soviet Military Policy in Eastern Europe', in S. Meiklejohn Terry, *Soviet Policy in Eastern Europe* (New Haven: Yale University Press).

Johnson, Paul M. (1981) 'Changing Social Structure and the Political Role of Manual Workers', in Triska and Gati (eds), *op. cit.*

Jones, Christopher D. (1981) *Soviet Influence in Eastern Europe: Political Autonomy and the Warsaw Pact* (New York: Praeger).

Kagan, George (1943) 'Agrarian regime of Pre-War Poland', in *Journal of Central European Affairs*, vol. III, no. 3.

Kahn, A. J. and Kamerman, S. B. (1981) *Child Care, Family benefits and Working parents: a study in cooperative policy* (New York: Columbia University Press).

Kamerman, Sheila B. and Kahn, Alfred J. (eds) (1978) *Family Policy: Government and Families in Fourteen Countries* (New York: Columbia University Press).

Kanet, Roger (1981) 'Patterns of Eastern European Economic Involvement in the Third World', in M. Radu (ed.), *Eastern Europe and the Third World: East vs. South* (New York: Praeger).

Kanet, Roger (1983) 'Eastern Europe and the Third World: the Expanding Relationship', in M. Sodaro and S. L. Wolchik (eds), *op. cit.*

Kaser, Michael (1976) *Health Care in the Soviet Union and Eastern Europe* (London: Croom Helm).

Kaser, M. C. and Schnytzer, A. (1982) 'The Economic System of Albania in the 1970s: developments and problems', in A. Nove, H. H. Höhmann and G. Seidenstecher (eds), *op. cit.*

Kaser, M. C. and Spigler, I. (1982) 'Economic Reform in Romania in the 1970s', in A. Nove, A. Höhmann and K. Thalheim, *The East European Economies in the 1970s* (London: Butterworths).

Kaser, M. and Zielinski, J. (1970) *Planning in East Europe* (London: Bodley Head).

Katsenelinboigen, A. (1977) 'Coloured Markets in the Soviet Union', *Soviet Studies*, vol. XXXIX, no. 1, January.

Kemeny, Istvan (1979) 'Poverty in Hungary', *Social Science Information*, 19, 2.

Kemeny, I. (1982) 'The Unregistered Economy in Hungary', *Soviet Studies*, vol. XXXIV, no. 3, July.

Kolankiewicz, George (1973a) 'The Polish Industrial Manual Working Class's in Lane and Kolankiewicz (eds), *op. cit.*

Kolankiewicz, George (1973b) 'The Technical Intelligentsia' in Lane and Kolankiewicz (eds), *op. cit.*

Kolankiewicz, George (1980) 'The Peasant-Worker in Poland: the New Awkward Class', *Sociologica Ruralis*, nos 1–2.

Kolankiewicz, George (1981) 'Poland, 1980: The Working Class under "Anomic Socialism"', in Triska and Gati (eds), *op. cit.*

Kolankiewicz, George (1982a) 'Employee Self-Management and Socialist Trade Unionism', in Woodall (ed.), *op. cit.*

Kolankiewicz, George (1982b) 'The Politics of "Socialist Renewal"', in Jean Woodall (ed.), *op cit.*

Kolosi, Tamas and Wnuk-Lipinski, Edmund (1983) *Equality and Inequality under Socialism: Poland and Hungary Compared* (London: Sage Studies in International Sociology).

Konrad, G. and Szelenyi, I. (1979) *The Intellectuals on the Road to Class Power* (Brighton: Harvester).

Koralewicz-Zebik, Jadwiga (1984) 'The Perception of Inequality in Poland 1956–1980', *Sociology*, vol. 18, no. 2.

Korbonski, Andrzej (1971) 'Bureaucracy and Interest Groups in Communist Societies: The Case of Czechoslovakia', *Studies in Comparative Communism*, vol. IV.

Korbonski, Andrzej (1974) 'The Prospects for Change in Eastern Europe', *Slavic Review*, XXXIII.

Korbonski, A. (1976) 'Leadership Succession and Political Change in Eastern Europe', *Studies in Comparative Communism*, Spring/Summer.

Korbonski, A. (1980) 'Eastern Europe: Soviet Asset or Burden? The Political Dimension', in R. A. Linden (ed.), *op. cit.*

Kosta, Juri (1982) 'Aims and methods of economic policy in Czechoslovakia 1970–78', in A. Nove, H. H. Höhmann and G. Seidenstecher, *op. cit.*

Kovrig, Bennet (1979) *Communism in Hungary: From Kun to Kadar* (Stanford, California: Hoover Institution Press).

Kramer, Mark N. (1985) 'Civil–Military Relations in the Warsaw Pact: The East European Component', *International Affairs*, vol. 61.

Kraus, Richard and Vanneman, Reeve D. (1985) 'Bureaucracy versus the

State in Capitalist and Socialist Reigmes', *Comparative Studies in Society and History*, vol. 27.

Krejci, Jaroslav (1976) *Social Structure in Divided Germany* (London: Croom Helm).

Krejci, Jaroslav (1982) *National Income and Outlay in Czechoslovakia, Poland and Yugoslavia* (London: Macmillan).

Krejci, Jaroslav and Velimsky, Viteslav (1981) *Ethnic and Political Nations in Europe* (London: Croom Helm).

Krisch, Henry (1982) 'Political Legitimation in the German Democratic Republic', in Rigby and Feher (1982), *op. cit.*

Kusin, V. (1973) *The Czechoslovak Reform Movement, 1968* (London: Macmillan).

Kusin, Vladimir V. (1978) *From Dubcek to Charter 77. A Study of 'Normalisation' in Czechoslovakia* (Edinburgh: University Press).

Kyn, O. (1975) 'Czechoslovakia' in H. H. Höhmann, M. C. Kaser, and H. Thalheim (eds), *The New Economic Systems of Eastern Europe* (London: C. Hurst and Co.).

Lane, David (1973a) 'The Role of Social Groups', in Lane and Kolankiewicz (eds), *op. cit.*

Lane, David (1973b) 'Structural and Social Change in Poland' in Lane and Kolankiewicz (eds), *op. cit.*

Lane, David (1976) *The Socialist Industrial State* (London: George Allen and Unwin.

Lane, David (1982) *The End of Social Inequality? Class, Status and Power Under State Socialism* (London: George Allen and Unwin).

Lane, David (1985) *State and Politics in the USSR* (Oxford: Basil Blackwell).

Lane, David (1985) *Soviet Economy and Society* (Oxford: Basil Blackwell).

Lane, David and Kolankiewicz, George (eds) (1973) *Social Groups in Polish Society* (London and Basingstoke: Macmillan).

Lane, D. and O'Dell, F. (1978) *The Soviet Industrial Worker* (London: Martin Robertson).

Lange, Oskar (1970) *Papers in Economics and Sociology 1930–1960* (Warsaw).

Leptin, G. (1975) 'The G.D.R.', in H. H. Höhmann, M. C. Kaser, and K. C. Thalheim (eds), *The New Economic Systems of Eastern Europe* (London: Butterworths).

Lewis, Paul (1973) 'The Peasantry', in Lane and Kolankiewicz (eds), *op. cit.*

Lewis, Paul G. (1979) 'Potential Sources of Opposition in the East European Peasantry', in Tökes (ed.), *op. cit.*

Lewis, Paul G. (1982a) 'Political Consequences of the Changes in Party–State Structure Under Gierek', in Woodall (ed.), *op. cit.*

Lewis, Paul G. (1982b) 'Obstacles to the Establishment of Political Legitimacy in Communist Poland', *British Journal of Political Science*, 12.

Lewis, Paul G. (1984a) 'Institutionalisation and Political Change in Poland', in Harding (ed.), *op. cit.*

Lewis, Paul G. (ed.) (1984b) *Eastern Europe: Political Crisis and Legitimation* (London and Sydney: Croom Helm).

Lewis, Paul G. (1984c) 'Legitimation and Political Crises: East European Developments in the Post-Stalin Period', in Paul Lewis (ed.) (1984b), *op. cit.*

Lewis, Paul (1985) 'Political Implications of the Popieluszko Affair', *Politics*, vol. 5, no. 2, October.

Liberman, F. G. (1962) 'The Plan, profits and bonuses', in D. Nove and D. Nuti (eds), *Socialist Economics* (London: Penguin).

Linden, Ronald H. (1980) *The Foreign Policies of Eastern Europe: New Approaches* (New York: Praeger).

Lipset, S. M. (1960) *Political Man* (London: Heinemann Educational Books).

Little, D. Richard (1976) 'Mass Political Participation in the U.S. and the U.S.S.R.: A Conceptual Analysis', *Comparative Political Studies*, vol. 8.

Lomax, Bill (1984) 'Hungary – the Quest for Legitimacy', in Lewis (1984b), *op. cit.*

Lovenduski, Joni (1986) *Women and European Politics* (Brighton: Wheatsheaf).

Lovenduski, Joni and Hills, Jill (eds) (1981) *The Politics of the Second Electorate* (London: Routledge and Kegan Paul).

Ludz, P. (1970) *The German Democratic Republic from the 60s to the 70s* (Cambridge, Mass: Centre for International Affairs, Harvard University).

Lukianenko, S. (1978) 'Financing and Administration of Social Security in Socialist Countries', *International Society Security Review*, vol. XXXI, no. 4.

McCartney, C. A. (1957) *October Fifteenth: A History of Modern Hungary 1929–1945*, 2 vols (Edinburgh: The University Press).

McCauley, Martin (1979) *Marxism–Leninism in the G.D.R., the Socialist Unity Party (SED)* (London: Macmillan).

McCauley, Martin (1983) 'Leadership and the Succession Struggle', in Martin McCauley (ed.), *The Soviet Union after Brezhnev* (London: Heinemann).

McCauley, Martin (1984) 'Legitimation in the German Democratic Republic' in Lewis (ed.) (1984b), *op. cit.*

McCauley, Martin (1986) 'The German Democratic Republic', in Martin McCauley and Stephen Carter (eds), *op. cit.*

McCauley, Martin and Stephen Carter (1986) *Leadership and Succession in the Soviet Union, Eastern Europe and China* (Armonk, New York: M. E. Sharpe Inc., and London: Macmillan).

McFarlane, Bruce (1984) 'Political Crisis and East European Economic Reforms' in Paul G. Lewis (ed) (1984) *Eastern Europe: Political Crisis and Legitimation* (London and Sydney: Croom Helm).

McGregor, James P. (1984) 'Polish Public Opinion in a Time of Crisis', *Comparative Politics*, vol. 17.

MacPherson, C. B. (1966) *The Real World of Democracy* (Oxford: Clarendon Press).

MacShane, Ian (1981) *Solidarity, Poland's Independent Trade Union* (Nottingham: Spokesman).

Manchin, R. and Szelenyi, I. (1984) 'Social Policy under State Socialism', in G. Espring-Anderson *et al.* (eds), *Comparative Social Policy* (Wisconsin: Sharpe).

Marrer, Paul and Montias, J. M. (eds) (1980) *East European Integration, East–West Trade* (Bloomington: Indiana University Press).

Marsh, David (1971) 'Political Socialization: the Implicit Assumption Questioned', *British Journal of Political Science*, vol. 1, no. 4, October.

Mason, David S. (1983) 'Solidarity, the Regime and the Public', *Soviet Studies*, vol. XXXV, no. 4.

Martin, A. (1977) 'Political Constraints on Economic Strategies in Advanced Industrial Societies', *Comparative Political Studies*, vol. 10, no. 3, October.

Meier, Viktor (1983) 'Yugoslavia's National Question', *Problems of Communism*, March–April.

Meiklejohn, Terry Sarah (ed.) (1984) *Soviet Policy in Eastern Europe* (New Haven: Yale University Press).

Mellor, Roy E. H. (1975) *Eastern Europe: A Geography of the Comecon Countries* (London and Basingstoke: Macmillan).

Melzer, Michael (1981) 'Combine formation in the GDR', *Soviet Studies*, vol. XXXIII, no. 1, January.

Meyer, Alfred G. (1966) 'The Functions of Ideology in the Soviet Political System', *Soviet Studies*, vol. XVII, No. 3, January.

Michalsky, Helga (1984) 'Social policy and the transformation of society', in Klaus von Beyme and Harmut Zimmerman (eds), *op. cit.*

Mieczkowski, B. (1975) *Personal and Social Consumption in Eastern Europe: Poland, Czechoslovakia, Hungary and East Germany* (New York: Praeger).

Milenkovitch, M. (1981) 'Yugoslavia and the Third World', in M. Radice (ed.), *Eastern Europe and the Third World: East versus South* (New York: Praeger).

Millard, L. Frances (1982) 'Health Care in Poland: from Crisis to Crisis', *International Journal of Health Services*, vol. 12, no. 3.

Minnerup, Gunter (1982) 'East Germany's Frozen Revolution', *New Left Review*, 132.

Misztal, B. A., Misztal, B. (1984) 'Urban Social Problems in Poland: the Macrosocial determinants', *Urban Affairs Quarterly*, vol. 19, no. 3, March.

Montias, J. M. (1979) 'Planning with material balances in Soviet-type economies', *American Economic Review*, December.

Montias, J. M. (1980) 'Economic Conditions and Political Instability in Communist Countries: Observations on Strikes, Riots and Other Disturbances', *Studies in Comparative Communism*, vol. XIII.

Moore, J. H. (1980) *Growth with Self-Management: Yugoslav Industrialisation 1952–75* (Clio).

Moore, Wilbert E. (1945) *Economic Demography of Eastern and Southern Europe* (Geneva: League of Nations).

Moreton, Edwina (1981) 'Foreign Policy Perspectives in Eastern Europe', in K. Dawisha and P. Hanson (eds), *op. cit.*

Morris, L. P. (1984) *Eastern Europe Since 1945* (London, Exeter: Heinemann Educational Books).

Morton, Henry W. (1979) 'Housing Problems and Policies of Eastern Europe and the Soviet Union', *Studies in Comparative Communism*, vol. XII, no. 4, Winter.

Mushaben, Joyce Marie (1984) 'Swords to Plowshares: The Church, The State and the East German Peace Movement', *Studies in Comparative Communism*, vol. XVII, no. 2.

Musil, Jiri (1980) *Urbanisation in Socialist Countries* (London: Croom Helm).

NATO Economics Directorate/Information Directorate (eds) (1980) *Economic Reforms in Eastern Europe and Prospects for the 1980s* (London: Pergamon).

NATO (1983) *External Economic Relations of CMEA Countries, a Colloquium* (Brussels, NATO).

Navarro, V. (1977) *Social Security and Medicine in the USSR* (Lexington, Mass: Lexington Books).

Nelson, Daniel N. (ed.) (1980) *Local Politics in Communist Countries* (Lexington: University Press of Kentucky).

Nelson, Daniel N. (1980a) 'Workers in a Workers' State', *Soviet Studies*, vol. XXXII, October.

Nelson, Daniel, N. (1980b) *Democratic Centralism in Romania: a Study of Local Communist Politics* (Boulder, Colorado: Columbia University Press).

Nelson, Daniel (1981a) 'Romania: Participatory Dynamics in "Developed Socialism"', in Triska and Gati (eds), *op. cit.*

Nelson, Daniel, N. (ed.) (1981b) *Romania in the 1980s* (Boulder: Westview Press).

Nelson, Daniel (1982) 'Communist Legislatures and Communist Politics', in Nelson and White, *op. cit.*

Nelson, Daniel, N. (ed.) (1983) *Communism and the Politics of Inequalities* (Lexington, Mass: Lexington Books).

Nelson, Daniel and Stephen White (eds) (1982) *Communist Legislatures in Comparative Perspective* (London and Basingstoke: Macmillan).

Noron, Andrew (1982) 'Social Welfare Provision in Poland', *Social Policy and Administration*, vol. 16, no. 3.

Nove, Alec (1980) *The Soviet Economic System* (London: George Allen and Unwin).

Nove, Alec (1983) *The Economics of Feasible Socialism* (London: George Allen and Unwin).

Nove, Alec, Höhmann, H. H. and Seidenstecher, Gertrude (1982) *The East European Economies in the 1970s* (London: Butterworths).

Nowak, Jan (1982) 'The Church in Poland', *Problems of Communism*, January–February.

Nuti, Domenico Mario (1981) 'Poland: Economic Collapse and Socialist Renewal', *New Left Review*, vol. 130.

Offe, Claus (1982) 'Some contradictions of the modern welfare state', *Critical Social Policy*, vol. 2, no. 2, Autumn.

Olson, D. M. and Simon, M. D. (1982) 'The Institutional Development of a Minimal Parliament: The Case of the Polish Sejm', in Nelson and White (eds), *op. cit.*

Pahl, Ray E. (1977) 'Collective Consumption and the State in Capitalist and State Capitalist Societies', in . Scase (ed.), *Industrial Society: Class, Cleavage and Control* (London: George Allen and Unwin).

Pakulski, Jan (1986) 'Legitimacy and Mass Compliance: Reflections on Max Weber and Soviet-type Societies', *British Journal of Political Science*, 16.

Parkin, Frank (1971) *Class Inequality and Political Order* (London: MacGibbon and Kee).

Parkin, Frank (1976) 'Market Socialism and Class Structure: Some Aspects of Social Stratification in Yugoslavia', in Faber (ed.), *op. cit.*

Parkin, Frank (1979) *Marxism and Class Theory: a bourgeois critique* (London: Tavistock Publications).

Perlmutter, Ames and LeoGrande, William M. (1982) 'Civil Military Relations in Communist Political Systems', *American Political Science Review*, vol. 16, no. 4.

Polonsky, Antony (1975) *The Little Dictators: The History of Eastern Europe Since 1918* (London and Boston: Routledge and Kegan Paul).

Porkett, J. L. (1979) 'Old Age Pension Schemes in the Soviet Union and Eastern Europe', *Social Policy and Administration*, vol. 13, no. 1.

Porkett, J. L. (1981) 'The Economic Lot of Polish Retired Workers', *Osteuropa-Wirtschaft*, vol. 26, no. 4.

Porkett, J. L. (1982) 'Retired Workers under Soviet-Type Socialism', *Social Policy and Administration*, vol. 16, no. 3, Autumn.

Pravda, Alec (1981) 'Political Attitudes and Activity in Triska and Gati (eds), *op. cit.*

Pravda, Alex (1982a) 'Industrial Workers: Patterns of Dissent, Opposition and Accommodation', in Tökes (ed.), *op. cit.*

Pravda, Alex (1982b) 'Poland 1980: From "Premature Consumerism" to Labour Solidarity', *Soviet Studies*, vol. XXIV.

Pravda, Alex (1983) 'Trade Unionism in East European Communist Systems: Towards Corporation?', *International Political Science Review*, vol. 14, no. 2.

Pryor, Frederic L. (1985) 'Growth and Fluctuations of Production in OECD and East European Countries', *World Politics*, vol. 27, no. 2, January.

Putnam, R. D. (1976) *The Comparative Study of Political Elites* (New Jersey: Prentice-Hall).

Radio Free Europe Research (1980–6) Background Reports.

Radio Free Europe Research (1980–6) Situation Reports.

Radu, M. (1981 'Romania and the Third World – the dilemmas of a free rider' in M. Radu (ed.) *Eastern Europe and the Third World: East vs. South*, *op. cit.*

Radu, M. (1981) *Eastern Europe and the Third World: East vs. South* (New York: Praeger).

Radvanyi, Janos (1981) 'Policy Patterns of East European Socialist Countries toward the Third World', in M. Radu (ed.) *Eastern Europe and the Third World: East vs. South, op. cit.*

Rakowska-Harmstone, Teresa (ed.) (1984) *Communism in Eastern Europe* (Manchester: Manchester University Press).

Ramet, Pedro (1982) 'The Czechoslovak Church under Pressure', *The World Today*, September.

Ramet, Pedro (1984) 'Church and Peace in the GDR', *Problems of Communism*, July–August.

Ramet, Pedro (1985) 'Disaffection and Dissent in East Germany', *World Politics*.

Revesz, G. (1975) in H. H. Höhmann, Kaser M. C. and Thalheim, K. (eds), *The New Economic Systems of Eastern Europe* (London: C. Hurst and Co.).

Richta, Radovan (ed.) (1969) *Civilisation at the Crossroads: Social and Human Implications of the Scientific Technological Revolution.* (Prague:).

Rigby, T. H. (1982) 'Introduction: Political Legitimacy, Weber, and Communist Mono-organisational Systems', in Rigby and Feher (eds), *op. cit.*

Rigby, T. H. and Feher, Ferenc (eds.) (1982) *Political Legitimation in Communist States* (London and Basingstoke: Macmillan).

Rigby, T. H., Brown, Archie and Readaway, Peter (eds) *Authority, Power and Policy in the USSR* (London and Basingstoke: Macmillan).

Rigby, T. H. and Harasymiw, B. (eds) (1983) *Leadership Selection and Patron-Client Relations in the USSR and Yugoslavia* (London: George Allen and Unwin).

Rosenblum-Cale, Karen (1979) 'After the Revolution: Women in Yugoslavia', in Volgyes (ed.), *op. cit.*

Rothschild, Joseph (1974) *East Central Europe Between the Two World Wars* (Seattle and London: University of Washington Press).

Rupnik, Jacques (1981) 'The Restoration of the Party-State in Czechoslovakia Since 1968', in Holmes (ed.), *op. cit.*

Rupnik, Jacques (1984a) 'Czechoslovakia: After 15 Years of Normalisation ... a Government Reshuffle', *Communist Affairs*, vol. 3, part 1.

Rupnik, Jacques (1984b) 'The Military and "Normalisation" in Poland', in Lewis (1984b), *op. cit.*

Rush, Myron (1974) *How Communist States Change Their Rulers* (Ithaca: Cornell University Press).

Rusinow, Dennison (1977) *The Yugoslav Experiment 1948–74* (London: C. Hurst and Co.).

Rusinow, Dennison (1985–6) 'Yugoslavia', in Martin McCauley and Stephen Carter, (eds) *op. cit.*

Sabel, Charles F. and Stark, David (1982) 'Planning, Politics and Shop-Floor Power: Hidden Forms of bargaining in Soviet-Imposed State-Socialist Societies', *Politics and Society*, vol. 11.

Sacks, Stephen R. (1976) 'Corporate Giants Under Market Socialism', *Studies in Comparative Communism*, vol. IX, no. 4, Winter.

Sacks, Stephen R. (1983) *Self-management and Efficiency: Large Corporations in Yugoslavia* (London: Allen and Unwin).

Sakwa, George and Crouch, Martin (1979) 'Sejm Elections in Communist Poland, an Overview', *British Journal of Political Science*.

Sanders, Irwin T. (1982) 'Church State Relationships in Southeastern Europe', *East European Quarterly*, vol. XVI, No. 1.

Sanford, George (1983) *Polish Communism in Crisis* (London: Croom Helm).

Sanford, George (1985) 'Poland's recurring Crises: an Interpretation', *The World Today*, January.

Sanford, George (1986) 'Poland', in Martin McCauley and Stephen Carter (eds), *op. cit.*

Scharf, G. Bradley (1984) *Politics and Change in East Germany: An Evaluation of Socialist Democracy* (London: Frances Pinter).

Schiavone, Giusseppe (1981) *The Institutions of Comecon* (London: Macmillan).

Schöpflin, George (1985) 'Hungary', in Martin McCauley and Stephen Carter (eds), *op. cit.*

Selucky, Rudolf (1972) *Economic Reforms in East European Industry* (New York: Praeger).

Seroka, Jim (1983) 'The Policy-Making Roles of the Yugoslav Federal Assembly: Changes, Trends and Implications', *Western Political Quarterly*.

Seton-Watson, Hugh (1960) *The Pattern of Communist Revolution* (London: Methuen).

Seton-Watson, Hugh (1961) *The East European Revolution*, Third Edition (London: Methuen).

Seton-Watson, Hugh (1975) *Eastern Europe Between the Wars 1918–1941* (Cambridge: Cambridge University Press).

Shabad, Goldie (1980) 'Strikes in Yugoslavia: Implications for Industrial Democracy', *British Journal of Political Science*, vol. 10, 3 July.

Shafir, Michael (1985) *Romania, Politics, Economy and Society, Political Stagnation and Simulated Change* (London: Frances Pinter).

Shafir, Michael (1985–6) 'Romania', in Martin McCauley and Stephen Carter (eds) *op. cit.*

Shoup, Paul (1968) *Communism and the Yugoslav National Question* (New York: Columbia University Press).

Shoup, Paul (1976) 'The Limits of Party Control: the Yugoslav Case', in Andrew C. Janos (ed.), *Authoritarian Politics in Communist Europe: Uniformity and Diversity in the Party States* (Berkeley: California University Press).

Simon, Maurice D. and Kanet, Roger E. (1981) *Background to Crisis: Policy and Politics in Gierek's Poland* (Boulder: Westview Press).

Simons, William B. (1980) *The Constitutions of The Communist World* (Germantown, Maryland: Sijthoff and Noordhoff).

Simons, William B. and White, Stephen (eds) (1984) *The Party Statutes of the Communist World* (The Hague: Martinus Nijhoff).

Singleton, Fred (1982) 'Objectives and Methods of Economic Policies in Yugoslavia 1970–80', in A. Nove, H. H. Höhmann, and G. Seidenstecher (eds), *op. cit.*

Singleton, Fred (1985) *A Short History of the Yugoslav Peoples* (Cambridge: Cambridge University Press).

Singleton, Fred and Carter, Bernard (1982) *The Economy of Yugoslavia* (London: Croom Helm).

Skilling, H. Gordon (1966) *The Governments of Communist East Europe* (New York: Thomas Y. Crowell Company).

Skilling, H. Gordon (1966) 'Interest Groups and Communist Politics', *World Politics*, 18.

Skilling, H. Gordon (1968) 'Opposition in Communist East Europe', *Government and Opposition*.

Skilling, H. Gordon (1971) 'Czechoslovakia's Interrupted Revolution', in R. Dahl (ed.) *Regimes and Oppositions*.

Skilling, H. Gordon (1976) *Czechoslovakia's Interrupted Revolution* (Princeton: Princeton University Press).

Skilling, H. Gordon (1977) 'Stalinism and Czechoslovak Political Culture', in Tucker (ed.), *op. cit.*

Skilling, H. Gordon (1984) 'Interest Groups and Communist Politics Revisited', *World Politics*, vol. 36.

Skilling, H. Gordon (1985) 'Independent Currents in Czechoslovakia', *Problems of Communism*, January–February.

Skilling, H. Gordon and Griffiths, Franklyn (ed.) (1971) *Interest Groups in Soviet Politics* (Princeton: Princeton University Press).

Smith, A. H. (1980) 'Romanian Economic Reforms', in NATO Economic Directorate/Information Directorate (eds) *op. cit.*

Smith, Alan H. (1983) *The Planned Economies of Eastern Europe* (London: Croom Helm).

Sobell, Vladimir (1984) *The Red Market: Industrial Cooperation and Specialisation in Comecon* (Aldershot: Gower).

Sodaro, Michael (1981) 'The GDR and the Third World – supplicant or surrogate', in M. Radu (ed.), *op. cit.*

Sodaro, Michael J. and Wolchik, Sharon L. (1983) *Foreign and Domestic Policy Development in Eastern Europe in the 1980s* (London: Macmillan).

Sontheimer, Kurt and Bleek, Wilhelm (1975) *The Government and Politics of East Germany* (London: Hutchinson University Library).

Staar, Richard F. (1982) *Communist Regimes in Eastern Europe* (Stanford, California: Hoover Institution Press).

Staar, Richard F. (ed.) (1982) *Yearbook on International Communist Affairs 1982* (Hoover Institution Press/Clio Press).

Staar, Richard F. (1984) *Communist Regimes in Eastern Europe*, 4th edn (Stanford, California: Hoover Institute Press).

Staar, Richard F. (1985) *1985 Yearbook on International Communist Affairs* (Stanford, California: Hoover Institution Press).

Staniszkis, Jadwiga (1981) 'The Evolution of Forms of Working Class Protest in Poland: Sociological Reflections on the Gdansk–Szczecin Case, August 1980', *Soviet Studies*, vol. XXXIII.

Staniszkis, Jadwiga (1984)0 *Poland's Self-limiting Revolution* (Princeton: Princeton University Press).

Stankovic, S. (1981) *The End of the Tito Era: Yugoslavia's Dilemmas* (Stanford, California: Hoover Institution Press).

Starrels, John M. and Mallinckrodt, Anita M. (1975) *Politics in the German Democratic Republic* (London: Praeger).

Stehle, Hansjakob (1985) 'Poland: Can the Church Point the Way?', *The World Today*, February.

Sugar, Peter F. (ed.) (1971) *Native Fascism in the Successor States 1941–1945* (Santa Barbara: ABC–Clio).

Summerscale, Peter (1981) 'The Continuing Validity of the Brezhnev Doctrine', in K. Dawisha and P. Hanson (eds) *op. cit.*

Szalai, Julia (1984) 'The Crisis of Social Policy for Youth in Hungary', *Critical Social Policy*, issue no. 9, Spring.

Szajkowski, Bogdan (1981) 'Albania, Bulgaria, Romania: Political Innovations and the Party', in Leslie Holmes (ed.), *The Withering Away of the State?, op. cit.*

Szczepanski, Jan (1961) 'The Polish Intelligentsia Past and Present', *World Politics*, vol. 14, part 2.

Szelenyi, Ivan (1979) 'Social Inequalities in State Socialist Redistributive Economies', *International Journal of Comparative Sociology*, vol. XIX, nos 1–2.

Szelenyi, Ivan (1983) *Urban Inequalities under State Socialism* (Oxford: Oxford University Press).

Tampke, Jürgen (1983) *The People's Republics of Eastern Europe* (London and Canberra: Croom Helm).

Taras, Ray (1984) *Ideology in a Socialist State: Poland 1956–1983* (Cambridge: Cambridge University Press).

Tismaneanu, Vladimir (1985) 'Ceausescu's Socialism', *Problems of Communism*, January–February.

Titmus, Richard (1974) *Social Policy: an Introduction* (London: George Allen and Unwin).

Tökes, Rudolf L. (ed.) (1978) *Eurocommunism and Detente* (London: Martin Robertson).

Tökes, Rudolf L. (ed.) (1979) *Opposition in Eastern Europe* (London and Basingstoke: Macmillan).

Tökes, Rudolf L. (1984) 'Hungarian Reform Imperatives', *Problems of Communism*, September–October.

Toma, Peter A. (1979) 'The Communist Party of Czechoslovakia', in Stephen Fischer-Galiti (ed.), *op. cit.*

Toma, Peter A. and Volgyes, Ivan (1977) *Politics in Hungary* (San Francisco: W. H. Freeman and Co.).

Tomiak, J. (1982) 'Educational Policy and Educational Reform in the 1970s, in J. Woodall (ed.) (1982a), *op. cit.*

Triska, Jan F. (1980) 'Eurocommunism and the decline of proletarian internationalism', in V. V. Aspatrurian, J. Valenta, D. P. Burke (eds), *op. cit.*

Triska, Jan F. and Charles Gati (eds) (1981) *Blue Collar Workers in Eastern Europe* (London: George Allen and Unwin).

Tucker, R. (1968) 'Paths of Communist Revolution', in K. London (ed.), *The Soviet Union: a Half Century of Communism* (Baltimore: Johns Hopkins Press).

Tucker, Robert C. (ed.) (1977) *Stalinism: Essays in Historical Interpretation* (New York: W. W. Norton & Co. Inc.).

Tyson, Laura D'Andrea (1980) *The Yugoslav Economic System and its performance in the 1970s* (Berkeley: Institute of International Studies).

Ulc, Otto (1974) *Politics in Czechoslovakia* (San Francisco: W. H. Freeman and Co.).

Vajna, T. (1982) 'Problems and trends in the development of the Hungarian New Economic Mechanism: a balance sheet of the 1970s', in A. Nove, H. H. Höhmann and G. Seidenstecher, *op. cit.*

Valenta, Jiri (1981) 'Czechoslovakia: a Proletariat Embourgeoisie?', in Triska and Gati (eds), *op. cit.*

Verba, Sidney and Goldie Shabad (1978) 'Workers' Councils and Political Stratification: The Yugoslav Experience', *American Political Science Review*, vol. 72.

Vergeiner, Walter (1978) 'Czechoslavakia' in Sheila B. Kamerman and

Alfred J. Kahn (eds) *Family Policy: Government and Families in Fourteen Countries* (New York: Columbia University Press).

Vienna Institute for Comparative Economic Studies (1983) *Comecon Foreign Trade Data 1982* (London: Macmillan).

Vienna Institute for Comparative Economic Studies (1984) *Comecon Data 1983* (London: Macmillan).

Volgyes, Ivan (ed.) (1975) *Political Socialisation in Eastern Europe: A Comparative Framework* (New York: Praeger).

Volgyes, Ivan (1978) 'Modernization, Stratification and Elite Development in Hungary', *Social Forces*, vol. 57, pt 2.

Volgyes, Ivan, (ed.) (1979) *The Peasantry of Eastern Europe: Volume II/20th Century Developments* (Oxford: Pergamon Press).

Volgyes, Ivan (1981) 'Hungary: the lumpenproletarianization of the Working Class', in Triska and Gati (eds), *op. cit*

Wädekin, Karl-Eugen (1982) *Agrarian Polities in Communist Europe: a Critical Introduction* (The Hague: Martinus Nijhoff).

Warsawski, Stanislaw (1983) 'Comecon: the Recent Past and Perspectives for the 1980s', in M. T. Sodoro and S. L. Wolchik (eds), *op. cit.*

Wesolowski, Wlodzimierz (1979) *Classes, Strata and Power* (London: Routledge and Kegan Paul).

Wettig, Gerhard (1984) Relations between the two German States', in Klaus von Beyme and Hartmut Zimmerman (eds), *Policy Making in the GDR* (Aldershot: Gower).

Weydenthal, Jan B. de (1979) 'The Workers' Dilemma of Polish Politics: A Case Study', *East European Quarterly*, vol. XIII, no. 1.

White, Stephen (1978) 'Communist Systems and the "Iron Law of Pluralism"', *British Journal of Political Science*, 8.

White, Stephen (1980) 'The USSR Supreme Soviet: a Developmental Perspective', *Legislative Studies Quarterly*, vol. 2, May.

White, Stephen (1986) 'Regime and Citizen', in McCauley and Carter (eds), *op. cit.*

White, S., Gardner, J. and Schöpflin, George (1982) *Communist Political Systems: An Introduction* (London and Basingstoke: Macmillan).

Wiatr, Jerzy and Przeworski, Adam (1960) 'Control and Administration in the People's Democracies', *Government and Opposition*, vol. I, no. 2.

Wiatr, Jerzy J. (1984) 'Mobilization of non-Participants during the Political Crisis in Poland, 1980–81', *International Political Science Review*, vol. 5, no. 3.

Wiedemann, P. (1980) 'Economic Reforms in Bulgaria: coping with the "Kj" problem', in NATO Economics Directorate/Information Directorate (eds), *op. cit.*

Wightman, Gordon (1983) 'Membership of the Communist Party of Czechoslovakia in the 1970s: continuing divergence from the Soviet model', *Soviet Studies*, vol. XXXV, no. 2, April.

Wightman, Gordon (1986) 'Czechoslovakia', in McCauley and Carter, *op. cit.*

Wightman, G. and Brown, A. H. (1975) 'Changes in the Levels of Membership and Social Composition of the Communist Party of Czechoslovakia 1945–73', *Soviet Studies*, vol. XXVII, no. 3 July.

Wolchik, Sharon (1981) 'Eastern Europe', in Joni Lovenduski and Jill Hills (eds.) *op. cit.*

Wolchik, Sharon L. (1983) 'Regional Inequalities in Czechoslovakia', in Nelson (ed.), *op. cit.*

Woodall, Jean (1981) 'New Social Factors in the Unrest in Poland', *Government and Opposition*.

Woodall, Jean (1982a) *Policy and Politics in Contemporary Poland: Reform, Failure, Crisis* (London: Frances Pinter).

Woodall, Jean (1982b) *The Socialist Corporation and Technocratic Power: The Polish United Workers' Party, Industrial Organisation and Workforce Control 1958–80* (Cambridge: Cambridge University Press).

Woodward, Susan L. (1983) 'Inequalities and Yugoslav Political Stability' in Nelson (ed.), *op. cit.*

Woolf, S. J. (ed.) (1968) *European Fascism* (New York: Random House).

World Health Organisation (1985) *World Health Statistics Annual 1985* (Geneva: WHO).

Zaninovich, M. George (1983) 'Yugoslav Succession and Leadership Stability', *Studies in Comparative Communism*, vol. XVI, no. 3.

Zaslavsky, V. and Brym, R. J. (1978) 'The Functions of Elections in the USSR', *Soviet Studies*, vol. XXX.

Zauberman, Alfred (1964) *Industrial Progress in Poland, Czechoslovakia and East Germany 1937–1962* (London: Oxford University Press).

Zebot, Cyril A. (1982) 'Yugoslavia's "Self-management" on Trial', *Problems of Communism*, March–April.

Zielinski, Janusz G. (1973) *Economic Reforms in Polish Industry* (London: Oxford University Press).

Zimmerman, Hartmut (1978) 'The GDR in the 1970s', *Problems of Communism*, March–April.

Zimmerman, Hartmut (1984) 'Power Distribution and Opportunities for Participation: Aspects of the Socio Political System of the GDR' in Klaus von Beyme, and Hartmut Zimmerman (eds) (1984) *Policy Making in the GDR* (Aldershot: Gower).

Zimmerman, William (1981) 'Soviet Relations with Yugoslavia and Romania', in M. Radu (ed.), *op. cit.*

Zukin, Sharon (1981) 'The Representation of Working Class Interests in Socialist Society: Yugoslav Labour Unions', *Politics and Society*, vol. 10.

Zukin, Sharon (1984) 'Yugoslavia: Development and Persistence of the State', in Harding (ed.), *op. cit.*

Index